# HOME GROWN

# Home Grown

## MARIJUANA
## AND THE ORIGINS
## OF MEXICO'S WAR
## ON DRUGS

*Isaac Campos*

THE UNIVERSITY OF
NORTH CAROLINA PRESS
*Chapel Hill*

The University of North Carolina Press has
been a member of the Green Press Initiative since 2003.

Library of Congress Cataloging-in-Publication Data
Campos, Isaac.
Home grown : marijuana and the origins of Mexico's war on drugs / Isaac Campos.
p. cm.
Includes bibliographical references and index.
ISBN 978-0-8078-3538-8 (cloth : alk. paper)
ISBN 978-1-4696-1372-7 (pbk.          )
1. Marijuana—Mexico. 2. Drug traffic—Mexico. 3. Drug control—Mexico. I. Title.
HV5840.M4C363 2012
363.450972—dc23    2011041766

cloth    16  15  14  13  12    5  4  3  2  1
paper    17  16  15  14  13    5  4  3  2  1

Parts of this book have been reprinted with permission in revised form
from Isaac Campos, "Degeneration and the Origins of the War on Drugs,"
Mexican Studies/Estudios Mexicanos 26, no. 2 (2010): 379–408.

THIS BOOK WAS DIGITALLY PRINTED.

# Contents

# Figures, Charts, and Tables

TABLES

# Acknowledgments

The research for this book would have been impossible without the support of many institutions and individuals. At the University of Cincinnati, the Charles Phelps Taft Research Center has been an extraordinary source of support, providing the money and time to complete this project. Thanks also go to my colleagues in the history department, as well as to our office staff, for their support and assistance. Many other institutions also helped fund this research. UCSD's Center for U.S.-Mexican Studies generously provided a fellowship that allowed crucial time for writing and research. The Mellon Foundation and the David Rockefeller Center for Latin American Studies at Harvard University were also remarkably generous in their funding of this project, as were the Harvard history department and Graduate School of Arts and Sciences. Thanks are also due to the U.S. Department of Education for a yearlong fellowship.

In Mexico City, the staffs of the Archivo General de la Nación, the Archivo Histórico de la Secretaría de Salubridad y Asistencia, the Archivo Histórico del Antiguo Ayuntamiento, the Archivo Histórico de la Facultad de Medicina de la UNAM, the Archivo General de la Secretaría de Relaciones Exteriores, the Archivo Histórico de la Secretaría de la Defensa Nacional, the Biblioteca Nacional de México, and the Biblioteca Miguel Lerdo de Tejada were all extremely helpful. At the U.S. National Archives in College Park, Maryland; the DEA Library in Arlington, Virginia; and the Getty Research Institute in Los Angeles, I also received valuable assistance. The staffs of the libraries at the University of Cincinnati and Harvard University were also indispensable. I'm especially indebted to interlibrary loan at Cincinnati, which always provided prompt and reliable service.

A very big thank you goes to my main teachers and mentors: John Womack, John Coatsworth, Paul Gootenberg, and Matthew Connelly. Their guidance over many years has been too wide-ranging and valuable to summarize in a sentence or two. I will thus simply say thank you. In Mexico, many individuals were kind enough to meet with me along the way and share whatever knowledge they could. Luis Astorga, Abigail Aguilar Contreras, Martín Barrón, Ignacio Chávez Jr., María Elena Medina Mora, María Cristina Sacristán, Guillermo Espinosa, and Carlos Zolla all shared their thoughts and often provided materials that were of use in this research. Special thanks are due to Ricardo

Pérez Montfort, who helped get my Mexico research started through a loan of his rich collection of primary materials. I also thank María Águeda Méndez for a library card and other help. Kate Doyle provided me with both fascinating work and a great example of how to make history matter. Farther north, conversations with Sven Beckert, David Courtwright, Lester Grinspoon, Jeff Jacobson, Friedrich Katz, Akira Iriye, Claudio Lomnitz, Ernest Small, Roger Owen, Pablo Piccato, Howard Shaffer, Joseph Spillane, Mauricio Tenorio, Steven Topik, and Eric Van Young were also illuminating.

Various colleagues were helpful with research and other critical support. Nicole Mottier, Amilcar Challú, Halbert Jones, Alec Dawson, Miki Cohen, John Lupien, Ev Meade, Paula De Vos, and Paul Ross all helped me acquire some important research materials. Moramay López-Alonso and Stephen Neufeld helped me navigate Mexico's tricky military archives. Hillary Smith and Rosalba Tena Villeda provided research assistance. Thanks to Jeremy Baskes (with an assist from Eric Zolov) for the book's title. Very special thanks also are due to Reanne Frank, whose help was invaluable. Sylvia Sellers-García, Sarah Jackson, John O'Connor, Boone Shear, Simon Rippon, José Ángel Hernández, and Paul Campos provided writing advice and help with editing, as did, less formally, Matt O'Keefe and Leah Stewart. John Chasteen and Margaret Chowning were also very helpful. Willard Sunderland, Wendy Kline, David Stradling, and Jana Braziel provided indispensable support of various kinds at Cincinnati, while Jennifer Malat, John Martin, Thérèse Migraine-George, and Gary Weissman furnished scholarly community. Additional thanks go to Jennifer for her help with the charts. Thank you also to the entire staff of the University of North Carolina Press, especially Elaine Maisner, who guided the publication of this book from the start.

Finally, the book is dedicated to my family in both the United States and Mexico. In Mexico, I owe a particular debt to Maricarmen and Angela Costero for housing me time and again, as well as to Maruchi, Rafael, and Luis Miguel Costero for many meals and good times. Thanks also to the brothers Sánchez and Mari Cruz Escudero for their hospitality. At home, Patricia, Carlos Manuel, and Elsa Inés provide love and perspective, without which I never could have finished this project. Patricia also deserves special thanks for designing the book's cover. Finally, my parents, Margarita Costero Campos and José Luis Campos, both scholars in their own right, made this sometimes idiosyncratic project possible with their unwavering support. I'm not sure how I would have done it without them. This book is therefore dedicated, above all, to them.

# HOME GROWN

# Introduction

This story begins with a little-known Spaniard who, in the sixteenth century, introduced a plant called cannabis to the Americas. It ends with Mexico's prohibition of that plant, by then called "marihuana," in 1920. There is a lot of ground to cover in between. Thus, I would like to begin, by way of introduction, with a brief outline of the plot.

Around the year 1530, a conquistador named Pedro Quadrado left his small village near Seville and traveled to the New World. After actively participating in the ongoing conquest of Mexico, Quadrado received a coveted *encomienda*, or royal tribute and labor grant, to undertake the cultivation of cannabis there. He thus became the first person to cultivate this species in the Americas.[1] That, anyway, is what he himself claimed, and probably with justification, for it was not until June 1545 that the Spanish Crown first ordered its subjects to sow cannabis in the New World.[2] For the Spanish, cannabis was first and foremost a fiber plant. They called it *cáñamo*. Tall, green, and gangly, of round seeds and "abominable smell," this was an extraordinarily common cultivar whose strong fibers, or hemp, made clothing, rope, and the broad and sturdy sails that powered the greatest sea-borne empire the world had ever known.[3] Thus began the long journey of cannabis through Mexican history, one that would eventually see its meaning and identity radically transformed.

The first signs of that transformation appeared in the 1770s. By then, cannabis had found its way into local medical-religious practice, and its seeds and leaves were sold by herb dealers under the name *pipiltzintzintlis*, or "the most noble princes." Though still cherished by Spanish officials as an industrial fiber, there were growing rumors that, for Indians, it also facilitated visions, communion with the devil, and sometimes madness. Prohibitionist edicts briefly raised the profile of these noble princes, but the name *pipiltzintzintlis* would soon fade into obscurity, as would (temporarily) the drug use of cannabis in Mexico.

A new generation of nationalist botanists would rediscover cannabis drugs during the 1850s. These men become interested in cataloging Mexico's "indigenous" natural wonders, and in the process they noted that "certain Mexicans" had begun smoking the stuff. The word *pipiltzintzintlis* was no longer in use, but two other local designations, both of which helped to reinforce the plant's apparent indigeneity, had emerged: *rosa maría* and *mariguana*.

1

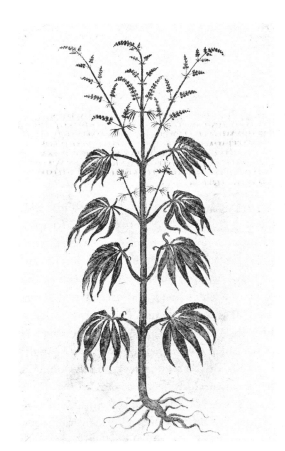

FIGURE I.1.
Illustration of cannabis
from the *Vienna Dioscurides*.
(Wikipedia Commons)

The former would also soon disappear, leaving the word *mariguana*, or *mari-huana*—or as it is now spelled in English, "marijuana"—to conquer the lexica of most of the Western Hemisphere.

Though these nationalist botanists saw potential value in this "local" drug plant, their writings would soon be overwhelmed by the view that this was a quintessentially indigenous "narcotic" causing madness, violence, and mayhem. In 1886, for example, a Mexican medical student delivered a thesis in the field of legal medicine on marijuana and the insanity defense, concluding that "the criminal responsibility of an individual in a state of acute marijuana intoxication should be exactly the same as that of the maniac," namely none. By 1898, Mexico City's leading daily could claim that "for years the press has described horrifying crimes, criminal eccentricities and suicides, which place before the court of public opinion individuals whose type oscillates between furious madmen and criminals worthy of being placed before the firing squad, and one after another case demonstrates that the murderer, the rapist, the insubordinate, the presumed suicide, and the scandalous acted under the influence of marihuana."[4]

During the late nineteenth and early twentieth centuries, hundreds of newspaper stories described marijuana's effects in similar fashion. The following report was typical:

A *MARIHUANO* ATTACKS FIVE GENDARMES

Yesterday on Chapultepec Avenue, around six in the afternoon, there occurred a major scandal.

The cause of the disorder was a cocky tough-guy [*valentón*] who was stoned [*grifo*] thanks to the influence of marihuana and who insulted all the passersby.

Two gendarmes attempted to reduce him to order and he attacked them with his knife, causing them significant injuries. The injured gendarmes were backed up by a pair of mounted police and another on foot.

The scandal then took on colossal proportions, for it became very difficult to disarm the *marihuano*.

When they finally reduced him to order, they took him to the Eighth Demarcation and confined him to a cell, it being necessary to hold him down with a straitjacket.[5]

Descriptions like this one of marijuana's effects not only were standard during the late nineteenth and early twentieth centuries but also went virtually unchallenged. As I demonstrate in chapter 4, a close analysis of more than four hundred Mexican newspaper articles — drawn from over a dozen publications, both liberal and conservative, and all describing the effects of marijuana — reveals that not a single article questioned this basic stereotype. Given that these papers were published in an environment of significant media competition and that they routinely lambasted each other for untruths and sensationalism, this unblemished record is quite extraordinary. Furthermore, there is evidence that lower-class Mexicans, most of whom were illiterate, were equally convinced of marijuana's frightening effects. As one commentator revealed in 1908: "The horror that this plant inspires has reached such an extreme that when the common people . . . see even just a single plant, they feel as if in the presence of a demonic spirit. Women and children run frightened and they make the sign of the cross simply upon hearing its name."[6]

Originally an industrial fiber symbolizing European imperial expansion, cannabis had been transformed by the dawn of the twentieth century into a quintessentially indigenous, and putatively dangerous, Mexican drug plant. Thus, in 1920, after labeling marijuana a threat to "degenerate the race," Mexican sanitary authorities banned the drug nationwide, seventeen years prior to similar legislation in the United States.[7]

■ For those readers familiar with the existing historical and social scientific scholarship on drugs in North America, much of this may come as a surprise. The War on Drugs is routinely described as "America's War on Drugs" and the drug problem as an "American disease," where "America" means the United States and the rest of the Americas have been cajoled or forced into cooperating.[8] Global drug prohibition has recently been portrayed as a kind of "informal American cultural colonization," while Latin America has been identified as a place where, prior to U.S. involvement, substances like marijuana and peyote were an accepted part of "Indian and Latin American culture."[9]

The problem is not that historians have looked deeply at the origins of drug prohibition in Latin America and gotten it all wrong. The problem is that historians simply have not looked deeply at the origins of drug prohibition in Latin America. Not a single monograph exists, for example, on the birth of these policies in Mexico.[10] This is a remarkable fact given the tremendous political, social, and economic costs that the War on Drugs have produced in that country over the last century. Drug prohibition is the sine qua non of the War on Drugs. Without prohibition, there is no black market, and without a black market, there are no "narcotraffickers" to demonize, no illicit drug users to incarcerate, and no national security threat to declare.[11] That is why scholars who date the War on Drugs to Richard Nixon's formal declaration of that "war" in 1971, or to the Reagan-era militarization of the conflict, are missing the forest for the trees.[12] Nixon merely intensified an antidrug crusade that formally began at the federal level in the United States (and Mexico) in the early twentieth century. Certainly that "war" became more militarized in the late 1980s, but neither was this completely new. Mexico's military, for example, had been eradicating drugs intended for the U.S. market since the late 1930s.[13] In sum, the origins of the War on Drugs lie in the legal and ideological roots of prohibition. With respect to marijuana in North America, those origins have their deepest roots in Mexico.

Marijuana also provides a simply fascinating case study for U.S.-based historians interested in the ideological foundations of drug prohibition. It is a substance whose inclusion among "Schedule 1" drugs in the United States is often cited as a fanatical excess of extremist drug warriors, an unscientific designation proving that politics, not rationality, drives the War on Drugs.[14] It is a compelling argument. After all, there is not a single death on record that can be attributed to overindulgence in marijuana, while serious research has long demonstrated that alcohol and tobacco are generally more habit-forming and unhealthy for their users than is cannabis.[15]

Yet despite today's typical view of marijuana as a "soft" drug in comparison to, say, the opiates and cocaine, Mexicans of a century ago believed it to be perhaps the "hardest" drug of them all, one that triggered sudden paroxysms of delirious violence. Could marijuana really have produced these effects? And, whatever the answer, what was it about the historical circumstances of the day that made such descriptions so eminently believable? How is it possible that not a single newspaper or scientific source seriously challenged their veracity? Finally, how did the radical transformation of cannabis's meaning occur in Mexico between the sixteenth and twentieth century? Where in the plant's long journey through Mexican history did these changes occur?

These are the questions around which this book is organized. By answering them, I hope to better explain marijuana's prohibition in Mexico, itself a key to understanding the origins of the War on Drugs in that country and, to a certain extent, in North America as a whole. Ultimately, the evidence will demonstrate that marijuana prohibition can only be described as a kind of "informal American cultural colonization" if one takes the radical step of considering Mexico as worthy of the "America" label as its powerful neighbor, for in this case the influence mostly flowed northward. Marijuana's prohibition in Mexico was, in short, home grown.

*Chapter 1*

CANNABIS AND THE

PSYCHOACTIVE RIDDLE

As I detail in chapter 4, marijuana caused violence, madness, and crime in nineteenth- and early-twentieth-century Mexico. This, anyway, is what the available historical sources overwhelmingly indicate. These ideas were widespread and appear to have cut across boundaries of class and ethnicity. There was almost no counterdiscourse, there were virtually no defenders of the weed, and there was remarkable continuity in the way this substance was portrayed, whether in newspapers or in scientific periodicals. Marijuana's effects were sometimes simply described as "madness," and, while hardly a clinical diagnosis, the dimensions of this particular brand of insanity were relatively consistent—irrational and sudden outbursts of violence, hallucinations, delusions, superhuman strength, and sometimes amnesia.

Given the sheer volume of reports on these effects and their overwhelming consistency, it is tempting simply to accept them at face value. In fact, with another subject or in another context, the overwhelming consistency of the evidence would already be proof enough of this drug's effects in that time and place. But in this case, we must proceed with caution, for there is significant dissonance here with more recent cannabis experience in North America. If marijuana was producing violent delirium a century ago, why isn't it producing those effects today? Furthermore, because we know that marijuana was used mostly by the lower class—people often considered criminal and violent as a matter of course by Mexican authorities—there is much reason to suspect that these claims were at the very least exaggerated. Yet the volume and consistency of the evidence is extraordinary, more extraordinary even than the flagrant, sometimes ostentatious prejudice of Mexicans a century ago.

But could cannabis really have caused these effects? Here we have a relatively simple question that has a decidedly complicated answer. One might expect otherwise. In fact, when I began this research, I expected the scientifically measurable effects of cannabis to be a straightforward control for understanding the past. My assumption went something like this: If we know the effects that a drug has in the present, then we will know what effects the drug had in the past, producing a perfect control for distinguishing between myth and reality in the historical archive. This, it turns out, was wrong.

Richard DeGrandpre has called this widespread misunderstanding the "cult of pharmacology" and has identified it as a key component in the genesis and longevity of misguided drug policies in the United States. The cult of pharmacology suggests that there is a direct and consistent relationship between the pharmacology of a substance and the effects that it has on all human beings. But as decades of research and observation have demonstrated, the effects of psychoactive drugs are actually dictated by a complex tangle of pharmacology, psychology, and culture—or "drug, set, and setting"—that has yet to be completely deciphered by researchers. For the sake of convenience, we might simply call that tangle the "psychoactive riddle."

This book seeks to decipher the psychoactive riddle of cannabis in nineteenth- and early-twentieth-century Mexico. Thus we must begin, ironically, with a few basic questions that will briefly delay our voyage into Mexican history. First, was the Mexican case unique? Was cannabis ever reported to produce similar effects in other times and places? Second, what can the latest science tell us about cannabis pharmacology? Does this drug even have the potential to produce the effects that were so often attributed to it in Mexico a century ago? The answers may surprise you.

■ Over many centuries and in many different contexts, cannabis has been reported to produce hallucinations, delusions, violence, and even permanent madness in its users. Take, for example, the *Pên-ts' ao Ching*, a Chinese pharmacopoeia compiled in the first or second century but attributed to Emperor Shen-nung (c. 2000 B.C.). There, readers are warned that "*ma-fên* (the fruits of hemp) . . . if taken in excess will produce hallucinations (literally 'seeing devils')." Later Chinese sources reported the use of cannabis by sorcerers "to set forward time in order to reveal future events."[1] Among medieval Muslims, almost every conceivable malady was attributed to the use of cannabis, including destruction of the mind, hallucinations, and insanity.[2] *The Thousand and One Nights*, which likely dates to Persia's Sassanid Empire (224–651),[3] popularized the view that cannabis produced dreamlike hallucinations that led users down the path to embarrassment and ridicule. Typical is "The Tale of Kazi and the Bhang-Eater" (*bhang* being cannabis), which recounts the exploits of a cannabis-eating fisherman. This particular bhang-eater lived a simple life, each day treating himself to three doses of bhang, one in the morning, one at noon, and one at night. On one of these occasions, while taking a nighttime walk, he confuses a swath of moonlight in the square outside his door for a river. After fetching his fishing gear, he begins to cast into the moonlight, only to have a dog take the bait. The animal soon drags the ridiculous man to what he thinks is the water's edge. Lest he be pulled in, he screams for help, rousing a crowd of neighbors who emerge from their homes only to witness the absurd scene. The same fisherman had earlier in his life been committed to an asylum after seeing visions of fish raining from the sky. Later he would accidentally urinate on a sultan while under the influence of bhang.[4]

During the early modern era, reports began to emerge in Western sources of the apparently pernicious effects of cannabis. According to historian James Mills, one of the more important accounts of this kind appeared in a little guide published, beginning in 1779, as the *Portable Instructions for Purchasing the Drugs and Spices of Asia and the East Indies*. Here, cannabis (bhang) was described as a "species of opiate in much repute throughout the East for drowning care. . . . The effects of this drug are to confound the understanding, set the imagination loose and induce a kind of folly or forgetfulness."[5] But the *Portable Instructions* also warned of more sinister effects. These had been reported a few years earlier by the British traveler and businessman John Henry Grose, whose work for the East India Company had apparently facilitated his observations on the subject:

> Bang is also greatly used at Surat, as well as all over the East, an intoxicating herb, of which it may be needless to say more after so many writers, who have fully described it: and it is hard to say what pleasure can be found in the use of it, being very disagreeable to the taste, and violent in its operation, which produces a temporary madness, that in some, when designedly taken for that purpose, ends in running what they call a-muck, furiously killing every one they meet, without distinction, until themselves are knocked on the head, like mad dogs. But by all accounts this practice is much rarer in India than it formerly was.[6]

According to Mills, the *Portable Instructions* was especially important to the diffusion of ideas about cannabis in the West because the work was repeatedly reprinted as an appendix to other similar guides that then circulated the globe in the baggage of European business travelers. For example, the *Portable Instructions* was appended to *The India Officers and Traders Guide in Purchasing the Drugs and Spices of Asia and the East Indies*, which became "the definitive guide to sailing from Britain, France, or America to India" and remained in circulation until at least the First World War. Grose's book, from which the above quotation was originally drawn, was also quite popular in its own right, published first in 1757, translated into French in 1758, and seeing three editions by 1772.[7]

In the nineteenth century, this developing lore achieved additional legitimacy thanks to the backing of some of the era's greatest intellectuals. In part, this was due to a confluence of historical factors, even an accident of history, that made cannabis into a substance of profound fascination for the "Western mind." This was a period, of course, that saw the interconnected ascendancy of science and colonialism, which manifested itself perhaps most obviously in the burgeoning field of Orientalism. It was also an era that saw a boom in the botanical sciences and pharmacology, producing the discoveries of countless wonder drugs. Cannabis was ideally suited to garner attention in this atmosphere. It was an Old World drug that had gained fame in *The Thousand and One Nights*, surely the most famous of "Oriental" sources. It was also a plant that appeared almost naturally inclined to reproduce the basic dichotomies at the heart of the Oriental-Occidental divide, for the species had two forms: in temperate regions, it appeared to produce mostly fiber; in the tropics, mostly drugs. As James F. W. Johnston explained in 1855:

> Our common European hemp (*Cannabis sativa*) . . . so extensively cultivated for its fibre, is the same plant with the Indian hemp (*Cannabis indica*), which from the remotest times has been celebrated among Eastern nations for its narcotic virtues. . . .
>
> In the sap of this plant . . . there exists a peculiar resinous substance in which the esteemed narcotic virtue resides. In northern climates, the proportion of this resin in the several parts of the plant is so small as to have escaped general observation. . . .
>
> But in the warmer regions of the East, the resinous substance is so abundant as to exude naturally, and in sensible quantity, from the flowers, from the leaves, and from the young twigs of the hemp-plant. . . . It grows well, and produces abundance of excellent fibre in the north, but no sensible proportion of narcotic resin. It grows still better, and more magnificently, in tropical regions; but there its fibre is worthless and unheeded, while for the resin it spontaneously yields it is prized and cultivated.[8]

In short, in the "East," cannabis appeared to naturally produce drug content fit for inducing revelry and escapism, while in colder climates, it yielded plentiful fiber ideally suited to industry and progress.

It should hardly be surprising, then, that probably the most influential source on the nature of cannabis during this era was not produced by a botanist but rather by Silvestre de Sacy, the most renowned Orientalist of the nineteenth century. In his "Memoir on the Dynasty of the Assassins, and on the Etymology of Their Name," Sacy argued that the origins of the word "assassin" were found in the word "hashish."[9] This argument was extraordinarily influential and did as much as anything to legitimize the view among Westerners that cannabis had the potential to produce at least fantastic visions if not violence in its users. It thus deserves a few moments of our attention here.

Sacy's theory was based in the history of a medieval Shiite Islamic sect called the Isma'ilis, popularly known as the "Order of Assassins." The Isma'ilis were much maligned during the Middle Ages by both rival Muslims and Christians. Among Muslims, they were portrayed as a secret conspiracy featuring complex initiation rites and bent on destroying Islam. Crusading Christians later elaborated on that unsavory reputation. The Isma'ilis themselves fueled the process with the adoption in the twelfth century of public assassination as a central tactic in their struggle against the Sunni Saljuq Turks. Though they did not pioneer this tactic, they did employ it in a most "spectacular and intimidating fashion," with young men (called *fidawi*) assassinating often important, well-guarded officials, most commonly in public places like mosques where the acts would therefore also serve as tools of intimidation.[10] It was all the more intimidating, of course, because the *fidawi* knew they would surely be killed in the process. They were, in short, probably the most famous "suicide bombers" of all time.

Predictably, the Isma'ilis became the targets of many choice insults, the most common of which were *malahida* (heretics) and *batiniyya* (meaning, more or less, "irreligiosity") but also, as Sacy later emphasized, *al-Hashishiyya*. Indeed, the first written use of the word *hashishiyya* appears in a polemic against the Isma'ilis in 1123.[11] This was a moment when hashish use was spreading around the Muslim world and gaining a reputation as low-class and antithetical to Islam.[12] There exists no evidence, however, that the Isma'ilis or, in particular, the *fidawi* assassins had anything to do with hashish. The original sources never explain why the word is utilized, and as historian Farhad Daftary has argued, it seems rather unlikely that warriors sent on such difficult and sensitive missions would have taken a potentially disorienting drug in order to carry them out.[13] Furthermore, *hashisha* was a term used as a general insult in the Arab world due to its association with heretics and the rabble of society. It thus seems most likely that the word was simply being employed in this pejorative sense rather than as an actual accusation of hashish use.

Sacy nevertheless speculated that the insult may have had some basis in the actual employment of hashish. Marco Polo's *Travels* provided the evidence. There, Polo described an "Old Man of the Mountain" who had created an impregnable castle with sumptuous gardens, rivers of milk and honey, and many young and beautiful virgins whose "duty was to furnish the young men who were put there with all delights and pleasures." The old man would keep scores of these youngsters at his court, all of whom were to become warriors, and he would describe to them the pleasures of paradise and explain that he had the key to it. Whenever he needed an enemy assassinated, he would have a group of these warriors secretly drugged with a potion so that they would fall into a deep sleep. He would then have them carried into the gardens of the castle so that when they awoke, they could experience the pleasures of paradise for a few days. The boys would later be drugged again and removed from the gardens, only to awake to the overwhelming disappointment of the real world. The old man would then promise their return in exchange for unwavering obedience. It was said that these young warriors thus became so fanatically loyal that they were willing to carry out virtually any task for their master, even if it meant they would perish in the process. Christian Crusaders had found in this legend an attractive explanation for the seemingly irrational behavior of the suicidal *fidawi*. Thus, stories began circulating in the late twelfth century among Christian sources, describing the Old Man of the Mountain, his magical potion, and his promises of paradise. The story went through several incarnations before Marco Polo's version became the standard European account.[14]

Though hashish is not actually mentioned in the tale, Sacy took the presence of the secret potion in the anecdote as evidence enough of the drug's critical role in producing visions of paradise. In fact, Sacy questioned the actual existence of the gardens themselves, arguing instead that they were probably just a product of young imaginations fueled by hashish. Here he echoed the basic reputation of cannabis as provided in the *Thousand and One Nights*. "What we know for certain is that even today, people who take opium or *hashish* can, even if covered in poverty's rags and staying in a miserable tavern, derive happiness and pleasures that are short nothing but reality."[15]

Sacy's great influence helped turn the Assassins legend into a crucial component of European writings on cannabis. But in the process, the moral of the story as it related to cannabis drugs was increasingly distorted, for other authors were considerably less shy about directly linking the frightening, suicidal assassinations of the *fidawi* to the effects of hashish. As the American poet and travel writer Bayard Taylor put it in 1854, "During the Crusades, [hashish] was frequently used by the Saracen warriors to stimulate them to the work of slaughter, and from the Arabic term of 'Hashasheen,' or Eaters of Hasheesh, the word 'assassin' has been naturally derived."[16] At midcentury, Ernest von Bibra and James F. W. Johnston both produced monographs on the world's intoxicants that summarized the existing knowledge of cannabis's effects. Both of them referenced Sacy's work prominently, with Johnston noting that "it is from such effects of this substance also that we obtain a solution of the extravagances and barbarous cruelties which we read of as practised occasionally by Eastern despots."[17] Sacy's study would in fact be cited as authoritative for more than a century after its publication. During the 1930s, Harry Anslinger of the U.S. Federal Bureau of Narcotics would famously employ the Assassins legend, both in his article "Marihuana: Assassin of Youth" and later during congressional testimony to help secure marijuana prohibition in the United States: "In the year 1090, there was founded in Persia the religious and military order of the Assassins whose history is one of cruelty, barbarity, and murder, and for good reason. The members were confirmed users of hashish, or marihuana, and it is from the Arabic 'hashshashin' [sic] that we have the English word 'assassin.' Even the term 'running amok' relates to the drug, for the expression has been used to describe natives of the Malay Peninsula who, under the influence of hashish, engage in violent and bloody deeds."[18]

Meanwhile, many other nineteenth-century sources reinforced the view that cannabis was a quintessentially Oriental substance that produced either visions or violence or both. Von Bibra, for example, claimed that "for Orientals, the common effect of hashish is of an agreeable, exciting character, inducing them to laugh, and increasing their appetite. For certain persons, however, hashish produces a contrary effect, rendering them quarrelsome and easily disposed to take up arms." Cited here was the case of two Bukharins aboard an Austrian steamer who, in the summer of 1849, had taken hashish and "suddenly become so wild that they killed several people before they could be subdued."[19] Alexander Dumas's wildly popular *The Count of Monte Cristo* also reinforced this view. In that work, hashish induced sleep, produced erotic visions, and enhanced music so that one might hear "the seven choirs of paradise." As Sinbad explains to Franz, "Taste this, and in an hour you will be a king, not a king of a petty kingdom hidden in some corner of Europe like France, Spain, or England, but king of the world, king of the universe, king of creation; without bowing at the feet of Satan, you will be king and master of all the kingdoms of the earth."[20] Dumas was also a participant in the famous 1840s meetings of the Club des Hashishins in Paris that brought together (among others) Théophile Gautier, Charles Baudelaire, and Honoré de Balzac to experiment with the drug. That club eventually produced a number of highly Orientalist writings on the subject, and Baudelaire would pithily sum up the supposed effects of hashish with his now famous phrase "Artificial Paradise."[21]

These views gained additional backing around midcentury by the first Western studies to scientifically appraise cannabis's effects. From India in 1838, William Brooke O'Shaughnessy announced the medical potential of cannabis in a work that would stimulate much new research into the drug. While O'Shaughnessy was mostly interested in cannabis as an effective medicine, he did note the warnings of Arabic and Persian physicians who had linked the drug to madness, impotence, and "numerous other evil consequences."[22] O'Shaughnessy's research in fact suggested that the drug produced a "singular form of delirium," especially in young, novice users. "This state is at once recognized by the strange balancing gait of the patient's; a constant rubbing of the hands; perpetual giggling; and a propensity to caress and chafe the feet of all bystanders of whatever rank. The eye wears an expression of cunning and merriment which can scarcely be mistaken. In a few cases, the patients are violent; in many highly aphrodisiac."[23] O'Shaughnessy argued that such effects varied considerably depending on the particular preparation ingested and the character of the user. In general, there was an inebriation "of the most cheerful kind," which inclined users to sing and dance, eat voraciously, and "seek aphrodisiac enjoyments," though in "persons of quarrelsome disposition it occasions, as might be expected, an exasperation of their natural tendency."[24] Indeed, as Europeans began conducting more controlled experiments into the effects of cannabis drugs, the impression that the substance could produce something resembling madness was only deepened.

This is certainly demonstrated by the most influential nineteenth-century medical text on cannabis, Jacques-Joseph Moreau's *Hashish and Mental Illness* (1845), a study based on the researcher's personal experience while experimenting with the drug. Moreau was trained in Paris as a physician, but his interest in mental illness and hashish was piqued by his extensive travels to the Middle East. He had also been a participant in the Paris meetings of the Club des Hashishins and was most likely the "Doctor X" mentioned by Gautier in his account of the group's activities.[25] Moreau became interested in hashish as a means of studying mental illness. He believed that the drug's effects would help researchers experience the symptoms of these disorders for themselves. "To understand an ordinary depression, it is necessary to have experienced one; to comprehend the ravings of a madman, it is necessary to have raved oneself, but without having lost the awareness of one's madness, without having lost the power to evaluate the psychic changes occurring in the mind."[26] Moreau argued that only on extremely rare occasions could mental patients be found with the capacity to reflect on their inner disturbances. However, he believed that hashish temporarily provoked precisely the same changes in the brain that were experienced by the mentally ill. This theory rested on his hypothesis that all mental illness was caused by "manic excitement" in the brain. This state he described as a "disintegration, a veritable dissolution of that mental structure known as the mental faculties," and something that was akin to the action of a solvent on another substance, "the separation, the isolation of ideas and molecules that formed a harmonious and complete whole when they were united."[27] Furthermore, Moreau believed, much as Aristotle had, that this state could best be described as a "sleepless dream."[28] "There is not a single, elementary manifestation of mental illness that cannot be found in the mental changes caused by hashish, from simple manic excitement to frenzied delirium, from the feeblest impulse, the simplest fixation, to the merest injury to the senses, to the most irresistible drive, the wildest delirium, the most varied disorders of feelings."[29]

Despite all of this, Moreau did not believe that hashish was especially likely to cause legitimate mental illness in its users. In an earlier article, he had argued that hashish, like other substances that affect the nervous system, could over the long term bring about permanent mental disorders. Such disorders were characterized by "an expressionless physiognomy, a depressed, lax, and languid countenance, dull eyes rolling unsteadily in their orbits. . . . Such are some of the symptoms characteristic of the *excessive* use of hashish." Yet Moreau emphasized that such effects as seen in Egypt were no different from those known in Europe to follow from the excessive use of alcohol. "Almost all Moslems eat hashish, a very great number of them are addicted to it to an unbelievably high degree and, yet, *it is extremely seldom* that one encounters persons upon whom the hashish has had the disastrous effects we have spoken about here."[30]

However, readers wondering about the effects of cannabis could easily have overlooked this nuance, for Moreau described the effects of hashish in eight stages through which users progressively lost control of their faculties and emotions. An initial stage featuring a pure feeling of happiness led eventually to "errors in time and space" in the third stage and the "development of the sense of hearing" in stage four. Here he described how the "crudest music, the simplest vibrations of the strings of a harp or a guitar, rouse you to a point of delirium or plunge you into a sweet melancholy."

From the first notes of this tune so deeply imprinted with sadness, I felt a chill go through my entire body. My excitement changed abruptly in character. Totally concentrated within me like a burning fire, the waltz evoked in me only sad thoughts, distressing memories. The faces of several of the people surrounding me reflected the sinister mood of my imagination. These people were just serious; others who were laughing at me seemed to be making faces and threatening me. They terrified me, and I nearly accused them of hostility toward me.[31]

The remaining stages accelerated toward a complete loss of control. In the sixth stage ("damage to the emotions"), for example, "a fact that ordinarily would at most have aroused our discontent now sends us immediately into a rage."[32] This circumstance would then be followed by the final two stages, featuring "irresistible impulses" and "illusions and hallucinations."[33]

Moreau's work is especially valuable because of his actual experimentation with cannabis drugs. It must nonetheless be read with some caution. For these experiments, he utilized an Egyptian cannabis preparation called *dawamesc*, something he described as a mixture of hashish extract with other substances: "In order to achieve the effects that the Arabs seek so ardently—because of the excesses they indulge in—cinnamon, ginger, cloves, some aphrodisiacs, and perhaps also, as Aubert-Roche seems to believe, powder of cantharides (Spanish fly) are added to this substance. I have heard it said by several people who have traveled in India that one never finds pure hashish there, that it is always mixed with the substances just mentioned, or even with opium, extract of Datura, and other narcotics. The addition of these various substances to hashish assuredly modifies its effects to quite an extent."[34] The lack of precision here is frustrating especially because Moreau is hardly the only source from the period to suggest that "hashish" was often something more than cannabis.[35] Even Sinbad's hashish in *The Count of Monte Cristo*, for example, was eventually described as being 50 percent opium.[36] This is a problem that plagues much of the early research and writing on cannabis. Furthermore, Moreau's citation of the "excesses [the Arabs] indulge in" also reinforces the basic point that even the best "science" of this period was deeply compromised by the prejudice of the day, particularly that of an Orientalist variety.

But it was not just Western sources that linked cannabis to violence and madness during the nineteenth century. In May 1891, the *Allahabad Pioneer*, an English-language newspaper published in British India, proclaimed that "the lunatic asylums of India are filled with ganja smokers," a belief that was, it turns out, widespread among both British colonialists and native Indians alike. Partly in response to this claim, which would be repeated before the House of Commons two months later, an Indian Hemp Drugs Commission (IHDC) was appointed by the British to investigate all things cannabis in the subcontinent.[37] In 1893–94, the commission performed a massive inquiry into the subject, questioning more than 1,300 witnesses and accumulating eight volumes of evidence. The final report famously concluded that the moderate use of cannabis was harmless; that excessive use, while injurious, was relatively rare; and that Britain should not prohibit cannabis in the colony. With good reason, drug policy reformers have since championed the extraordinarily thorough IHDC report as a model of rationality.[38]

But while the IHDC's conclusions are relatively straightforward, the extraordinary quantity of evidence that inspired them proves significantly more complex. The commission actually found widespread belief in British India, particularly among native Indians, that even the moderate use of cannabis drugs was harmful to users. Also widespread was the belief that the excessive use of cannabis could incite unpremeditated crime or "homicidal frenzy," and more popular still was the view that the use of cannabis eventually led to madness.[39] The commission would investigate all of these claims in depth, eventually concluding that, while exaggerated, all of them had at least some basis in fact. Thus, while moderate use was deemed relatively harmless, the commission argued that "the excessive use of hemp drugs may, especially in cases where there is any weakness or hereditary predisposition, induce insanity."[40] Similar conclusions were reached with respect to the moral effects of the drug, including its purported relationship to crime. While "moderate use produces no moral effects whatever," the commission argued that "excess leads directly to loss of self respect, and thus to moral degeneration," and, "occasionally, but apparently very rarely indeed, excessive indulgence in hemp drugs may lead to violent crime."[41]

Though the commission concluded that cannabis should not be prohibited in India, this was not because the drug was considered totally harmless but rather because the harms of prohibition were deemed to outweigh the benefits. Crucial here was the philosophy of John Stuart Mill, whom the commission cited at length to justify its position: "To be prevented from what one is inclined to . . . is not only always irksome, but always tends, *pro tanto*, to starve the development of some portion of the bodily or mental faculties." It is nevertheless quite noteworthy that one-third of the commission, and two of the three Indian commissioners, objected to these conclusions, arguing that the actual effects of cannabis were much closer to the widespread popular view than the final report had suggested.[42]

Over the coming decades, research in India would mostly agree with the IHDC's dissenting minority. The most interesting of these studies appeared just a decade later. The author was George Francis William Ewens, superintendent of the recently opened Punjab Lunatic Asylum. Though Ewens declared the IHDC report a landmark "in which the various inferences deducible were discussed in a most thorough and able manner," he nonetheless disagreed sharply with its conclusions. "The smallest practical experience of insanity among natives of India is sufficient to convince one that these conclusions in this particular were mistaken and that excessive indulgence in any form of hemp drugs is a very frequent cause of mania." Ewens's study also demonstrated that far from being a product of Orientalist fantasy, the belief that the use of cannabis could produce insanity and violence was widespread among ordinary Indians. "The number of cases is remarkable, in which the insanity is attributed . . . by the relatives who come to see the patients or by the patients themselves after recovery, to the use of those drugs." It was, he argued, "a widespread belief, which as far as I can gather has always been held, both among the general population and also among European medical men practicing among them, that an excess in the use of these intoxicants . . . is the cause of an enormous proportion of the cases of insanity occurring in the country."[43] Of particular interest were the ninety-three case reports that he abstracted in an appendix to the study. The similarity of many of these cases to those reported in Mexico around the same time is noteworthy. Patient #12, for example, "murdered his wife in a fit of mania from *bhang*." Patient #13 "had been for a long time addicted to the use of *charas* [another cannabis preparation] and suddenly one day attempted to stab a Sheikh who was preaching against the use of drugs. A fairly quiet and reasonable man, but subject to attacks of extreme violence, with delusions of personality." Patient #22 "owned to being addicted to *charas* and *bhang*, and that when in a state of *nasha* [intoxication] he killed his wife, smashed her head in but remembers nothing of it," etc. The cases are also striking for the number that apparently displayed delusions of grandeur in a manner highly reminiscent of the bhang-eaters in the *Thousand and One Nights*. Case #25 suffered "delusions of being king of the Jogies, and possessor of six enormous rubies, each worth a king's ransom. Dresses in rags, and paper crowns, etc." Case #32, "known as a notorious consumer of *bhang*," suffered "delusions of being king of Delhi and of the Punjab." Case #54, though "a beggar," had "delusions of great possessions," and so on.[44]

Over the coming decades, other reports would emerge from India, Africa, and North America linking cannabis to madness and violence, but these would also be increasingly challenged.[45] A military study of the use of marijuana by soldiers in the Panama Canal Zone, for example, concluded in 1925 that the links between cannabis and deleterious effects had been wildly exaggerated. "There is no evidence that marihuana as grown and used here is a 'habit-forming' drug in the sense in which the term is applied to alcohol, opium, cocaine, etc., or that it has any appreciably deleterious influence on the individuals using it."[46] Growing skepticism with respect to earlier studies was also demonstrated in a 1937 report before the Cannabis Subcommittee of the League of Nations Advisory Committee on Traffic in Opium and Other Dangerous Drugs. "It is true that some directors of lunatic asylums in Egypt and British India have estimated the number of psychoses due to the abuse of hashish at 15% or even 30% of all the cases admitted in the course of a year, but it is generally held by the experts of Western countries that this percentage must be exaggerated, and that many cases of schizophrenia are dissimulated under the erroneous diagnosis of toxic insanity."[47]

It was, however, at this very same time that the Federal Bureau of Narcotics (FBN) in the United States and its crusading head, Harry Anslinger, were in the process of publicizing the frightening effects that marijuana supposedly had on its users. In the summer of 1937, Anslinger published his "Marihuana: Assassin of Youth," an article in which he claimed that in at least two dozen recent cases of "murder or degenerate sex attacks, many of them committed by youths, marihuana proved to be a contributing cause."[48] Reflecting the uncertainty of the times, a major report commissioned by the mayor of New York City just a few years later found no link between marijuana and such heinous acts, though that report was suppressed by the FBN. The American Medical Association, under pressure from Anslinger, also condemned it.[49]

The next twenty years would see the perceived links between cannabis drugs, insanity, and violence begin to fade from public discourse in the West. By the 1950s, even Anslinger had begun to back down somewhat from his earlier claims, placing more emphasis on the supposed likelihood that cannabis use would lead to the use of harder drugs like heroin. This was the so-called stepping stone or gateway theory that remains prevalent today, at least in popular discourse.[50] With the upsurge of marijuana use among middle-class white youth in the United States during the 1960s, these earlier discourses and the draconian laws they spawned became increasingly controversial, a fact that surely helped to make marijuana and notions of what would soon be referred to as "reefer madness" symbolically powerful for the counterculture and its opponents.

But serious reports of "cannabis psychosis" had not completely disappeared. In the late 1950s in South Africa, Frances Ames studied the effects of orally ingested cannabis on a number of novice users with no history of mental illness. Among other outcomes, the subjects experienced feelings of panic, paranoia, delusions, visual hallucinations, and even depersonalization. Ames compared these reactions to manic and schizophrenic states. A decade later, reports emerged on a particularly interesting set of cases involving American soldiers in Vietnam. There, during 1967 and 1968, psychiatrists John A. Talbott and James W. Teague examined twelve cases of "acute toxic psychosis," which were closely linked to the ingestion of cannabis. In each of the twelve cases, the subject had taken cannabis for the first time and shortly thereafter experienced a series of psychotic symptoms ranging from anxiety and delusions to hallucinations and depersonalization. In one case, a soldier smoked a cigarette containing the drug and immediately experienced a "burning, choking sensation in his throat" and began to feel extremely anxious and suspicious. After going to a civilian bar, he became afraid that the Vietnamese there were going to do him harm. He then fled the bar "in terror." He was soon before the psychiatrists, who found him to be experiencing rapid, disjointed thought and to be repeatedly returning to his fears of being harmed.

A second case was more remarkable. Here, a sentry on guard duty smoked some marijuana with another soldier, whom he eventually shot to death. Shortly after smoking the marijuana, the victim, who was apparently wearing a shirt that read "Ho Chi Minh," began teasing some nearby children and saying that he was the esteemed North Vietnamese leader. The sentry became confused by this and asked the victim if he was in fact Ho Chi Minh. The victim then showed him his shirt with the name written across it. The sentry lifted his rifle and shot him several times. He then ran back to the base carrying the T-shirt with the name on it, pronouncing himself a hero. Other soldiers then went with him to see the body and there found the other sentry's corpse with several gunshot wounds to the chest.

All twelve cases examined by Talbott and Teague involved subjects who had smoked marijuana for the first time. Ten of the twelve experienced delusions and paranoia. Only two of the patients had any prior history of psychiatric problems. All of the subjects fully recovered within forty-eight hours, with the exception of one patient whose symptoms endured for eleven days. The cases produced some puzzlement from both Talbott and Teague and other psychiatrists in Vietnam. If these cases had been caused by cannabis, they wondered, why had there been essentially no reports in the psychiatric literature of similar reactions in the United States over the past three decades? Might this kind of acute cannabis psychosis be peculiar to Vietnam? A number of hypotheses were offered that alone or in combination might have helped to reconcile the data. First, it was noted that Vietnamese cannabis tended to be about twice as strong as the marijuana smoked in the United States, and about half the time it was mixed with opiates. This combined with the peculiar stresses of the Vietnamese setting might have helped to trigger the severe reactions among soldiers. Second, the lack of reporting in the United States might have resulted from the illegality of cannabis and the reluctance of psychotic patients to report on their own marijuana use. Talbott and Teague in fact argued that these reactions were probably underreported in Vietnam for the same reasons, with all but the most severe negative outcomes being handled without recourse to psychiatric care. Furthermore, a lack of awareness of cannabis's potential to produce such reactions might have led doctors to completely overlook it as a potential causal factor. The authors noted a recent case of a woman on an American college campus who turned up at the hospital in a similar psychotic state after having smoked cannabis for the first time. In that case, the doctor who treated her had no knowledge that cannabis might have been the cause and did not look into the case further since she recovered relatively quickly.

In the end, Talbott and Teague concluded that these reactions should be causally attributed to the ingestion of cannabis for several reasons: all of these cases occurred immediately after the patients had smoked cannabis for the first time; the condition was self-limiting and the "signs and symptoms had a definite toxic, organic quality"; and, finally, the patients recovered completely and the condition did not recur. They determined: "Cannabis derivatives, as a causal or precipitating agent, should be considered whenever a young person presents with an acute toxic psychosis with paranoid features. Since possession of the drug is illegal, accurate histories may not be obtainable, but the physician must be alert to the possibility of marihuana psychosis in cases resembling acute schizophrenic reaction, acute paranoid psychosis, or acute toxic-metabolic psychosis."[51]

One must remain extremely skeptical of these conclusions, particularly given the fact that 50 percent of Vietnamese cannabis preparations were said to contain opiates. The study nonetheless is important because the cases so closely resemble the kinds of adverse reactions that were reported in Mexico, India, and various other locations in the past.

While there had certainly been very little reporting on such phenomena in the United States over the previous thirty years, Talbott and Teague were not the only researchers to suddenly become interested in the cannabis-psychosis connection, particularly as the drug became increasingly controversial in the United States during the 1960s. That revived interest ushered in a new era of more controlled and serious study of cannabis botany and pharmacology that would greatly improve our understanding of this drug and its effects.

■ In 1970, in the *New England Journal of Medicine*, Andrew Weil published a fascinating paper that examined various adverse effects experienced by marijuana users. Based on his work with hundreds of patients during his time both as a medical researcher in Boston and as a practicing physician in San Francisco, Weil argued that adverse reactions to marijuana were not uncommon. Obviously, Weil was not the first person to make such a claim, but his research was especially interesting because he had found not only that these effects were often misdiagnosed by clinicians as "acute cannabis psychosis" but also that these misdiagnoses were actually responsible for the onset of more severe and debilitating symptoms in patients. Weil argued that by treating a patient as if he or she were experiencing "cannabis psychosis," clinicians managed to produce precisely that outcome in a kind of self-fulfilling prophecy.

Panic reactions were the key here. According to Weil, probably 75 percent of the adverse reactions to cannabis that he had observed had come in this form. Patients experiencing severe panic would become fearful that they were losing their minds or dying, and such reactions could become sufficiently intense to simulate acute psychosis. Weil estimated that in an environment where marijuana use was largely accepted, such reactions were probably extremely rare, occurring perhaps 1 percent of the time. But in an environment where marijuana use was considered more deviant, the rates might reach as high as 25 percent. He argued that all physicians should assume an adverse reaction to marijuana to be a panic reaction "unless proven otherwise." "This diagnosis not only is by far the most likely on a statistical basis but also represents the only condition whose outcome is crucially dependent on the initial response of the physician. Panic states can always be terminated by simple reassurance. If the doctor approaches the patient as a psychiatric emergency (by administering tranquilizers or urging hospitalization), he will often prolong the panic by inadvertently confirming the patient's fears of a mental breakdown."[52] Here was suggested nothing short of a solution to marijuana's psychoactive riddle as constituted in the United States of the late 1960s.

Weil richly illustrated this point with two fascinating case studies. The first involved a twenty-four-year-old medical student recently arrived to San Francisco from New York City. Prior to his move west, he had tried marijuana but had never experienced any intoxication. Not long after arriving in San Francisco, he went to a party and there smoked a lot of strong marijuana. He started to feel strange and to have difficulty communicating with others and soon became convinced that he was experiencing an "acute psychotic reaction." He then took himself to the hospital and was treated by another resident with Thorazine, an antipsychotic medication. The next day he awoke still experiencing severe anxiety and was given Librium, an anxiolytic. Throughout the day he showed little improvement and routinely asked anyone within earshot if they thought he was losing his mind. Finally, as evening approached, another physician became involved and defused the situation by calmly explaining to the young man that he was merely experiencing an unusually intense marijuana high that was now dissipating. "The patient gratefully accepted this reassurance and improved so rapidly that he was able to assume his externship duties the following day. Afterward he agreed that he had been 'letting [himself] get frightened' but said he would not smoke marihuana again 'for some time.'"[53]

A second, equally interesting case involved a thirty-seven-year-old housewife whose fifteen-year-old daughter had convinced her to try hashish. The woman was extremely reluctant but also very curious to try the drug. The daughter provided some hashish, which the two shared, the daughter eating about three times as much as her mother. After about an hour, the mother began to feel panic and soon became convinced she'd been poisoned. She called the family physician, who instructed her to take a cab to the hospital. Upon arrival, she was experiencing a continuous heart rate of 140 beats per minute. Her physician then injected her with an antipsychotic medicine and had her admitted to the psychiatric ward. After another four days of experiencing agitation and a depressed mood, she fully recovered.[54]

As Weil argued, both cases suggested just how important the role of "set" (the user's psychology) and "setting" (both social and cultural) could be in the experience of marijuana intoxication. In the first case, the young medical student's symptoms improved almost immediately upon authoritative reassurance that he was not losing his mind. In the second, the housewife's inexperience and reluctance to take hashish contributed to her rapid descent into panic. The potential unreliability of dosage in predicting outcomes of cannabis intoxication was poignantly illustrated by this latter case, for the daughter had consumed about three times as much hashish as her mother but reported only experiencing a "good time" for about six hours.[55] In this way, Weil vividly illustrated how a psychoactive agent like cannabis interacts with the psychology of the user and the sociocultural environment where the drug is ingested. The symptoms of the medical student surely were intensified due to his knowledge of something called "toxic psychosis." Similarly, the housewife's reaction was probably fueled by the deviant reputation of cannabis among people of her age, background, and social standing.

This is not unusual among drugs. In his insightful book on the subject, psychopharmacologist Richard DeGrandpre refers to this phenomenon as the "placebo text." In DeGrandpre's view, the placebo text is "any unwritten cultural script that, like a religious text, informs a group's beliefs and expectations about a given drug, animating the 'drug effects' once the substance is taken." "If by *placebo effect* one means an outcome produced not by a drug but by beliefs and expectations about a drug, then a placebo text becomes the cultural teachings, however subtle, that inform these beliefs and expectations. According to this view, once a substance is taken, beliefs and expectations join with the first-order pharmacological effects of the substance to mediate or animate the immediate and long-term effects attributed to the drug."[56]

This phenomenon first began to receive significant scholarly attention in the 1930s, particularly from pioneering sociologist and drug researcher Alfred Lindesmith. Lindesmith had become convinced that many of the perceived effects of drugs were a direct product of the drug user's expectations. As an example, he cited a study of drug addicts in New York that demonstrated that the relationship between the taking of opiates and the experience of withdrawal symptoms was in fact extremely tenuous. Here, two groups of addicts had their regular morphine doses surreptitiously altered by researchers. Those in one group were made to believe that they were receiving their regular daily dose of morphine, but over the course of several weeks, that dose was in fact being reduced to complete placebo. Despite the removal of the drug, many of the patients experienced no signs of withdrawal whatsoever and were convinced they were still receiving their regular dose. Those in the second group continued to receive their regular dose but were misled to believe that it was being decreased over time. Many of these patients complained loudly of the painful withdrawal symptoms that were being caused by the dose reduction, though none had actually taken place. From evidence like this, Lindesmith theorized that while a physical withdrawal process did exist, its relationship to "addiction" required both the recognition of those symptoms and a learned and socially mediated response to them. As DeGrandpre has elegantly explained, this response had to involve the cognitive phenomenon of concern over that withdrawal and the behavioral phenomenon of responding to that withdrawal with more drugs, creating a "biopsychosocial circuit" necessary for addiction to occur. "For example, an individual may experience little physical withdrawal following opiate use, or . . . a person might interpret withdrawal as a sign of impending drug dependence and subsequently reduce or quit his or her drug habit. If, on the other hand, a withdrawal experience causes an individual to become obsessed with the prospect and experience of withdrawal—and to continually use in order to avoid it—the circuit will be completed, with the learning process now occurring repeatedly, thus reinforcing the drug habit at all three levels: physiological, cognitive, and behavioral."[57]

Though studies of this kind are more difficult to perform today due to ethical considerations, recent work on drug effects in animals has continued to demonstrate the importance of environment on drug effects, whether on addictive behavior, mood, or even lethality. One study using rats, for example, showed that the lethality of cocaine is not merely dose dependent but is contingent upon the circumstances of the drug use. In this particular study, two groups of rats were injected with high doses of cocaine. In the first group, the rats had unlimited access to cocaine and could choose to take an injection as often as they desired. In the second group, the rats had no choice in the matter. Instead, these animals were paired with a rat from the first group and given injections of cocaine at precisely the same dose and rate at which their first group partner chose to take the drug. In other words, each pair of rats would take precisely the same dose, but only one of the partners took the cocaine in a voluntary manner. The outcome of this experiment was quite extraordinary—none of the rats who self-administered the cocaine died, but the exact same doses of cocaine produced death in five of thirteen of their involuntary partners. The same researchers conducted a similar experiment with morphine in order to measure differences in dopamine levels and other brain activity in the two groups. Again, significant differences were found between the animals that took the drugs voluntarily and those that were compelled to do so.[58] The experiment showed clearly that factors other than pharmacology were critical in determining the outcomes of drug use, even lethal overdose.

Many other fascinating animal studies of this kind have been conducted. One of the most interesting was performed by John Falk at Rutgers University, who gave rats a choice of self-administering cocaine or water, a choice that was signaled, as is often done in these kinds of studies, by the appearance of another stimulus (in this case, a light). In his initial experiments, Falk found that the rats chose the cocaine every time. But then he found that he could substitute ethanol, caffeine, or nicotine and produce the same response from the rats. This made him suspicious that perhaps the results were not being produced by the drugs but rather by the light stimulus. He thus devised an experiment to provide a choice between cocaine and water. With no further stimulus, the animals chose cocaine every time. He then paired the choice with a light stimulus. After conditioning the rats to choose the cocaine on the flash of the light, he then paired the light stimulus with the water. Remarkably, the rats then chose the water every time. Clearly, the environmental cues surrounding the cocaine use had come to trigger the compulsive drug-taking behavior more than the drug itself had.[59]

In another study, patterns of drug use among macaque monkeys were shown to be closely related to the place of the animals in their social hierarchy. While all the animals used cocaine when given the opportunity, only the subordinate animals used heavily. In another experiment, it was found that animals significantly reduced their drug taking when simply given the choice of a sweet-tasting alternative. Here, the apparently highly addictive qualities of cocaine observed in a context devoid of recreational choices was shown to almost disappear in a more enriching environment containing satisfyingly sweet alternatives to cocaine abuse.[60]

In short, responses to drug use are conditioned by much more than simply the substance being consumed and the related dosage. This is the essence of the psychoactive riddle. Sometimes this fact is easy to recognize. For example, most of us have observed that the same dose of alcohol can produce remarkably distinct effects on two different people at a party. Where a few shots of whiskey can produce a joyful intoxication in one person, the same whiskey can produce anger and belligerence in someone else. Here the differing psychological set of the cases would appear crucial, and in truth, other stimuli could conceivably have produced similar effects in these hypothetical individuals. The joyfully intoxicated subject might have acted similarly in the context of, say, his or her best friend's wedding or some other significant event. The belligerent drunk might have become equally violent after listening to a certain kind of especially aggressive music. But in this instance, and at this particular party, it appears clear to all observers that alcohol was the trigger for each of these very distinct moods. Similarly, many of us have seen or even experienced the compulsive behavior that can be produced by gambling, but gambling does not require the ingestion of any drugs at all.

In fact, perhaps the closest relative to Mexico's marijuana madness (as described a century ago) is the phenomenon of "amok," something that has been linked to cannabis and other drugs but that has been shown to require no drugs whatsoever. As mentioned earlier, John Henry Grose, in the late eighteenth century, described cannabis as a substance used in Surat that produced "a temporary madness, that in some, when designedly taken for that purpose, ends in running what they call a-muck, furiously killing every one they meet, without distinction, until themselves are knocked on the head, like mad dogs."[61] Today, of course, the phrase "to run amok" is a widely used figure of speech referring to someone or something that has gotten out of control. But historically it has been used to describe a very real psycho-cultural phenomenon indigenous to the Malay archipelago and nearby territories. It was first noted by Western observers during the Age of Exploration but continues to garner the attention of twenty-first-century medical anthropologists. And while it is no longer predominantly associated with psychoactive drug use, the phenomenon looks remarkably like those descriptions of marijuana-induced violence so common in late-nineteenth- and early-twentieth-century Mexico.

Recent scholarship has defined amok as "a sudden mass assault," where an individual, after a period of brooding, attacks those around him or her in an outpouring of more or less random violence. This is generally followed by claims of amnesia on the part of the individual. Amok is perhaps the most famous of the so-called culture-bound syndromes, a group of known but rather bizarre behaviors that are restricted to specific cultural geographies. There is considerable debate over whether such behaviors should be classified as psychiatric disorders or as a "socially learned, culturally channeled and sanctioned means of expressing normally forbidden emotions." In a recent article on the phenomenon, Kevin Browne has noted that, whatever the preferred model, amok is widely understood as "a variant of a worldwide, biological disorder on which cultural trappings are layered."[62] The Malay origins of amok have been identified in training for warfare, which was adopted from the Hindu states of India long before contact with Europeans. After the introduction of Islam into the peninsula in the fourteenth century, amok sometimes became a form of religious fanaticism where infidels were slaughtered in wild outbursts of violence. Descriptions of amok later became a regular part of European travel accounts in Asia. These generally involved an almost totally unexpected attack by a knife-wielding Malay that would last until the *pengamok*, as these individuals were then called, was either killed or overwhelmed and subdued. The behavior has yet to be fully understood and numerous theories have been forwarded to explain it, from it serving as a means of carrying out suicidal wishes to it being a manifestation of mental illness or drug (including alcohol) abuse.[63]

In his seventeenth-century chronicles of the "exotic pleasures" of the Orient, Engelbert Kaempfer described amok in relation to opium abuse:

> I have spoken about opium and its common use by the Persians and Indians. I add an abominable abuse that thrives among the dark Indians: bru-

talizing the spirits in order to acquire the audacity to perpetrate murder. When tired of their own life or injuries, they dedicate themselves to seeking death through the punishment and death of others. For this purpose they swallow a lump of opium from which the intention conceived is stimulated, reason is disturbed, and the spirit is freed from restraining. The result is such that with dagger in hand they rush like raging tigers into the streets and are bent on slaughtering whomever they meet, whether friend or foe, until they themselves are struck and laid low by someone else. This act, a frequent sight among the inhabitants of Java and the farther Orient, is called Hamuk. The very sound of the word terrifies anyone there who hears it. For if a person sees a murderer, he cries out at the top of his voice the word Hamuk in order to warn those unarmed to flee and take care for their lives, while whoever is armed and courageous is expected to run and slay the beast.[64]

It is in these and similar descriptions of amok that we find some of the closest parallels to the supposedly marijuana-induced violence of modern Mexico. This greatly complicates our endeavor here, for while it clearly shows that outbursts of this kind were linked to cannabis and other drugs in diverse contexts, recent ethnographic research also demonstrates that amok and other similar phenomena definitively exist and in fact require no drugs at all for their inspiration. We are thus faced with the confounding possibility that marijuana may have been intimately involved in such incidents in Mexico without actually playing any real causal role in their denouement.

None of this is meant to suggest that drugs do not play an important and sometimes predictable role in triggering certain behaviors. As DeGrandpre emphasizes, while the placebo text is critical, drugs do have demonstrable pharmacological properties—a fact that greatly enhances the effectiveness of the placebo text. "If placebo effects are mobilized by beliefs and expectations, then what could be better than an active drug for launching the placebo effect?"[65] Weil's research certainly suggested that set and setting were critical determinants of cannabis's effects in humans. But what of those panic reactions that he found so common among the adverse responses to marijuana? Were these more linked to the nature of cannabis pharmacology or to the environment in which that drug use occurred?

At the time of Weil's research, these questions were in fact still quite difficult to answer. A few years earlier, Martin Keeler had published a study in the *American Journal of Psychiatry* in which he examined the cases of eleven college students who had experienced unpleasant symptoms after using cannabis. These ranged from panic attacks and paranoia to depersonalization and delusions. One nineteen-year-old subject reported that "during a marijuana reaction he became convinced that his internal organs were rotting and that he would die," a sensation that was somehow related to his "conviction that he had done evil things." A twenty-three-year-old woman reported having "the horrors" while intoxicated with marijuana. "She described this as a feeling that indescribably evil things would happen to her because of the kind of person she was." In another case, a twenty-two-year-old man "became convinced that his taking the drug was part of some gigantic plot but that he did not know what the plot was." More disturbingly, several of these individuals demonstrated a recurrence of such symptoms after the transient marijuana intoxication had subsided. Two had become schizophrenic after using marijuana, LSD, and amphetamine.[66]

Yet Keeler struggled to contextualize these findings within the existing scientific literature on marijuana. The state of the research simply did not allow it. While there existed many studies from other parts of the world describing psychotic reactions to cannabis, these had not been sufficiently controlled—it was still not clear how common such adverse reactions were or what dosage tended to be involved, nor were sufficient details about the users in question available.

> There is no accurate or reasonably accurate way of determining how many acute difficulties occur during or immediately after marihuana use. Most of these reactions do not come to medical attention. There are great differences in the potency of different preparations. The populations from which the reports of adverse reactions in this study are derived might be defined as university nonconformist. These individuals are of superior intelligence, more than average education, and not delinquent in the usual sense. It is not justified to assume that adverse reactions would be the same in this group, a delinquent group in a large city of the United States, and the urban poor of Morocco.

In other words, marijuana's psychoactive riddle was utterly unsolvable given the current state of research. One could not be sure whether the drug had actually caused these effects or if it simply precipitated them in predisposed individuals. It was in fact quite possible that the effects had *preceded* the cannabis use.[67]

But as controversy over marijuana use increased, so did the number of researchers looking to answer these questions. In 1967, H. Isbell and colleagues utilized newly synthesized synthetic tetrahydrocannabinol, or THC, one of the key active ingredients in cannabis, to measure the effects of the drug in a laboratory setting. The researchers found that at high doses, psychotomimetic responses were achieved in most users.[68] A year later, Andrew Weil, Norman Zinberg, and Judith Nelson performed what was probably the first double-blind laboratory study on the effects of marijuana. Weil and colleagues, like Keeler, noted the significant problems that had attended cannabis study to date. They were especially concerned that research into the drug's effects had relied on orally administered cannabis when most users actually smoked the drug, and no study to date had ever employed double-blind, controlled conditions. After correcting for these problems, their conclusions diverged quite significantly from earlier reports, with no psychotomimetic reactions whatsoever: "Marihuana appears to be a relatively mild intoxicant in our studies. If these results seem to differ from those of earlier experiments, it must be remembered that other experimenters have given marihuana orally, have given doses much higher than those commonly smoked by users, have administered potent synthetics, and have not strictly controlled the laboratory setting." They also put much emphasis on the important role that set and setting appeared to play in the experience of marijuana intoxication and how this fact had greatly prejudiced studies like Ames's 1958 work in South Africa. "The researcher who sets out with prior conviction that hemp is psychotomimetic or a 'mild hallucinogen' is likely to confirm his conviction experimentally, but he would probably confirm the opposite hypothesis if his bias were in the opposite direction. Precautions to insure neutrality of set and setting, including use of a double-blind procedure as an absolute minimum, are vitally important if the object of investigation is to measure real marihuana-induced responses."[69]

Nonetheless, experimental design was not the only impediment to better understanding. Here is where marijuana's peculiar pharmacology comes into play. While in the 1960s, only THC had been identified as a critical psychoactive element in cannabis, research of the last few decades has demonstrated that cannabis chemistry is remarkably complex. It is now recognized that cannabis contains over four hundred chemical compounds, sixty-six of which are unique to the plant. The latter are called "cannabinoids" and include four compounds particularly crucial to the plant's psychoactivity: delta-9-tetrahydrocannabinol, delta-8-tetrahydrocannabinol, cannabinol, and cannabidiol. Delta-9-tetrahydrocannabinol is the most prevalent of these compounds and produces the majority of the plant's psychoactive effects. It is thus often referred to simply as THC. As THC ages, it breaks down into cannabinol, which is also psychoactive but about ten times less so than THC. Cannabidiol (CBD) is the second most prevalent of the active agents, accounting for up to 40 percent of a given plant's psychoactive content.[70] It was originally believed that CBD was not psychoactive. More recent studies have shown conclusively that CBD is an active agent but that it interacts with THC in complex ways. CBD can simultaneously augment certain effects of THC while diminishing others.[71] By itself, CBD is an anxiolytic.[72]

Humans and many other species, from chickens and trout to fruit flies, feature cannabinoid receptors in the brain and immune system. The cannabinoids in marijuana bond with these receptors, triggering activities within particular cells and inhibiting certain brands of nerve impulses. These changes trigger others. For instance, THC affects the dopamine system much like the opiates and nicotine do and may enhance or inhibit gamma-aminobutyric acid (GABA) as alcohol does, though the precise effects on these systems are not yet fully understood.[73] These receptors, of course, did not evolve so that humans and other animals could enjoy using cannabis. The body actually creates its own cannabinoids that bond with them. The most well-known of these has been named anandamide. Anandamide and cannabinoid receptors are especially prevalent in the hippocampus and cerebellum, both of which affect the memory and motor functions of the brain. Anandamide is also found in the thalamus, which influences pain and emotion, though very few cannabinoid receptors are found there, suggesting that anandamide bonds with other receptors as well.[74]

These various psychoactive properties and their interrelation perhaps help account for why the reported effects of cannabis vary so widely. For example, Michael Lyons recently surveyed 2,500 subjects who had smoked cannabis a minimum of five times and found extraordinary variability in the symptoms reported. He and his investigative team provided their subjects with a survey listing a broad range of symptoms and then asked the users if they had ever experienced them while taking cannabis. These effects and the percentage of users reporting them were as follows: relaxed or "mellow" (93 percent); sociable (71 percent); lazy (65 percent); drowsy (62 percent); euphoric (61 percent); unable to concentrate (56 percent); creative (56 percent); laugh/cry (55 percent); paranoid (53 percent); increased sex drive (48 percent); guilty (43 percent); anxious (40 percent); confused (38 percent); energetic (38 percent); jumpy (30 percent); depressed (28 percent); confident (24 percent); dizzy (23 percent); hear/see things that are not there (18 percent); "keyed-up" (17.4 percent); out of control (17 percent); nauseous (9 percent); irritable (7 percent).[75] These results largely conform with other studies of the same kind.[76]

A few things stand out from the above survey data. First, there is an incredible variability of experience reported by cannabis users. The drug can make users feel both energetic and lazy, euphoric and depressed, relaxed and paranoid, confident and anxious. Second, while negative symptoms like paranoia are less common than more positive ones like euphoria, over half of respondents reported having experienced the former and fully 18 percent reported seeing and hearing things that were not there, two symptoms commonly associated with psychosis.

Psychosis is a condition that is most commonly linked to schizophrenia but that is also connected to many other mental disorders. Intoxicants, especially the class of drugs known as hallucinogens, can produce hallucinations and delusions of a kind that might otherwise be connected to psychosis. Psychiatrists now refer to such effects as psychotomimetic. Today, if subjects are aware that their hallucinations have been produced directly by a drug, their condition is not classified as psychosis but as "substance intoxication." If such symptoms persist, the condition might then be classified as a "substance-induced psychotic disorder."[77] While it's now clear that cannabis can produce psychotomimetic symptoms, it's not known how often users experience them. Most research suggests that such responses are most common among novice users, particularly those who eat a dose of cannabis. Eaten cannabis requires considerable time to take effect, which often leads novices to ingest large amounts of the drug before normal symptoms begin to be experienced. Overdose is not uncommon in such situations with paranoia and hallucinations as potential results (though no death has ever been attributed to cannabis ingestion).[78]

But over the course of the 1970s and early 1980s, new evidence began to accumulate of an apparent relationship between cannabis use and actual psychosis. In 1974, Gurbakhsh Chopra and James Smith published a study that identified by far the largest number of cases of apparent "cannabis psychosis" in the literature. Their research centered on admissions to the Addiction Research Clinic in Calcutta between 1963 and 1968. There, they found that 11 percent of patients admitted to the clinic, or about two hundred individuals, had arrived "with psychiatric symptoms that occurred following the reported use of a cannabis preparation." The authors found that most of the patients had taken large doses of cannabis and then experienced a state not unlike the well-known "alcoholic blackout" in that they engaged in conversations and complex activities but had no memory of having done so. They had then been admitted to the clinic either on their own or on their family's recommendation. Chopra eventually interviewed all of these patients in order to obtain a "complete medical, psychiatric, and social history for each." Though the authors admitted that the process was at times complicated by the agitated state of the patients, they eventually came to the conclusion that "cannabis psychosis" was a very real phenomenon.[79]

To demonstrate this, they divided the patients into three categories. The first group, about 34 percent of the subjects, had been in good health and had no history of mental problems. According to the authors, their symptoms were "typical of an acute toxic psychosis." These included delusions, hallucinations, depersonalization, excitement, and confusion. Symptoms disappeared within a few days, and the patients returned to normal. A much larger second group, about 61 percent of the total, did have previous psychiatric problems, typically "schizoid," "sociopath," or "unstable personality." These patients at first experienced symptoms like those in the first group, but the condition was more prolonged, lasting up to several weeks. Once the apparent cannabis-related symptoms subsided, the underlying psychiatric issues manifested themselves with greater intensity, "with schizophrenic and paranoid symptoms being those most prevalent." Some of these patients eventually relapsed into the original acute condition after a few months' time. A third group, about 5 percent of the sample, were patients with overt psychosis. Not all had been hospitalized previously but might have been in a Western context. Most of these patients had smoked low-grade cannabis, following which "their tenuous contact with reality was severed and they were no longer able to function in society even at their previous marginal level. Symptoms of irrational behavior, volubility, indifference to family and self, withdrawal, incessant craving to smoke marihuana, coupled occasionally with violent responses to minimal or supposed provocations, were superimposed upon their previous psychotic symptomatology. For a few, the drug-induced symptoms—the toxic psychosis—became so prominent that they temporarily obliterated the underlying symptomatology." The authors presented one illustrative case in detail, this of a thirty-year-old man from the group with no history of psychiatric problems. "He was admitted with symptoms of confusion, garrulity, incoherent speech, constant laughing, restlessness, insomnia, and occasional outbursts of violence directed to those around him." After a short time, the symptoms subsided, but when the patient returned to cannabis use some weeks later, the symptoms again returned. Since abstaining from the drug, he had experienced no further recurrences.[80]

This final point was critical. Almost all of the patients recovered their former mental status and maintained it as long as they abstained from cannabis. "Those patients who reverted to the use of cannabis after discharge from the clinic almost always again developed an acute toxic psychosis." In addition, some of the patients from the second and third groups, those with some psychiatric history or overt psychosis, experienced a worsening of their previously existing psychiatric condition. The authors admitted some uncertainty in that the temporal sequence of events could not be fully verified. That is, there was a chance that for many of these patients, cannabis use had been a symptom of "psychotic decompensation" rather than a cause. But even given that caveat, they concluded that there were enough cases with no preexisting psychopathology, and enough similarity between the symptoms of all the patients, that "it seems likely that the clinical entity of 'cannabis psychosis' does, in fact, exist."[81]

No other study to date has identified nearly as many examples of "cannabis psychosis." In a 2004 survey of all the existing research on this question, Wayne Hall and Louisa Degenhardt found a total of only 397 such cases reported worldwide, 200 of these coming from the Chopra and Smith study, which, in their opinion, had not sufficiently proven cannabis to be the causal mechanism.[82] Hall and Degenhardt also found that the symptoms of "cannabis psychosis" in the literature were extremely mixed and almost always disappeared during abstinence from the drug, suggesting that these were cases of acute intoxication rather than "psychosis." Ultimately, the authors found "no compelling evidence . . . that there is a specific clinical syndrome that is identifiable as a 'cannabis psychosis,'" and they concluded that if such syndromes do exist, they are "rare or they only rarely receive medical attention in western societies."[83]

Of course, the distinction between an actual "cannabis psychosis" and an "acute intoxication" that looks very much like "psychosis" would hardly be significant under the historical circumstances we are interested in here. Again, despite the significant doubts that cannabis can actually precipitate "psychosis," there remains widespread agreement that cannabis can produce psychotomimetic symptoms. In his excellent and dispassionate survey of the scientific research, Mitch Earleywine has provided one of the best summaries of the existing state of knowledge:

Cannabinoid intoxications can also mimic certain aspects of psychoses like schizophrenia. These psychotic disorders typically include odd thoughts, auditory hallucinations, and inappropriate emotions. An odd thought typical of psychosis must be completely implausible within the person's culture. For example, a psychotic individual might have the odd thought that other people are inserting ideas into his head. Auditory hallucinations usually include hearing voices that do not exist. Inappropriate emotions might include smiling when frightened or sad. Large doses of eaten marijuana or hashish can create comparable symptoms but this cannabis psychosis is not the same as schizophrenia. It usually lacks the formal thought problems and inappropriate emotions. It also dissipates relatively quickly, while schizophrenia remains a chronic mental illness. Other drugs, particularly the hallucinogens, create these symptoms as well. LSD, mescaline, and psychedelic mushrooms lead to erratic thoughts and strange speech patterns typically found in psychotic individuals. Extended use of cocaine or amphetamine can also lead to the paranoid, irrational behavior common to some forms of schizophrenia.[84]

But other significant evidence has accumulated linking cannabis to actual psychosis, in particular schizophrenia. An important breakthrough in that research came in 1987 when a longitudinal study of more than 45,000 Swedish military conscripts revealed a statistically significant relationship between the use of cannabis and the risk of developing that disorder.[85] The data indicated that in comparison to people who had never used cannabis, the relative risk of developing schizophrenia was about six times higher for individuals who had used the drug more than fifty times. However, the authors acknowledged that their study did not prove a causal relationship. As had been suggested in the major Indian studies of nearly a century before, use of cannabis may have been a symptom rather than a cause. It was suggested that perhaps as those predisposed to schizophrenia began experiencing symptoms of the disorder, they might have self-medicated with cannabis. Similarly, cannabis might have merely helped exacerbate schizophrenic symptoms in those soldiers who were predisposed to it. The fact that rates of schizophrenia have not risen in countries that have seen a significant rise in cannabis use remains one of the strongest indications that cannabis does not cause schizophrenia in individuals who are not already predisposed to the illness.[86] Nevertheless, the study showed convincingly that some kind of relationship did exist between the drug and that condition.

Research has since delved more deeply into the question. In the most recent meta-review of the literature on the subject, Jennifer McLaren and colleagues analyzed the ten major cohort studies that have closely examined this question. They conclude that the cannabis-schizophrenia link has been consistently demonstrated. But these studies have also suggested that cannabis is only causal in that "cannabis produces psychotic disorders in individuals who possess an underlying vulnerability to psychosis." Again, were there a causal link involving all users of cannabis, rates of schizophrenia should have increased as rates of cannabis use have increased, but this has not been the case. Nevertheless, the literature reveals "consistent and robust evidence of an association between cannabis and psychosis; cannabis use was generally shown to precede psychotic symptoms; and a dose-response relationship was evident."[87]

The reasons for this link remain uncertain. It is still quite plausible that at least part of the relationship can be explained by the use of cannabis by schizophrenics to self-medicate. McLaren and colleagues argue that this theory neither accounts for the whole relationship nor stands as the most plausible explanation for it but acknowledge that it may be an important part of the dynamic. Of particular interest on this point is a recent Australian study that found a bidirectional relationship between cannabis use and schizophrenia— cannabis use predicted schizophrenia, but schizophrenia also predicted cannabis use.[88] In fact, studies in the United States have found schizophrenics to have rates of drug abuse about five times higher than the general population and to be about six times as likely to use illicit drugs.[89] Other recent qualitative studies have found that despite considerable evidence that cannabis can exacerbate some of the hallmark symptoms of schizophrenia (like auditory hallucinations and delusions of various kinds), schizophrenics themselves find the effects of cannabis helpful and cite self-medication as a reason for their use of it.[90] In his 2008 study of schizophrenic cannabis users, William Costain found that some of his subjects claimed to better hear the voices in their heads while using cannabis. For psychiatrists, this is considered a worsening of psychotic symptoms, but for these schizophrenic patients, the effect was considered a relief. "Patients used cannabis to enhance hallucinations, and this was associated for them with themes of spirituality, creativity, clarity, power, and control."[91] Nathalie Francoeur and Cynthia Baker recently found that schizophrenics reported a number of positive symptoms from the use of cannabis, including relaxation and an enhancement of their concentration.[92] But as McClaren and colleagues have argued, self-medication probably tells only part of the story. In fact, some potential biological evidence for the link has recently been identified, with researchers having found elevated levels of anandamide in the cerebrospinal fluid of schizophrenics and also higher densities of CB1 receptors in their prefrontal cortexes.[93]

But what does this mean for the perception of the cannabis-psychosis connection in everyday life? Obviously, a sixfold increase in relative risk as was indicated by the Swedish study is significant, but overall the numbers suggest that the relative risk of schizophrenia for cannabis users nevertheless remains small. For the more than 45,000 soldiers studied in Sweden, the baseline relative risk of schizophrenia was less than 1 percent. Thus, among those 45,000 soldiers, there were only 274 total cases of schizophrenia, and among these, just 21 were in the group of high cannabis consumers. In fact, only 49 of the schizophrenic subjects had ever used cannabis at all. In that study, cannabis was only the third most reliable predictor of schizophrenia, trailing both "existing psychiatric conditions" and "divorce." In a more recent meta-review of the research into the cannabis-schizophrenia link, Hall and Degenhardt estimated that the use of cannabis increases the relative risk for schizophrenia in the average individual from 7 in 1,000 to 14 in 1,000.[94] These are not insignificant increases, but neither do they put most cannabis users at an especially high risk of developing that disorder.

It also must be kept in mind that the relationship between cannabis and psychosis is not unique among psychoactive drugs. As already noted, there is a very high correlation between schizophrenia and substance abuse in general, especially tobacco. There is also some evidence for a causal link between other drugs and psychosis, though these vary in strength. For example, the causal link between alcohol and psychosis appears to be weaker than that between cannabis and psychosis, but the link between amphetamines and psychosis is considerably stronger than that for cannabis.[95]

These results nonetheless remain extremely interesting given our purposes here. The best controlled research to date indicates that cannabis clearly can produce psychotomimetic symptoms. Furthermore, there is a correlation between cannabis use and schizophrenia, whatever the reason. Assuming that correlation has always existed, it seems plausible that it has at times reinforced the belief in places like Mexico and India that cannabis "caused" madness. If we then consider the reality of the psychoactive riddle and the importance of the "placebo text" in producing drug effects, it seems eminently plausible that these circumstances could have produced seemingly psychotic responses in Mexicans a century ago, much as Weil showed that expectations among late-twentieth-century cannabis users had led otherwise routine panic reactions to spiral out of control. As David Castle and Nadia Solowij explain with respect to cannabis and its psychotomimetic potential, "The experience of intoxication with any psychotomimetic substance is influenced, inter alia, by dose; previous experience (and hence expectation of effect); the personal characteristics of the user (e.g. personality); and the context in which the drug is taken."[96]

Of course, Weil's subjects did not then go on violent rampages through the streets. Such responses would obviously have been more a product of set and setting than of the cannabis alone. We are thus drawn back into Mexican history to explore these critical variables.

*Chapter 2*

CANNABIS AND THE

COLONIAL MILIEU

By the sixteenth century, cannabis was known throughout much of the world as a medicine, fiber, and intoxicant. Though not present in the Americas until after the Spanish conquest, eventually this plant would take on all of these roles in Mexico as well. But cannabis would only gradually emerge into Mexican history, as scattered plantings slowly fused with local lifeways. The slow pace of this emergence ensured that this drug's historical trajectory would be steered by the peculiar architecture of Mexican colonial life, where medicine, religious practice, and intoxication were inextricably linked in a complex and perennial struggle for political control.

This chapter thus describes not only the emergence of cannabis in Mexico but also the political, economic, and cultural structures that would guide the plant's inconspicuous yet defining passage through nearly three hundred years of Mexican colonial history. Here I also examine the critical dynamic of religion, medicine, and political control that infused the relationship between the three major cultures that collided in sixteenth-century New Spain. That story introduces us to the various intoxicants that laid the groundwork for cannabis's reception there, from powerful hallucinogens used for divination in indigenous medical practice to alcohol and tobacco, two drugs that generated tensions between the desire of authorities to regulate the spiritual and temporal lives of the people and the increasingly obvious profit potential of popular vice. Through this atmosphere, cannabis eventually would emerge as a divinatory substance rumored to produce visions, supernatural encounters, and sometimes madness.

■ As a source of food, fiber, oil, and drug, humans have found cannabis useful since the dawn of agriculture. The plant's botanical flexibility, allowing its survival in a wide range of soil types, altitudes, and climates, has combined with its many uses to make this hardy weed one of the world's most widely culti-vated plants. Over centuries of human intervention, it has been carried into radically different climates and selectively bred for certain desired character-istics, resulting in remarkable morphological transformations. Many of these same plants eventually escaped from cultivation and, in the wild, reverted in some respects to their original forms.[1] These processes have produced a great variety of specimens with diverse phenotypic and chemical compositions, some that produce strong fiber, some that produce strong drugs, and some that produce both.

Cannabis has also proven quite adept at propagating itself over the mil-lennia. Wind pollination allows seeds dropped by humans, birds, or rivers to be fertilized at significant distance from the original source, even if no male plants spring up adjacent to females. And cannabis can survive in a diversity of soil types, from altitudes of 10,000 feet right down to sea level. Even the morphological characteristics of individual strains appear to be highly mal-leable, quickly adapting to distinct climatic conditions.[2] However, this poten-tial for self-sufficiency has not kept cannabis away from human activity. On the contrary, cannabis thrives in precisely the types of environments that ac-company human settlements—sunny open spaces and loamy soils rich with nitrogen from human waste. Richard Evans Schultes provides the most suc-cinct observation on this point: "As [man] unconsciously bred the quick grow-ing weeds capable of utilizing soils high in nitrogen, he also unconsciously carried them about from place to place and gave them previously unparal-leled opportunities to . . . build up into super-weeds."[3]

It is generally agreed that cannabis originated somewhere in "central Asia," a usefully vague designation that includes the many far-flung but plausible sites of genesis, from the area surrounding the Caspian Sea to parts of Siberia and the Himalayas.[4] While the roots of the word "cannabis" lie probably in the more western areas of this "central" region, the earliest evidence for its utilization by humans has appeared somewhat farther east in what is today northern China. Here, archaeological evidence indicates the use of canna-bis for fiber as early as 4000 B.C.[5] Over many millennia, the use of canna-bis as a fiber, food, medicine, and intoxicant dispersed it throughout most of the Old World. By the Age of Exploration, hemp had became indispensable to shipbuilding, where only flax could rival its utility for the construction of salt-resistant ropes, hawsers, sails, and nets. By the seventeenth century, each British warship was said to require 180,000 pounds of rough hemp for its complete outfitting. Cannabis fiber had thus literally become the stitching of maritime empire.[6] This fact above all helped to further disperse the plant to the New World. It would arrive first in New Spain, where the peculiar structures of Mexican colonial life would guide its historical trajectory, transforming it from an industrial fiber symbolizing imperial expansion and might to a psychoactive medicine rumored to facilitate communication with the devil.

■ The Spanish conquest and colonization of Mexico brought together European, indigenous, and African culture in most spheres of life. The diverse but in many ways similar relationships enjoyed by each of these traditions with medicine and drugs was no exception. As Gonzalo Aguirre Beltrán has demonstrated, these three medical traditions had perhaps as many traits in common as in contrast, with all of them mixing rational approaches to healing with recourse to the supernatural.[7] This combination of medical practice, materia medica, and religious belief helped to ensure that drugs would become critical nodes of dispute within the colonial struggle for political hegemony. And that they were, with prohibition edicts emerging against various medico-religious substances that too readily facilitated ecstatic experiences of a non-Christian nature. These conflicts are crucial to this story because as cannabis eventually emerged into Mexican life and culture, it had to pass through the dust raised by these ongoing battles.

Let us then begin with the Spanish, who introduced European medical conceptions that involved an almost total balance between natural and supernatural etiologies of illness. In Aguirre Beltrán's estimation, for Spaniards this was true "as much within the lecture hall as on the street" and meant that Spanish conceptions of illness were based in "an inextricable combination of science and religion."[8] Even some of the most advanced minds of sixteenth-century European experimental medicine continued to consider the importance of witches and demon possession in the origins of infirmity.[9] Though deeply rooted in Europe, many of these beliefs gained a strong foothold in the Americas and in fact endure to the present. The belief, for example, in *mal de ojo*, or the idea that one person could bewitch another simply by looking at him or her in a particular way, remains common today in Mexico but has roots traceable at least as far back as the writings of Saint Thomas. The equally common belief that God might allow the devil to possess sinners also had European roots, as did common traditions like the carrying of saints' relics to cure and ward off illness.[10]

Indigenous practice in Mexico also combined natural and supernatural notions. Spanish chroniclers were famously puzzled by what they saw as a contradiction between the seemingly unlearned mind of the typical Indian and that same mind's encyclopedic knowledge of Mexico's rich plant and animal life.[11] The majority of scholars who have studied indigenous medical practice have focused on this rational aspect of pre-Hispanic traditions. Yet indigenous communities often saw poor health as a punishment directly doled out by the gods for some kind of misbehavior, with illnesses taking forms that were appropriate to the angered divinity's character. For example, Tlaloc, the god of rain, was believed to cause ailments related to humidity or the cold. Such belief was common not only within the Mexica cultural sphere but within the Zapotec and Mayan as well.[12] In smaller indigenous communities, illness was often attributed to human malevolence and witchcraft. Like their Spanish counterparts, indigenous doctors often began their diagnoses by weighing likely natural causes against the chance that there might have been some kind of supernatural intervention to produce the illness. Oftentimes, this search for answers led healers, and sometimes patients, to ingest one of the many powerful hallucinogenic materials available in the region. These materials were believed to facilitate the divination of causes through communication with particular gods.[13]

Finally, in those traditions that accompanied West African slaves to Mexico, illness was often understood as punishment contrived by angry gods or ancestors. As in Spanish and indigenous traditions, African doctors needed to identify the god or ancestor who had caused the illness and from that information determine an appropriate cure. But the African tradition also placed particular emphasis on treatments that involved spirit possession. Certain individuals, when possessed by particular gods, would become mediums through which those gods verbally communicated and thereby revealed the origins of the ailment in question. Aguirre Beltrán demonstrates how in Mexico, this particular emphasis on possession sometimes mixed with indigenous traditions to create new syncretic practices.[14]

Thus we see how the Spanish, indigenous, and African medical traditions all blended aspects of the "rational" and the "supernatural" in their approaches to medicine and that, while distinct, they had enough features in common to facilitate the formation of syncretic cultural forms.[15] That syncretism became the hallmark of medical practice among colonial *curanderos*, or healers. For that reason, medical practice and medicinal drugs almost immediately became the objects of intense regulation by Spanish authorities. As Aguirre Beltrán has noted, the Inquisition was created to maintain norms of conduct along lines determined by Spanish custom, and while the Inquisition's jurisdiction was only supposed to involve matters of religion, "folk medicine, born of revelation and pregnant with the most profound mysticism, [was] an object of continuous and tireless persecution."[16] These elements—this critical mixture of ritual, rationality, and the supernatural—were central components of the early history of drugs and medicine in Mexico, bringing these substances into the regulatory gaze of authority at a remarkably early date.

In this atmosphere, healers became controversial figures. During the colonial era, it was widely understood that *curanderos* could be the source of both health and sickness. The public was well aware that the healing powers of the *curandero*, with his or her remarkable knowledge of the "mystical causes of illnesses" and spectacular ability to communicate with the gods, came with a price—those powers could also be utilized to do harm. It was understood, particularly among ordinary folk, that the *curandero* might very well use that power, at the behest of a client, to purposefully bewitch, injure, or even kill.[17]

Interestingly, drugs have long been understood to have a similarly bipolar nature. The Greek root of the prefix "pharmaco" simultaneously means both "medicine" and "poison," something that was quite clear to Paracelsus, who noted that "in all things there is poison, and there is nothing without a poison. It depends only upon the dose whether a poison is poison or not."[18] For many substances, this duality is obvious. Before and after the conquest, for example, tobacco was smoked or chewed to provide energy and pleasure, used as a remedy against poisonous wounds, and employed as a poison to kill insects and incapacitate deadly snakes.[19] Of course, religious belief often hinges on some kind of dualism of this sort as well. Not surprisingly, then, this ambivalent zone occupied both by *curanderos* and certain medicinal substances, this zone that mixed good and evil, was a constant point of dispute and confusion for Spanish authority. The sixteenth-century physician Juan de Cárdenas, for example, wondered how the Indians could have discovered the wonderful medicinal properties of tobacco, speculating that "some angel advised its use to the Indians, or some demon who was also an angel was involved; since it liberates us from diseases, it truly seems to be like an angelic medicine, or a remedy created by demons."[20]

One especially troubling point of conflict in this regard was the use of native hallucinogenic plants for divination in medical practice, a custom that brought out important parallels with previous European experience. As noted earlier, hallucinogens are substances that can, in certain doses, produce psychotomimetic effects, especially visual, tactile, aural, or gustatory hallucinations. There remains significant disagreement over how to classify the 180 or so substances of this kind known to be used by humans, both because there is considerable diversity within this general group and because their effects often vary tremendously, depending on the size of the dose ingested and the culture that dictates their use. But of those 180 substances, the majority are used in the Americas, and more than half are used in Mexico. Mexico, in fact, boasts the richest tradition of such drug use in the world.[21]

The Spanish who arrived in the sixteenth century found that indigenous *curanderos* took hallucinogenic substances like peyote (*Lophophora williamsii*) or ololiuhqui (*Rivea corymbosa*) to divine the causes of illness. Again blurring the lines between materia medica and the supernatural, these substances were not merely viewed as miraculous in their powers but were understood to be the personification of gods. That is, the substances themselves were seen as "persons" whose ingestion thus constituted a kind of ritual cannibalism (the parallels with Catholic communion are striking). Peyote users were thought to temporarily gain the omnipotence of the god in question, thereby acquiring critical knowledge otherwise withheld from humans. In the case of ololiuhqui, the god would appear to its user and explain the etiology of the illness at hand.[22] The friars did their best to discourage all of this, emphasizing the close ties between these substances and the devil. But, as Fernando Cervantes has argued, because the Indians believed that all deities simultaneously wrought good and evil, the friars' arguments merely reinforced the notion that these mushrooms facilitated communication with the gods. For Indians in Mexico, "evil and the demonic were in fact intrinsic to the divinity itself. In the same way as in Hinduism Brahma represented both creation and destruction, or in the works of Homer there was no clear distinction between the concepts of theos and daimon, so, too, Mesoamerican deities represented both benevolence and malevolence, creativity and destructiveness."[23] The drugs' very real hallucinogenic effects of course helped to confirm such notions all the more.

Europeans were not unfamiliar with the utilization of certain natural substances for purposes of witchcraft and divination, especially in ancient times.[24] Thus ololiuhqui had been compared by Mexico's first Royal Protomédico, or "First Physician," Francisco Hernández, to the *Solano furioso* (*Solanum manicum* or stramonium) first identified by Dioscorides and that later was said in Europe to be "used by witches to induce visions that they claimed were actual happenings."[25] But while Europeans were familiar with the use of certain powerful hallucinogens, the Mexican countryside produced a wealth of such substances that was, again, unmatched by any other area of the world, from the mushroom known as *teonanácatl* or "God's flesh," through peyote and ololiuhqui, to the mysterious *pipiltzintzintlis* or "most noble princes," about which much more is discussed below.[26]

In the *Florentine Codex*, compiled by Bernardino de Sahagún and a group of informants drawn from the ranks of the Indian nobility, a number of these substances and their remarkable effects were described. Sahagún and his collaborators called them *hierbas que emborrachan* or "herbs that intoxicate."

> There is a plant called *Coatl xoxouqui* which produces a seed called *Ololiuhqui*: this seed intoxicates and maddens [*enloquece*]; they put it in people's drinks in order to do harm to those to whom they want to see bad things happen; and those that eat the seeds see visions and horrible things: witches put it in the drink or food of those whom they hate in order to do them harm: this herb is medicinal and its seed is effective against gout when ground and applied at the location of the malady.
>
> There's another herb ... that is called *Péyotl*: it is white, it grows in the north: those who eat or drink it see horrible or comic [*de risas*] visions: that intoxication lasts two or three days and later it recedes: it is a common food of the *Chichimecas* and it gives them energy to fight and not have either hunger or thirst.[27]

Nine other plants are described by Sahagún and his native informants in similar terms: *tlápatl* and *tzitzintlápatl*, both of which were said to intoxicate and cause perpetual madness; *míxitl*, which caused vomiting and later paralysis, "and if he who eats it has his eyes open at the time, he will not again be able to close them, and if he has them closed, he will not again be able to open them"; *teonanácatl*, which would intoxicate, cause visions, and inspire lust; *tochtetepo*, which was put into drinks to kill people and used by witches to bewitch; *atlepatli*, which was also deadly; *aquiztli*, which if urinated or spit on by someone, caused that person's face and body to swell up; *tenxoxoli*, which provoked vomiting and bleeding; and finally *quimichpatli*, which was also deadly. All of these, like peyote and ololiuhqui, were also said to be medicinal in some specific way.[28]

These substances produced significant anxiety among Spanish and religious authorities, as demonstrated by the various prohibitions that would eventually be aimed at them. The exact nature of that anxiety is of course impossible to definitively pinpoint. However, and paradoxically, some of it appears to have stemmed from the fact that the practice, ideology, and symptoms of hallucinogen ingestion in colonial Mexico so closely resembled some aspects of the practice, ideology, and symptoms of Christian worship among the Spanish. In fact, generally speaking, Spanish spiritual authorities often were most perturbed by those rituals that demonstrated excessive congruence between European and indigenous belief or practice. Lack of distinction rather than excessive distinction was often seen as especially troubling. For example, Franciscan friars of the early conquest period were famously optimistic regarding the potential for salvation among the Indians in part because of eerie similarities between Mexica religious rituals and those of the Catholic church. The Mexica administered sacraments, designated major and minor priests, maintained monasteries, and celebrated ascetics and chaste women. But soon, that optimism gave way to a deep pessimism as widespread evidence of Indian backsliding was uncovered. In the minds of Christian authorities, those same similarities now looked like obvious signs of diabolical intervention intended to forestall conversion. The gods of the Indians were, as Sahagún put it, "lying and deceitful devils," tricking the Indians with practices that mimicked those truly Catholic ones. Thus, in his *Historia natural y moral de las Indias* (1590), the influential Jesuit José de Acosta argued that the more similar to Christian practice a competing religion appeared, the more clearly its origins were diabolical.[29]

Such similarities were undeniable in the realm of drugs. While the friars at the front lines of the spiritual conquest might deplore the fact that Indians consumed sacred mushrooms in order to be possessed by the deity that resided within them, the most devout Catholics often welcomed possession by demonic forces as a means of purging the soul in preparation for the afterlife. As Fernando Cervantes has noted, "Such diabolical instigations . . . were seen as clear symptoms of spiritual progress. Indeed, the more powerful and vivid were the demonic attacks, the more worthy of respect and admiration were those who suffered them."[30]

Antonio Escohotado has in fact argued that the roots of anti-drug ideology throughout the West reside in the similarities between Christian communion and pagan religious rites that involved actual hallucinogenic substances. According to this theory, while the Christians were offering the body of Christ devoid of psychoactive content, competing religions offered a brand of communion featuring organic material that reliably produced ecstatic experience. Here the Christians demanded faith while the competitors provided immediate results.[31] It is a fascinating theory, but Escohotado perhaps underestimates the ability of faith to produce ecstatic experience on its own. Most scholars today see spirit possession as a kind of sacred theater acted out to the expectations of a particular culture. But that does not mean the experience of the possession is not very real to the participants. Similar explanations have been offered for other phenomena such as the involuntary behavior, convulsions, and insensitivity to pain routinely observed in the mesmerists and hysterics of the nineteenth century and in the violent amok outbursts of the Malay peninsula already discussed in chapter 1.[32] In these various examples, it has been argued that subjects play out socially expected or sanctioned roles but not because they are "faking it." They truly experience the various phenomena in a kind of culturally derived placebo effect, much like what can occur thanks to the interaction between drug, set, and setting.

Whatever their origin, as anxieties about drugs were stoked in New Spain, prohibitions followed, providing still more fodder for a developing "placebo text." That process began in earnest in New Spain on June 19, 1620, when the Inquisition formally banned the use of peyote and similar substances throughout the viceroyalty.

> Seeing that, said herb, nor any other can possibly have by nature such virtues and efficacy that is attributed to the stated effects nor to cause the images, ghosts, and representations with which are founded said divinations, and that in those one obviously sees the effects of the suggestion and assistance of the Devil, author of this abuse, taking advantage of, first of all in order to introduce it easily ... indians and their inclination toward idolatry, and overcoming later many other people ... we mandate that from here forward no one of whatever social status can use said herb, peyote, nor any others for the same or similar effects, under no title or color nor shall they encourage indians or other persons to take them understanding that if they do so ... we will proceed against the rebellious and disobedient ... as against persons suspected of violations against the Holy Catholic faith.[33]

Over the next two centuries, dozens of proceedings were carried out against individuals for the use of peyote, ololiuhqui, and various other divinatory substances. It was through this milieu that cannabis would eventually emerge.

But hallucinogens were not the only controversial drugs in circulation. Alcohol, of course, had a long history in Mexico prior to the Spanish invasion. While our knowledge of pre-Hispanic traditions remains greatly circumscribed by the deficiency of the available sources, William Taylor has convincingly demonstrated that alcohol was an extremely important component of pre-Hispanic cultures, standing at the center of religious ritual and restricted under sometimes extraordinarily severe sumptuary laws. Two basic patterns of alcohol use appear to have reigned in pre-conquest Mexico. In some communities, its use was restricted to the nobility with penalties ranging from whippings to death for commoners who drank or noblemen who became drunkards. Other communities allowed widespread drunkenness on ritual occasions but at no other time, with significant but less severe penalties for violators.[34]

The latter custom stood at the center of a distinction between Spanish and indigenous concepts of "moderation," and as Taylor has argued, this distinction appears to have been crucial in the development of Spanish stereo-types painting drunkenness as "a natural inclination of Indians" and "a barbarous vice of a barbarous people." For the Spanish, moderation meant the frequent, even daily imbibing of alcohol, but never drinking so much as to become drunk. For many indigenous communities, on the other hand, moderation meant the drinking of alcohol only on ritual occasions but with the intention of achieving drunkenness on those special days.[35] As one seventeenth-century Spanish observer commented, "If the Indians drank pulque the way Spaniards drink wine (which is not the case, nor has it been, nor is there any hope of their ever doing so) it could be permitted . . . but these are Indians and it is proven that their custom is to get drunk, and it is for that reason that they drink."[36]

However, while the Spanish found much to lament in the drinking practices of the indigenous commoners, so too did the representatives of the pre-Hispanic nobility who observed that adherence to sumptuary restrictions on drinking crumbled apace with their own power and influence. As Spanish dominance grew, indigenous elites began to view the widespread violation of these traditional restrictions as a root cause of growing disorder and demographic decline within Indian communities. Spanish observers similarly believed widespread alcoholism to have played an important part in the demographic collapse of the sixteenth century. The shared consternation of the two ruling classes had reason only to increase over time, as many peasant communities began celebrating Christian holy days with the kind of generalized, heavy ritual drinking previously associated with indigenous religious celebrations. Whether a sign of syncretism or protest, these events only helped to heighten elite concerns regarding alcohol while fueling increasingly negative commentaries on the baleful effects of this substance.[37]

The Mexica had referred to pulque as *centzonttotochtli*, meaning "four hundred rabbits," in order to emphasize their belief in the infinite number of ways that alcohol could affect its users. Imported Spanish understandings mingled with such notions to construct a seemingly endless number of consequences attributed to alcohol during the colonial era, from violence and rebellion to incest and idolatry.[38] Specifically, Spanish observers argued that drinking inhibited civilized judgment and allowed people to be ruled by more primitive, animal drives.[39]

Fears of disorder were certainly not altogether misplaced. Eighteenth-century criminal records from rural Oaxaca and the areas around Mexico City indicate that alcohol played a role in 18 percent of murders and 60 percent of assaults.[40] The perception of a connection between crime and alcohol appears to have been fueled also by the rules of legal proceedings that considered alcohol, much like insanity, to be an attenuating circumstance. The records suggest both that this situation inspired lawyers to pursue the alcohol defense and that ordinary Mexicans began to either internalize the belief or, like their lawyers, recognize the utility of the claim that alcohol was responsible for their indiscretions. The most common defense was to claim that one had been drunk and could not remember having committed the crime. Others claimed temporary insanity under the influence of alcohol. As one defense lawyer argued, his client "was so drunk and so beyond himself that he behaved like a lunatic, like an automaton or a brutal machine whose movements were completely lacking in reason and free will."[41] The relationship between these two states of mind would remain a crucial and contentious issue at the heart of debates regarding alcohol in Mexico right into the twentieth century. However, we should note that disorderly drinking made up only one part of the alcohol story in colonial Mexico. In stable peasant communities where ritual drinking on Catholic holy days continued to follow traditional patterns, social restrictions regarding "moderation" and drunken behavior appear to have kept violence and alcoholism at a minimum.[42]

In any case, the Spanish influence on the history of alcohol in Mexico stands out in two particular spheres. First, the introduction of wine and distilled spirits during the sixteenth century probably encouraged antisocial patterns of drinking among Indian populations.[43] Unlike pulque, these products were not associated with the community norms that limited the drinking of alcohol to special occasions and that frowned on frequent, European-style "tippling."[44] Second, Spanish taxes on alcohol sales created an important source of income that was not easily forsaken by the authorities. By 1579, measures were being taken to try and limit the abuse of alcohol, particularly in Mexico City, and other comparable restrictions appeared with some frequency over the next half century. But these laws labored against protections given to alcohol dealers by many local and viceregal authorities who found these tax revenues too lucrative to surrender.[45] This would remain a recurring theme over the coming centuries.

But other themes too look familiar when viewed with knowledge of future developments. Mexico City, for instance, became known during the colonial era as a center of excessive drinking, where merchants from outside the city found relief from the restrictions on alcohol consumption of their rural village communities. Furthermore, Indians and violence were closely linked to this urban vice. Taylor reports the lament of a late-seventeenth-century parish priest who claimed to see several dozen drunk and severely injured Indians every night in the local hospital.[46]

The case of tobacco also proves important, though its history in Mexico demonstrates a number of distinctive characteristics. Most important, that history reveals how a practice that was decidedly alien to Europeans, tied to local religious belief and practice, and capable of producing great physical harm could nevertheless gain widespread acceptance by the Spanish. Given all that we have seen regarding alcohol, the amount of conflict caused by tobacco seems remarkably modest in comparison. After all, prior to the conquest, smoking was unknown to Europe, and probably the rest of the world, while in Mesoamerica the use of tobacco was intimately related to indigenous medical and religious practice.[47] Like the various divinatory substances treated above, tobacco was sometimes seen as the personification of deities. Furthermore, this was a substance that played an enormous role in economic life. As Carlos Martínez Marín has noted, "The role of this low intensity stimulant was preponderant in the pre-Columbian society of America: tobacco was present at all moments of the life cycle, from birth to death; in the same way it was present in the economic and social structure, in the political functions of the State and of the community, in war, and in all religious ceremonies, in mythological thought, in cosmic understandings, in magic, in everything."[48]

In 1492, the Taíno Indians famously offered tobacco to the Spanish upon first contact in the present-day Bahamas. Early Spanish reactions to the use of this substance varied greatly. While Bartolomé de las Casas emphasized Indian claims that the plant reduced hunger and fatigue, another chronicler, Pedro Mártir de Anglería, noted that "the *behique* [Taíno priests] eat an intoxicating weed that, upon being snorted in powder form, makes them crazy like Furies, making them murmur that they have heard various things from their *zemes* [spirits or ancestors]."[49] Because of tobacco's intimate relationship with native religious practice, the church initially associated it with the devil. But for whatever reason, concern about the use of the drug was tempered, and the measures taken to regulate its use were in fact quite modest. In New Spain and Peru, some initial prohibitions against the use of tobacco within churches and prior to Communion were promulgated, and in the 1580s, the clergy were expressly prohibited from smoking prior to Mass. But as the use of tobacco was gradually stripped of its sacred character, the church softened its already quite moderate stance, and by 1725, most of the earlier prohibitions had been rescinded.[50]

Perhaps the church's more measured approach was conditioned by the relatively rapid adoption of the habit by the Spanish. Shortly after the conquest, Europeans began to experiment with tobacco, a habit to which they eventually took with great enthusiasm. Initial use was mostly related to medicinal applications, of which there were numerous. But soon, perhaps due in large part to the habit-forming qualities of the practice, use evolved in more recreational directions. The primary nodes of global diffusion were, as often happens, ports, where medicinal employment quickly faded into recreational use. Interestingly, in these early years, the practice was seen in the Americas as something "very base and low class, and something of slaves and tavern drinkers and people of little worth [*consideración*]." While the practice would be taken up in northern Europe by elites toward the end of the sixteenth century, this low-class reputation apparently continued for some time in Mexico, where even two hundred years later the observation could still be made that tobacco was mostly smoked by "the poor and people of middling means [*conveniencias*]," who were said to have taken on the vice for entertainment's sake and to relieve them of their troubles. Gradually the habit was adopted by the higher classes and, in the 1700s, by women as well. By the middle of the eighteenth century, annual consumption had grown significantly, by 1761 weighing in at over two million pounds.[51] Of this considerable figure, about half could be attributed to consumption in Mexico City.[52]

Interestingly, Mexicans were unique among global tobacco consumers in their utilization of cigarettes. In Europe, pipe smoking and snuff had emerged as the most common means of taking tobacco because those methods were far more economical at a time when the importation of tobacco leaves was still very expensive.[53] In Mexico, of course, price was never a problem, and early colonial smokers most commonly used some kind of hollowed-out cylinder, whether of cane, silver, clay, or wood, to smoke their tobacco. However, because such media tended to deliver overpowering doses of smoke, they gave way to the rolling of tobacco in corn husk, the classic means of smoking among the Maya. But preparing these cumbersome contraptions was difficult and time-consuming; thus, this practice was gradually overtaken by the rolling of tobacco in paper. It was at the beginning of the eighteenth century that a man named Antonio Charro began to roll cigarettes in his Mexico City store and sell them ready to smoke. This proved perhaps the most critical development in Mexican, and even world, tobacco consumption. After 1780, the practice began to spread to the rest of Latin America; by 1840, it had become fashionable in France; and in the twentieth century, it took hold in Europe, the United States, and eventually the rest of the world.[54]

In 1642, Spanish bishop-viceroy Juan de Palafox suggested tobacco's potential as a source of revenue, but it was not until the middle of the next century that this potential began to be seriously pursued. Proposals to monopolize the Mexican trade were raised in the 1740s and some half-measures were taken beginning in 1761, but it was the loss of Havana to the British in 1762 and the subsequent need for new sources of revenue that finally resulted in a full-scale monopoly. From the Crown's point of view, the monopoly was a resounding success—from 1776 to 1809, it accounted for between 12 and 22 percent of total state revenue.[55]

This then was the environment through which cannabis would eventually emerge, a cultural nexus of both acceptable and unacceptable forms of intoxicant use, where notions of healing, profit, social control, and the supernatural interacted in complex ways. While this atmosphere clearly helped to determine cannabis's historical trajectory, the diversity of drugs and responses to them in colonial Mexico suggests that no single precedent could have been expected to serve as a template for its reception there.

■ As noted in this book's introduction, it was a little-known conquistador named Pedro Quadrado who claimed to have first introduced cannabis to Mexico. This would have taken place sometime in the 1530s. For the Spanish, cannabis was valued above all as a source of strong fiber used in the production of various products, none more important than the sails and ropes that powered the imperial navy. Thus in 1545, the Spanish Crown officially mandated its cultivation in the Americas: "We order the Viceroys and Governors that they mandate the cultivation of hemp and flax in the Indies, and that they get the Indians to apply themselves to this farming and to weaving and spinning flax."[56]

Quadrado's efforts mostly failed, something he later blamed on the death of four (probably Indian) slaves.[57] Other attempts followed, though cultivation remained small-scale and isolated. In 1587, for example, a certain Manuel de Rodas asked authorities in Atlixco, Puebla, for the use of six Indians to help him undertake the production of hemp there.[58] The results of that request are unknown, but perhaps not completely by coincidence, it was in Atlixco that a family called Hernández began growing and manufacturing hemp during the seventeenth century. There at the basin of Popocatépetl, central Mexico's towering, 18,000-foot volcano, the Hernández clan found the plants to grow "abundant and leafy," and from them they made cords for lamps, traces, cinches, and various other products that were sometimes requested from Mexico City. Production continued successfully until, in 1761, the last remaining member of the family, Don Juan Joseph Hernández, died.

With Don Juan Joseph went the production of hemp fiber there and perhaps in all of Mexico.[59]

But the demise of the Hernández farm did not mean the complete demise of cannabis in Atlixco. In a process that was likely replicated in other spots around Mexico since Quadrado first introduced the species, some members of the Hernández workforce had discovered the plants to be medicinally useful. Perhaps they had been tipped off by the plant's famed "abominable smell."[60] Whatever the cause, before long the Indian employees of the old farm had taken some samples home and begun cultivating their own medicinal cannabis in the sunny corners of their gardens.[61]

By the middle of the eighteenth century, Indians around the region had begun referring to cannabis with the name *pipiltzintzintlis* and were employing it for purposes of divination. As a result, the *pipiltzintzintlis* had been banned by the Inquisition, eventually becoming notorious for producing visions and even madness in users.[62] But neither the Inquisition nor other Spanish authorities appear to have had any idea that this substance was derived from cannabis. In fact, when Spanish investigators discovered that the Indians of Atlixco had adapted hemp to their own medicinal needs, the news was received with great enthusiasm, for it suggested that the locals might be willing to expand their cultivation of the species. Yet these same Indians were convinced that such cultivation was illegal unless undertaken with special permission from the Crown.[63] In short, by this point there appears to have developed a disconnect between official views of cannabis and those of ordinary folk in New Spain. The latter apparently understood this plant to be persecuted by the Inquisition under the name *pipiltzintzintlis* and therefore banned, while the former, ignorant of the link between cannabis and that notorious divinatory substance, expressed surprise that anyone could think that hemp production was illegal.

The Crown very much hoped to undermine the popular impression because a new initiative was under way to establish hemp production in the Americas. The new effort was intimately linked to the larger issues that defined the period of the Bourbon Reforms. The perennial sea-borne conflict with Britain during these years had put a premium on the outfitting of the Spanish navy, while growing oceanic commerce was driving up demand for outfitting within the private merchant marine. At the same time, a rapidly expanding population in Spain was also growing the market for all of those hemp and flax products used domestically. Yet Spanish production had not increased to meet the rising demand, creating a situation in which Spain was servicing a growing percentage of its hemp and flax needs through imports of both raw and manufactured products from abroad. That situation violated the basic principles of economic autarky that still dominated the era, but initial efforts to increase cultivation of these species within Spain were proving unsuccessful.[64]

Thus, on January 12, 1777, the Crown demanded that the original law of 1545 be heeded: "The King orders . . . that the Indians and mixed populations of the towns of those dominions apply themselves to the sowing, cultivation, and exploitation of hemp and flax so that those fruits, as primary materials, can be brought to Spain free from any import or export taxes, in order to foment the manufacture of cloth, canvas, and rigging of which so much is needed both in the Peninsula and in those vast dominions."[65]

Eleven months later, Viceroy Don Antonio María de Bucareli y Ursúa instructed the governors of New Spain's various districts to promote that cultivation: "So that the news reaches all of the jurisdictions under your control, make it known through a decree in the county seat, and in every one of the villages that constitute [your district], that not only is the cultivation and exploitation of hemp and flax not prohibited, but that His Majesty wants, and it will be very much to his Royal Pleasure and Sovereign Approval, . . . that the Indians, as well as Spaniards and the rest of the mixed races [castas], promote and dedicate themselves particularly to their cultivation and commerce."[66]

These orders received an immediate and enthusiastic response from officials throughout Mexico. Authorities in San Juan Teotihuacán, for example, reported that in Texcoco there was ideal land for the cultivation of the two species. A mission near San Miguel el Grande in Guanajuato reported that about a dozen haciendas in the area could cultivate the species without interfering with any of the traditional wheat production there. Cholula also claimed ideal conditions for cultivation while noting that the local inhabitants were well schooled in weaving and would happily take to crafting secondary materials out of the raw hemp and flax.[67] In dozens of other districts, the orders to cultivate were warmly received.[68]

But despite this enthusiasm, certain obstacles greatly hindered the project's potential for success. First, while some hemp cultivation had occurred in Atlixco, investigators found no evidence that it had occurred anywhere else in Mexico. Flax was somewhat more familiar, with growers in Tacuba and Xochimilco having been located, but, in the former, the species had been cultivated only for its medicinally useful seeds. Indeed, Tacuba's growers were quite unaware that there was any other use for these plants.[69]

To this lack of experience was added the additional impediment that the cultivation and treatment of cannabis to produce fiber was far more complicated than simply getting the plants to grow successfully in Mexico.[70] As instructions provided with the orders indicated, cultivation had to take place in well-watered, fertile lowlands, but these were not to flood, either. The plants were to be sown close together so that they might grow tall and narrow because stockier plants produced hard, woody fibers of low quality. Yet the plants could not be too close together or they might suffocate one another. Here the authorities noted that this distinction was "learned more through experience than through teaching." A series of steps had to be followed, from guarding the young plants against birds to distinguishing between male and female specimens, beating the crops to harvest their seeds, and treating them with water and sun to extract the fiber. Even the final treatment proved complicated because the hemp poisoned the water utilized for this purpose and made it quite dangerous to future consumers, whether human or animal.[71]

But clearly, the greatest impediment to the realization of a new hemp industry was a consistent lack of seeds.[72] Reports from Cholula during March 1778 of ideal conditions and enthusiasm among the locals but no seeds were typical. Such reports were received from around Mexico over the next two decades.[73] The search for the raw material even led potential cultivators to New Spain's pharmacies, only to find some flax but no hempseed.[74] The lack of seeds thwarted repeated orders in 1777, 1779, 1787, 1792, and 1795 for production to get under way.[75]

These problems deserve considerable emphasis because they help us to periodize this history. As we shall see, by the second half of the nineteenth century, the presence of cannabis in the Mexican countryside would be sufficiently ubiquitous to help convince various observers that this substance must be indigenous to the region. Yet as we have seen here, in the late eighteenth century, cannabis and even hempseed were extremely rare in Mexico. There were only pockets of cultivation, and while hempseed typically appeared in European pharmacopoeias, Mexico's pharmacies simply did not have enough of the raw material on hand to provide a basis for industrial production.

Despite all of these difficulties, a considerable amount of hemp was sown in Mexico during this period — certainly enough, in any case, to turn this plant into a common feature of the countryside over the next century, especially given cannabis's ability to propagate itself. Shortly after the initial order of 1777, reports began to arrive from throughout Mexico that some cultivation had begun. In Papantla, Veracruz, hemp plants had been successfully cultivated and were sent to Mexico City as samples in 1778. By April of that same year, a mission near San Miguel el Grande had successfully grown some hemp despite a lack of the tools normally required for the job. Even on the Pacific coast, in San Blas, where it was concluded that the climate was simply wrong for the production of high-quality hemp, some plants were nevertheless sown. And as the century came to a close, efforts were bearing some modest fruit in places like Monte Alto, Guerrero.[76] Other areas reported having been provided with seeds to get the planting started. About thirty pounds of hempseed were supplied to growers near La Piedad, Michoacán, while Tacuba received about eight pounds of seed and other growers received similar allotments.[77] However, the majority of production was concentrated on about sixty-four acres of land in Chalco near Mexico City, where the Royal Factory of Hemp and Flax was created in 1781. There, cultivation eventually became quite significant. For example, in 1783, about ninety bushels of hempseed were sown in Chalco, and in 1787, nearly 4,400 pounds of hemp were harvested and sent to Veracruz for shipment to Spain.[78]

Meanwhile, the plant's adoption into local pharmacopoeias helped to initiate a transformation of cannabis's reputation among elite Mexicans. Once seen exclusively as an industrial fiber symbolizing imperial expansion and might, gradually cannabis would develop a reputation as an indigenous drug plant capable of provoking disorder and madness. That process began in the early 1760s. Roughly two centuries after what was widely believed to have been the failed introduction of cannabis to New Spain, José Alzate found, to his great surprise, that Indians around Mexico City were eating preparations of cannabis called *pipiltzintzintlis* in order to see visions and commune with the supernatural.

■ José Antonio Alzate y Ramírez was born on November 20, 1737, in Ozumba, New Spain, a little town within the old province of Chalco where, later, cannabis would be cultivated in large quantities under royal mandate and guidance. His father was an emigrant from Guipúzcoa, Spain's Basque country. His mother, who was also born in Chalco, was a relative of Sor Juana Inés de la Cruz, arguably colonial America's greatest intellectual. Alzate's own life was filled with intellectual pursuits and achievement. At fifteen, he received his bachelor of arts degree, and three years later, in 1756, he acquired another bachelor's in theology. In the same year, he was ordained a Catholic priest.[79] Like so many intellectuals of that era, he demonstrated tremendous interest in both science and letters. He studied and practiced astronomy, archaeology, botany, and zoology. In 1768, he began publishing what was probably Hispanic America's first Enlightenment literary journal. Over the coming years, he would publish widely on a variety of topics, leaving a rich scientific legacy in Mexico.[80]

Alzate had surely heard of the *pipiltzintzintlis* long before he began his research into their nature, for they had been the subject of prosecutions by the Inquisition for decades. Yet among the various divinatory plants of Mexico, the *pipiltzintzintlis* were among the most mysterious. They had appeared before the Inquisition seemingly out of the blue in the late seventeenth century and by Alzate's time had still not been formally identified. Alzate did not know it, of course, but by the end of the eighteenth century, the word *pipiltzintzintlis* would again disappear completely from the records. Inquisition files described the plant as a cultivated herb whose roots were used to make a hallucinogenic drink that led users to see "bad things" and speak in absurd ways. Fray Agustín de Vetancurt, in his *Teatro Mexicano* (1698), was the only Spanish chronicler to mention the plant, noting that it was dioecious and had properties similar to those of peyote, with its leaves being used, among other purposes, to inspire divination.[81] By Alzate's day, the *pipiltzintzintlis* were believed to produce a range of troubling side effects, from uncontrollable laughing fits and stupidity to a kind of "furious madness," the latter being the most common effect according to Alzate. Writing in 1772, he described their use as follows:

> The abuse of the pipiltzintzintlis is one of those relics of paganism that is preserved among some of the Indians; that much is expressed by the edicts published by the prelates in this kingdom, and most recently in 1769, in which the parish priests are called upon to employ all of their energies in uprooting this superstition at the center of which hinges [*va de por en medio*] the spiritual health of the Indians, and we can add to that their temporal health as well. . . . There is no doubt that the temporal health [of the Indians] is also a central concern here [*va de por medio su salud temporal*]. The violent effect of the narcotics proves this sufficiently; it has not been but a few months since a person to whom they administered the pipiltzintzintlis, I do not know for what purpose, in perhaps too great a dose, lost their mind [*perdió el juicio*].[82]

The 1769 edict to which Alzate referred had been published by Archbishop Don Francisco Antonio Lorenzana y Buitrón. The edict had reiterated a prohibition on the use of the *pipiltzintzintlis* along with other "idolatrous" customs engaged in by Mexico's Indians. Stiff penalties were instituted for failure to report such activities—twenty-five lashes and a month's jail for Indians and excommunication for everyone else. And so that no one could claim ignorance of these rules, they were to be posted publicly and read aloud on a designated festival day. The list of prohibited behaviors was extensive, the following being only a short excerpt:

> Celebrating a pact ... with the Devil; or executing superstitious Cures that rely on generally unhealthy methods [*en lo natural inconducentes para la sanidad*]; or misusing the Pipiltzitzintles [*sic*], Peyote, Hummingbirds, or Roses, or of other Herbs or Animals; or faking Miracles, Revelations, Ecstasies, and entrancements, or turning to others so that they divine things far away, in the future, or hidden, or doing [such things] on their own; or carrying edible Offerings, Dolls, Wax or incense to the caves, hills, springs, pools, or Rivers, with the intention of giving them to the air, or other elements; or worshiping certain Animals, or inanimate beings [*cosas*], violating the First Precept of Decalogue, and the solemn profession, that they made in the Sacrosanct Baptism, in which they renounced the Devil, and his pomp; or allowing themselves to be taken by the abuse that is practiced in certain parishes in the Medicine called *Papas*, that they put in the tangled hair of others [*les hacen en algunos cadejos de la cabeza*] with certain ingredients, and they assure that they will die when they find them.[83]

Reflecting his peculiar background as a priest and Enlightenment scientist, Alzate sought to determine, through empirical investigation, whether the reputed effects of the *pipiltzintzintlis* were natural or supernatural. When he acquired a sample, he noted that this supposedly miraculous substance actually amounted to little more than a small pile of leaves and seeds. Examining it closely, he clearly recognized the features of the common European hemp plant. To verify his initial observation, he planted the seeds in his garden, and indeed, from them grew classic samples of cannabis, "the same," he noted, "as in Europe."[84]

The discovery was perhaps disappointing. This was, after all, an era of intense European botanical exploration and enthusiasm. Spurred forth by Carl Linnaeus's efficient and rational new binomial system of plant classification, Europeans of those days had caught botanical fever, setting out to "discover" and name new species for the sake of science and personal glory.[85] But despite the wonderfully exotic name, Alzate had merely discovered one of the world's most common cultivars.

In New Spain, it was a novel discovery nonetheless. As much was confirmed shortly thereafter when a group planning an expedition to Sonora approached Alzate in search of hempseed. Those in the group had hoped that during their trip they might successfully sow hemp along the Pacific coast but had no idea where to find the necessary raw material. At that time, it was widely believed that, beyond the private gardens of a few scattered botanical enthusiasts, cannabis was not grown in Mexico. This was a belief that would persist for some time. Given his recent findings, Alzate suggested they simply visit the city's indigenous *herbolarias*, or herb dealers, and ask for the *pipil-tzintzintlis*. Much to their surprise, they came away with several bushels of hempseed, which, we may presume, were eventually sown along Sonora's sun-drenched coast.[86]

Returning to his library, Alzate found that the link between cannabis, mystical visions, and even madness was not altogether novel. Writing in 1689, the French physician and poet Peter Petit had suggested that the "nepenthe" offered by Helen to Telemachus and Menelaos in *The Odyssey*—that "mighty medicine" so powerful that "whosoever drinks of it, that day he weeps not, though father and mother die, and though men slay brother or son before his eyes"—might have been derived from cannabis. Helen claimed to have acquired it from Egypt, "where many medicines grow that are mighty both for good and ill."[87] Cannabis was indeed grown in Egypt and, according to Petit, used to forget melancholy and life's worries through agreeable visions: "Forests, fountains, gardens and meadows, adorned with the most beautiful flowers . . . in a word, the veritable Fortunate islands, or more properly stated, an actual paradise of Mohammed."[88] Additionally, Valmont de Bomare, in his *Universal Dictionary of Natural History* (1767), cited Engelbert Kaempfer's widely read travels, which indicated that the seeds of cannabis were mixed with food in the East Indies "and if eaten in abundance they excite the user to the point of delirium."[89]

For Alzate, these reports proved that the effects of cannabis were overwhelmingly a product of the plant's nature rather than any supernatural intervention. Yet he did not completely rule out demonic influence. "It would be folly to assert that in some instances the effects of hemp on the Indians are not aided by the spirit of darkness, through that implicit or explicit pact that some of them can contract with him; but normally, we should confess that, for the most part, the effects and visions are purely natural. Piety, rationality, and judgment [*la crítica*] tell us that we should not label as supernatural all of those things that do not extend beyond the limits of nature."[90]

The episode provides a fascinating glimpse into the quiet emergence of cannabis into Mexican life and culture during the colonial era. Alzate's investigation and the almost total lack of other sources that refer to cannabis drugs during the period make clear that this process took place largely beyond the gaze of official or literate Mexico. They also demonstrate that, since its sixteenth-century introduction, cannabis had been incorporated into local medico-religious practice in a manner that linked it to the many other psychotomimetic substances of the region. Alzate's description of the *pipiltzintzintlis* would have fit seamlessly with Sahagún's sixteenth-century passage on the "herbs that intoxicate." In short, from the first recorded use of cannabis in Mexico as a psychoactive drug, it was associated with hallucinations, madness, deviant religious practice, and the devil.

While we have seen that cannabis does have the potential to produce psychotomimetic effects, it should nevertheless be noted that some of the effects accorded to the *pipiltzintzintlis* might very well have been produced by substances other than cannabis. In fact, ethnobotanists have disagreed on the true identity of the *pipiltzintzintlis* as described in the Inquisition files. Aguirre Beltrán has argued that the word *pipiltzintzintlis* was most likely a synonym for ololiuhqui,[91] while R. Gordon Wasson has hypothesized that the word was actually used to refer to *Salvia divinorum*, a substance still used for divination in the mountains of Oaxaca.[92] Ethnobotanist José Luis Díaz also explored this question, but, apparently unlike Wasson or Aguirre Beltrán, he was aware of Alzate's work on the subject. Díaz concluded, probably correctly, that Wasson, Aguirre Beltran, and Alzate could all have been correct, with the word *pipiltzintzintlis* serving as a synonym for all three substances. It was, he notes, hardly unusual during this period for a single word to be used to describe multiple plants having what were understood to be similar properties.[93] Others have also made this observation. At the turn of the twentieth century, for example, renowned Mexican botanist José Ramírez found that at least two different plant species were commonly referred to as "ololiuhqui" in Mexico. This, he argued, was hardly surprising, given that it was "a general rule that the common indigenous names of plants should generally be taken to be generic names" and that it was typical for multiple species to receive the same appellation.[94] Given Alzate's credentials, his presence in the period in question, and the great detail with which he describes his research, we have little reason to doubt the veracity of his account.[95] Yet, at the same time, had cannabis always been the source of the *pipiltzintzintlis*, we would expect, given how common the species was in Europe, that the Inquisition authorities would have noticed. Díaz's multiple species thesis is thus probably the correct one. Perhaps cannabis was sometimes used as a substitute for other psychotomimetic drugs when these were in short supply. This is precisely what Carl Lumholtz found in the 1890s among the Indians of Mexico's Pacific coast. There he observed the Tepecanos substitute cannabis for peyote when they could not acquire the latter. In fact, they called cannabis *Rosa*

*María*, a designation that had commonly been used during the colonial era to refer to peyote.[96]

What, then, happened to the name *pipiltzintzintlis*? To my knowledge, it does not appear in any source after the eighteenth century. This question will surely never be answered definitively, but we might hypothesize that the original name fell out of favor over time thanks to the prohibitions instituted against it. We know that certain substances, especially those that had been proscribed by Spanish authorities, eventually were given Christianized names in Mexico, whether through syncretism or simply to help protect their identity and cultivation. Thus, ololiuhqui gained the designation *Nuestro Señor* (Our Father), *los Ángeles* (the Angels), *María Santísima* (Mary Most Holy), and *Semilla de la Virgen* (Seed of the Virgin). *Salvia divinorum* is today most often referred to as *Yerba María* (Mary's herb).[97] Peyote came to be called *Santa Rosa María* (Saint Mary Rose), *Santísima Trinidad* (the Most Holy Trinity), and, like *Salvia divinorum*, *Yerba María*.[98] Also quite interesting from this perspective, of course, is that cannabis itself began to be called *Rosa María* and *mariguana* in the nineteenth century.

However, before leaving Alzate, we should note his proposed solution to the problem of the *pipiltzintzintlis* and their use by the Indians for divination. As he argued: "The prohibition of its use is very necessary as long as the Indians continue to believe in its diabolical effects. But is it not well known that prohibitions incite more and more the desire to do that which is prohibited, for that malice to which we have such propensity?" This, of course, is an argument that is still heard with some frequency today regarding the wisdom of sumptuary restrictions, be they of alcohol, marijuana, or anything else. In lieu of prohibition, Alzate thus proposed that the Indians be educated to understand that the effects of this substance were natural and that the devil played only as much of a role as the user allowed. This, he argued, was necessary because without such knowledge, Indians would continue to be tricked into devil worship by the natural effects of the drug. As an example, he noted that cannabis seeds were widely used in European medicine as an effective remedy against gonorrhea and other ailments. He wondered how much of this seed had been prescribed by physicians at the royal medical hospital and how many Indians had thereafter been driven further into their superstitious beliefs due to the very real efficacy of the drug. Would not the fact of being cured by cannabis only have reinforced the belief that the drug's effects were supernatural? He thus thought it all the more important to teach the Indians that these effects were purely natural, for as long as they associated those effects with diabolical intervention, they would be tempted to take the drug for purposes of divination. Ultimately, drugs like the *pipiltzintzintlis* were, in Alzate's opinion, "bad for being prohibited, and not prohibited for being bad."[99]

In this manner, cannabis's reputation began to be transformed. The plant had arrived in Mexico as an industrial fiber symbolizing imperial expansion but by the eighteenth century had begun to be categorized with the many other divinatory and hallucinogenic plants of Mexico. This appears to have been a direct result of Mexico's peculiar political and cultural environment where a nexus of religion, healing, and political control deeply colored that society's relationship to drugs.

■ Before we leave colonial Mexico, we must answer a final question: Could Mexico's drug-producing cannabis stock have really been derived from plants that were originally introduced for the production of hemp fiber? After all, in most places where cannabis is grown for fiber today, the THC levels in those plants rarely rises above .3 percent, a level insufficient to produce significant psychoactive effect in users. Furthermore, these cannabis plants are usually monitored strictly in order to ensure consistently low levels of psychoactivity. Given the modern politics of cannabis, that monitoring is crucial to the well-being of the industrial hemp industry.[100]

Certainly, today the difference between drug and fiber cannabis is clear-cut. But such distinctions were not so consistently maintained in the past. Historically, traditions of cannabis drug use have been overwhelmingly situated in hotter, tropical climates, while colder, temperate regions have mostly known cannabis as a fiber-producing plant. Speculation began long ago on the origins of this dichotomy: Was cannabis more likely to produce drug content in hot climates? Or was it that the difference between tropical and temperate strains of the plant was simply a matter of culturally based selection pressures? The question was especially tricky because it was believed that in hotter climates, cannabis tended to produce more of the sticky resin that carries the majority of a plant's cannabinoid content. This latter observation suggested that while there might have been particular selection pressures for drug-producing plants in tropical locations, those pressures might have been sparked by the natural tendency of the plant to exude more resin in those places. It also suggested, of course, that plants long grown for fiber in temperate climates might be turned into drug-producing plants under hotter conditions.

Researchers have recently been better able to test these hypotheses. It has been discovered, for example, that plants bred over time for fiber tend to be high in cannabidiol (CBD) and low in tetrahydrocannabinol (THC). When this discovery was made, it was believed that CBD was not psychoactive, thus presenting a ready-made means of determining fiber versus drug strains. A formula was then developed that distinguished between fiber and drug plants using the ratio of THC to CBD.[101] These innovations enabled researchers to test not only if the ratios of cannabinoids remained constant within given environments but whether or not these levels would be altered by exposure of like strains to diverse environmental conditions.

Probably the most thorough study of this question was carried out by Ernest Small on drug and fiber strains of cannabis collected from fifty different countries. Growing the plants on a farm in Ottawa, Canada, Small confirmed the existence of two clearly distinct types of cannabis, which, respectively, conformed to the high THC (drug) or high CBD (fiber) formula. The former came overwhelmingly from tropical drug stocks, while the latter had been acquired mostly from temperate, fiber-producing strains. Other studies confirmed this general pattern.[102] However, and most important for our purposes here, Small also found a third strain displaying high levels of both compounds. Furthermore, most of these plants had come from Northern Hemisphere stocks used for the production of fiber, seed, and oil rather than of drugs.[103] These findings, of course, suggest that fiber stocks must sometimes have carried sufficient cannabinoid content to intoxicate users, both because we now know that CBD is psychoactive and interacts in dynamic ways with THC, and because some fiber strains of cannabis have historically contained significant levels of both cannabinoids.

The evidence also suggests potential variability of cannabinoid content within individual strains. Small reported a few notable cases of variation within a number of his samples, with some apparent "fiber" strains having one or two plants conforming more closely to what he had defined as drug-plant characteristics.[104] He also reported that one of his experimental strains, which had been grown in both Ottawa and Mississippi under controlled conditions, had produced different cannabinoid levels in the hotter and colder climates, respectively. In the hotter climate, the same strain produced roughly twice as much THC. Small argued that this was likely due either to the production of more resin in the South or perhaps to drought conditions in Mississippi, which caused the lower, less potent leaves of the plants to fall off. In either case, the hotter weather resulted in specimens with higher net drug content.[105]

Indeed, even studies that have confirmed the existence of these basic types and the general stability of the THC to CBD ratios have also noted that environmental factors may produce especially high or low production of the active agents.[106] Other studies have also confirmed some variability within strains while noting the considerable fluctuations in cannabinoid output at different stages of a given plant's development. For instance, researchers at the University of Mississippi have shown that the cannabinoid output of particular plants is in fact cyclical, with THC or CBD levels (or both) rising and falling during the maturation process.[107] Other work has revealed great variation in the cannabinoid output of individual plant parts, though this output still follows the general THC/CBD ratio of each plant "type."[108]

The development of cannabis drug cultures in Mexico occurred over the course of centuries, a period that plausibly would have allowed for cannabis strains observed as having higher drug content to be selected for. Furthermore, as we will see, even by the end of the nineteenth century the quantities of cannabis smoked to achieve drug reactions were considerably higher than those ingested today, with users sometimes smoking entire cigarettes of cannabis on their own. Finally, in light of the recent discoveries that CBD is, contrary to previous understandings, psychoactive, the ratio of THC to CBD does not provide a foolproof distinction between drug- and fiber-producing plants. As Small indicated to me in response to my queries on the subject, it has been observed that many strains of cannabis used for preparing hashish are actually very high in CBD. Indeed, a 1971 work by Patricia S. Fetterman and colleagues demonstrated that Turkish strains of cannabis conformed to the "fiber-type" THC/CBD ratio. Turkey, of course, has a long history of hashish use.[109] For his part, Small believes it unlikely that European fiber strains of cannabis would have been the source of Mexico's drug-producing cannabis. However, he did suggest the possibility that seeds brought from Spain might have been infiltrated with drug-cannabis stock, especially given the proximity of the Iberian Peninsula to North Africa, where cannabis drug use was common.[110] Since we do not have any evidence of cannabis drug strains being imported to Mexico at any time prior to 1920, it seems most likely that some of these strains imported for fiber eventually became drug-producing plants, thanks to one or more of the mechanisms suggested above.

■ The colonial era thus saw the emergence of cannabis into Mexican life and culture. Cannabis strains originally imported for the production of fiber appear to have been adopted into local pharmacopoeias in a manner that almost completely eluded the gaze of the authorities or literate Mexicans. That process brought cannabis into a cultural nexus where drug use, religion, and political control all mingled uneasily. By the end of the eighteenth century, the plant had come to be called *pipiltzintzintlis* in some circles and was associated with divination, visions, and even madness. These were some of the effects that would eventually define marijuana's reputation a century later. But it would be nearly eighty years between Alzate's research and the next known reference to cannabis drug use in Mexico. To that period we now turn.

*Chapter 3*

THE DISCOVERY

OF MARIJUANA IN

MEXICO

In 1854, the Mexico City daily *El Correo de España* informed its readers that Alexander Dumas, with his ability to make fashionable just about anything, had turned hashish into the latest European fad. Dumas's descriptions in *The Count of Monte Cristo*, suggesting that hashish produced pleasant dreams and sensations of "indescribable well being," along with the plant's exotic name and origins, had produced a veritable "hashishmania" among the European cognoscenti. But to *El Correo*'s surprise, a local botanical authority revealed that Mexico produced its own somewhat less prestigious version of the stuff:

> To spoil the illusions of those who allowed themselves to be seduced by the magic of orientalism, we're not sure which untimely botanist came to explain that the real hatchis grows in the valleys of [our] hot country disguised by the prosaic name mariguana, and that not only has it cast out [*esparcido*] spirals of narcotic smoke from the pipe of Haroun al-Raschid, but also in lost hours it has filled with delight the Indians of Chilpancingo, and entertained the innocent inhabitants of La Acordada in their moments of tedium. This circumstance will result in hatchis, or haschisch, or mariguana, losing much of its fabulous prestige.

As was the custom of the day, the journalists took it upon themselves to sample the local product, but "despite having each of us smoked a mariguana cigarette, we have not reached that summit of happiness that the French novelist promised us, nor even gotten beyond inhaling the smoke of a bad flavored weed of hardly select odor."[1]

It's not clear from whom *El Correo* had learned this information, but almost surely it was either Leonardo Oliva or someone who had read his recently penned *Lecciones de farmacología* (1853–54), for that was only the second published source since Alzate's 1772 work on the *pipiltzintzintlis* to clearly identify the use of cannabis as a drug in Mexico. Much had changed since Alzate's essay. The Age of Reason had spawned a generation of scientifically inclined Mexicans who, after securing independence from Spain, were inspired to focus their attention and talents on the Mexican interior, to map the nation's cultural dimensions, to list the nation's resources, and to celebrate *lo mexicano*, whatever that might turn out to mean. Their publications provide a window into the life and culture of the great illiterate majority. Mostly, even with this improved perspective, observers failed to discern the presence of cannabis either as a wild plant or drug in Mexico. But cannabis did become visible from one specific viewpoint: that of nation-building botanical scientists like Oliva. These researchers set out in search of Mexico's long-famed botanical riches and, like Alzate, found cannabis (now called marijuana) ensconced in local medical practice and culture. These circumstances helped to cement marijuana's reputation as an indigenous drug plant, and, for these researchers, this made it a potentially valuable component of a truly national materia medica. But, as *El Correo*'s story indicated, such would not necessarily be the response of Mexican elites in general.

In this chapter, I examine the processes that led to marijuana's nineteenth-century "discovery." The evidence suggests that if marijuana smoking had occurred in Mexico prior to the 1840s, it was extremely rare, enough so to remain completely outside of the historical record. But marijuana's discovery also illustrates that from very early on, this drug's history would play out within a highly fraught transnational intellectual environment. Here we see that, for a brief moment in the 1850s, the nationalist objectives of Mexican elites might have allowed for the celebration of marijuana rather than its total demonization. But, as with Mexican nationalism more generally, there was a fundamental contradiction when all of this was reflected off a European standard of modernity, a contradiction that, as we will see in subsequent chapters, would plague marijuana's history right down to its prohibition in 1920.

■ Carl Linnaeus's creation in 1753 of a parsimonious method for classifying plant species provided a starting point for the processes that would ultimately lead to marijuana's nineteenth-century discovery in Mexico. In *Species Plantarum*, Linnaeus obliterated a confusing system of botanical nomenclature with a simple formula that assigned a single binomial to each of the 5,900 species of plants known to Europeans at the time. This elegant system created a straightforward means by which travelers could add discoveries to the list of known species and thus helped to inspire a new era of exploration to the interior of the continents by scientifically inclined Europeans.[2]

The impact on Latin American science and nationhood was profound. Three separate botanical expeditions to the Americas were commissioned by the Bourbon kings of Spain—the Expedición Botánica a los Reinos de Perú y Chile in 1777, the Expedición de Nueva Granada begun in 1782, and the Expedición Botánica a Nueva España, from 1787 to 1803—all of which contributed significantly to the development of science among the soon-to-be independent republics.[3] The most important of such expeditions was Alexander von Humboldt's from 1799 to 1804, which collected over 60,000 plant specimens, 3,000 of which were unknown to Europe at the time.[4] Humboldt's daring exploits, melding the rational pursuit of knowledge with the romantic courting of danger, captured the imagination of the West. As Marco Polo and Columbus had done before, Humboldt piqued Westerners' interest in exotic lands and peoples, inspiring intellectuals ranging from Victor Hugo to Charles Darwin. He also inspired nationalism in the Americas by defending the New World against attacks of inferiority from the Old, prompting Simón Bolívar to dub the German naturalist the "true discoverer of America."[5]

As the nineteenth century wore on, subsequent generations of Mexican scientists took inspiration from Humboldt, for they often found themselves promoting and defending the worth of their country against a new wave of European criticism that followed in the wake of national independence. The arrival of scores of European travelers and businessmen, who often published their criticisms of Mexico's environment and society, helped fuel what was already a strong nationalist impulse to map and catalog Mexico's wealth of natural wonders.[6] Thus, like previous Europeans who had traveled to the interior of continents in search of plants to classify, Mexico's elites ventured into the provinces to catalog their own nation's remarkable botanical riches.

Though much cannabis had been sown in late-eighteenth-century New Spain, and though the plant could by then be found in some local pharmacopoeias, the reports of various naturalists suggest that it remained a patchy presence in the Mexican countryside at the turn of the nineteenth century. Humboldt, who traveled through New Spain in 1803, failed to notice it, commenting that up to that point "there [had] not been cultivation of either hemp or flax in Mexico."[7] Writing just before the turn of the century, the Spanish botanist Vicente Cervantes more accurately described hemp as being "cultivated in Cuernavaca and a few other places in the realm," yet he provided no information to suggest that he had anything more than a standard European textbook knowledge of the plant.[8] Josepho Mociño, who was born and raised in New Spain and who together with Martino Sessé led a scientific expedition through the viceroyalty between 1799 and 1804, gave good reason to believe that the "narcotic" properties of the plant were mostly unknown to Mexicans at the time. In an 1801 address in Mexico City, he stated that "among the narcotics [of Mexico] we have the opium poppy, the leaves of *Cicuta* (*Conium Maculatum*), *yerba mora* (*Solanum Nigrum*), *toloache* (*Datura stramonium*), and tobacco."[9]

Other sources over the next several decades confirm the plant's patchy distribution. It is noted in the 1820s as a typical wild plant of Sinaloa's temperate climate, but an 1832 list of materia medica in Puebla fails to cite it.[10] An 1837 geography of Aguascalientes makes no mention of cannabis as either a wild plant or a medicinal herb.[11] Neither does a similar report on Guanajuato in the 1840s, though later in that decade, "wild hemp" was reported to grow in the nearby state of Colima.[12] Sources that we would expect to have mentioned cannabis smoking had it been known also consistently fail to mention it. It is almost totally absent from the literature on Mexican customs by Guillermo Prieto and Manuel Payno, despite copious references to alcohol and other vice.[13] It is also absent from accounts by foreign travelers and soldiers. For example, the Reverend William Bingley detailed the vices of Mexicans and "Indians," including drinking, gambling, and sloth, while Albert G. Brackett, a soldier in the Mexican-American War, described soldiers, gambling, and alcohol and noted that "the numerous plants, so new and strange to me, possessed great attractions, and I was, with others, often led astray with regard to their names and peculiarities," yet both failed to mention cannabis. The same was true of G. F. von Tempsky, who recounted the "bloodlust" and drinking of Indians while also providing detailed descriptions of prisoners and soldiers, the two demographics that would eventually be most closely linked to marijuana.[14] Two other travelers provided especially telling omissions or "non-references" to cannabis smoking. In chapter 1, I quoted Bayard Taylor on the effects of hashish, for in 1854 he had published an article on the subject. Yet in that same year, he published a travel account of his time in Mexico in which he richly described its people and their habits without ever noting the use of cannabis.[15] Similarly, in 1844, the French traveler Mathieu de Fossey published his *Viage a Méjico*, in which he offered detailed descriptions of vice, especially the drinking of alcohol. But he would not mention the use of "mariguana" in Mexico until the publication of a second travel account in 1857. While in Colima, he noted that tobacco was not cultivated there but that "ordinary folk [*la gente del pueblo*] smoke the leaves of a plant called mariguana which provides them a drunkenness full of hallucinations and of agreeable sensations." More ominously, he also noted that the plant sometimes caused those with feeble brains or who abused it to have "accesses of frenzy," and thus it had been forbidden among prisoners as they tended "to throw disorder into the jail when they arrive at the peak of delirium." Echoing *El Correo de España*, Fossey also noted that this plant was the same as "the haschich of the Orient of which Alexandre Dumas speaks in Monte-Cristo."[16] It seems that sometime between the publication of his first and second books, the practice had come to his attention for the first time.

Finally, Humboldt provided perhaps the best evidence that cannabis smoking was mostly unknown in Mexico during this period. Though in the original edition of his *Ensayo político sobre el reino de la Nueva España* (1811) he had mistakenly claimed that hemp cultivation had not occurred in Mexico, by the publication of the third edition (1836), he had been corrected by better-informed authorities, a fact that he explained in the footnotes.[17] Yet despite an important passage in the original text in which he also noted that a variety of cannabis was cultivated in other parts of the world for its drug content, no amendment to the third edition was made to indicate that such use was also known in Mexico. It certainly seems that those same informants who had corrected him on Mexico's history with industrial hemp would not have failed to mention the narcotic use of cannabis had they been aware of it.[18] All of this, along with the fact that marijuana smoking is not mentioned in any published text until the 1840s, indicates that if this practice had already appeared in Mexico before then, it was still extremely rare.

But gradually the forces that Linnaeus and Humboldt had done so much to set in motion combined to make the use of cannabis, whatever its extent, gradually more visible to elite observers. Almost immediately upon independence, nation-building Mexican elites had begun to express considerable interest in the nation's "indigenous" drug plants. Extraordinary knowledge of materia medica had of course long been viewed by outsiders as a quintessential characteristic of Mexico's Indians. Cortés had famously advised the Crown that it need not send any physicians to New Spain, for the Indians were expert enough in this regard.[19] But with independence, local medicinal knowledge and material became a potential source of the national wealth and therefore a key node of incipient Mexican nationalism. In 1825, for example, Vicente Cervantes founded the National Museum, whose mission was to promote botanical research. Upon Cervantes's death in 1829, Vice President Anastasio Bustamante became the museum's head of natural history and botanical studies, and shortly thereafter he coedited an index of Mexico's plants in both Spanish and Nahuatl.[20] Similarly, the Academy of Surgical Medicine of Puebla had been founded in 1824 with the goal of publishing an "indigenous pharmacopoeia" in order to "identify the qualities of Mexican plants so as to substitute them for those originating abroad." Despite great political instability in Mexico, efforts in this direction were continued under the presidency of Vicente Gómez Farías, who in 1833 founded the Establishment of Physical and Mathematical Sciences as part of a program of education reform. The new institution, which featured a field of study in medicinal plants, was conceived of as a crucial tool for the mapping of the Mexican nation. Finally, in 1838, the Academy of Pharmacy was founded, an organization whose principal duty was to create Mexico's first national pharmacopoeia.[21]

The academy's *Farmacopea mexicana*, completed in 1842 and published four years later, richly illustrates these developments. In its introduction, the authors lament that it had "not been long since everything in this city, excepting nature itself, was Spanish." Specifically, they referred to defective medicinal formularies from Spain that failed to take into account the local products available in Mexico. "Seeing as this Academy is Mexican, it has carefully endeavored, whenever good conscience has permitted it, to substitute indigenous substances for the exotic, and clarify the legitimate names of those medicines that for a long time have been distributed by pharmacists without prejudice to medical practice as substitutes for products that otherwise would have come from abroad."[22] Mexico's famed botanical riches had the potential to provide both an extraordinary comparative advantage and a truly Mexican contribution to European civilization. This had profound meaning for elite Mexicans of that age, something that was perhaps illustrated by the conspicuous inferiority complex that also imbued the *Farmacopea*'s introduction. The authors spoke of "overcoming their timid modesty" in putting together such a volume, "despite having neither protection from the authorities, nor national models on which to base their work, nor funding beyond their own private purse, without even, it must be confessed, sufficient literary education."[23] This was not an unusual sentiment among the new crop of nationalist scientists of that period. Though the recently founded Geographical and Statistical Society of the Mexican Republic could count Humboldt himself among its members, in the inaugural issue of the society's *Boletín* the editors expressed hope that "the civilized nations of the world will . . . do us the justice of viewing with a certain indulgence the imperfection of our first essays in such difficult material."[24]

Though cannabis was of course originally a foreign import, its gradual adoption into local medical practice had imbued it with a certain indigeneity by association. It is thus hardly surprising that the first published reference to *mariguana* as a drug would appear in the *Farmacopea mexicana*. While no specific reference to marijuana smoking was made in the volume, the plant's leaves were identified as "narcotic."[25] Tellingly, *Cannabis indica* (aka *Rosa María, Cáñamo del pais, mariguana*) and *Cannabis sativa* (aka *cáñamo*) are there classified separately within a list of "The Most Common Elemental Medicines." *Cannabis sativa* was Linnaeus's binomial and had by that time become synonymous with European fiber-producing varieties of the plant.[26] The *Farmacopea* noted that its seeds were "emulsive."[27] *Cannabis indica* had been coined by Lamarck and was most often used to describe drug-producing cannabis strains, as was done by the *Farmacopea*.[28] All of this suggests that drug cannabis was by 1842 known to be used in Mexico, despite its absence from all other sources.

Real proof of such use would only appear in 1846 with a report that marijuana smoking had caused a recent outbreak of laziness in the military, and then not again until the publication of Leonardo Oliva's two-volume *Lecciones de farmacología* in 1853–54. Like the *Farmacopea*, Oliva's *Lecciones* exuded the nationalism of the period. Oliva, who was the chair of the Department of Pharmacology at the University of Guadalajara, argued that illnesses and the natural products necessary to cure them would always be found in the same regions, for all things indigenous to a particular area would have acquired their characteristics through their interaction with the same environment. Quoting Pliny the Elder, Oliva suggested the nationalist implications of this general philosophy: "I do not concern myself here with the drugs that they bring us from India or Arabia or any foreign land. I am not interested in remedies that originate so far from home; those were not created for us."[29]

Oliva recognized the comparative advantage of Mexico's varied climates and soils to produce a diversity of natural remedies. He contrasted this potential with that of the "frozen countries of the poles" that were, because of their cold climates, destined to rely far more on medical material imported from warmer foreign lands. However, the desire to exploit this advantage required that Mexican scientists be willing to take seriously the knowledge of country folk and Indians, whose empirical approach to these remedies had long been scorned by scientific medicine. "It is not rare to see illnesses which have been combated assiduously, energetically, and philosophically by physicians, finally surrender, as if through magic, to a concoction at which the physician scoffs, composed of simple ingredients and prepared by some old woman."[30] It should be the object of science, Oliva believed, to take up such knowledge and perfect it through experimentation.

He was also very much dissatisfied with the state of Mexican medicine in the middle of the nineteenth century. He argued that little had been accomplished since Mario Mociño had fifty years earlier criticized the lack of an official Mexican materia medica, and he lamented the humiliation of being forced to study foreign pharmacopoeias.

> How it is that our men, with their blind hatred of servitude, which they believe pursues them like a specter and which they somehow identify everywhere, nevertheless pay their respects to that servitude in the realm of the natural sciences, the realm from which such obeisance should remain furthest! But this is not all, for they ambush [us] to the point of the ridiculous, writing seriously on substances and species which to us are unknown, dismissing as vulgar precisely those medicines that we do use, attributing the effects of the latter to the former while preferring the foreign, even though these result far inferior to our own indigenous products.[31]

Given all of this, Oliva's inclusion of marijuana demonstrates as clearly as any other source that this drug was by then seen as an indigenous product. But despite his desire to tap into local sources of knowledge, Oliva's own research into the drug did not go much beyond the consultation of published European texts: "Murray has already made known its [physiological] properties: even the emanations of the plant, of which there are copious quantities, are said to cause violent headache and the first signs of intoxication." Drawing from Jacques-Joseph Moreau's *Hashish and Mental Illness*, Oliva noted that cannabis could "at times . . . occasion both moral and physical hallucinations: one sees what does not exist or one sees incorrectly what does exist." Other European works were also cited, in particular William Brooke O'Shaughnessy's Indian research and his claims to the drug's effectiveness in cases of tetanus, rheumatism, rabies, delirium tremens, and Asiatic cholera. However, Oliva did provide one critical piece of new information: "The leaves smoked, as is done by the Hottentots according to Sparrman, and as do certain Mexicans [*algunos mexicanos*], produce intoxication and illusions without bringing on the gastric irritations or other negative effects of alcoholic beverages." This reference to *algunos mexicanos*, only the second known reference to the smoking of marijuana in Mexico, reinforces what other sources from the period had already indicated—that this practice was still quite rare in Mexico—while his failure to mention any specifically Mexican understandings of the drug's physiological or medical qualities also suggests that these properties were not yet widely known to elite Mexicans of the day.[32]

Oliva was also the first person to speculate in print on the origins of the name "marihuana," an etymology that to this day remains unexplained. Oliva argued that the word was simply a synonym for "*Rosa María*," combining the roots *mari*, meaning "María," and *huana*, meaning "rose," though he admitted he did not know to what language the latter word might belong. Nonetheless, he asked rhetorically if this "Americanized" form did not suggest that the plant had passed to Mexico from Asia prior to the conquest.[33] Since Oliva's time, various other theories have been proposed to explain the word's origins. In 1926, a Mexico City medical student named Ignacio Guzmán suggested that the term was derived from a combination of the Nahuatl words *mallín*, meaning "prisoner," and *hua*, meaning "property."[34] This theory remains among the more intriguing, since the Spanish *r* is generally written with an *l* in Nahuatl (for example, Maria = Malia).[35] Shortly thereafter, Francisco Santamaría, in his dictionary of Mexican idioms, admitted that no one had produced any clear answer to this question. However, he did cite what was perhaps the most common going theory—that the name derived from the slang terms for a soldier, "Juan," and that of his female companion, "María." Santamaría also made a second, more interesting observation—that there was an island in the Bahamas called "Hariguana [*sic*]."[36] In fact, the island was called "Mariguana," though if one looks at a map today, such an island does not exist.[37] Since the middle of the twentieth century, that island has been more frequently referred to as Mayaguana, which was its original indigenous name. That designation had originally been used by Europeans, but in 1633, and for unknown reasons, the island was called "Mariguana" in a grant made by Cardinal Richelieu. The latter spelling stuck for several centuries until gradually the indigenous designation was readopted.[38] The existence of a Bahamian island called Mariguana is intriguing since it hints at a potential Caribbean origin for the diffusion of cannabis smoking to Mexico, a theory that has been suggested elsewhere by alternative etymologies of the same word. It has been argued, for example, that the word *marijuana* derives from the Portuguese term *mariguango*, which supposedly meant "intoxicant,"[39] a theory that on its surface appears plausible since cannabis use does appear to have developed quite early on in Brazil among African slaves.[40]

But all of these theories have major shortcomings. To begin, it is highly unlikely that the term came to Mexico by way of Brazil. I have not been able to determine on what this *mariguango* theory is based, and a review of Portuguese dictionaries from various eras provides absolutely no evidence that such a term has ever existed.[41] Furthermore, although the importance of African influence on cannabis use in Brazil is quite well founded, no such influence is at any time evident in Mexico. The most common word used for cannabis in Brazil, *maconha*, a term whose origins lie in West Africa, never appears in Mexico as a synonym for marijuana. Likewise, the practice of using water pipes to smoke the drug, as was typical in Africa and then Brazil, also fails to appear in Mexico at any time within the period of this study.[42] Thus, there is almost no evidence, beyond coincidence, to suggest that the word *mariguana* was derived either from the Bahamian island of the same name or as a product of Luso-Caribbean influence on Mexico. Guzmán's Nahuatl theory is intriguing, but, on the other hand, there is no known use of the word *malihuana* in reference to cannabis. If "marihuana" was merely a hispanicization of an indigenous word, should we not have found some evidence of the original term still in use somewhere in Mexico?[43] The common theory cited by Santamaría linking *mariguana* to the word "Juan" is also lacking because the spelling of marijuana with a *j* in Mexico has always been extremely rare and, to my knowledge, nonexistent prior to the twentieth century. Indeed, the use of the *j* with this term appears to surface originally in U.S. newspaper stories during the decade beginning around 1910. If the term was meant to denote "Juan," why was the word never spelled with a *j* in Mexico? Furthermore, while the earliest extant reference to marijuana smoking in Mexico does involve soldiers, this was not the only group connected to its use. And none of the earliest references, to the best of my knowledge, make a point of connecting the drug exclusively to the military.

At the same time, various other equally speculative theories have been forwarded to explain the origins of the term. Some have claimed that "marijuana" was originally a slang term for cheap tobacco in northern Mexico.[44] Another scholar, in a decidedly idiosyncratic piece, has claimed *mariguana* was derived from a combination of various Arabic terms.[45] All of these theories, while perhaps intriguing, are nevertheless based in pure speculation. Indeed, we could harness other scraps of evidence to make equally justifiable claims of our own. For instance, in his work on Mexico's sixteenth-century ethnic groups, Manuel Orozco y Berra noted a people in the Tamaulipas region called the Mariguanes who "sowed corn, beans, squash, lived in huts, and manufactured rough crockery."[46] Shortly after their appearance in the sources of the late sixteenth century, the Mariguanes disappear from the historical record. Might the origins of this word be found among these people? We might also play with linguistic clues. For example, if we turn to the language of the now extinct Opata people of western Mexico, we find some remarkable potential for speculation. Here exists, for example, the word *mariguat*, which means "father of the daughter."[47] Could this word have been the root of *mariguana*? It is a theory based on almost nothing, yet it is as valid as any of the others.

The use of the term "*Rosa María*" in reference to cannabis does suggest that the *mari* of *mariguana* is indeed the standard abbreviation for "María" used in compound names. This suggests that like so many other divinatory substances in Mexico, cannabis was eventually given a Christianized name, probably in an effort to hide its identity. As we have seen, certain divinatory substances, particularly those known to possess what are today classified as hallucinogenic properties, were persecuted with great enthusiasm by Spanish colonial authorities. That persecution, as well as syncretism, appears to have inspired the emergence of new, more Christian-sounding names for these plants. Thus, we saw in chapter 2 how various drugs began to be called by names that included the words "María" or "Virgin" or various other standard Christian designations (for example, *Semilla de la Virgen*, *Santa Rosa María*, *Yerba María*, and the like). During the colonial era, cannabis acquired the appellation *pipiltzintzintlis*, a name that was synonymous with a powerful divinatory substance persecuted by the Inquisition. Given the early adoption of cannabis into local pharmacopoeias, its subsequent identification with the proscribed *pipiltzintzintlis*, and its known movement into the divinatory rituals of certain indigenous groups, it seems most likely that cannabis gradually acquired a more Christian-sounding name, one that incorporated the word "María" quite prominently, as either a defense mechanism against persecution or as a result of the forces of cultural syncretism that so colored the histories of the other divinatory substances described above. This theory also leaves room perhaps for the Nahuatl term *huan*, meaning "property," to play a role, for the conjunction might form a word meaning something not unlike "Mary's weed," a designation quite similar to those cited above as synonyms for other divinatory plants. All of this, of course, remains highly speculative. But it is speculation that conforms to the historical reality of substances like marijuana in colonial Mexico, where medicine was intimately linked to religious belief and practice and where these close relationships guaranteed constant conflict with authority. Certainly Oliva's theory and his work on marijuana in general demonstrate how cannabis had by the mid-nineteenth century been "Mexicanized," despite its foreign origins.

Oliva's work also helps us to sum up several of the main arguments of this chapter. First, while the use of marijuana appears to have been increasing in Mexico, it was still rare. Second, while the practice was rare, new nationalist institutions and initiatives were gradually making the use of this drug more visible to elite observers. Third, because these institutions and initiatives were incubated within a larger nation-building context, the presence of marijuana as a "Mexican" medicine was implicitly understood in a relatively positive light. Yet, and fourth, because these scientific figures were simultaneously looking abroad as they more intensely examined Mexican nature and society, they served to bring foreign ideas to bear on the developing history of this drug in Mexico.

That European influence served to exacerbate a critical contradiction in Mexican nationalism. Nation-building Mexican elites, as they mined European texts like those of Moreau and O'Shaughnessy for information about marijuana, not only received Persian, Arab, and Indian notions about this substance but also learned of them as translated through the powerful Orientalist lens of nineteenth-century European science. Orientalism, of course, functioned in part to establish difference between western Europe and the "Oriental" other.[48] That is, the Orient was the anti-Europe and thus "uncivilized" and "premodern." At the same time, these Mexican researchers were thoroughly engaged in a self-conscious, nationalist endeavor to hoist Mexico, they hoped, up to the heights of modern European civilization. Marijuana, as we have seen, being a purportedly "Mexican" medicinal plant, was implicitly celebrated in these texts as a substance that might help Mexico free itself from an ongoing "servitude" to European medical practice. Marijuana fit into the nationalist endeavor because it provided a certain "uniqueness" that was at the same time a valuable contribution to modern science. This was the essence of the tricky balance that plagued the nationalist project in peripheral nations like Mexico. As Mauricio Tenorio-Trillo has demonstrated in his book on Mexico's participation in world's fairs, a country like Mexico had to toe a very fine line, demonstrating a national uniqueness that justified independence and celebration while not being so different as to make it incompatible with "an approved cosmopolitanism and modernity."[49]

For Oliva, marijuana clearly provided a certain amount of this obligatory uniqueness. After all, the word "marihuana," in his estimation, seemed to suggest that this substance had been in use in Mexico since pre-Hispanic times. But the European texts made it eminently clear that, alternatively, this plant could simply be viewed as a Mexican version of a thoroughly "Oriental" substance that inspired "artificial paradises," was smoked by the Hottentots, and occasionally provoked irrational outbursts of violence. Of course, at this time, Europeans were in the business of seeking out the world's miracle drugs, in particular those that might be found in exotic locales like India or Mexico.[50] Because they too were celebrating the medicinal qualities of substances like this, the contradiction inherent in this process for Mexican nation builders had only begun to reveal itself. But as we shall see, when civilizational hierarchies became increasingly codified by science over the coming decades, this link between Mexico's cannabis and the Orient (first made by Alzate in the

1770s) would become an increasingly powerful source of anxiety for Mexico's national architects.

An 1859 publication by Crescencio García, a former medical student at the University of Guadalajara, provides a final example to illustrate all of these points. García spent much of the 1840s traveling through the Bajío (west-central Mexico) and studying the flora of that region. Perhaps inspired by Oliva, with whom he most likely studied and with whose work he was clearly acquainted, García eventually undertook an investigation into certain medicinal substances used in the region and the manner of their employment.[51] "Thanks are in order for Nature's Architect," he exclaimed, "who decided to enrich our soil, for we have no need to import any medicines at all! . . . Humboldt said it correctly: 'Mexico with its [botanical] products can maintain the rest of the world.'"[52] Also like Oliva, and the various nationalist botanists who went before them both, García believed strongly in the necessity of establishing an authentic Mexican materia medica. "It is now necessary that we break free from the servile yoke that obliges us to follow the lead of foreign medical practice; it is indispensable that we dedicate ourselves to the cultivation of legitimate medical practice, stripping it of the vices and defects of which it suffers, and not leave aside the observations of our own practicing physicians." But García also exhibited the self-consciousness typical of the era:

> Even though I recognize that only an official Academy or other literary body could adequately carry out a work of this kind, the desire to serve my country and science was stronger than my timidity, and after all it is high time that we Mexicans put aside all that dissuades us from writing, for it is necessary to confess that this is what keeps us behind in nearly all of the branches of literature, and for no other reason than that we desire that all of our works be perfect and complete, and the obstacles to achieving this in our first efforts thus results in no one wanting to put their name on the line in an environment that demands the sublime and does not accept anything less.[53]

Though he chastised Oliva for relying too heavily on European sources, García's research certainly was not wholly original. In fact, he plagiarized Oliva's *Lecciones* significantly. But he did interview Indians and country people, and his efforts yielded information as yet unknown to Mexican or European science. He learned that "among us Mexicans," marijuana was sometimes "administered to positive effects by some midwives in cases of sluggish births, principally when the pusillanimity obstructs the physiological passage through the uterus." He also noted that the leaves of the weed were smoked, sometimes with tobacco, by Arabs and in Mexico, "principally in the prisons of the Island of Mescala and Guadalajara. . . . It is said that under the drug's influence there is a propensity toward happy ideas, and one of the most common effects is that it provokes gales of laughter that last the entire period of intoxication which can last at times for three or four hours. In some individuals it produces a kind of furious delirium, in which case one can suppress this effect by administering a lemonade. When used habitually marijuana produces apoplexy and the brutification of the spirit." Finally, García claimed, incorrectly, that among the "ancient Mexicans" marijuana had been used to anesthetize victims prior to their sacrifice.[54]

García's work provides a fitting bookend to the first half of the nineteenth century, for it fuses all of the main themes we have encountered so far. There is a celebration in this text of marijuana's apparently Mexican authenticity, with Oliva's theory on the etymology of the term being copied and García's incorrect claim that marijuana was utilized as an anesthetic among the "ancient Mexicans." And this, of course, followed on the heels of his thanks to "Nature's Architect" for endowing Mexico with sufficient indigenous materia medica to obviate any dependence on foreign medicine. Finally, despite all of this, García nonetheless revealed the timidity of a generation of scientists who were desperately eager to establish Mexico's uniqueness while proving its compatibility with the modern, civilized national models provided by Europe.

This era thus saw remarkable advances, in institutions, nationalist initiatives, and knowledge about materia medica, all of which helped to make marijuana considerably more visible to nonusers despite the plant's continued marginality in Mexico. This process helped to solidify its reputation as an indigenous drug plant with indigenous qualities. Botanists began to cite marijuana as a typically "Mexican" substance and would continue to do so over the coming decades, as evidenced by its inclusion in the Mexican botanical collections sent to the World's Fairs of 1855 (Paris) and 1876 (Philadelphia).[55] However, while for nation-building botanists of the middle nineteenth century that indigeneity signaled a potential source of untapped wealth, in the minds of many this was also a sign of potential danger. That double-edged sword paralleled the fundamental contradiction that the Indian question produced for nationalist Mexicans over the coming decades, and all of this would play an important role in the rapid demonization of marijuana in Mexico.

*Chapter 4*

THE PLACE OF MARIJUANA

IN MEXICO, 1846–1920

*A MAN POSSESSED*

*We read in* El Pabellón Nacional *that last Saturday around 11 in the morning, there was a great disturbance in San Pablo plaza of this capital city; that the people ran as if they were pursued by an African lion and that the author of such a scandal was a soldier who, under the influence of mariguana, and with knife in hand, frantically attacked the passersby, wounding people left and right.*

*The same newspaper notes that a gendarme attempted in vain to detain the man on Molino Bridge, but far from succeeding, he received a wound in the back, and the possessed soldier could not be captured until, with a club, another gendarme applied a powerful blow to the man's head.*

— *"Un hombre energúmeno,"* El Monitor Republicano,
    *March 29, 1888*

Though Mexican sanitary officials would eventually prohibit marijuana because it supposedly threatened the well-being of the entire nation, use of the drug was not especially widespread among Mexicans of the late nineteenth and early twentieth centuries. That fact was first suggested to me by the relative scarcity of marijuana references in the historical archive. I discovered that one could spend days on end searching through a particular archival collection without finding a single reference to this drug. Of course, just because a subject rarely appears in the archive does not necessarily mean that it was absent during the period in question. Ironically, a scarcity of references could plausibly be attributed to a subject's *ubiquity*. As another historian warned me years ago: camels are only rarely mentioned in the Koran. However, in the end, my initial suspicions were confirmed. Ubiquity, it turns out, was definitely not the problem.

This chapter draws on a diversity of historical sources, as well as the latest digital tools, to provide the best possible outline of marijuana's place in Mexican society between the first evidence of its smoking in 1846 and its nationwide prohibition in 1920. The chapter's core feature is my close analysis of nearly six hundred newspaper articles, from more than a dozen publications, that discuss marijuana in some way. These were drawn from a larger survey of more than 40,000 newspaper issues. Though marijuana use was not especially widespread during this period, its profile was nonetheless extremely well defined: it was overwhelmingly associated with two closely related demographics (prisoners and soldiers) and two closely related effects (madness and violence). Furthermore, the drug's effects were often portrayed in quite lurid, sensational detail. The above press clipping was typical: a madman "possessed," running through the streets like a lion, knife in hand, with the newspapers casually reporting the apparent facts. Perhaps most extraordinary of all, there was virtually no counterdiscourse to such descriptions. In this chapter, I set the table for the second half of the book, where I seek to explain all of these curious facts.

■ As we've seen, marijuana smoking in Mexico was not noted in a published source until 1846. Where in Mexico the practice first appeared is unclear. However, it is suggestive that almost all of the earliest references to Mexican marijuana smoking come from either the capital or a relatively narrow, six-hundred-mile Pacific coast stretch running roughly from Puerto Vallarta south to Acapulco. As noted in chapter 3, Crescencio García said marijuana was smoked in the prisons of Guadalajara and the Jaliscan island of Mescala; *El Correo de España* found it in the state of Guerrero and Mexico City's Acordada neighborhood; while Mathieu de Fossey noted the practice along the Pacific coast in Colima.[1]

All of this geographic coincidence is certainly intriguing but hardly sufficient to draw any conclusions, for the precious few extant references to marijuana in Mexico between 1846 and the mid-1870s do not provide enough evidence for us to reach any solid conclusions. While the drug's profile was on the rise, Marijuana's most striking feature during the second half of the century remained its absence from most of the sources where one would expect to find it had it been a common feature of Mexican life. These include the accounts of foreigners fixated on vice,[2] studies on vice and hygiene by Mexican researchers,[3] and descriptions of intoxication within the popular literature of the period.[4]

However, the extant sources do suggest that marijuana's reputation was becoming more widely established in Mexico. Two sources are especially poignant in this regard. The first is an 1874 debate between the prominent medical-legal scholars Rafael Rébollar and Marino Zúñiga concerning Article 527 of the newly minted Federal Penal Code. That article sought to punish acts that caused serious consequences—like blindness, madness, or a permanent handicap—but that did not at the same time endanger the life of the victim. Zúñiga objected because he claimed that there did not exist a means of causing such serious injury without in fact endangering someone's life. Rébollar responded that this was actually easily accomplished, citing as one example the use of "certain substances" to produce madness or "idiotism" in individuals. Zúñiga then mocked Rébollar's ignorance and noted that while certain substances like opium and atropine could produce madness, those effects were only temporary. To that, Rébollar provided this important response: "We don't believe that Mr. Zúñiga would go so far as to deny that plants that produce madness might exist. The plant kingdom, among us [Mexicans], is, it can be said, unexploited. . . . And it is also a fact that the Indians know the virtues and properties of many plants unknown to botany. Well informed and reliable people have assured us that in the states of Guanajuato, Monterey [*sic*] and others, marihuana employed in certain ways produces madness, and permanently unlike in the cases of atropine or opium." To this, Zúñiga could only respond with further mockery, noting that while "in the opinion of *persons*" marijuana might cause madness, this was a fact that he could not either confirm or deny, having no knowledge of the subject.[5]

Similarly, in 1886, a student at Mexico's National School of Medicine named Genaro Pérez wrote a thesis on "whether or not the abuse of marihuana can impel the committing of a crime, and if the *marihuano* (what the common people call someone who habitually smokes this plant) should be considered irresponsible for any of his actions." It was a question that had gained his interest, he explained, because it had "begun to forcefully attract the attention of medico-legal investigators" and because it had yet to be studied by the "European professors."[6] The final point is especially telling because there did already exist by the 1880s a rather large European literature on the effects of cannabis. But in Mexico, as Pérez would demonstrate, there remained some doubt as to whether or not the "marihuana" reputed to cause crime and madness was actually cannabis or some other substance. Pérez's thesis, like Zúñiga and Rébollar's earlier dustup, suggests that this was an important transitional moment. Marijuana's reputation for causing violence and madness, and even its true identity, had yet to be completely settled in Mexico.

As Mexican newspapers began dedicating more print to straight news stories and yellow journalism toward the end of the century, published reports on marijuana and its effects became much more common. Nonetheless, marijuana continued to play a relatively minor role in published discourse in comparison to other forms of vice. To measure just how minor, consider the data from a newly available resource—more than a dozen Mexican newspapers digitized by Readex in partnership with the Center for Research Libraries.[7] At the time of this research, sixteen dailies had been digitized spanning the years 1805–1922 for a total of 47,707 text-searchable newspaper issues, most of which were published during the yellow press era. Since each issue contains dozens of articles, the database allows the full-text searching of upward of one million newspaper stories, making possible a relatively profound study of marijuana's prevalence and reputation within the media. Combined with other sources, the findings provide an excellent outline of marijuana's place in Mexican life during this period (readers interested in the methodology of my work here can find a much more detailed explanation in the appendix).

The newspapers analyzed were published in two different eras: an earlier period dominated by highly political content that saw very little print dedicated to simple news reports, and a second era that began roughly around 1880 and that was characterized by modern publishing technology, yellow journalism, and a division between official, subsidized newspapers and independent papers of both liberal and conservative leaning.[8] To illustrate the diversity of the publications sampled, the basic political affiliations of the papers published in the second, more "yellow" era are listed in Table 4.1.

To get a sense of marijuana's prevalence within the public discourse during these years,[9] I first performed a very basic keyword search and noted the number of raw hits for each in the database. Table 4.2 represents the findings. As the table demonstrates, marijuana had almost no presence in the media prior to the yellow press era. Though during that period, vice was obviously a much less frequent aspect of the press, we see that marijuana references were still greatly outnumbered by references to drunkenness and pulque, the typical drink of the Mexican working class, appearing about 1 percent as often as those other words. After 1880, when vice was a much more common feature of the newspapers, there were only 763 marijuana citations in more than 36,000 issues. It appeared 4.5 percent as frequently as alcohol and 10 percent as frequently as pulque. Chart 4.1 clearly illustrates these contrasts.

## TABLE 4.1. POLITICAL AFFILIATION OF NEWSPAPERS

| Subsidized/Official | Independent-Liberal | Independent-Conservative |
|---|---|---|
| El Imparcial | El Monitor Republicano | El País (Catholic) |
| Mexican Herald | Two Republics | La Voz de México (Catholic) |
| Nueva Era (Madero years) | Nueva Era (Díaz years) | Excelsior |
| El Diario (Madero years) | El Diario (Díaz years) | La Revista de Yucatán |
| | El Dictamen | |
| | La Patria | |

Sources: For *El Monitor Republicano, El Imparcial, La Voz de México,* the *Mexican Herald,* and *Two Republics,* see P. Smith, "Contentious Voices amid the Order," 29, 35, 37, 96, 136. For *El Dictamen,* see Bueno, "On the Selling of Rey Momo," 102 n. 22; and Valles Ruiz, *Los aires de la transición,* 27–28. For *El Diario, El Imparcial, Nueva Era,* and *El País,* see Knight, *Mexican Revolution,* 2:391. For *Excelsior,* see Vital, "Victoriano Salado Álvarez," 511. *Excelsior* aligned itself as a critic of the Constitutionalist regime upon its founding. On *Excelsior* and also *La Patria,* see Navarrete Maya, *Excelsior en la vida nacional,* 26–28. On *La Patria,* see also Aguilar Plata, "La imagen de Porfirio Díaz en la prensa capitalina," 148.

The numbers largely conform to what sources outside of the press suggest—that by the end of the century, marijuana's reputation was well known, but the drug was not widely used outside of prisons and soldiers' barracks. A few sources can help to illustrate this point. During the 1890s, the ethnographer Carl Lumholtz traveled along Mexico's Pacific coast documenting the geographic features and cultures that he encountered. There he made numerous references to vice of many kinds but mentioned the intoxicant use of marijuana only once. In fact, Lumholtz specifically noted that the drug's users were of a somewhat circumscribed demographic: "The leaves of this injurious narcotic are smoked throughout Mexico, but mostly by criminals and the depraved."[10] Similarly, Julio Guerrero, in his *La génesis del crimen en Mexico,* documented in great detail the worlds of Mexican vice and crime around the turn of the twentieth century, but he failed to mention the use of marijuana even once. At times, the drug's absence is quite conspicuous. For example, when he discusses the tendency of Mexico City's inhabitants to ingest large quantities of stimulants in order to cope with the valley's climate, he mentions coffee, chocolate, tea, pulque, beer, and wine but fails to mention marijuana.[11] Federico Gamboa's wildly popular 1903 novel *Santa,* surely the most important literary work on Mexican vice during the Porfiriato, also fails to mention

## TABLE 4.2. REFERENCES TO VICE IN THE MEDIA ("RAW HITS"), 1805–1922

*Pre-Yellow Press Era (1805–79)*
*Total Issues Available: 11,646*

| KEYWORD | NUMBER OF RAW HITS |
|---|---|
| Drunkenness | 861 |
| Pulque | 781 |
| Alcohol | 225 |
| Whiskey | 53 |
| Opium | 68 |
| Morphine | 20 |
| Marijuana | 8 |
| Peyote | 3 |
| Cocaine | 1 |
| Toloache | 1 |

*Yellow Press Era (1880–1922)*
*Total Issues Available: 36,061*

| KEYWORD | NUMBER OF RAW HITS |
|---|---|
| Alcohol | 17,143 |
| Drunkenness | 9,941 |
| Pulque | 7,377 |
| Whiskey | 3,555 |
| Morphine | 2,782 |
| Marijuana | 763 |
| Opium | 585 |
| Cocaine | 93 |
| Peyote | 12 |
| Toloache | 8 |

*Source*: Readex/CRL: World Newspaper Archive.

## CHART 4.1. REFERENCES TO VICE IN THE MEDIA ("RAW HITS"), 1880–1922

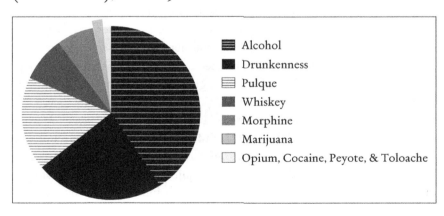

- Alcohol
- Drunkenness
- Pulque
- Whiskey
- Morphine
- Marijuana
- Opium, Cocaine, Peyote, & Toloache

marijuana, despite its emphasis on the close relationship between intoxication (drunkenness) and the environments, both high and low, of prostitution. Still another glaring absence comes in the work of the lithographer José Guadalupe Posada. While Posada did produce one character named "Don Chepito Mariguano," who is analyzed in depth in chapter 7, I have been able to find only one other reference to marijuana in all of Posada's work, despite that work being heavily attuned to scandal and vice and aimed at popular tastes and subjects.[12] Finally, even Mariano Azuela's classic novel *Los de abajo* (1915), which consistently describes an alcohol-soaked revolutionary environment, contains only a single reference to the use of marijuana. That reference, like so many others, again emphasizes the circumscribed social world with which marijuana was associated. At a moment in the novel when the injustices that forced so many soldiers into the federal army are being recounted, a degenerate soldier is described as a constant marijuana smoker.[13] Like Lumholtz's quote above, the single reference emphasizes both the marginality of marijuana's use at the time and its association with the most degraded members of Mexican society, in this case impressed federal soldiers.

Certainly the number of newspaper stories that referred to marijuana increased significantly at the end of the century, but this surely had as much to do with the press's growing obsession with scandal as anything else.[14] Chart 4.2 represents the number of articles that mention marijuana (585 total), organized by newspaper and year from 1878 to 1920. Clearly, there was a significant upsurge in coverage of marijuana around 1897. This is what we would expect given that *El Imparcial*, the signature modern newspaper of the yellow press era in Mexico, was founded in the previous year. But the chart also demonstrates several other points of interest. First, note how few articles were produced in a given year by any given paper. This reiterates what we already noted above: that marijuana clearly was present in Mexico but was a relatively unusual feature of the public discourse. Second, coverage of marijuana does not appear to have varied significantly between newspapers of different political persuasions. Table 4.3 reiterates this last point as it represents the percentage of available issues in which marijuana appeared, organized by newspaper, for the entire collection.

Not surprisingly, the newspapers with percentages below 1 were those whose publication runs occurred mostly or totally prior to *El Imparcial*'s founding in 1896. References to marijuana in the other papers appear in 1.3–3.6 percent of issues, the highest scores involving three "official" papers that published under Presidents Díaz, Madero, and finally Huerta, with the strongly Catholic and oppositionist *El País* in that group as well. Note that

## CHART 4.2. VARIANCE IN MARIJUANA NEWS COVERAGE IN RAW NUMBERS, 1878–1920

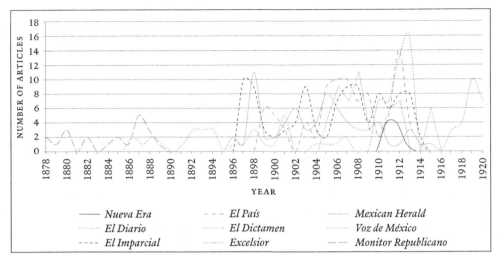

*Source*: Readex/CRL: World Newspaper Archive.

all three major political persuasions are represented from top to bottom. Because the newspaper database does not contain every issue of every paper, I also calculated the percentage of issues per year and per paper that referenced marijuana. Those results are represented in Chart 4.3. Again, there is an obvious uptick in coverage at the end of the century with a peak roughly between 1906 and 1914. The one clear anomaly, the 1910 spike in *El Diario*'s coverage, is easily explained: only sixty-nine total issues of that publication are available for that year. Thus, most likely, a normal year's worth of marijuana coverage was randomly packed into the few available issues. Overall, however, marijuana's presence in the media appears to have been consistently minor.

Some sources did occasionally claim that the use of marijuana was spreading, but none provide anything like a reliable measure. In 1879, *El Monitor Republicano* wrote that marijuana had "spread a lot" in Guanajuato but offered no evidence to back up that claim. In his 1886 thesis, Genaro Pérez noted that he had decided to study whether or not marijuana use could lead to criminal behavior, a question, he said, which had "begun to forcefully attract the attention of medico-legal investigators." But it isn't clear if the increased attention was because of expanding use and reputation or simply because legal debates over the role of intoxicants in crime were on the rise.[15] At various points, the

## TABLE 4.3. FREQUENCY OF MARIJUANA REFERENCES BY NEWSPAPER

| Newspaper | Total Issues | Articles on Marijuana | % That Reference Marijuana |
|---|---|---|---|
| El Diario | 1,428 | 52 | 3.6 |
| Nueva Era | 562 | 15 | 2.6 |
| El Imparcial | 5,653 | 134 | 2.4 |
| El País | 5,433 | 131 | 2.4 |
| El Dictamen | 3,733 | 61 | 1.6 |
| Excelsior | 1,686 | 25 | 1.5 |
| Mexican Herald | 6,896 | 86 | 1.3 |
| La Patria | 803 | 1 | .1 |
| La Voz de México | 6,788 | 50 | .7 |
| La Revista de Yucatán | 319 | 2 | .6 |
| El Monitor Republicano | 4,210 | 21 | .5 |
| El Universal | 2,457 | 2 | .08 |
| El Siglo Diez y Nueve | 4,062 | 2 | .05 |
| El Diario de México | 3,568 | 0 | 0 |
| Two Republics | 233 | 0 | 0 |
| La Mosca Parlera | 16 | 0 | 0 |

Source: Readex/CRL: World Newspaper Archive.

newspapers made what was obviously intended to be an alarming declaration: that marijuana had moved out of the prisons and barracks and into the upper classes. But there is almost no evidence to back that claim, which itself was belied by its appearance in both 1908 and 1919.[16]

The data does suggest that from very early on, the use of marijuana was associated overwhelmingly with prisoners and soldiers.[17] Chart 4.4 represents all the newspaper articles that referred in some way to the demographics of marijuana use between 1854 (the first time marijuana is cited in the Readex/CRL newspaper sample) and March 1920, when the drug was banned nationwide (424 articles in total). The first bar for each group represents all of the data. For the second bar, I excluded 132 "repeat" stories—that is, stories that re-reported an event already covered by the same or a different newspaper.

CHART 4.3. VARIANCE IN MARIJUANA NEWS COVERAGE BY
PERCENTAGE, 1878–1920

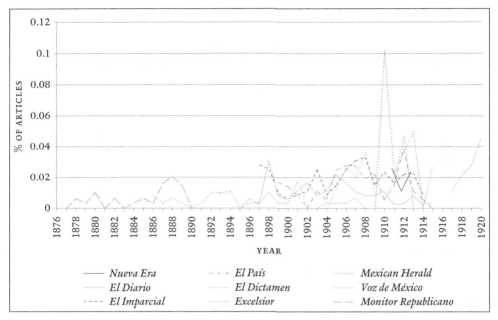

*Source*: Readex/CRL: World Newspaper Archive.

The second bar thus controls for especially sensational stories that might have inflated the numbers for a particular demographic. Both series produce roughly the same demographic proportions.

As Chart 4.4 demonstrates, prisoners and soldiers vastly outnumbered all other demographic groups connected to marijuana. The next closest category was "the lower classes," a broad and vague designation that overlapped with most of the other key demographics. Only one of the top categories suggests anything but lower-class antecedents, that of "public official," and that category was almost entirely an artifact of a single high-profile case in 1913 that was covered for weeks by the press. Thus, when "repeat" stories are removed, that category plummets from twenty-eight references to only two. In short, marijuana was associated overwhelmingly with prisoners and soldiers and, more generally, with the "lower-class" segments of Mexican society.

Geographically, the data is less clear. As noted already, most of the scant mid-nineteenth-century references to marijuana smoking came from either Mexico City or west-central Mexico. In the most serious and thorough study of marijuana during the period, though one confined to its use in the military,

# CHART 4.4. DEMOGRAPHIC CHARACTERISTICS OF
# MARIJUANA USERS AS REPORTED IN THE PRESS, 1854–1920

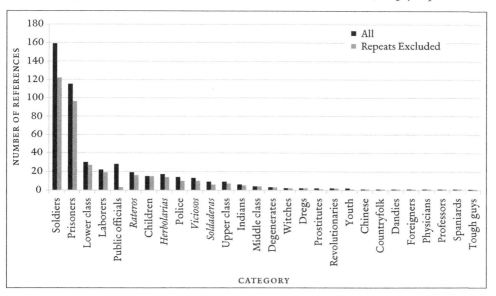

*Source*: Readex/CRL: World Newspaper Archive.

the physicians Adolfo Nieto and Eliseo Ramírez claimed that marijuana was mostly used by soldiers from Mexico City or by those who had passed through the capital during military service.[18] My newspaper survey supports this claim but is deeply biased toward those results because most of the available publications were based in the capital. Thus, of 500 stories that refer to the location of marijuana use, 331, or 66 percent, refer to sale or use in Mexico City. It's impossible to know exactly how much hometown bias accounted for this figure, but an interesting comparison is provided by *El Dictamen*, published in Veracruz. There, 55 articles mention the geography of marijuana use, and of these, 23, or 42 percent, refer to use in the city of Veracruz, while 9, or 16 percent, refer to use in Mexico City. *La Revista de Yucatán* was published in Mérida but produced only two records that referred to marijuana (one in Yucatán and one in Mexico City). If we control for the inevitable hometown bias of the newspapers, it is noteworthy that there are reports from all over the country of marijuana use. The data displayed in Chart 4.5 excludes all references to Mexico City as well as references to Veracruz that appeared in *El Dictamen*. Again, the first bar for each location refers to all of the available articles, while the second reflects the data after subtracting 27 "repeat" stories.

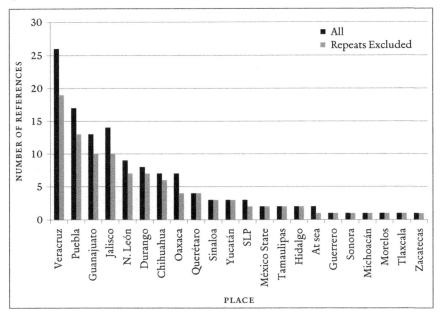

*Source*: Readex/CRL: World Newspaper Archive.

It is certainly interesting that out of 129 total articles, more than 26 (20 percent) came from Veracruz. If the patchy data from the mid-nineteenth century suggests that west-central Mexico was the center of marijuana use, the patchy newspaper data from the yellow press era suggests that, outside of Mexico City, the real hotbed was the central gulf coast. Neither conclusion is especially convincing. We should also note that bigger cities were connected to marijuana much more often than rural areas: of the twenty-six Veracruz references, twenty-three came from the city of Veracruz; twelve of fourteen Jalisco references came from Guadalajara; and six of nine Nuevo León references came from Monterrey, though surely these numbers are, at least in part, an artifact of the urban nature of newspaper reporting. In the end, there is nothing to refute Nieto and Ramírez's claim that Mexico City was the center of marijuana use, but on this point the available evidence is very shaky indeed.

How did Mexicans go about smoking marijuana during this period? Nieto and Ramírez provide an excellent summary along with a rare description of the specific cannabis that was favored for smoking:

There exist various types of this weed; but the most well known among the habituated are: one of a pale yellow similar to the peel of a lemon; and the so-called "flower pot" marihuana, dark and reminiscent of old oregano. Both are employed in their natural form, that is to say, without preparation, in cigarettes of normal length, but two or three times thicker than normal, made with the pure weed or mixed with tobacco rolled in light brown-yellow paper [*papel de estraza amarillo claro*]. Other times the weed is packed into the wrapping of normal cigarettes which have been previously emptied of their contents.

*Dawamesc, Hafioun* and the rest of the Oriental preparations are unknown among our marihuana smokers, and only in one case that was referred to me by Dr. Felipe López was tobacco or marijuana used which had been saturated with alcoholic tincture of cannabis.

The smokers sometimes do so alone; but more often, they form groups of two or more and they smoke a single cigarette (Juana, Juanita, *grifo* or "rice taco with garbanzo beans"), that they pass from mouth to mouth until everyone has taken three puffs of smoke, or, more rarely, until the cigarette has been smoked completely.[19]

This basic outline of the culture of marijuana use combines most of the key elements typically described by the sources.[20] However, one detail that Nieto and Ramírez did not mention but that appeared in many other descriptions was the custom referred to as "refining" the drug. This entailed the chewing of *piloncillo* or *panela*, that is, unrefined brown sugar. The *Mexican Herald* described it in the standard terms while adding that publication's typical sensational flare: "Sometimes to make the effects of marihuana more terrible, smokers 'refinar' (to refine). This they do by taking a draught of smoke, which they swallow, then a bite of 'panela' or any other sweet stuff and a very little sip of water, in succession. The effects are so terrible that smokers attack and attempt to kill everybody. They attack even their own shadow. A regular marihuana smoker is sure to go crazy, never to recover his mind again, in less than three months."[21]

Certainly the most common means of ingesting marijuana was through smoking, though on a few occasions it was rumored to be mixed in tea, coffee, or pulque.[22] Another important aspect of the Mexican culture of marijuana use supposedly involved the taking of just three inhalations of smoke. When a user did this, he was said to *darse las tres*, or "take the three." Supposedly this was precisely the amount necessary to send a person into a frenzy.[23]

As we've seen, such smoking usually took place within the confines of prisons and soldiers' barracks, though one idiosyncratic source at the end of the period under discussion did suggest something quite different for upper-class users: "So, for example, a group of high-class smokers had rented a room in a big old monastic house; to arrive at the designated room, to which they only went at night, one had to pass through some long and dark corridors that once upon a time were the cloisters of the convent. The room was upholstered in black and adorned with human skulls and bones, and when the regular attendees introduced a new initiate, they used, like lamps, some pots in which they ignited alcohol mixed with salt so that the greenish flame would have a macabre effect on the future smoker."[24]

The main marijuana dealers in Mexico City were by most accounts the *herbolarias* of the city's markets. In 1880, it was reported that the *herbolarias* of the Volador market were selling, in addition to some useful medicinal items, many poisonous ones, including marijuana. This would be an ongoing concern of the authorities right up till the revolution, with *herbolarias* being cited as the most identifiable purveyors of the weed.[25] *Herbolarias* were generally said to collect the cannabis in the wild, a plausible claim given that marijuana grew wild in much of the country by the end of the nineteenth century.[26]

There were other sources of supply, however. Petty dealers working on the streets or from private residences, theaters, small stores, or stalls on the street (ostensibly dedicated to other commerce) were also cited and occasionally arrested under state and local law.[27] There were also individuals who attempted to smuggle marijuana into the prisons, barracks, or military hospitals in small or large quantities. Sometimes these were *soldaderas* (the girlfriends and wives of soldiers), sometimes they were the soldiers themselves, and other times they were nondescript individuals.[28] More rarely there were reports of large quantities of marijuana being brought into the city. In December 1899, for example, *El País* reported that two "Indians" from Querétaro had been captured on Matamoros Street with 140 kilos of the weed. But big busts of this kind were relatively unusual.[29] Querétaro was noted on a few occasions for its high-quality marijuana, but it was only one of a number of places where the drug was reported to grow especially potent or to be cultivated specifically for export to Mexico City. These included Puebla, Michoacán, and Guanajuato (especially Celaya), along with the outskirts of the capital itself.[30] Finally, pharmacies sold marijuana, but those transactions were highly restricted by the reigning sanitary codes. Only rarely were pharmacists said to be supplying illicit users with the weed.[31]

With respect to gender, the use and sale of marijuana had very conspicuous contours. In the newspaper stories that mentioned the sex of individuals

## CHART 4.6. SEX OF INDIVIDUALS LINKED TO MARIJUANA IN THE PRESS

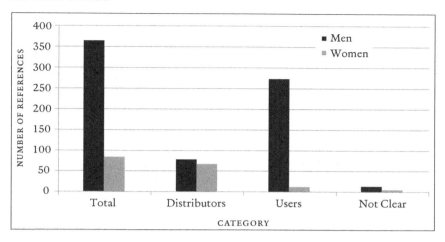

*Source*: Readex/CRL: World Newspaper Archive.

## CHART 4.7. DISTRIBUTION OF USERS AND DISTRIBUTORS AMONG MEN AND WOMEN

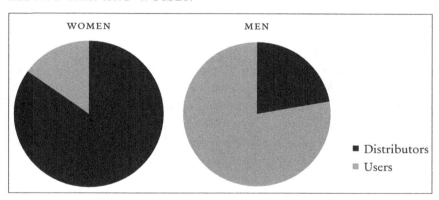

*Source*: Readex/CRL: World Newspaper Archive.

either selling or using marijuana (423 total articles), men far outnumbered women, as Chart 4.6 demonstrates. Despite their underrepresentation overall, women were disproportionately represented among distributors of the drug. While they were referenced in only 13 percent of the stories that identified the individuals involved, they constituted 43 percent of the reported drug distributors. Most men, by contrast, were users. Chart 4.7 neatly illustrates the contrast.

## CHART 4.8. EFFECTS OF MARIJUANA AS REPRESENTED BY THE MEXICAN PRESS, 1854–1920

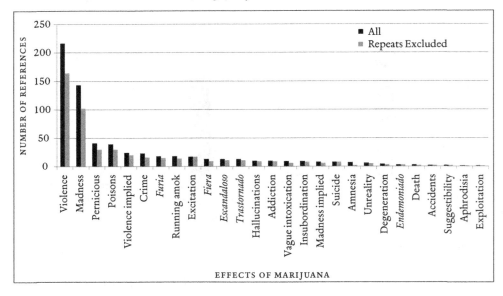

*Source*: Readex/CRL: World Newspaper Archive.

Thus, during this period, marijuana was overwhelmingly associated with prisons and soldiers' barracks, and the most stereotyped marijuana dealer was the female *herbolaria*, though its sale was linked to various other types of small-time dealers as well. While there were more male dealers than female overall, when women were involved with the drug it was overwhelmingly as distributors rather than as users. This is probably mostly a reflection of the drug's use in overwhelmingly male environments as, overall, there were more male distributors than female reported. And though marijuana's presence was relatively discreet in comparison to other forms of vice, a well-stereotyped culture of use had also emerged. As we will see in the coming chapters, all of these factors contributed in some way to the demonization of marijuana in Mexico during this period.

But nothing contributed more to that sinister reputation than the effects that were attributed to marijuana's use. Here the newspaper survey once again provides some very telling data, with 422 of the surveyed articles having mentioned the drug's effects. Chart 4.8 represents the number of articles that cite each of the listed effects, with a count taken both with and without "repeat" articles (definitions for these effects can be found in the appendix). As

## CHART 4.9. EFFECTS OF MARIJUANA WITH CONSOLIDATED CATEGORIES

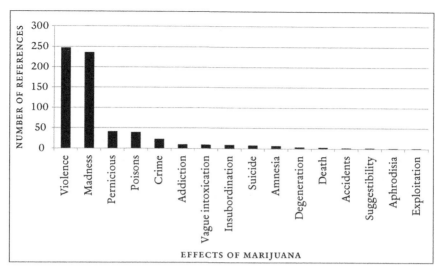

*Source*: Readex/CRL: World Newspaper Archive.

is evidenced by the chart, violence and madness were the two most common effects linked to marijuana, and by a wide margin. The next highest number was produced by the "pernicious" category (used for vaguely described negative effects), and, given the rest of the data, surely the most common "pernicious" effects in the minds of writers and readers were violence, madness, or a combination of the two. Note that of more than four hundred articles that mention the effects of this drug, not a single one suggests that those effects were anything but negative. This is quite extraordinary.

There was significant overlap in many of the categories with several of the words being closely related. For example, *furia* and *fiera* could usually be assumed to refer to a kind of "madness" (again, see the appendix), though in my initial analysis I counted them separately. In Chart 4.9, I consolidated the closely related categories to show the numbers with more inclusive definitions of "violence" and "madness." This view of the data is even more striking: clearly, violence and madness were the two effects most often attributed to marijuana. But what kind of "violence" was this, and what did the press mean by "madness"? It's best to start with the latter because the madness that was described by the sources, if described in detail, was almost always a violent one. And, as we'll see, when references to madness did not mention violence, it was usually because the symptoms were not described in detail.

Of course, as we saw in chapter 2, claims that cannabis caused a kind of "madness" in Mexico date back all the way to Alzate in the 1770s. Furthermore, most of the earliest nineteenth-century references to marijuana also noted this effect, if somewhat vaguely. But as references to marijuana became more common toward the end of the century, these vague comments gave way to more detail. Marijuana madness might, for example, involve outlandish, insubordinate behavior by soldiers. On November 14, 1878, *El Monitor Republicano* reported that, on the second of that month, the soldiers of the Fifteenth Battalion had been called to order for inspection, and in the process, one soldier, who was "excited by marijuana," broke ranks and began shouting seditious messages to the troops. A captain tried to reduce him to order only to receive bayonet wounds to the hand and hip. Others then responded with gunfire and wounded their seditious comrade. In the scuffle, two other soldiers managed to desert. The paper lamented that earlier press reports of the incident had suggested the occurrence of a serious case of sedition, for in fact it was just a man "driven mad by mariguana."[32]

More commonly, marijuana madness involved smokers who experienced an "access of delirium" and then performed a sudden and irrational act of violence. These often included simple descriptions like the following, which appeared in *La Voz de México* on January 19, 1888: "A wretched soldier who smoked marijuana experienced an access of delirium during which he murdered two of his comrades and injured two others."[33] Reports of this kind were almost always presented in a matter-of-fact way, as with the following report that appeared on March 21, 1899, in *El País*: "Yesterday afternoon the jury was announced for the trial of José Buendía who, while serving time in Belén, smoked some marihuana and, criminally deprived of the faculties which God gave man, turned into a madman and attacked two of his fellow prisoners, burying a knife into them and causing their deaths."[34] Or consider a case reported by *El Imparcial* on December 15, 1899, in which a former soldier named Eulalio Andagua came back to the barracks to visit his old friends, but when he arrived he was "turned into a madman for having smoked marihuana." He then attacked a guard who had to fire a shot for reinforcements. Andagua was captured and placed in a holding cell, but there he tried to kill himself by repeatedly smashing his head against a wall.[35]

Such cases were very similar to another genre of marijuana madness often reported in the press that involved smokers getting upset by a slight insult and responding with violence. As *La Voz de México* reported on January 22, 1891, an inmate of the Tlatelolco military prison in Mexico City felt insulted by one of the guards, so he attacked and wounded him with a knife. "It appears that Torres was drunk or crazy as a consequence of having smoked marijuana which, as is well known, puts people into a state of delirium tremens."[36]

Most cases of this kind involved soldiers, prisoners, or individuals performing violent acts against others with whom they were acquainted in some way. But another more frightening form of marijuana madness was also present, one that looked remarkably like the "running amok" of the Malay Peninsula described in chapter 1. This response to marijuana was especially frightening because any ordinary citizen could become a victim of the violent outburst. The clipping that began this chapter is a classic example, but there were many others. A similar story was reported by *La Voz de México* in 1901:

> Yesterday afternoon a group of curious people surrounded a man who appeared to be suffering a fit of madness.
>
> That individual, turned into a beast, launched himself at the passersby, attempting to dismember them, tearing their clothes and hitting them.
>
> Three porters who were on the corner quickly acted, jumped him, and held him down, tying his arms and legs until he was converted into a veritable bundle.
>
> The anger of the individual in question was then turned on himself and with bites he tore apart his own arms until a straitjacket could be put on him.
>
> Margarito Trujano, which is the name of the individual in question, was not crazy, rather, as was discovered later, he was crazy under the influence of marihuana which he had smoked in large quantities.[37]

Similar cases were sometimes reported that didn't involve violence against strangers but bordered on it. As *El Imparcial* reported in 1904:

> Manuel Guerrero and Florencio Pino are given to smoking marihuana. Yesterday each of them smoked three cigarettes of this weed, and upon finishing them they found themselves crazy and almost raging [*furiosos*].
>
> As they walked along Camelia Street they believed themselves to be the bravest men in the world and they began insulting everyone who passed nearby. In the end they attacked each other, causing various injuries.[38]

As should already be clear from the above examples, the press commonly described marijuana smokers degenerating into something like a wild animal. An August 1903 report from the *Mexican Herald* offers a case in point:

> Yesterday morning Corporal Victoriano Reyes of the second cavalry arrived at his home in Tacubaya after smoking a "marihuana" cigarette with

some friend and began to beat his wife because she had not bathed his pet dog. The woman cried for help and then the mad soldier bit her, severing her right ear and a large part of the left cheek. At that moment a gendarme appeared on the scene, but Reyes attacked him and bit a large slice of flesh from his arm. The gendarme had to call another policeman by firing his pistol and after half an hour's struggle the rabid corporal was taken in a straight jacket to the police station.[39]

In July 1908, *El Imparcial* described a marijuana smoker who displayed "simian movements" and "claws" and who had been driven into a violent and atavistic frenzy by the weed.[40] Another especially noteworthy series of articles had appeared in the same paper a decade earlier, in May 1898, when a *soldadera* named Laura Veraza entered the barracks in Mexico City and, apparently while under the influence of marijuana, attacked various soldiers with a knife, killing one and gravely injuring two others. *El Imparcial* described the woman as a monster who "more than a human appears to be a wild beast [*fiera*]."[41] The paper began calling Veraza *La Fierita* (The Little Wild Animal), and her behavior was described as typical of the "instinctual criminals" that filled Mexico's lowest classes.[42]

Such outbursts were sometimes attributed to the user seeing horrible visions or experiencing terrible delusions. In 1893, *La Voz de México* reported on a porter who, according to his wife, had been smoking marijuana for about eight months, gradually increasing the dosage throughout. His character began to change and he became ornery and mean. He then stopped eating normally and had a hard time even chewing food. One day he experienced a terrible frenzy and was taken to the police station because he wanted to murder his wife and children. He was then transferred to the hospital, where he told his story: When he started using marijuana, he explained, he saw beautiful visions despite the terrible headaches it gave him. But before long, his pleasant hallucinations began to transform into horrifying ones where flowers morphed into bloody, severed heads. Then his family started to look like giants, midgets, dogs, and parrots that attacked him. All of this had led to the murderous frenzy that forced his hospitalization.[43] Similarly, in 1901 the *Mexican Herald* reported the following: "Among the misguided youths, both male and female of this city, are a number who have become addicted to the *marihuana* habit, and who congregate in the early morning hours before dawn on various plazas and smoke this poisonous weed, which produces a sort of insanity for the time. A youth addicted to this habit, was told the other night that he was pursued by brigands, and in his terror, he leaped into a sewer drain, nearly drowning before he could be extricated."[44]

Yet quite often, specific "mad" effects were not even described. In such cases, an understanding of the details was apparently taken for granted. In July 1893, for example, *La Voz de México* reported that a clerk in a small grocery store forced a twelve-year-old boy to smoke some marijuana just to see what would happen. The boy "became crazy upon feeling the effects of such a prejudicial weed."[45] Dozens of stories casually referred to marijuana's maddening effects in this manner.[46] Many simply suggested that "everyone" already knew what those effects were.[47] Surely the press expected the audience to imagine symptoms like those described in the more detailed stories above: a "madness" that was sudden, temporary, and usually violent. Only rarely did the sources specifically cite marijuana as a cause of long-term insanity.[48]

When marijuana was described as a cause of violence without any specific reference to madness, the cases were for the most part indistinguishable from those above. Consider the following brief snippets: February 2, 1887—a soldier shoots another for telling him to stop smoking marijuana; February 19, 1887—a soldier smokes some marijuana and takes up a sniper's position outside the barracks, killing three and wounding five; August 3, 1894—in Belén prison, an inmate high on marijuana violently attacks two prisoner-guards; January 11, 1897—a marijuana smoker throws a homemade bomb at a police officer; July 17, 1897—a drunk and stoned man attacks a stranger on the street like a "furious lion" and disembowels him with a knife; August 28, 1898—marijuana is cited as the chief cause when a man stabs a policeman to death; November 19, 1900—a stoned soldier attacks another with a knife; December 17, 1901—a man smokes marijuana and then stabs a woman to death; June 13, 1904—a woman smokes marijuana in Guadalajara and attacks two policemen with a long blade; June 21, 1905—a marijuana smoker in Durango takes a knife and tries to murder a woman; February 16, 1906—a Guanajuato municipal guard smokes some marijuana and murders a Protestant minister; October 26, 1906—a man smokes marijuana, then savagely beats his grandfather; February 6, 1907—in Veracruz a prisoner "drunk on marijuana" has an argument with a guard and stabs him four times; February 23, 1910—a marijuana smoker murders a woman and skins the corpse.[49] And so on. The headlines themselves told a frightening tale: "Murder," "Effects of Marijuana," "With a Sickle," "Bloody Drama," and the like. Again, while the cases cited here did not specifically use the word "madness" to define these particular incidents, the writers and their audience surely made little distinction between these cases and those that specifically cited the "delirium" caused by marijuana.

In short, marijuana was overwhelmingly associated with violence and madness during this period, and the reports of its effects often contained quite sensational and bloody detail. Users were routinely described as "furious madmen" or even as having degenerated into something akin to a wild beast. Nonetheless, there existed almost no counterdiscourse to challenge these notions. How was this possible? Did no one find the reports of frenzied violence or the descriptions of marijuana users as wild beasts unconvincing? The answer appears to be no. How might we explain this?

*Chapter 5*

EXPLAINING THE MISSING

COUNTERDISCOURSE I

THE SCIENCE OF DRUGS

AND MADNESS

In the late nineteenth and early twentieth centuries, vice assumed many forms in Mexico. Foreign soldiers participating in the battles of the 1860s emphasized its presence. One Argentine volunteer in the forces fighting Maximilian lamented widespread drunkenness in the Mexican army, rampant smuggling of alcohol into soldiers' barracks, and the failure of military authorities to stamp out these practices. On the other side of the conflict, an American declared gambling and laziness the universal vices of Mexico.[1] Mexican critics no doubt provided the most nuanced denunciations of vice. Dogs, beggars, and prostitutes had given Mexico's capital the feel of a "Turkish" city, according to *El Diario del Hogar*. The same paper also decried the "barbarity" of bullfights and cockfights and applauded their prohibition in Michoacán while blaming gambling in part for the "contagion" of suicide that it claimed was gripping the country. A newly composed *zarzuela* would also treat the gambling theme, "each character a playing card . . . making evident the terrible consequences of that vice."[2]

The origins of vice too were legion. According to the critics, climate, boredom, hard work, laziness, wealth, and poverty all played a causal role. While the Argentine volunteer cited the effects of ignorance, climate, and physical labor as the causes of drinking in the army, an observer for the 1864 Scientific Commission of Pachuca emphasized the boredom that led miners to seek diversion in alcohol.[3] According to one young scholar at the medical school, ennui also led the lazy children of the rich to drink and gamble away their lives.[4] Even music could prove the catalyst to further pleasure seeking in alcohol and tobacco. José Gabriel Malda's novel *Recuerdos de la vida bohemia* recounts the life of a young man named Adrián driven to alcoholism by Bellini's opera *Norma*: "Adrián had not missed a single note of the work, and elevated to an atmosphere as yet unknown to him, there was revealed within his face a profound anxiousness." The moment produced a "prolonged echo" in the young man's soul, and when the soprano performed her aria, "his eyes sparkled with a divine fire, his lips trembled, his cheeks lit up, and sweat poured from his face; his beating heart threatened to drown him, tears covered his countenance . . . the moment of inspiration had arrived, that moment that decides the future of men. Adrián loved art, like a warrior loves the battlefield despite the fact that it might kill him."[5]

Adrián's plight richly represents the significant ambiguity that characterized understandings of vice in Mexico during this period, as well as the way that popular understandings of intoxication closely dovetailed with contemporary medical theories. Vice could be of the rich or of the poor, of the hard working or of the lazy, and it could result from substances or emotions. When one character in Malda's work explains to a young woman that "her glances were making him drunk, her caresses driving him mad," this was not meant as an entirely figurative description.[6] Highly influential in Mexico, Pedro Mata y Fontanet, the founder of forensic medicine in Spain, engaged during the middle nineteenth century in charged debates comparing the strength of the angry to that of the mad, or the pulse rate of the person in love with that of the nymphomaniac.[7]

As we saw in the last chapter, marijuana played a relatively limited role in Mexican life throughout this period, yet understandings of that drug and its effects were highly consistent. The fact that marijuana triggered a kind of "madness" in its users that often resulted in delirious acts of violence was almost taken for granted by most Mexican sources. Somehow, prior to the drug's prohibition, no counterdiscourse ever emerged. The present chapter is the first of two that seek to directly explain this curious fact. Here, I focus on the science of drugs and insanity as it was understood in late-nineteenth- and early-twentieth-century Mexico. Not only did that science fully justify the typically lurid descriptions of marijuana's effects, but it was highly congruent with more popular understandings of intoxication. All of this helped make the stereotyped mad *marihuano* an eminently plausible character in the universe of Mexican vice.

■ Given the long history of alcohol in Mexico and its widespread use, Mexicans could not help but view marijuana in part through the prism of powerful and well-established discourses on that substance. Indeed, the Spanish term *embriaguez*, which literally means "intoxication," in practice usually meant intoxication by alcohol unless qualified to mean otherwise.[8] National period writers were well acquainted with alcohol's Mexican history. Francisco

Ortega, for instance, in a prize-winning essay for the Mexican Athenian Society in 1845, described the pre-Hispanic familiarity with alcoholic beverages along with the famously severe penalties prescribed for abuse, emphasizing that it was the introduction of distilled spirits (to both Mexico and the rest of the world) that had led to the rapid diffusion of alcohol abuse.[9] José Fernando Ramírez, a contemporary of Ortega's, also concluded that, "abandoned to that vice, the corruption, the disorder, and the destruction of the indigenous races was felt."[10]

For nineteenth-century researchers, these themes provided a useful introduction because their continued pertinence seemed obvious. Ramírez claimed that nearly all crimes against persons in Durango were committed by people under the influence of alcohol; Ortega cited foreign statistics to conclude that drinking was the "road to crime"; and Manuel Domínguez y Quintana, an 1860s medical student in Mexico City, forwarded the widely accepted argument that alcohol provoked crimes that broke down the social cement.[11] This link between crime and alcohol would remain a central theme of Porfirian discourses on delinquency. In fact, it has been argued that no social problem more concerned Porfirian authorities than alcoholism, and certainly the same could be said about many of the leaders who emerged victorious from the Mexican Revolution.[12]

While concerns about alcohol were nothing new, the nineteenth century saw an evolution of these toward a concept based in medical science and theories of public hygiene. Medicalization resulted in much more detailed descriptions of alcohol's effects, with these usually portrayed as developing in stages and eventually leading to some type of madness. In 1870, for example, medical student Jesús Barrera described the three stages of drunkenness in his thesis on the subject. In the first stage, the pulse increased, ideas were "exalted," and the genitals were excited. The second stage involved a more severe intoxication whose effects were variable and depended on the person in question. "In some this excitation is transformed into furor, and the subject surrenders himself to violent acts of which he will later have absolutely no memory; in others this stage is accompanied by a type of stupidity, with almost complete loss of the voice and a prostration of his strength." Finally, there was a stage of "grave intoxication" characterized by apoplexy, low pulse, and a respiration that invoked a "death-rattle."[13] The precise details of these three stages had come into Mexican thinking apparently through the work of Johann Christoph Hoffbauer, and this basic schema endured right through the Porfiriato.[14]

One of the most frightening consequences of alcohol abuse as described in the nineteenth-century medical literature was delirium tremens, which occasionally affected drinkers. Delirium tremens sometimes occurred after an overdose of alcohol by someone unaccustomed to drinking it but most often affected hard-core alcoholics who had suddenly been deprived of drink. As Barrera explained in his medical thesis: "When this delirium develops slowly, the patient is sad, uneasy, the members are agitated with a particular type of nervous tremble. These symptoms are followed by the delirium. In some, it is calm; in others, and this is the case of the majority, the patients become furious, they yell, they're tormented by hallucinations of eye and ear, they threaten and beg to be freed from the imaginary dangers that threaten them, from the phantoms that pursue them."[15] Following such an episode, the patient either recovered completely or remained demented permanently. Barrera also described what he called the "epileptic form" of alcoholism — a kind of madness experienced by an alcohol drinker that lasted for weeks. Much as we saw with late-nineteenth-century Indian research on cannabis's effects (see chapter 1), Mexican experts sometimes had difficulty distinguishing the effects of alcohol from the possibility of some preexisting mental illness. Barrera himself noted that "this convulsive form can take on actual epileptic character, and because of that character alone it is impossible to know if the epilepsy is symptomatic of alcoholism or caused by something else."[16]

Writing at about the same time, Domínguez also emphasized the importance of delirium tremens and quoted the descriptions of one of his medical school instructors on the symptoms of this condition. Like the marijuana descriptions of the Porfiriato, these symptoms again blurred the line between intoxication and madness, human and beast. "Normally . . . one finds these patients tied to a bed wearing a straitjacket, shouting, insulting anyone whom they see in the distance, trying desperately to break free from their bindings as if to launch themselves against all of them, and with an angry countenance, their eyes red and brilliant, their lips trembling and sometimes frothing, their hair disordered as their position dictates, in the end they appear as excited maniacs, or perhaps as chained but ferocious wild beasts." According to Domínguez, these patients explained their behavior by claiming "that everyone around them insults them and laughs at them; or if they are in a hospital, they blame the malevolence of the patient next to them, or the nurse who attends them, or any other person. There are in these people, therefore, illusions and perhaps even hallucinations; they are truly madmen." Yet they were madmen who could describe their own condition in terms highly compatible with contemporary medical theory. "The delirium has a particular character in the beginning: it is a reasoned delirium, because the patient is conscious that he is suffering hallucinations. Most remarkably, despite their limited intellectual abilities, they define this delirium as Pitcairn did long ago, saying that they are dreaming while awake. But as time goes on, the lucid intervals become shorter and shorter, until they result in continual madness."[17]

Throughout the period of this study, madness and alcoholism were routinely connected in Mexico. As we saw in chapter 1, the Indian Hemp Drugs Commission of 1893–94 was formed after a member of the British Parliament alarmingly declared that the lunatic asylums in India were "filled with ganja smokers." But in the 1840s, Ortega illustrated to Mexicans the gravity of the alcohol problem in the West by pointing out that half the madmen in lunatic asylums in Britain were there because of alcohol.[18] During the Porfiriato, Mariano M. Martínez argued in his medical thesis that "degenerated beings produce other degenerates, and this inheritance cannot be applied with more certainty than in the field of the drinkers. The multitude of madmen that fill the insane asylums testify to this, where it is hardly possible to find even one case where alcohol has not taken a more or less active part in either the condition of the patient or in that of their ancestors."[19] Statistics from Mexico's own insane asylum provided a quantitative basis for such claims. In his 1887 study of madness in Mexico, Mariano Rivadeneyra argued that over half the inmates at the San Hipólito mental hospital suffered from some kind of alcoholic-related insanity.[20]

Though surely few Mexicans actually read these scientific studies, the basic concepts nonetheless melded seamlessly with more popular descriptions of drunkenness and alcoholism. For example, in his classic novel *Los bandidos del Río Frío*, Manuel Payno described the "Saint Monday" experience of a choleric, Mexico City artisan named Evaristo. In Payno's depiction, Evaristo's day at the *pulquería* takes him gradually through the three stages of drunkenness, from "happy and nothing more," through "drunk," to "delirious." At each stage, Evaristo becomes more out of control, first losing all his money to gambling, then being beaten severely in a street brawl for dancing provocatively with another man's wife, and finally going home and taking out his humiliation on his own "saintly" bride. At the climax of the episode, his wife is forced to get down on her knees and beg for her life. "Evaristo, mad, delirious, drove a chisel several times into her chest, leaving her only enough breath to utter 'Jesus, Jesus help me!' as she fell to the floor bathed in her own blood." Payno goes on to explain that Evaristo had been suffering hallucinations from the mixture of alcoholic drinks, and "in that way, mad, frenetic, he uttered incoherent words, he searched for tools, pieces of wood, hammers, in order to destroy, injure, triumph in the face of those threatening visions."[21]

Antonio Salinas y Carbó's work also suggested that a three-stage concept of alcoholism was familiar to Mexico's lower classes. This, he explained, had become apparent when, in a recent trial, a police officer was asked to define drunkenness.

[The police officer] answered, guided only by common sense . . . and he divided [drunkenness] in three stages: the first, that he called *estar tomadito*, when one has drunk very little, and winds up happy and very talkative; the second, *a medios chiles*, when one drinks more, and then fights with everyone, they sway when they walk, and they start acting crazy; and the third, when they become completely drunk, in fact in this case they fall down and pass out asleep. Incredible! [*¡Cosa singular!*] This man, completely lacking in education, and only directed by his own criteria, had demonstrated the periods of drunkenness, but expressed in his own words.[22]

The three stages of alcohol intoxication were also commonly cited in the newspapers of the Porfiriato, whether in longer articles on the ravages of alcohol abuse or in more casual references to drink. Thus, in 1892, a story by Luis Vergara Flores in *El Diario del Hogar* described the movement of a drinker through stages of "drunkenness," "tragicomedy," and "actual madness":

The delirium arrives along with a tenacious and rebellious insomnia; visual hallucinations characterized by images of weird animals, mice, rats, snakes that swarm imprudently over the bed of the patient. The most common and most frequent is the delirium of persecution. Relatives, friends, and compadres become invisible enemies for these strange madmen, who lie in wait for an opportunity to poison, stab, or do them just about any harm; they dream of astute thieves who are attempting to steal from them all of their goods and immense property. They hear filthy insults, criminal imprecations, insolent sayings, infernal phrases: This obliges the patients to try and hide themselves, to run or to take up arms to defend themselves against these supposed enemies, whom they attack violently, swinging vainly in the air, against walls, or trees, or innocent people.[23]

Delirious episodes of this kind were also reported in the press. Suffering from delirium tremens, a man in Guanajuato was reported to have chopped his family into pieces with an axe and then been found eating his own son. Another story described a "furious madman" who was found to be drunk after running around in the street threatening random pedestrians with a pistol. Under the headline "dangerous madman," *El Diario del Hogar* reported the story of a furious drunk who could be subdued only by multiple police offi-

FIGURE 5.1. "Very interesting news of the four murders by the wretch Antonio Sánchez in the town of San José Iturbide, Guanajuato State." (Reprinted in Roberto Berdecio and Stanley Appelbaum, eds., *Posada's Popular Mexican Prints* [New York: Dover, 1972], 44)

cers. In addition, newspaper stories sometimes casually referred to the various stages of drunkenness in a manner that suggests that these were common knowledge.[24]

The medical literature's descriptions of alcoholic delirium, or the portrayals in the press of remarkable crimes committed by madmen or drunks, also find numerous parallels in José Posada's penny-press lithographs. Indeed, Posada often portrayed the same stories found in the Mexican press but in a manner consumable by his mostly illiterate audience. The man in Guanajuato who, suffering delirium tremens, murdered his family with an axe and then ate his infant son was not only featured in *El Diario del Hogar* but also portrayed strikingly by Posada (Figure 5.1). Here we see the man, hair on end, eyes bulging, surrounded by flying, diabolic apparitions, as he begins devouring his own baby.

Such apparitions had been common fare of popular depictions of gruesome crimes in Europe since the Middle Ages, but they were also found in the medicalized descriptions of alcoholic hallucinations in this period under discussion.[25] Other works by Posada also demonstrate the diffusion of these discourses into sources available to the poor and illiterate. An 1890s broadside seemingly depicts Payno's Saint Monday drama, as a wife falls to her knees in

FIGURE 5.2. "Woman praying to the Virgin of Guadalupe as her husband (?) rages madly." (Reprinted in Roberto Berdecio and Stanley Appelbaum, eds., *Posada's Popular Mexican Prints* [New York: Dover, 1972], 32)

prayer while her drunken husband, hair on end, eyes bulging, rages through their home (Figure 5.2). Another broadsheet depicts a man, surrounded by demons, as he poisons his family, while yet another displays a knife-wielding lunatic—again, eyes bulging, hair on end—being swallowed by the earth for the murder of his children and his parents (Figures 5.3 and 5.4).

In his interviews of criminals at Belén prison, Carlos Roumagnac found that inmates demonstrated similar conceptions of alcohol and its effects. One man confessed that he had been getting drunk since the age of sixteen, drinking pulque during the daytime and harder alcohol at night. "Then he would become very tired, and whenever someone offended him, he would have the desire to fight them." Another prisoner described his awareness of the loss of control brought on by alcohol and how this drug could lead to unexpected consequences and injuries. Having taken to drink as a youngster, this prisoner eventually murdered a man in a fight. While on the run in Pachuca for several years, he endeavored to never get drunk, "so that nothing would wind up happening to him, because he was a long way from home and he didn't want to wind up either in jail or injured."[26]

All of this raises an important question: was the popular view influenced by the science, or did scientific writers simply medicalize popular views? Most

FIGURE 5.3. "Horrible and frightful episode!! A despicable son poisons his parents and a servant in Pachuca!" (Reprinted in Roberto Berdecio and Stanley Appelbaum, eds., *Posada's Popular Mexican Prints* [New York: Dover, 1972], 39)

FIGURE 5.4. "The earth swallows José Sánchez for murdering his children and his parents." (Reprinted in Roberto Berdecio and Stanley Appelbaum, eds., *Posada's Popular Mexican Prints* [New York: Dover, 1972], 41)

likely it was a little of both, though the general dearth of sources on popular attitudes makes such a determination extremely difficult. Whatever the case, here we see how popular and scientific discourse melded seamlessly to create a "commonsense" view of alcoholism and drunkenness in late-nineteenth- and early-twentieth-century Mexico. Given what we have learned of the "psychoactive riddle," we should expect that an element of self-fulfilling prophecy then began to intervene here, where popular conceptions fueled certain behaviors, which, in turn, reinforced popular conceptions. Ultimately, all of this helped to legitimize a concept of "marijuana madness" that exhibited numerous parallels with the discourse on alcohol and its effects.

In fact, sources from the period often conflated the effects of alcohol, marijuana, and other drugs with little differentiation, as in this story published by *El Monitor Republicano* in June 1882: "For many years gambling, alcohol, and mariguana have continued to be a permanent cause of quarrels, fights, and accidents that disturb the order that should reign in this [military] hospital. All restrictive measures have failed completely, and the strictest vigilance has not managed to prevent the introduction of cards, dice, and liquor which, as is well known, are the principal elements with which the soldier sustains and activates his vices."[27] Similarly, in 1891 *La Voz de México* reported that an inmate in the Tlatelolco military prison had attacked a guard with a knife. "It appears that Torres was drunk [*ebrio*] or crazy as a consequence of having smoked mariguana which, as is well known, puts people into a state of delirium tremens."[28] In 1898, *El Imparcial* reported on the case of Laura Veraza, aka *La Fierita*, a woman who had attacked several soldiers in the barracks and who, when doing so, appeared "drunk and actually what looked more like high on marijuana."[29] A year later, the same paper covered the sensational murder trial of José Buendía and commented on the widespread belief among Mexicans of all classes that intoxication exonerated individuals from blame in criminal situations:

> No matter how much he is asked, he answers that he doesn't remember a thing, that he was drunk and that he had smoked marijuana, the poor wretch did not understand that even then the divine and human laws maintain his immense responsibility.
>
> In effect, it is a belief among men of the lower classes and even among many of the more elevated social stations, that it serves as an exoneration or at least a significant excuse to say: I did such a thing because I was crazy from intoxication.

But who was responsible for that madness?

He who gets intoxicated knowing that alcohol, or marihuana, or morphine are supposed to lead them to such extremes.[30]

Similarly, *El Dictamen* of Veracruz reported on a corporal named Telésforo Carreón who got angry when a madam of a local brothel refused his romantic advances. Carreón soon was brandishing a knife and threatening the woman, who then called for the aid of a policeman. The officer was forced to summon backup to subdue the man and get him into a jail cell. Once there, he continued his mad tirade: "He appeared crazy, for he tried to kill himself by smashing himself against the walls of the cell where he was placed, demonstrating that he was in the highest level of excitation due to alcohol or the weed known by the name of 'marihuana' of which they assure us he was fond of smoking." After this scene at the jailhouse, it took five men to transfer him to the barracks, "for he was in such a state of madness, it was impossible for two men to control him."[31] The same paper would later note another case where a man ran amok, eventually charging into a restaurant and stabbing someone nearly to death. "The criminal upon being asked his name said it was Juan Martínez. He was poorly dressed and everything he does suggests that either he is under the effects of alcohol or marihuana, or that he is not right in the head."[32]

On June 5, 1896, in the hall of the Chamber of Deputies in Mexico City, Trinidad Sánchez Santos, the strongly anti-vice publisher of the Catholic daily *El País*, delivered a speech to Mexico's various scientific societies where he defined alcoholism as "the pathological state that results from the ingestion of intoxicating substances, such as spirituous drinks, morphine, cocaine, mariguana, etc."[33] A decade later, his newspaper would praise *El Imparcial* for celebrating marijuana's prohibited status in Mexico City but asked why that publication and others did not also support the total prohibition of alcohol, a drug that, the paper argued, produced roughly the same consequences. In 1917, *Excelsior* would make a similar argument.[34] At times, then, marijuana was hardly distinguished from other drugs.

Yet at other times, it was clearly delineated based on various measures. For *El Imparcial* in 1898, the distinction was based partly on class. "If one were to collect statistics on the people that use and abuse morphine, laudanum, ether, and cocaine; if a medical specialist were to publish his observations on the fabulous growth of such manias within the upper and middle classes of society, we would find that alcoholism on the one hand and alkaloids on the other, cause as many ravages as epidemics." But such consequences were even worse among the lower classes, a subject that led directly to a discussion of marijuana.

Marihuana, nefarious weed, lamentable like a Lucrezia Borgia; diabolical tempter, with effects more intense than alcohol, poison consumed clandestinely by proletarians who seek to realize their paradises in the hell of impulses that the terrible drug produces.

Marihuana is the gloomy and brutal pleasure of the prisoner, the degenerate, and unfortunately of our troops. Not forgotten are two or three tragedies which occurred in barracks and crimes perpetrated against officers or soldiers, whose determining cause was the homicidal insanity of a [marihuana] smoker.[35]

*El Diario del Hogar* argued that pulque on its own was bad enough, but mixed with marijuana it became especially deadly.[36] Similarly, *El País* commented on the terrible criminal effects of alcohol, which led for some to prison time, where even worse vices, like smoking marijuana, were acquired.[37] The same paper later argued that the introduction of marijuana and alcohol into the prisons had terrible consequences, but marijuana's were worse: "Well understood is how serious [a problem] that clandestine commerce is, much more so with respect to the poisonous marihuana, which predisposes persons who smoke it to scandal and crime." And later in *El País*, a Dr. G. Benítez would describe marijuana's effects in great detail, from hallucinations and delusions to the lashing out labeled here as "running amok," concluding that "the effects of acute alcoholism are child's play in comparison to those of marihuanism."[38]

Various other factors also distinguished alcohol from marijuana. Alcohol had been used for centuries in Mexico, and thus the discourse surrounding it was far more diverse and developed. Commentaries on the baleful effects of marijuana tended to be simple and efficient: the drug caused madness and violence and was an undisputed, pernicious force in society. Anti-alcohol campaigns, by contrast, were forced to rely on a much more diverse array of arguments. For example, commentators often emphasized the consequences of alcoholism for families and the working class, as fathers used their earnings to buy alcohol instead of food and clothing for their children. There were also consistent references to the effects on health of alcohol abuse. Domínguez y Quintana's 1870 medical thesis provided a comprehensive list of the social and physical maladies associated with alcohol abuse, including the breaking down of the social cement; the fact that alcohol attacked all classes; the formation of pterygia (a yellowish lesion) in the eyes; the fact that workingmen were especially vulnerable to booze; the fact that alcoholic fathers abandoned families, which then inspired the prostitution of wives and daughters; and the fact that the abused children of alcoholics grew up bent on exacting some kind of revenge on society. A 1901 primer for schools enumerated all of these themes and more:

17. Alcohol leads one to lose their vision by simply drinking it.
18. It produces paralysis, trembling, and convulsions.
19. It speeds aging and makes you die young.
20. The person who drinks alcohol loses their memory and intelligence.
21. Many times they end up crazy.
22. They turn out lazy for work and useless.
23. They lose their dignity and turn themselves over to every type of crime.[39]

While in some ways this more diverse set of arguments served as extra ammunition for anti-alcohol campaigns, they were also necessary because there was significant resistance to efforts to restrict or prohibit alcohol, something that clearly could not be said with respect to marijuana. Alcohol was widely used and was therefore big business in Mexico, and had been so since the colonial era. Ortega reflected on this problem in the 1840s, comparing the nineteenth century's alcohol problem with the same issues prior to independence and lamenting that even with stronger enforcement mechanisms, Mexico could hardly control alcohol abuse: "Would this improved effort [*elemento*] be enough to destroy those inspired by the great interest that the makers and distributors of spirits have in developing the baneful industry on which they depend?" *El Diario del Hogar* editorialized along similar lines in the late Porfiriato: "*La codicia rompe el saco*; if in order to increase public revenues, or for a poorly understood idea of freedom of commerce, we forget to procure the betterment of our customs, we will have made a transcendental error that history and posterity will condemn irremissibly."[40] Resistance would also come from the many people who recognized the positive side to alcohol ingestion. Of this, there were plenty of signs in Mexico. In 1888, for example, *El Diario del Hogar* ran a laudatory piece on the great men of history and their favorite alcoholic beverages. The same paper published recipes for pulque and wrote positively on that beverage's international marketing potential. In the late Porfiriato, *El Diario del Hogar* also lamented a pulque shortage in the district of Tacubaya, because that drink was often seen as a hygienic substitute for the community's polluted water supply.[41] On the other hand, save for a few references to medicinal cannabis, the entire discourse on marijuana was negative.[42]

Finally, from a symbolic standpoint, and within an international frame of comparison, no matter how much ink might be spilled lamenting the impending consequences of alcoholism for the nation, a national alcohol problem was somewhat less problematic than one related to a drug like marijuana. Where commentaries on marijuana often associated that drug with the Orient and therefore, by definition, with the world's anti-Europe, articles on alcohol routinely cited England, putatively one of the most civilized nations on earth, as having the world's worst drinking problem. Thus, already in the 1840s, Ortega was citing heavily from European studies and providing details of the alcohol problem in England, Ireland, Scotland, France, Belgium, and the United States.[43] As will continue to be obvious as we move forward in this story, the Mexican elite were highly attuned to Mexico's place in the "competition of nations," and while an alcohol problem might threaten its ability to compete, it did not symbolically disqualify it from the club of civilized modernity. But marijuana, with its quasi-Oriental identity and its reputation as the "Mexican opium," was another story.

Psychiatric research and writing also helped to conflate the effects of marijuana, alcohol, and other drugs. While the newspapers clearly were not seeking to define "insanity" in a precise, scientific way, the symptoms they described did conform in large part to the scientific concept of madness as understood in Mexico at the time. More specifically, descriptions of intoxication looked very much like "delirium," a condition that was defined as an outward symptom of madness but that could also stem from other causes. In a 1901 textbook for Mexican students of legal medicine, Román Ramírez explained that while the words "madness" and "delirium" were often used interchangeably, in truth delirium was an active manifestation or symptom of madness. Thus, "passive lunatics" were not said to be delirious, though they were certainly mad. Further complicating matters, delirium might result from causes other than insanity. Thus, a distinction was made between "vesanic" and "non-vesanic" delirium. "Vesanic delirium pertains to insanity; non-vesanic delirium appears in febrile ailments like the measles, scarlet fever, smallpox, typhus, pneumonia, meningitis and acute intoxications from alcohol, chloroform, belladonna, marihuana, etc." According to Ramírez, non-vesanic delirium like that associated with fevers or drugs was a "non-essential" symptom of the condition in question and therefore distinct from vesanic delirium, which was "many times the principal or unique symptom of insanity.... In general vesanic delirium has a chronic course, it recurs frequently, each time more seriously, and it dominates the entire life of the individual and becomes his nature. Nonvesanic delirium is transitory and accidental like the illness that produces it." However, he warned that "none of the above distinctions are absolute."[44]

Clearly a key factor was the duration of the symptoms, something that physicians still consider critical when distinguishing "psychosis" from the psychotomimetic effects that might be produced by certain drugs. The distinction was, of course, a fine one and never to my knowledge elaborated upon by the press, but it was nonetheless typical of more technical writing on madness at the time. In an 1899 lecture at the National School of Medicine, Carlos Viesca y Lobatón forwarded an argument reminiscent of Ramírez's while dividing the types of deliria into various categories. In the following passage, he describes the "furious delirium" caused by fevers and intoxications. The description should by now look familiar: "In [cases of] furious delirium the feverish person attacks through words or actions the imaginary beings that he believes surround him, the people who are around him, himself, or he directs blows against the inert objects that he believes are animate and which have taken on the most extravagant forms; it is characterized by the excitation that dominates his entire being, by the rapid and irrational acts that are performed and by a physiognomy more or less in harmony with his altered ideas; all of this mixed, we can say, with the retinue of other symptoms of the illness." Viesca went on to argue that marijuana could trigger this state, but so did many other drugs and conditions, including mental illness. Of the intoxications that most often produced delirium, he cited alcoholism, lead poisoning, morphine, cocaine, and "haschisch (cannabis-indica) among certain oriental peoples; among us that plant of mournful memory consumed in the prisons and known by the vulgar name marihuana." He also would distinguish between "maniacal delirium" and "melancholic or depressive delirium." Marijuana intoxication clearly belonged to the former category:

The characteristic of the maniac is an overexcitement of the ideas, feelings, and decisions. The complete disequilibrium in the exalted faculties produces the most diverse and abstruse manifestations of that infernal personality, fulminated by the curse of the prophets and object of the incantations of witches and fortune tellers. In order to contain these wretched beings the straitjacket was invented. When the mania is primitive it constitutes a form of madness or else it manifests itself through accesses, and in both cases generally the causes are recognized as: epilepsy, cretinism, dementia, alcoholism, general paralysis, and the abuse of marihuana.[45]

Thus, marijuana madness (and that of drugs in general) was not its own clinical entity but rather a basic manifestation of stereotyped "delirium." The press demonstrated this fact on numerous occasions when it noted that a person was "either a madman or a *marihuano*," the two categories being mostly indistinguishable. For example, on July 6, 1904, *El País* reported the case of Miguel López, a prisoner on death row for murder who had recently exhausted all of the possible appeals of the sentence. Since then, he had been acting strange and detached.

> Yesterday morning . . . he went into the workshops courtyard. A certain mystery was noted in him, and according to certain witnesses, he showed signs of madness, for he pronounced incoherent words. The opinion of others is that López had smoked two marihuana cigarettes and to that was attributed his weird countenance and delirium.
>
> Whatever the case, the fact is that suddenly, and without giving time for anything, he stood up from the stool in which he was sitting and with his shoemaker's knife [*chaveta*] stabbed himself two times in the chest.[46]

But, again, despite the many similarities between marijuana delirium and that produced by other substances, the former was frequently distinguished as being especially pernicious. On this, one final example is worth noting. In the 1890s, the physician Máximo Silva wrote his *Higiene popular* (published in 1917), a book that treated the problem of "hygienic education," a central concern of the revolutionary sanitary authorities, who would eventually prohibit marijuana nationwide. Silva neatly summed up how marijuana's reputation differed from that of other drugs, despite their many similarities:

> The delirium produced by marihuana, generally similar physiologically to that of all the narcotic drugs, opium, solanaceas, alcohol, is characterized, nevertheless, by two uniquely fatal symptoms: marihuana stimulates action and multiplies the personality. Opium enervates and makes one drowsy; solanaceas provoke feverish and unconscious delirium; alcohol after its unsure and hesitant action depresses and strikes down, but marihuana due to an abominable concession, not only preserves the will, but multiplies the means of exercising it. It centuplicates the personality and stimulates action. Imagine, as in a hellish vision, a diabolic mob, whores, ruffians and murderers with their personalities multiplied and compelled to act thanks to the effects of the drug.

Ultimately, this particular characteristic was especially frightening because of the social background of most marijuana smokers: "One should not suppose that the beatific souls and balanced spirits are going to exalt their personalities by means of marihuana." Though deeply rooted in class and racial prejudice, Silva's theory nevertheless hinged on the critical variables of "set" and "setting," though these terms had yet to come into use. While all drugs were dangerous and could produce delirium in their users, ultimately marijuana was especially dangerous because it accentuated the tendencies of the people who used it, and, as explored further in the next chapter, marijuana was overwhelmingly associated with a class of people considered to be dangerous, degenerated, and criminal as a matter of course.[47]

All of this demonstrates that popular discourses on marijuana and its effects were thoroughly supported by current scientific theory on insanity and the effects of drugs in general. This proved especially important because there was far less Mexican research on marijuana itself. During the period under discussion, only one study was actually published based on original research with marijuana smokers, that being Genaro Pérez's 1886 medical thesis. A second important study, by the physicians Adolfo Nieto and Eliseo Ramírez, reviewed the scientific literature on marijuana while providing anecdotal evidence from the Mexican context as evidence, but their work was not presented in public until a month after marijuana's prohibition in 1920.

Nonetheless, from the beginning, Mexican authorities could back their claims about marijuana with recourse to the European literature on cannabis/hashish, and this they did. During the 1850s, Leonardo Oliva had classified marijuana as *Cannabis indica*, "the same Hashish of India or weed of the fakirs," and had drawn on the works of Moreau and O'Shaughnessy to describe the drug's medical applications and intoxicating effects. In his thesis, Genaro Pérez quoted extensively from the European sources to back his opinion that marijuana produced a kind of madness that could lead to criminal behavior. He included long quotations from the doctors Auguste Voisin and Henry Liouville, for instance, who had witnessed rabbits lose weight, agility, activity, and eventually their lives after being given daily doses of hashish. Voisin also experimented with humans and described the symptoms of intoxication at length: "Under the acute intoxication the users stir constantly, they speak with an extreme volubility, they have fits of laughter, they turn themselves over to uncontrolled dancing and erotic demonstrations and they are prisoners of vivid hallucinations. *Sometimes, on the contrary, a furious delirium is observed*. A deep sleep or stupor follows this agitation."[48] Chronic hashish use, according to Voisin, caused melancholia. Voisin also compared hashish intoxication to that of opium but "with its own special character. . . . The hashish smoker is mainly a pederast."[49] Pérez cited various other French works, from observations made by one of Voisin's students at Cairo's insane asylum, to the research of Ajasson de Grandsagne and Brierre de Boismont, who together concluded that hashish produced precisely the eight stages of intoxication outlined by Moreau in *Hashish and Mental Illness*.[50] In borrowing from the European scientific literature, Pérez reproduced some of the Orientalism embedded in those sources. After citing Egypt, Algeria, Turkey, and Tunis as the countries outside of Mexico where the drug was smoked, he also recounted the standard story of the Old Man of the Mountain who "used a drink with which he intoxicated his followers in order to make them believe that he had the power to transport them to the Paradise of Mohammed, as long as they provided him their blind faith and a loyalty without limits." He also associated the drug with "Oriental" hedonism: "It produces a type of ecstatic delirium, and it is considered by the Arabs to be the source of all things sensual [*voluptuosidades*], and of all the immaterial enjoyments."[51]

Yet while European studies influenced Mexican researchers, clearly Mexican discourses did not simply derive from the importation of European opinions. As we've seen, already in the eighteenth century cannabis had been linked to madness in Mexico, and some of the first references to its smoking in the mid-nineteenth century did the same. In the 1870s, Rafael Rébollar suggested that marijuana was an indigenous substance "unknown to botany" and yet reputed to cause madness. Similarly, in the 1880s, the *costumbrista* writer Hilarión Frías y Soto would argue that marijuana was definitively *not* the same substance as the cannabis described in the European sources, yet he insisted that marijuana produced insanity in its users.[52] Later, in an 1897 issue of *Revista médica*, José Olvera made the argument that while cannabis use might have certain negative consequences in other parts of the world, these were especially pronounced in Mexico. "The use of Indian hemp is found in all the regions where the plant grows and it is consumed as a solid or liquid, or as smoke, moreover I believe in no part of the globe does it produce such fatal effects as in the Mexican Republic. It's true that in other regions the delirium that marihuana produces is a turbulent one, but in our country it reaches a fury, terrible and blind impulse that leads to murder."[53] Finally, to my knowledge, the press never cited the European sources and yet reported on hundreds of cases of violence or madness produced by the drug. In short, the European science gave a certain authority to various claims about marijuana's effects, but those claims mostly had an organic, Mexican basis. Mexican science contributed little to the debate but only because, as noted already, almost no one studied marijuana's effects in a serious, scientific way. Pérez's

1886 thesis was the one exception, but it had virtually no discernible influence on Mexican thought prior to 1920.[54]

■ Thus, we see how the scientific discourses of the age fully supported the typical reports of marijuana's effects. Marijuana was not unique among intoxicants in its purported tendency to produce madness and violence. Especially striking were the deep similarities between the reported effects of this drug and those of alcohol. Yet the discourse around marijuana did stand out in that it was almost universally negative. Within published sources, there were no defenders of its recreational use and, as we will see, no opposition to its prohibition. While the effects of alcohol and marijuana were often conflated, overall the latter's reputation was more consistently negative and dangerous. In the next chapter, I explain why.

*Chapter 6*

# EXPLAINING THE MISSING

# COUNTERDISCOURSE II

## PEOPLE, ENVIRONMENTS,

## AND DEGENERATION

*THE CAPITAL'S INHABITANTS WERE*
*DRIVEN MAD BY MARIJUANA*

*Against whom was he fighting, that man who with simian movements attempted to defend himself against fantastic enemies? The same enemies that he swore endeavored to tear out the tongue which he struggled to clutch between his hands?*

*He's high on marijuana [*está enyerbado*] — said the people running behind and surrounding him at a safe distance.*

*Indeed, the man appeared prisoner of a mad fury, and with his eyes pressing out of their sockets, his skin yellow and dry, his disordered hair and clothing, he presented an image more terrifying than one can imagine.*

*Suddenly he launched himself against the onlookers, and he would have killed the woman around whose throat he had latched his claws were it not for four tough, strapping men who managed to drag him off of her.*

*The battle then took on almost epic proportions. The* marihuano *reaching deeply for strength from his feeble body, struggling among the men, while the crowd whistled and guffawed seeing how the madness of the depraved man only increased each time a street urchin, already well aware of the symptoms of marijuana intoxication, simulated the action of drawing from his mouth long threads which he extended along his arms.*

*The* marihuano, *staring straight at the boy, seemed to regain his strength and alternating between laughs, sobs, and howls fought until he finally collapsed to the ground with his tongue hanging from his foaming mouth.*
—El Imparcial, *July 17, 1908*

The above drama was not drawn from a pulp novel. It was reported, quite seriously, in *El Imparcial*, Mexico's leading newspaper, a publication that at its height claimed a daily circulation of more than 100,000 (in a city with fewer than half a million total inhabitants). How much of the story was true is difficult to say. Even more uncertain is what typical Mexico City readers thought of this or other similar descriptions. Did they immediately view them as sensational exaggerations, or did they find them quite believable, even in their most fantastic details?

Reports of marijuana users degenerating into a more primitive state of being were hardly uncommon in late-nineteenth- and early-twentieth-century Mexico. The *marihuanos* of news reports routinely became "ferocious" or "rabid" while engaging in grotesque acts of violence. But if such reports were understood to be gross exaggerations, why were they never challenged? Why was there no counterdiscourse?

One key explanation, and the subject of this chapter, lies in marijuana's overwhelming association with prisoners, soldiers, and *herbolarias* and the environments where these people lived, worked, and suffered. Prisons and soldiers' barracks were themselves fraught with symbolism, having well-developed reputations for injustice, unhygienic conditions, violence, and vice, while *herbolarias* were synonymous with Indian Mexico and tended to stimulate ancient fears of malevolent witchcraft. Most important, these people and environments occupied uncertain space at the juncture between civilization and barbarity, a space where Mexico's claim to modern, European status might be questioned. They were therefore all positioned to resonate profoundly with the idea of "degeneration," a social-scientific concept that both justified and fueled descriptions of rabid and ferocious *marihuanos*. Thus, while it is impossible to know exactly how a Mexican in July 1908 understood the above newspaper clipping, the ubiquity of the degeneration discourse and marijuana's connection to it suggest that such fantastic details were likely taken quite seriously.

■ It was no coincidence that the 1920 law that prohibited marijuana nationwide was titled "Dispositions on the Cultivation and Commerce of Substances That Degenerate the Race." Degeneration was in many ways the key concept behind that legislation. At its most elemental, the idea of degeneration stood at the crossroads of progress and decline, fueled by the concern that accelerating modernity and civilization might, paradoxically, turn back the evolutionary clock. Of course, anxiety about the decline of humans from a more perfect form is a very old concern in the Western tradition.[1] But in the globalizing environment of the late nineteenth and early twentieth centuries, a period highlighted by both industrialization and colonialism, that dialectic took on renewed urgency. In this atmosphere, as Daniel Pick has noted, "evolutionary theories, as expounded by Chambers, Spencer and Darwin were often explicitly progressivist, even if they popularly and outrageously could arouse, despite themselves, images of simian humanity." Here, degeneration became a central concern of scientific, medicalized social analysis throughout the Atlantic world, "an empirically demonstrable medical, biological or physical anthropological fact" rather than merely a philosophical problem.[2] Yet while it might have been believed to be empirically demonstrable, the idea was nevertheless articulated in remarkably diverse, often contradictory ways and, critically, at multiple levels of analysis.

The French and Italian strains of this discourse most powerfully influenced Mexican manifestations of these ideas. The psychiatrist Benedict Augustine Morel's *Traité des dégénérescences physiques, intellectuelles et morales de l'espèce humaine* (1857) inaugurated an enormous technico-scientific literature on this idea in France and elsewhere and was widely influential in Latin America.[3] From Italy came the perhaps even more influential work of Cesare Lombroso, who developed the concepts of the "born criminal" and of "atavisms" that he argued lurked within, and manifested themselves upon, the bodies of deviants.[4] Morel and Lombroso were only the most influential of thinkers on a subject that in some ways dominated European thought on crime, urbanization, and medicine during the late nineteenth century.[5] Both traditions emerged from the particular historical circumstances of their time, "a complex process of conceptualizing a felt crisis of history," according to Pick.[6] In France, that crisis was brought about both by the rapid expansion of population in Paris during the first half of the nineteenth century and by the years surrounding the revolutions of 1848, a period when liberal progressivism appeared doomed. The former inspired great anxiety among the bourgeoisie, for "the Paris population seemed to contain immutably alien races, peoples constitutionally incapable of settling, a tribe of vagabonds and nomads," inspiring a general fear of the "mob" among the upper sectors of society.[7] The turmoil of 1848, a product of the regular upheavals in France since 1789, had fueled a growing pessimism and a belief that democracy could result only in "turbulent decadence."[8] Those anxieties were intensified later in the century after the disastrous war with Prussia. That war turned concern about population in another direction, toward a fear that France's low birthrate doomed it to defeat in the face of a more vigorous and aggressive Prussian neighbor. Similarly, Lombroso's theories arose out of the struggle to unify Italy in the second half of the nineteenth century, the desire to turn "peasants into Italians," and the need to bring stability to a country that had suffered through twenty-eight different governments in its first thirty-two years of existence.[9]

That these circumstances, both the French and Italian, might produce theories that resonated with Mexican thinkers of this period should be of little surprise, for the Porfiriato was in many ways defined by parallel concerns. Mexico's first fifty years of independence had been characterized by constant upheaval and highlighted by grave doubts about the viability of democracy there. At the same time, fear of foreign invasion from the north and a general dread regarding the quality of Mexico's population and its potential for modernity continued to fuel anxious inquiries into the state of the nation. In short, the popularity of these theories in Mexico was not merely a product of their prestigious European origins but derived from like historical contexts at approximately the same moment in time.[10]

Critically, degeneration was often articulated at multiple levels of analysis simultaneously. In some ways, the concept typified the "medicalization" of social analysis that accompanied the rise of positivism during the nineteenth century, when social and biological infirmities were often conflated. In France, as Robert Nye has argued, this "medicalized" vision "made it possible for observers to pass easily from a case of individual 'degeneracy' to degeneration as a collective problem," which "encouraged the appraisal of social problems from the view of national interest, thrusting, as it were, issues of domestic health and external security into an identical frame of analysis."[11]

A concept like "degeneration," of course, can be fully articulated only within some kind of comparative relationship, for something can appear degenerated only in comparison to a more healthy or fully constituted other. Here too the multiple levels of analysis, both external and internal, become apparent. Externally, comparisons could turn on axes varying from civilizations, to nations, to political formations; internally, oppositions were based on ethnicity, gender, and ultimately human versus beast. Indeed, while writing *Orientalism*, Edward Said noticed that the "deviant" populations of nineteenth-century Europe were in many ways seen as internal "Orientals." "The Oriental was linked . . . to elements in Western society (delinquents, the insane, women, the poor) having in common an identity best described as lamentably alien."[12] Pick too noted this fact, concluding that "the object of the racial anthropology that emerged in this period was not only Africa or the Orient but also the 'primitive' areas and groups within the home country."[13]

For Mexican thinkers, removed from the preoccupations of external empire, these "primitive" internal elements were certainly the focus. But Mexican elites also contributed a kind of colonial discourse of their own regarding Mexico's Indian past. Mauricio Tenorio-Trillo has called this "an ad-hoc complement for late nineteenth-century Western orientalism" and has shown how the idea that Mexico's nineteenth-century Indians had degenerated from a great past was a fundamental component of nationalist writings and architectural representations from the period. These ideas allowed Mexican anthropologists and scientists to negotiate the tricky problem of how to engage the dominant European scientific debates of the period. The problem was delicate because the desire to engage these debates indicated Mexican efforts to be "modern"; but these discussions revolved around racist, civilizational hierarchies that labeled Mexico—a country full of ruins and dark peoples evoking comparisons to Egypt rather than France—as *pre*modern. Furthermore, Mexico's elite thinkers had to find a solution that continued to justify the miserable political and economic realities of life for Mexico's indigenous peoples as well as the strong racial hierarchies that continued to rule social life in general. Linked to a strain of the degeneration discourse, the idea that the ancient peoples of Mexico had been strong, brave, and noble thus served a useful purpose, as it allowed Mexican elites to argue that the nation's racial stock was good but had degenerated due to either the political and economic failures of earlier regimes or the acquired habits and customs of the natives. The former, of course, had supposedly already been remedied, while the latter might be effectively educated or scrubbed away.[14] Such thinking thus closely linked Indians and their mestizo descendants to the "Oriental," as is evident in Federico Gamboa's novel La llaga, which, as we will see later in this chapter, makes explicit the link between degeneration and marijuana. As Gamboa put it, Mexico's "great national majority" were the "heirs of sensual and bloodthirsty [carniceras] races—the Arabs and Indians."[15]

In practice, degeneration could mean any number of things during this period in both Mexico and Europe. For Morel, the idea was extraordinarily complex and involved innumerable conditions, symptoms, and habits, from pointed ears and suicidal tendencies to alcohol abuse. In the long run, idiocy, sterility, and death resulted. However, further complicating the picture, these "symptoms" were also sometimes "causes." For Morel, their elemental origins were found deep within the individual; they were hidden and often imperceptible, usually in flux and evolving through different manifestations at different levels of the family tree.[16]

Lombroso's notions were best distinguished from Morel's by his fatalistic insistence on the biological origins of "atavisms" among certain members of the population. Like Morel, Lombroso was concerned with a wide array of maladies that jeopardized national prosperity, from superstition to murder, but he categorized these as holdovers from earlier eras that could not be remedied through education or other "hygienic" interventions. Furthermore, Lombroso put much more stock in the idea that such atavisms were physically visible on the "born criminal."[17] This he famously claimed to have discovered while examining the skull of a notorious Italian brigand: "I seemed to see all of a sudden . . . the problem of the nature of the criminal—an atavistic being who reproduces in his person the ferocious instincts of primitive humanity and the inferior animals. Thus were explained anatomically . . . the insensibility to pain, extremely acute sight, tattooing, excessive idleness, love of orgies, and the irresponsible craving of evil for its own sake, the desire not only to extinguish life in the victim, but to mutilate the corpse, tear its flesh and drink its blood."[18]

As the concept of degeneration developed in Mexico, it reflected many of the different strains found in Morel, Lombroso, and their various colleagues and followers.[19] Newspaper references to the concept displayed the transnational character of the discourse, as such citations often appeared within articles drawn directly from the foreign press. Thus, articles were produced on declining birthrates and the unhealthy watering down of a nation's stock through immigration.[20] Degeneration was also understood as a general condition that involved bad government, bad racial stock, and "degenerated customs."[21] Some articles combined all of these elements.[22] At the same time, "good" racial stock could mean a more "pure" stock of good blood, or a good mixture of various "good" stocks, or the addition of "good" stock to "bad" stock.[23] Too much civilization or "soft comfort" was believed to cause degeneration as well.[24] And, of course, degeneration was also understood as something that befell even great nations, though it perhaps best defined the old civilizations of the Mediterranean and, especially, the Orient.[25]

While these meta-level consequences were frequently cited, the Mexican press was equally rich with more Lombrosian descriptions on the level of the individual. A piece by Lombroso was reprinted in *El Diario del Hogar* that explained that the poor were born without the same aspirations as the rich. While this condition ensured their poverty, it also helped them to weather it.[26] Depictions of "atavisms" were also extremely widespread. One story, drawn apparently from the U.S. press, told of a black missionary from the United States who returned to Africa to convert souls there, but renewed exposure to his native environment brought out the primitive within and he fell right back into the cannibalism of his ancestors.[27] Indeed, atavism usually implied the recrudescence of bloodlust. Arguments against bullfighting often cited the threat of such regressions and cautioned that the gory spectacle tended to bring out the primitive, bloodthirsty tendencies of the population.[28] These various arguments often displayed the enduring influence of Lamarckian notions of evolution through acquired characteristics.[29]

Perhaps the richest concentration of these different notions is found in Julio Guerrero's highly influential 1903 study, *La génesis del crimen en México.* Guerrero used the concept of degeneration to refute the widespread notion that laziness was an inevitable consequence of the Mexican climate.[30] In the process, his work vividly demonstrates how the concept was simultaneously understood as a social, political, economic, physical, and hereditary malady. Guerrero argued that Mexico's tumultuous post-independence era had sown the seeds of laziness. The constant fighting had left huge swaths of country-side vacant and small villages overrun by the "refuse" of the cities, criminals fleeing from other parts of the country, and crippled victims of the fighting. These immigrants were "veritable monsters" who terrified the healthy and honorable families, who then isolated themselves, with no choice but to in-breed. Thus, to the already vice-ridden lower classes were added the crippled and monstrous refuse of the civil wars and the now-inbreeding, formerly honorable but rapidly degenerating populations of the countryside. As in the tales of medieval travelers, Guerrero described the small towns where one came across "children with two heads, joined twins, idiots; macrocephalics, albinos, creatures with harelips and feet without toes or hands with six fingers, tuberculars, syphilitics, scrofulous, midgets and hunchbacks." This was a truly nightmarish scene where just a few miles from the capital, one's train might be surrounded by "swarms of blind blenorrhoeals, with purulent and vacuous eye sockets; they surround the train that is halted, and bewilder the passengers with monotonous supplications, audible mumblings accompanied by the squeaking of a violin."[31]

These horrible sights were just one aspect of a countryside drowning in misery that forced a wave of immigrants into Mexico City, causing an over-crowding comparable to "Chinese cities." The situation helped to drive wages down so that workers were forced to live in miserable conditions despite being employed. Starving, naked children, "like the savages of Polynesia," dotted the city streets. Workers began to slow down the pace of their labor for fear of finishing the job and being left unemployed. The vicious competition for survival then led to the relaxation of morals among the population, which in turn produced alcoholism and more degeneration of customs and health, destroying families and ultimately resulting in greater laziness.[32]

Guerrero's chapter on "atavisms" developed along similar lines, with political shortcomings having sparked the decline into primitive behaviors. He begins with a long historical explanation of governmental corruption and incompetence that helped to spawn the civil wars and upheavals of the nineteenth century. Those upheavals led Mexicans to the conclusion that only force could protect their interests and lives.

> This armed fight without quarter, bloody and desolating, of seventy years, produced with the daily repetition of its dramatic spectacles a profound impression on the Mexican spirit. The brain filled up with scenes of fighting, blood, gunfire, battles, escapes, murders, fires, robberies and rapes. . . . As a psychic consequence of those scenes were born grudges that never could be turned off, projects of vengeance which like a ferocious tic brought with it reminiscences of death in the middle of the celebrations; it killed the happiness in the bottom of the soul and exacerbated the latent misanthropy that in Mexico is produced by the climatic nervousness. In the middle of that environment of hatred were born, in the same way that the panther develops in the tropical jungles or the crocodile in the swamps, regressive types from Vandalic times.[33]

For Guerrero, the most "celebrated" people of any country merely represented the accumulation of all of the characteristics typical of that nation. Thus, the United States had produced an Edison and Britain a Shakespeare. Mexico, on the other hand, produced remorseless murderers. "These monstrous criminal types, were nothing other than cases of the hypertrophy of a bloodthirsty instinct, developed in a large sector of Mexican society, although at a much lower grade, but which has removed from them the repugnance for the sight of blood and has made the agony of the victim captivating [*interesante*]." This was the result simply of the biological laws of heredity:

> The human races, upon adapting themselves to the environment in which they develop, take on a physical type and a uniform character which is conserved or repeats itself anatomically and physically through the centuries, and despite the external forms of the civilization. . . .
> In Mexico's Central Plateau of thoroughly dry, hot, and luminous air which disturbs the nerves; where meditations are darkened by the abuse of tobacco, alcohol, and coffee: with the irritation of an eternal and fruitless fight for life; and until recently, with a desperate and almost centenary impotence to form a plexus of social solidarity; the character of a great part of the society has degenerated and the ferocious tendencies of the Aztecs have reappeared. After ten generations there has returned to pal-

pitate in some of the chests of our compatriots the barbarous spirit of the adorers of Huitzilopoztli; of those of the sacred springs when they went by the sad sound of their *teponaxtle* [drum] on their [missions to capture] prisoners [*razzias*] in the regions of Tlaxcala and Huejotzingo, in order to open their chest with obsidian knives, to pull out the heart and devour it in a holocaust to their gods. Three centuries of mass and the barracks were ultimately very little for the complete evolution of character in those masses; and if today reappears the Sarmatian Attila in the peasants of Silesia, in our political battles there has reemerged in the multitude at the same time as the indomitable warrior of Ahuizotl the bloodthirsty priest of Huitzilopoztli.[34]

To this had been added the bloodlines of savage and brutal Spanish conquerors who, in the sixteenth century, had been gathered from the prisons of Andalusía and sent to the Americas, where, despite the sermons of friars and the laws of the Crown, they slaughtered with reckless abandon. From all of this emerged Mexico's typical mestizo along with political struggles "more barbarous than even those found in black Africa," where military engagements became as ferocious as "African and Asiatic wars." Santa Anna was the ultimate example. His initial exploits became those of "a ferocious brute [*bestia*], who corralled, feels the bloody congestion of a maddened beast [*fiera*], and lashes about with its fangs without knowing what it's tearing into, and in order to assault its enemies it fixes its claws even at the inanimate objects that surround it." For Guerrero, Attila the Hun failed to perform as many brutal acts as Santa Anna, though "that was fifteen centuries ago." Ultimately, these were the instincts that, thanks to the political and social convulsions of the nineteenth century, had begun to appear in Mexico's criminals whose crimes were overwhelmingly of a violent nature, manifesting themselves in bloody street brawls and stabbings.[35]

Thus, in Guerrero we find nearly all of the elements that combined to define the degeneration discourse in Mexico. Ultimately, degeneration could result in atavisms that almost literally transformed human beings into beasts. The animal came from within, but that biological inheritance was drawn out by social and political circumstances. There was constant potential for the true, bloodthirsty nature of the average Mexican to rise to the surface. Here we see degeneration's multiple levels of articulation at work. While the focus might be on the specific behavior of a criminal or *caudillo*, the actions resulted from political and economic failures and, ultimately, depended on the core nature of the civilization. Where the United States produced an Edison, Mexico produced remorseless killers. Finally, Guerrero helps to further illustrate how Mexico's Indian past provided a kind of internal "Orient" that paralleled the external portion of European degeneration discourses. When speaking of Mexican savagery, the obvious comparisons were with "Asiatic and African" brutality.

Drug use, including alcohol, also played an important role as both a cause and symptom of degeneration. Alcohol was widely cited as a substance that degenerated entire races and placed the security of the nation at risk. It was thought to cause crime, madness, and death while leaving the seed of degeneration in the children of alcoholics, leading those children eventually to the abuse of other drugs. Populations might thus become so physically weakened as to make them vulnerable to conquest.[36] In 1899, the physician Ricardo Suárez Gamboa argued that "the great family of the degenerated offer delirious reactions of extreme variance, which need nothing more than a pretext to develop themselves. . . . From the most inferior degenerate, the idiot, up to the most superior degenerate, the genius, all of them offer the characteristic of mental disequilibrium and of eclipses of free-will in the face of instinctive impulses." Already degenerated, these souls were unable to resist the allure of intoxicants. Alcohol, morphine, and marijuana abuse then sparked the emergence of those instinctive impulses.[37]

Trinidad Sánchez Santos, who defined "alcoholism" as the "pathological state that results from the ingestion of intoxicating substances, such as spirituous drinks, morphine, cocaine, marijuana, etc.," explained in 1896 how the damage (lesiones) caused by "alcoholism" was passed down from generation to generation, how degenerated individuals were more likely to fall prey to "alcoholism," and that the consequences of all of this were madness, decrepitude, and ultimately a kind of spiritual weakness that made them the likely victims of tyranny. "Deprived of free-will, better said volitional energy, [the alcoholic] will be the universal slave, tied always to a servitude to all whims, tyrannies, abuses, and cruelties."[38] Such direct links between degeneration and drugs would eventually be critical to the emergence of prohibitionist policies in Mexico.

But arguably more important still was marijuana's extremely close association with prisons and soldiers' barracks, two environments understood to be highly degenerated in their own right. These were the main locations of marijuana use in Mexico, and they were understood in remarkably similar ways. They were both seen as comparative measures of Mexico's civilizational advancement; they were institutions populated through injustice and governmental incompetence that primarily affected society's most marginalized actors but also citizens at higher positions on the social scale; and, finally, these institutions, dotted by vice, immorality, and disease, featured some of the most squalid, unhygienic conditions in Mexico. Prisons in particular came to be used by critics of the Díaz regime as potent symbols of degeneration. Thus, marijuana's close association with these people and institutions helped to reinforce its reputation as a degenerating element in Mexican life and society.

José Joaquín Fernández de Lizardi's masterpiece, *El Periquillo Sarniento* (1816), provides perhaps the best starting point for examining how prisons were understood in nineteenth-century Mexico. Often considered to be the first truly Latin American novel, *El Periquillo Sarniento* features many elements of *costumbrismo*, a style of writing that described the features of everyday life in Mexico. *Costumbrismo* would flourish in the nineteenth century as Mexicans sought to establish the parameters of what in fact it meant to be "Mexican." Within such writings, prisons often played an important role. They were in short a significant part of even the earliest nationalist imaginings in Mexico.

Like many prison critics who would follow in his footsteps, Fernández de Lizardi's portrayal was probably based in part on personal experience, for he had spent six months in jail for publishing criticisms of the Spanish viceroy.[39] Ultimately, he touched on most of the themes that would dominate writing about Mexican prisons throughout the nineteenth century, beginning with his protagonist being wrongfully accused of a crime and winding up in jail because of it. Fernández de Lizardi described prison as a "deposit of iniquity and malice" where prisoners of all races and classes mixed alarmingly. "There were in that courtyard a million prisoners. Some white, others dark; some partly dressed, others decent; some naked, others wrapped in their blankets; but all of them pale and with their sadness and desperation painted in the emaciated colors of their faces."[40] The unsanitary conditions were highlighted by ubiquitous vermin and open containers of human excrement. Yet many of the prisoners had adjusted to the situation, gambling with passion, singing, and even dancing by hopping around in their shackles. Legal proceedings were tortuously slow, and innocent prisoners were often kept in jail for months, even years. Also present were the notorious "presidents," alpha-prisoners selected by the administration to keep order who often utilized that power despotically for personal profit. Later, these presidents could not help but invoke comparisons to the Porfiriato's notorious and hated *jefes políticos*, who played a similar role in municipalities across the country. Finally, there was the brutality to which prisoners were subjected, El Periquillo himself having a vat of urine poured on him by other prisoners while he tried to sleep.[41]

Manuel Payno, another important *costumbrista* writer of the nineteenth century, also wrote about prisons and their conditions. He too had first-hand experience with Mexico's penitentiaries, though his was in an official capacity—he had been commissioned during the 1840s by a reforming Santa Anna to study the prisons of the United States.[42] Originally published as a serial during 1845–46 and then revised and republished, his novel *El fistol del diablo* describes Mexico as it was roughly between 1833 and 1856, and with respect to prisons it told a story not unlike Fernández de Lizardi's.[43] In Payno's version of the basic template, an innocent girl is wrongly accused of a crime by her jealous and vengeful neighbors. This lands her in La Acordada jail (later known as Belén), which is described as hell on earth: bloody cadavers lying just within the prison gates from the routine brawls that take place; a disturbing mixture of accused prisoners and those already convicted of crimes; the corruption and filth within the establishment; and the seemingly endless wait for the legal authorities to process her case.[44] Payno's masterpiece, *Los bandidos del Río Frío*, published in the 1890s, describes Mexico City's juvenile poorhouse (essentially a juvenile prison) in similar terms.[45]

Writing of this kind about prisons touched a sensitive nerve in nineteenth-century Mexico and would eventually resonate deeply with the degeneration discourse, for prisons were often perceived through a lens of international comparison and as a measure of Mexico's advancement as a civilized nation. As Payno noted, "In every country justice has its places of punishment established under different systems, depending on each country's level of civilization; but it would take too long to engage in material descriptions. Prisons are always places of horror, of misery, and of grief."[46] However, he argued that in Mexico, the conditions were particularly bad, for while according to both "civilization" and "religious maxims" the object of prisons was to reform rather than cause suffering, Mexico was "where the innocent begin suffering untold sorrows from the moment they are accused, while the real criminals always find a thousand ways to evade punishment."[47]

Descriptions of soldiers' barracks, the other centers of marijuana use in Mexico at this time, were hardly distinguishable from those of prisons. Soldiers usually landed in the barracks as a consequence of injustice, for the levies that produced a large percentage of the troops were notoriously unfair and corrupt. In his medical thesis, Agustín García Figueroa contended that the remarkable injustice of the levies was ultimately the result of Mexico's constant upheavals, which had forced the rapid recruitment of soldiers. The idea of a levy was not in itself unfair, he argued, but rather the fact that it was aimed overwhelmingly at *los desheredados*, or Mexico's most marginal, "disinherited" elements. The ranks of the impressed included workers, drunks, and criminals from the cities as well as country people who, while not initially immoral, were ignorant enough to be almost immediately corrupted by the culture of the barracks. Other members of the military landed there only because, according to García Figueroa, they either wanted to work but could not find employment or were simply too lazy to be employed. For these men, a miserable payout of some twelve pesos justified becoming "a slave" in the armed forces.[48] As the Porfiriato wore on, individuals were often portrayed as having been forced into the army by the corruption and despotism of local political bosses, a fact credited for sowing much revolutionary discontent.[49] Julio Guerrero also cited the levies as the source of the highly immoral elements of the army, blaming the nation's "administrative incompetence" for the situation, though he believed that ultimately the military could serve as a site of "regeneration," much like the prison system was supposed to do.[50] Another thesis writer, Leopoldo Ortega, also lamented that the levy in Mexico was used to impress children, the old, and the infirm.[51] In 1889, Alfonso Luis Velasco called marijuana and prostitutes the only consolation for soldiers impressed into the army, a sentiment that was reiterated both by Federico Gamboa in his novel *Suprema ley* and by the Porfirian press.[52]

Also like prisons, the barracks were the site of tremendous filth. Ortega argued that poor hygiene killed many more soldiers than bullets, while García Figueroa cited the parasites found all over the soldiers in medical examinations.[53] Francisco Domingo y Barrera noted the lack of ventilation and sunlight, overcrowded conditions, miserable diet, and excess of moisture in Mexico City's barracks as typical causes of infirmity among the troops.[54] García Figueroa wrote scathingly about the "ugly" *soldaderas* who followed the troops and provided for many of their needs through pillage. These services just highlighted the government's failure to take care of its soldiers. "The *soldaderas* on campaign are as useful to the army as they are pernicious for the towns [*poblaciones*]. The governments of Mexico have never been able to cover the necessities of their belligerent armies; the Mexican soldier on campaign lacks everything, and if he maintains himself indomitable it is only because of the patient resignation that so characterizes the indigenous race. Poorly equipped, poorly paid and without the right to gather his own resources, he marches trusting that female providence that in spite of the civilians and property rights, cover the primary necessities of the belligerent."[55] Here again we see how elements of the degeneration discourse began to creep into the analysis, with government failures having set off a chain reaction of degenerate behaviors. According to García Figueroa, the ugly *soldaderas* led the soldiers to believe that the only pleasure to be derived from relations with the opposite sex was the pure genital sensation of the act, thus spawning homosexuality, whose signs were found in the effeminate behavior and dress of soldiers, as well as the syphilitic lesions surrounding their mouths and anuses. The levies brought children into the ranks, which promoted pederasty. And syphilis was further spread by the entrance of society's most degraded prostitutes, women from the poorest corners of Mexico City who lived like "lizards" in shacks on the edge of town.[56]

Finally, of course, prisons and soldiers' barracks were united in their overwhelming association with marijuana, which was routinely smuggled in along with alcohol and other contraband. Such smuggling was a constant theme in the press over these years, and it continually earned the attention of prison and military authorities who attempted to stem the tide through various means.[57] For example, an 1898 effort to busy Belén's female prisoners through the manufacture of cigarettes was also conceived of as a means of preventing the smuggling of marijuana cigarettes into the prison.[58] Prison employees were routinely disciplined or fired for the smuggling or sale of marijuana. In August 1907, a guard at Belén was reprimanded for allowing the introduction of seven marijuana cigarettes.[59] The following spring, another guard was fired after allowing a prisoner to receive a package containing sixty-five cigarettes of the weed.[60] In late October 1908, a riot in the notorious "Bartolinas" section of the prison was blamed on the use of marijuana and alcohol. The warden considered the failure to prevent the introduction of these substances a particularly serious error because of the type of extremely dangerous men held in that section. In light of recent efforts to "moralize" the prison authorities, the firing of the involved employees was again recommended.[61] The following February, prison authorities continued to lament the corruption connected to the entry of marijuana into the prison. The introduction of marijuana and alcohol was said to be widespread. Most recently, an employee had been found hiding two large bags of the weed under a vat on the prison roof, which he clearly intended to smuggle into the building.[62] One employee became the subject of quiet surveillance as the numbers of "scandals" inside his area of the prison had increased since he took the job. In October 1910, he was caught passing a cloak to a prisoner within which was found a bag of marijuana measuring thirty by ten centimeters. The employee was immediately fired, "since the violation should be considered of the most grave, not only for the disloyalty evident in the carrying out of his duties, but also for his going against the measures dictated by the Mayoralty [*Alcaldía*] causing grave and transcendent harm to the prisoners and the order of the establishment."[63] Around the same time, the prison barber was also fired for smuggling marijuana into the building.[64]

The military had a long if sometimes contradictory record on these matters. In 1875, for example, a controversy emerged at the military prison of Santiago de Tlaltelolco over the existence of an official cantina within the prison walls. It is not clear if the cantina's liquor was supposed to be sold to inmates or just to the guards, but its presence was blamed for a number of brawls.[65] The military code of justice specifically forbade the use of "intoxication" as an extenuating or attenuating circumstance if that intoxication was contracted voluntarily. The penalties for simple drunkenness were also significant. Article 516 of the 1879 version of the code decreed one year of prison for any officer who became incapable of carrying out orders due to drunkenness. A repeat offense would get him banned from the military. For corporals and sergeants, the penalty was to be six months of arrest, a year for repeat offenses. Public drunkenness was also penalized, and, more severely still, drunkenness that led to "scandals and fights" could inspire expulsion from the military for officers and arrest for lower-ranked members of the troops.[66]

In 1882, a prohibition on the introduction of marijuana, cards, and alcohol to the military hospital was reiterated in order to cut down on insubordination, fights, and "disasters." The move was prompted by the May 21 death of a soldier who, "as a consequence of an attack of delirium from using marijuana," fell to his death in the courtyard of the institution. Meanwhile, *El Monitor Republicano* reported that for years, gambling, alcohol, and marijuana had caused fights and accidents in that institution, even though the "strictest vigilance" had been established to prevent their introduction, with "all of those people capable of giving themselves over to the commerce of prohibited objects" being searched on their arrival to the prison, exempting only officers from the drill. But, in the end, the officers were found to have been introducing these materials all along.[67] In 1882, various measures were decreed by the military in Oaxaca after incidents of desertion, insubordination, and attacks on superior officers were attributed to the use of marijuana. Orders were then given to root out the plant where it was grown and suppress its sale in pharmacies.[68] A slightly revised military code of 1893 contained roughly the same provisions on "intoxication," but perhaps reflecting the growing importance of marijuana, it now defined *embriaguez*, a term usually associated with alcohol, as "any transitory perturbation of the mental faculties procured voluntarily."[69] Two years later, a guide to military jurisprudence outlined the difference between civil and military law on this point. "In the common code it is required always that the agent, that is, the person who commits the infraction, do so voluntarily; in the code that we study here it is not always necessary. So for example, a man in a state of complete drunkenness or whose brain is affected by having smoked marihuana (*Cannabis indica*), if he kills another, even if he doesn't know what he's doing, he is punished."[70]

Finally, in the summer of 1894, the Secretariat of War sent a letter to the federal sanitary council in hopes of encouraging a crackdown on the sale of marijuana in Mexico City's markets. "The vice of marihuana smoking spreads among the troops in an alarming way, despite the determination with which the authorities seek to prevent [*persigue*] the introduction of that substance to the barracks, but seeing that it is so easy to hide it and its acquisition does not present any difficulty at all, as it is sold freely in the markets, it becomes almost impossible to extirpate a harm of such transcendence, if the appropriate authority does not pursue a radical solution."[71] The letter inspired a visit to the city's markets by officials from the sanitary council who found that, indeed, marijuana was freely available.[72] In the meantime, the military continued to punish violators of its own rules, jailing soldiers for a month at a time for introducing marijuana to the barracks, a problem that was counted among the typical *malas costumbres* of the troops.[73] But the sale in the markets and the drug's use by soldiers would remain a perennial problem.[74] In 1907, one authority even lamented that efforts to stamp out yellow fever in the barracks by covering up the windows (to keep mosquitoes out) were undermined when soldiers removed those covers in order to smuggle marijuana into the institution.[75]

A likely explanation for the drug's initial popularity in these institutions was that it was more easily smuggled than alcohol. Furthermore, unlike alcohol, which stayed on one's breath long after it had been ingested, the smell of marijuana tended to drift away rapidly and thus carried less risk of detection.[76] We might also speculate that only in environments such as these would a substance with such a sinister reputation be imbibed. Perhaps a feedback loop began to emerge between the drug's menacing reputation, which would make it more or less anathema to all but society's most marginal elements, and its subsequent association with those elements, which then reinforced its sinister reputation. Reports sometimes emphasized that inmates began using the drug only once exposed to the prison or barracks, not beforehand. In this way, it appears to fit in with homosexuality, which, while certainly engaged in outside of prison, could be flaunted within it.[77]

Prisons and soldiers' barracks were thus understood in remarkably similar ways. They were filthy, unhygienic, and unjust centers of vice that housed the most marginal elements of Mexican society. There was also significant crossover between these environments as soldiers regularly served as guards in the prisons and introduced marijuana to those institutions.[78] Finally, the discourses resonated deeply with the idea of degeneration and in the process reinforced marijuana's link to that theory and all that came with it.

That process transpired most vividly in writing about Mexico City's Belén Jail (formerly La Acordada).[79] During the Porfiriato, Belén's unhygienic conditions and corruption were a regular theme of the oppositionist press, which often based its assessments on personal experience, its writers routinely being jailed under the unofficial censorship codes of the period.[80] For these writers, the conditions within Belén served as a useful allegory for the perceived injustice and cruelty of the Díaz regime as a whole. For example, in the spring of 1893, *El Diario del Hogar* published a series of articles on the fate of the so-called political prisoners (that is, members of the press imprisoned for their writing), which, not coincidentally, produced a spate of references to marijuana.[81] But for our purposes, the work of Heriberto Frías proves the most valuable example of this genre in part because it was uniquely informed by the author's firsthand experience not only with these institutions but also with drugs, the military, and the standard corruptions of the Porfiriato.

Frías had gained fame when he wrote a candid account of the Tomochic Rebellion, an uprising in the state of Chihuahua that was eventually crushed with great prejudice by the federal army. Frías had actually been a member of those federal forces and had thus witnessed the episode firsthand. But Tomochic was only the most noteworthy highlight of Frias's generally remarkable life story. Born in 1870 to a solidly middle-class family in Querétaro, Frías nonetheless spent much of his childhood in Mexico City, where he had been enrolled by his father in the prestigious National Preparatory School. After his father's sudden death left the family penniless, Heriberto was forced to sell newspapers and magazines on the streets of the capital to make ends meet. There he was introduced to a rougher side of life. Caught stealing five pesos from his employer, he was eventually sentenced to eight months in Belén. There he found a niche by writing letters and verse for prisoners and prison administrators. But that experience also familiarized him with gambling and the use of marijuana, activities of which he may have even partaken himself.[82]

Once out of jail, a friend of his father's secured him a place as a student at the National Military Academy. In January 1889, he officially joined the army, where he frequently found trouble due to his drunkenness. That vice led to stints in both the military prison of Santiago de Tlaltelolco and, once again, Belén. He eventually participated in the incident at Tomochic. The barbarity of that episode disillusioned Frías and helped to inspire another alcoholic binge, for which he was "scorned even by the soldiers of the garrison." Angered by the official version of the military events, he wrote his own eyewitness account and sent it to the oppositionist paper *El Demócrata* in Mexico City, which ran the story in several installments during 1893. Though published anonymously, it was not long before the government found out who was responsible and Frías was briefly condemned to death, a sentence that was later changed to a court-martial.

Discharged from military service, he returned to Mexico City in 1894 looking for work in the newspaper business, eventually finding a job at *El Demócrata* where he easily fit in with the bohemian lifestyle of the writers there, who, it seemed, were constantly drinking and smoking (tobacco).[83] *El Demócrata* had made a name for itself with withering critiques of the status quo in Mexico. A series of these articles in early 1895 earned Frías another stint in Belén, from where he penned thirteen new articles on the conditions within the prison.[84] Thus, in Frías we have a rare case indeed: a commentator on marijuana and its effects who was both familiar with the drug, possibly as a user, and who had spent significant time in prisons and soldiers' barracks.[85]

Frías's account from Belén emphasized the already well-established critiques of prison life, from the snail's pace of the legal process to the bloody brawls, epidemics, inedible food, pederasty, homosexuality, corruption, and common use of alcohol and marijuana.[86] As was typical, marijuana was portrayed as only one of a number of factors that contributed to the daily horrors of life in Belén, part of a tableau of degenerating elements that led to the emergence of more primitive forms of life inside the prison walls. An example of this was a type of prisoner that Frías called El Nahual. Appropriately, the title *nahual* (or *nagual*) traditionally referred to a kind of indigenous priest known for metamorphosing into various animal forms, wreaking havoc, and transforming back again into a human state, with the scars of the metamorphosis still evident. The *nahual* had first been cited in post-conquest sources by Bernardino de Sahagún, who described him as being especially malevolent.[87] Frías described El Nahual as "the most abject of thieves," a kind of filthy and disgusting hyper-kleptomaniac who brought together "all that is deformed and monstrous in Belén jail," a street urchin despised by all the inmates, before whom "even the prisoners experience a chill as if they were seeing a hairy tarantula." Of all the frightening and filthy characters in Belén, El Nahual stood alone in his wretchedness: "hunched over his bony frame; dragging indolently his legs dressed in shreds of greasy, gray underwear; on his back a red shirt lacking the buttons necessary to hide his pitiful breast; and on his bald head a piece of a felt hat casting a shadow over a sallow face of lively eyes, beardless and snub-nosed." El Nahual was "a beggar, except without the anxiety and pain of hunger; he is a thief except without any purpose; he is a murderer, but without passion or ambition of riches; and if he is given to all of the vices imaginable and commits every kind of betrayal, it is only because these acts are depraved and therefore serve as adornments in his descent into greater degrees of wretchedness. They are the luxuries of a total perversity." In his filth and rags, he "sniffs around like a skinny dog, his body annihilated by marijuana and other vices."[88]

Marijuana played a similar complementary role in the story of Miguel Guttman, a poet and well-known resident of the prison. From the beginning, Frías emphasized that Guttman was legitimately demented. "One of those mad martyrs but without resignation, disposed by virtue of the dull work of their accumulated bitterness, year after year, to return to those who they believe have been their persecutors and hangmen, all the harm that they imagine they have done to them. Oh cheerless, terrible, sinister madmen who write verses by wetting their burins in their own blood!" Again echoing the degeneration discourse, Frías asks rhetorically what could have caused such madness, answering that it had been an accumulation of factors beginning with heredity, followed by heartbreak and the experience of jail, and, as these elements gradually drove Guttman deeper into sadness, "he turns to that sad intoxication to which all of the desperate of prison turn, to marijuana." It is the marijuana that makes him feel happy but also that drives him deeper into madness. "The smoke of the cigarette inhaled with an anxious thirst bathes the cells of his brain, making them vibrate madly, enervating his sensitivity, killing his memories, and submerging him in hazy Oriental ecstasies that sweetly prostrate him, transforming his solitary confinement [bartolina]. The dementia progresses." He escaped from Belén briefly but soon wound up back in jail, gradually accumulating more elements of madness in the experience of betrayals, rebellions, stabbings, tears, and more marijuana, that "fateful intoxication that accentuates his sinister dementia of hate for the entire world."[89]

Matching its somewhat limited role in the press of this period, marijuana, for Frías, was only one of many lamentable factors within the prison walls, but one that clearly accentuated the overall wickedness of that institution. This fit the larger object of El Demócrata's efforts to highlight Belén as a landmark of the injustices of the current regime. It also fit the well-established prison discourse that ran through both the academic and literary portrayals of prison life prior to the 1890s. The two other major anecdotes relating to marijuana in Frías's account provide similar lessons. In one, a young boy is "seduced" by several others, perhaps given marijuana to make him unconscious, and then raped. In another case, two of the toughest prisoners in the jail, the inseparable best friends Juan and Romualdo, meet to say goodbye, for Juan has been granted an early release. The two share a friend and lover in a prostitute on the outside named Chole, and Juan asks Romualdo, who is smoking a marijuana cigarette, if he has any messages for her. He also tells his friend to cut down on the marijuana habit or it will become a vice. Romualdo, taking the cigarette from his mouth and throwing it to the ground, replies: "You know what you can say to Chole? Here . . ." and he stabs his friend to death. Romualdo is then himself killed by a group of "presidents."[90]

Belén continued to be a critical flashpoint for conflict between the oppositionist press and the Díaz regime throughout the Porfiriato.[91] One of the best examples of this genre was probably the last, as it appeared in the pages of *El Diario del Hogar* just as the Díaz regime was beginning to crumble. The paper's editor, Filomeno Mata, had drawn the ire of the authorities in December 1909 for warning all members of the oppositionist press that criticism might land them in jail. Ironically, the warning led to the shutting down of his paper and the jailing of Mata's son and then of the publisher himself. The paper remained closed for six months while Mata languished in Belén. After his release, Mata succeeded in publishing a string of long, powerful articles that chronicled the conditions at the prison. The classic elements were listed: the corruption of guards, the months spent by prisoners simply awaiting trial, the filth, the pederasty, the violence, and, of course, the marijuana, which entered the prison through the corruption of the guards and led to frequent assaults within the institution. With respect to the drug, the series placed the blame squarely on living conditions within the institution, drawing testimony from the inmates themselves. "It is not the habit of maddening oneself nor a special delight in obtaining in one's sleep agreeable nightmares that which obliges them to use marijuana, rather the infinite number of bedbugs that fall from the ceiling, and that, with the smoke from the marijuana, either die or move away. This means nothing less than if they disinfected the cell blocks [*galeras*] every day, if it was possible to do so sufficiently to undermine the plague of bedbugs, perhaps in that manner many of those who now use that foul weed to defend themselves from the parasites would stop using." The piece also emphasized that it was no good to prohibit the introduction of the weed into the building, "because the jail regulations, like all of the laws, are evaded daily, and ten cents are sufficient to obtain within Belén jail a cigarette capable of driving three individuals mad."[92]

The paper reprinted the first of these articles, claiming that a flood of new subscription requests had poured in with its original publication, and the theme was continued right through the fall and into the initial uprising that would eventually spiral into the Mexican Revolution. Here again the conditions within Belén served as a metaphor for the corruption of the present regime and a rhetorical device in support of the growing "no-reelection" campaign. As Mata put it in his inaugural piece of the series: "Given the administrative corruption of political fiefdoms [cacicasgos], the only means of combating it is to prohibit reelection and in that manner the citizens will not be victims of arbitrary authority."[93]

The oppositionist press thus used marijuana as a potent symbol of all that was wrong with prisons, which themselves had come to represent all that was wrong with the Díaz regime. Those associations would remain important to the victorious factions of the revolution who would consistently seek to position themselves in opposition to Díaz and his policies. As much was evidenced at the Constituent Congress of 1916–17, where the Jaliscan delegate Federico Ibarra praised the foundational work done by Mata and El Diario del Hogar while unleashing a diatribe against the degeneration of the Mexican race through alcoholism, gambling, and prostitution, a process that he claimed had been carried out intentionally by the Porfirian authorities to maintain their power in perpetuity.[94]

■ But other factors also contributed to marijuana's deep resonance with the idea of degeneration. Chief among these was the plant's continued association with Indian Mexico, indigenous drugs, and, most important, the herbolarias who sold them. In sum, the belief that marijuana was a typical drug of ancient, "Indian" Mexico only augmented its potential for sparking the frightening consequences of degeneration.

Though not indigenous to Mexico, marijuana had been integrated into enough aspects of "Indian" life to make that misconception possible. In 1874, for example, Hubert Howe Bancroft published a book on "wild tribes" among Pacific coast Indians in North America. There, while discussing various "Chichimec" groups in northern Mexico, Bancroft described the process by which one family gained the permission of another for their respective children to marry:

When a young man desires to marry, his parents make a visit to those of the intended bride, and leave with them a bouquet of flowers bound with red wool; the bride's parents then send round to the houses of their friends a bunch of mariguana, a narcotic herb, which signifies that all are to meet together at the bride's father's on the next night. The meeting is inaugurated by smoking; then they chew mariguana, during which time all preliminaries of the marriage are settled. The following day the resolutions of the conclave are made known to the young man and woman, and if the decision is favorable, the latter sends her husband a few presents, and from that time the parties consider themselves married, and the friends give themselves up to feasting and dancing.[95]

As noted already, Carl Lumholtz also observed the ritual use of marijuana along Mexico's Pacific coast during the 1890s. "The Tepecanos still keep up their feasts, but celebrate them privately, as the 'neighbors' ridicule their customs. . . . The sacred cactus hikuli (peyote) is used by them and called by this name. As recently as three years ago the Tepecanos themselves went for the plants, but now they buy them from the Huichols. A form of common hemp called *mariguana* or *rosa maria* (*Cannabis sativa*) sometimes takes the place of hikuli. The leaves of this injurious narcotic are smoked throughout Mexico, but mostly by criminals and the depraved."[96] Lumholtz also noted the general use of marijuana among the "superstitions" of Mexico's western Bajío region. These practices, which Lumholtz described as "a mixture of Spanish and Indian notions," included the following, which he learned of in Tequila, Jalisco:

It does not require especial skill to bewitch a person. The harm can be done in most any way. Nor is it difficult to cure, because the saliva applied to the patient's armpit is a sure cure. The only difficulty is in settling matters with the party who did the bewitching. The healer comes either on Thursday or Friday or Tuesday, because on other days he does not hear the sorcerers and witches. He arrives at eight o'clock, just about the time when the owls begin to fly about. He may find the witch on the first night and make arrangements with her at once; or he may have to work hard hunting her most of the night, or even every night for a month or longer. With some people six months are required for a restoration. The healer places the ill man's sandals soles up, reverses his shirt and drawers, and recites the credo backward in order that the owl may come down for him to catch her. Then he gathers a great heap of old rags, to which he adds some mariguana, a plant which many persons carry with them in their girdles as a protection against sorcery. When the pile is ready he sets fire to it and the house is filled with smoke. All the inmates have to leave it, except the ill one, who no longer knows whether he is ill or well. The fee for such a cure is, in Tequila, ten dollars, and the patient has also to provide the material to produce the smoke. Even if he does not recover, he has always given the healer something for his trouble, as a rule, three or five dollars.[97]

Such practices, though rarely reported in published sources, surely helped to imbue marijuana generally with a certain indigeneity. But for more casual observers, probably the most important sign of marijuana's indigenous identity was not the actual ritual use of cannabis by Indians but the presence of marijuana in the wares of the country's *herbolarias*. As José Antonio de Alzate discovered (see chapter 2), *herbolarias* had been distributing cannabis in Mexico since at least the eighteenth century, and though they were not always Indian, they were deeply associated with Indian Mexico. Since the conquest, as noted earlier, Spanish observers had been astounded by the remarkable botanical knowledge of Mexico's Indians, and the possession of such knowledge quickly became a quintessential marker of indigeneity in Mexico. Alzate had described *herbolarias* as "Indian women in the market who sell herbs and other little medicinal things and who play the role of the druggists of Europe."[98] Harking back to the conflicts over medicinal practice and religion in the early colonial period, *herbolarias* were also often tied to witchcraft. In the nineteenth century, their activities came into conflict with the professionalizing fields of medicine and pharmacy, a situation that made their role in society that much more controversial.

Perhaps the best representation of the nineteenth-century discourse on *herbolarias* appears in Manuel Payno's novel *Los bandidos del Río Frío*. Payno's *costumbrista* masterpiece was originally written in serial form between 1889 and 1891 and thus takes the standard twists and turns of such works, with many short stories tied together throughout the book.[99] The story of interest to us here begins on a small family farm outside of Mexico City. The lady of the house, Doña Pascuala, is the daughter of a Spanish priest (prior to taking his vows) and a woman who died shortly after childbirth. The husband is a full-blooded Indian, a relative of the great Aztec emperor Moctezuma II, "but with his flashes of thought and wisdom" he helped justify the belief that "they were almost people of reason."[100] Doña Pascuala is at the center of a medical mystery that has confounded all of central Mexico: she is pregnant but at nine months could not give birth, nor at ten, nor at eleven or twelve months. By the time she reaches the thirteenth month of pregnancy, the baby has given no signs of ill health, but it appears that Doña Pascuala might herself burst. The newspapers have even begun reporting the story. All of this eventually helps to bring Mexico City's most famous physician to the farm, a certain Dr. Cordoniú. The doctor's Catalan name neatly identifies him as a practitioner of modern, European medicine. But before long, Cordoniú too is despondent at his inability to either explain or cure Pascuala's condition. He eventually takes the case to the National School of Medicine, where the faculty is also left baffled. In the face of his shameful inability to deal with the case, Cordoniú eventually retires to his home, instructing his servant to send away anyone who might call regarding Pascuala's case. She is on her own.

Then her Indian husband, Don Espiridión, intervenes, declaring that he never trusted Cordoniú to resolve anything: "That's not what I call a cure . . . and I've never had faith in doctors. We don't have any choice but to turn to the witches. No matter how much everyone says that there are no witches, I believe that there are and the facts prove that there are. Every day we see them; and above all only they know how to cure the illness that you have." The witches in question are a pair of *herbolarias* whose life story Payno describes in detail. The two had emerged from a little neighborhood on the outskirts of Mexico City where the houses were made of mud and looked more like refuges for animals than humans. "It never ceases to be surprising that such a poor and degraded population lives on the banks of this great capital. It is made up absolutely of those who were called *macehuelas* since the days of the Conquest, that is, those who worked the land; they weren't exactly slaves, but it was the most abject class of the Aztecs, that, as the most numerous, has survived now so many years and conserved its poverty, its ignorance, its superstition and its attachment to its customs; their proximity to the capital has not served either to change their habits or their situation, nor to provide them any amenities." These were the poorest of the Indians, people who made a living selling mosquitoes gathered from the nearby waters, people who had never fully learned the Catholic faith or to read and write or hardly to speak Spanish and who had barely conserved any of their ancient traditions, either. Their ways were a strange mixture of Indian and Spanish traditions. From here the *herbolarias* had emerged and for whatever reason had begun gathering and studying the effects of medicinal plants, first by experimenting on dogs and then eventually on people. They would travel around the region gathering their wares, and they gradually developed a reputation for efficacy. Business boomed, and soon they had been able to move into a more comfortable home where they were protected from the elements. "It was Asiatic luxury, or better said, Aztec. The middle-class families prior to the Conquest did not live any better." Their curing methods involved a mixture of empirical knowledge and recourse to the supernatural. The position of the moon or a prayer to the Virgin of Guadalupe might be the key to a cure. But their methods were effective, and they proved stiff competition for the city's physicians. They soon also gained a reputation as witches.

Eventually, Don Espiridión calls on them to examine his wife. This they do, asking her innumerable questions, some of them quite bizarre and difficult to answer, while examining her physically, often inspecting "the parts of the body furthest from the place where the problem should have been located." They soon come up with a number of remedies that include the slaughter of a rooster at midnight, the blood of a lizard, the lighting of candles in honor of the Virgin of Guadalupe, and of course various herbs. None of these remedies have any positive effect. They therefore decide that the problem can be solved only through direct consultation with the Virgin of Guadalupe. "Don Espiridión knew nothing of this. His wife hid it from him fearing that he would tell the people of Tlalnepantla and they would make fun, for among the functionaries there were now Masons who believed only in the Great Architect of Nature and had advanced to the point of denying the apparition of the Virgin."

Here we see the crucial distinction between the supposedly modern, rational world of Europeans and the premodern world of Indians in which the *herbolarias* occupied their traditional space. Just as the Spanish had been amazed by the botanical expertise of Indians despite their supposedly primitive condition and belief systems, modern Mexicans of the nineteenth century were drawn to the *herbolarias* for their know-how but feared them for their antiquated beliefs. But now those antiquated beliefs involved an old-fashioned syncretic Catholicism. As Payno explained, this in fact was the most dangerous element of all.

The Virgin of Guadalupe is of course Mexico's syncretic religious symbol par excellence. The Virgin had supposedly appeared before an Indian named Juan Diego in the sixteenth century, precisely at the spot where the goddess Tonantzin had been worshiped. According to Payno, this was where,

in front of the goddess who was carved out of a great piece of granite, they had many ceremonies and dances, and on a certain day of the year, they ended the religious festivals with the sacrifice of 100 children from one month to two years old, who had their throats cut on one of the sacrificial stones, with obsidian and flint knives. The goddess would not be content without the tribute of this innocent blood and she threatened those who resisted taking their children with rains, hail, thunder, and a thousand calamities. The mothers, despite their grievous sobs, that some historians say were heard all the way to Texcoco, rushed to take their children and they turned them over to the savage priests of the goddess.

The cult of the Virgin of Guadalupe had taken the place of this bloodbath, but for people like the *herbolarias* described by Payno, those descended from the poorest of the Aztecs, those raised in neighborhoods fit only for wild animals, there was sometimes some confusion. The older of the two here, in fact, did not distinguish between Guadalupe and Tonantzin and often referred to "Madre mía, Santa María de Guadalupe Tonantzin." Thus, not surprisingly, after consulting with the Virgin, she became convinced that the only way to save Doña Pascuala was to sacrifice another child to the goddess. Only then would Pascuala's baby be born safely. Pascuala initially objected to this plan but, eventually, terribly desperate as she was, agreed to allow the *herbolarias* to seek one out on December 12, the Feast of the Virgin of Guadalupe. According to the *herbolarias*, a lost child would appear only if it were truly the Virgin's will. Pascuala was convinced. And, indeed, on that day, a lost child appeared, was captured by the older of the *herbolarias*, and was thrown into a field, where it was sure to be devoured by wild dogs. That night, miraculously, Pascuala's baby boy was born healthy and strong.[101]

This was the essence of the *herbolaria* in nineteenth-century Mexico, just as it had been at the start of the colonial era. In the 1850s, a certain Dr. Villa described the medicines and superstitions of Indians in remarkably similar terms, then poignantly disparaged such healers as "the men of mariguana." In an 1850s geography, Emilio Pineda painted a similar picture of Indian medicine and witchcraft:

The Indians [of Chiapas] differ very little from those of the rest of the Republic. . . . There are among them certain people learned in their knowledge of medicinal and poisonous plants, which they maintain with a profound secrecy, barely transmissible from parents to children, and they practice with mysterious and shady tools. They cure dropsy by various means, gangrene, migraines, gout, and many other ailments incurable for some physicians. They have with respect to many plants and animals the same concern as the ancient Mexicans, which perhaps was inherited from the Greeks, transmitted to us by Dioscorides; but they do not resemble those who they ironically call *godfathers* in the Department of Veracruz, for these, in addition to . . . fomenting the worry and superstition of those people, are infamy, fraud, and deceit all in one. The rest of the people view these sages with a respect mixed with fear and distrust: they believe that they are the cause of plagues and domestic calamities; and in secret they give them the insulting name *witches*.[102]

Since the colonial period, botanical investigators had nonetheless relied on *herbolarias* for their knowledge. For his *Teatro Mexicano*, Fray Agustín de Vetancurt had gathered together *herbolarias* to learn what he could from them about Mexico's medicinal plants.[103] But, not surprisingly, this knowledge was also disparaged. Guillermo Prieto, that other great *costumbrista* writer of the nineteenth century, described how Manuel Muñoz, the son of one of the founders of the National School of Medicine, had in the 1830s demonstrated a profound interest in the customs of ordinary Mexicans, including their medicinal practice—this "despite" his modern medical title as a surgeon. But because of the disdain with which the "grand physicians" of the nineteenth century approached folk medical practice, Muñoz published far less on the subject than he otherwise might have.[104]

In fact, one of the first tasks undertaken in the 1840s by Mexico's newly inaugurated sanitary council was the formation of a commission to investigate the role of *herbolarias* in the distribution of medicines in Mexico. On February 1, 1843, that group presented its findings. The researchers reported that "in these places there have existed since time immemorial small stands [*tiendas*] commonly known as *herbolarias* in which without any precautions are sold to everyone whatever they want . . . [such as] purging nut [*Jatropha curcas*], hemlock and many other substances which have active properties [*efectos enérgicos*]."[105] The sanitary council's investigative team worried that these medicine dealers, when faced by requests from customers for substances that they did not have on hand, often substituted for the desired plants with others that, "while sometimes appearing similar on the outside, had exactly opposite effects once employed [by the patient]."[106] The group considered prohibiting these establishments under the council's mandate to prevent the distribution of medicines by anyone but licensed pharmacists. However, taking into account that *herbolarias* had been practicing their trade in Mexico without interruption "since time immemorial" and that they performed a useful service by providing the community with freshly gathered materials for medical practice, the committee chose instead to suggest a set of oversight mechanisms to regulate this trade. These included the requirement that *herbolarias* register and receive a license from the municipal government. On receiving said license, the registrants would be given a list of plants whose sale was permitted by the council. Only licensed *herbolarias* would be permitted to sell the officially sanctioned substances, and the trade would be monitored by a newly formed commission charged with visiting the operations of the registrants.[107]

Such remained the policy of the sanitary council for decades. An 1883 council regulation governing the distribution of dangerous medicines noted that it was also imperative to "take note of the sale of every type of plant and other medicinal product, many of which are toxic or abortive, and which the merchants who dedicate themselves to this business, known commonly as '*Herbolarias*,' sell without any restriction whatsoever." But rather than ban the activities, the council instead created a "list of products that *herbolarias* can only sell to pharmacists." That list included *cabalongas* (*Thevetia peruviana*), *codos de fraile* (*Thevetia yccotli*), cicuta (hemlock), *cintul* (*Veratrum frigidum*), *cebolleja* (*Veratrum officinale*), *beleño* (henbane or *Hyoscyamus niger*), belladonna (*Atropa belladonna*), toloache (jimsonweed), *yerba de la puebla* (*Senecio canicida*), *yerba mora* or *Solanum nigrum* (black nightshade), *zoapatle* (*Montanoa tormentosa*), and marijuana.[108]

*Herbolarias* would continue to be associated with marijuana over the coming years, helping to maintain the drug's folkloric status and indigeneity by association. In September 1894, for example, *El Diario del Hogar* lamented that marijuana was sold at the public markets by the *herbolarias* to anyone who wanted it. In 1903, the *New York Times* reported on the link in an article with the conspicuous title "Doctors of Ancient Mexico," while in the same year *El Imparcial* noted the following: "But more common than the sorcerer is the witch that during certain hours of the day sells in the markets herbs to cure 'the air,' others against indigestion, others in order to bewitch or unbewitch, and others to give good fortune, others for criminal uses, and in reality if they produce one effect it is madness, like marijuana, or to kill the unfortunate women who believe in their effects, like *zoapatle*, which brings to the doors of the maternity hospital not a few dying women."[109] Similarly, shortly after the sensational 1908 incident that began this chapter, the poet José Juan Tablada wrote a remarkable piece on the "black masses" of marijuana, where he described a smoking parlor where new users were introduced to the drug by *herbolarias*. "Various ancient *herbolarias*, veritable witches of Goya, supply the poison; an old initiate, with black face, bloodshot eyes, and grimacing like a Japanese mask runs the ritual and directs the beginners."[110]

Tablada again illustrates how the link between marijuana and *herbolarias* served to reinforce the reputation of both as being quasi-Oriental in nature. Tablada in fact was part of a larger intellectual movement that emphasized parallels between Mexico and the Orient. As Mauricio Tenorio-Trillo puts it, "In truth, *Japonisme* and Mexican exoticism had been simultaneously observed since the 1876 World's Fair in Philadelphia. By then, the links that organizers or visitors found between the Orient and Mexico were well established as a cognitive sphere. Many Mexicans and foreigners had found Japanese, Chinese, or Hindu connections in native Mexican pottery, architecture and languages. World Orientalism knew no real boundaries within the realm of the exotic."[111] In 1913, Rubén Darío, another Latin American poet with similar Orientalist proclivities, wrote a similar if somewhat less sensational piece in the Buenos Aires daily *La Nación*. The article dealt with drugs in general but also specifically cited marijuana intoxication in Mexico, comparing it directly to the running amok of the Javanese after their use of opium.[112] Meanwhile, the Colombian poet Porfirio Barba Jacob took up residency in Mexico City and there enjoyed "Indian and Chinese fantasies, together with marihuana and Gibran poems."[113]

■ In 1910, Federico Gamboa completed his novel *La llaga*, or "The Ulcer," a work that provides the most poignant literary representation of the various themes running through this chapter.[114] Gamboa was deeply influenced by the naturalism of the French novelist Emile Zola. Naturalism, which sought to portray the dark side of society (poverty, crime, vice, and the like) with the aid of scientific data, was particularly well suited to the intellectual climate of Mexico at the time. Typically, naturalist novels portrayed characters whose lives were undermined by social forces over which they had little control.[115] But Zola was also perhaps France's greatest literary purveyor of notions of degeneration, incorporating both the more "internal" and protean visions of this malady (à la Morel) and the characteristically Lombrosian belief in degenerated physical features and atavisms that signaled the inherent criminality of certain individuals.[116] Gamboa saw himself as the "Mexican Zola,"[117] and the influence is clear in *La llaga*.

Set within the notorious military prison of San Juan de Ulúa in Veracruz, Gamboa's novel uses that filthy and corrupt environment as a metaphor for the underside of the "progress" that had come to define the Porfiriato.[118] Early in the novel, a young publisher of an opposition newspaper named Gregorio Báez is brought to the prison to serve an indefinite sentence for having become too critical of his state's powerful governor. That indiscretion had landed Báez in a frightening environment surrounded by men who were, as an older inmate explained it, "beasts, but . . . while they don't attack us, they are inoffensive beasts . . . to a point." As in Julio Guerrero's work, these "beasts" were generally safe to deal with, but there was a frightening uncertainty involved, typified by the understanding that this safety only applied "to a point." These were degenerated men who, "for ethnic misfortune, ignorance, cerebral inferiority, bad moral and physical inheritances," were nevertheless happy in that environment. "How horrible! . . . not only do they have their few primitive necessities covered, but actually true amusement: they reminisce, gamble, drink, smoke . . . even 'marihuana' — [a friend] told him in confidence, promising him that when they came into contact with the wicked weed, '*mota*,' it would be an impressive and unique spectacle."[119]

Here we see degeneration in vivid detail, as these primitive men find happiness in the sloth of the prison:

> There were laughing mouths that, thanks to their size, simulated bloody and pustulous wounds that would have burst in that sun and with their emanations should have poisoned the air; lips so thick and coarse, that one could say they pertained to voracious and flesh-eating beasts; maxillary and cheek bones that depicted [*acusaban*] unbreakable wills of steel; eyebrows like savage jungles, that concealed sunken, lashless eyes, Chinese-like eyes, of alarming strabism, big and serene eyes like a ruminating cow, facing the sadness of the twilight, lying upon the furrows.
>
> And the skulls?
>
> Had Gregorio understood something of this, he would have believed himself truly in hell; but, ignorant and all, with astonishing certainty, he divined that in those asymmetries, protuberances, and cavities was rooted the genesis of evil, of that ancient and incurable evil, eternal and infinite evil . . . but why, Lord? . . . There in those skulls . . . undoubtedly one could decipher the origins of races and of bygone eras that, like an endless curse, are left behind by a sad heritage, degenerations and scars.

This was the essence of degeneration, the physical symbol of "the majority" who "for lack of means cannot evade the harsh implacability of ancestral stigmas and atavisms, and they pay for the errors of their parents; those for whom when things are not going too badly in their gray and anonymous lives, still engender children who are going to become delinquent and wind up in prisons and gallows."[120]

Typically, marijuana was not portrayed as a ubiquitous, everyday presence in the prison but instead as the terrifying stimulant whose introduction into that milieu brought the savagery of these men to the surface. The crucial scene reads like a fever dream. A series of impromptu lectures among the inmates on the barbarity of prison conditions is suddenly cut short by a growing murmur that refracts through the prison walls: a barely audible, almost primitive chanting of a well-known marijuana *corrido*'s "barbarous verses": "So stoned am I [*marihuano estoy*], I can't even lift my head." Wrenched from their lectures, the prisoners begin to scramble for the safety of shelter and weapons. "Wherever you can, but quickly! . . . Take these clubs, and if someone approaches you, hit them, whoever it is. Hit them hard, and hit them in the head. . . . It's marihuana!" The prisoners slip into the building's angled shadows as the "satanic ritual" approaches its climax. A dozen prisoners in a circle, each taking three long drags from the "heavy and bitter" smoke, "enough to make the strongest mind reel and undermine reason in the most impulsive and implacable of dementias," their hair beginning to stand on end, their eyes bulging out from their sockets, their mouths devouring large bites from a shared block of sugar. "Sparkling eyes from within these horrifying grimaces told of every imaginable madness and crime." Gamboa explained that it was marijuana, "the wicked weed already familiar to the Egyptians and Marco-Polo; '*la mota*' or Indian hemp that the naturalists have classified as being the same as hashish; the producer of madness [*la yerba enloquecedora*] that—in contrast to opium which depresses, and alcohol, which momentarily excites but then depresses and brings down [*anonadar*] the user—centuplicates the personality and stimulates brutal and delirious acts."[121]

As the scene continues, the dozen begin to break from their circle without disrupting their chanting: "The chief devil, with his twenty-five brothers, has come to take the whole lot of the *marihuanos*"; and then they explode out against the rest of the prisoners, attacking with makeshift weapons as the inmates scramble and fight for their lives among screams, curses, and guffaws. Behind the sounds of flesh tearing, bones splitting, and pouring blood can be heard the incessant chanting: "Through here she passed, through here she used to pass, that little *marihuanita* who consoled me." In the middle of the chaos, a particularly religious inmate known to the rest as "the Sexton" is "chased down by two of the beasts, who, inflamed by bestial lust, . . . proceeded to perpetrate their ignominy on him." Finally the prison gate opens and the soldiers burst in, the major screaming for the *marihuanos* to surrender or die. But far from surrendering, they attack, only to be repelled by a huge blast that shakes the prison. One of the men, his knee shattered by a bullet, rolls in the blood and mud, chanting, "The *marihuanita* who consoled me." And on the ground in the middle of the wreckage is found a package, with a colorful label much like any normal pack of cigarettes: "Mosquetero Factory—Cannabis Indica—medicinal cigarettes for the treatment of asthma, cough, and snoring—Regeneration, of Pachuca, E. de H."[122]

Gamboa likely meant for the label to serve either as a symbol of the commercial corruption and cynicism so associated with the underside of capitalist "progress" or as an explicit reference to the Flores Magón brothers' revolutionary newspaper of the same name, suggesting what was likely to result from their efforts on behalf of Mexico's irremediably degenerated masses.[123] In either case, the package, and the scene as a whole, neatly illustrates the dichotomies and anxieties that were at the heart of the degeneration concept and that so profoundly resonated with the discourses on marijuana, prisons, soldiers' barracks, and *herbolarias*. Degeneration served as a kind of fluid adhesive to link all of these different realms. While modernity and progress were so badly desired, there was considerable anxiety that the fundamental, almost Oriental nature of the Mexican population might undermine modern progress. Worse still, accelerating modernity might somehow unleash savage, atavistic tendencies. Of these, almost anyone might fall victim, just like the innocent passersby with a *marihuano* loose in the streets. Together these factors probably made the typical media reports of rampaging *marihuanos* eminently believable to Mexicans a century ago. Yet the question remains: did these violent, marijuana-fueled outbursts actually occur? That question is explored in the next chapter.

*Chapter 7*

## DID MARIJUANA REALLY
## CAUSE "MADNESS" AND VIOLENCE
## IN MEXICO?

Reports of men made mad by marijuana, running amok through the streets, while appearing implausible from a twenty-first-century vantage point, were, as we've seen, largely justified by the social-scientific thought of late-nineteenth- and early-twentieth-century Mexico. This raises an important question: did marijuana really produce these effects? As noted in chapter 1, in most circumstances we would consider hundreds of unchallenged reports sufficient to prove the existence of a given phenomenon. But this case is complicated by two factors: first, while marijuana remains widely used, reports of it triggering violent rampages in Mexico or anywhere else have become a thing of the past. Second, marijuana was mostly used by Mexico's most marginal social sectors, but nearly all of the extant sources were produced by a small class of literate elites whose disdain for lower-class, illiterate Mexicans was often palpable.

We've already seen that cannabis can produce psychotomimetic effects and that, given the right "set" and "setting," it is not impossible for it to have triggered violence in the past. But we cannot fully solve cannabis's psychoactive riddle without controlling for the obvious elite-bias of most of the sources considered here. Ideally, we could turn to dozens of detailed criminal case files containing testimony from marijuana users and other witnesses to determine what really happened. Unfortunately, the archives have not preserved records of this kind.[1] Instead, therefore, I will seek to overcome some of the bias in the source base by examining, as much as possible, lower-class opinion on marijuana, as well as those sources most likely to have some real insight into marijuana users and their environments. The sources demonstrate that little distinguished lower- and upper-class opinion on this weed and its effects, suggesting that, indeed, marijuana at some times probably contributed to violent episodes and "mad" behavior.

In the final years of the nineteenth century, emigrants from the Mexican countryside poured into a rapidly expanding Mexico City. Like much of the Western world, Mexicans were experiencing the anxieties, excitement, and dislocations of a globalizing modernity. New streetcars shimmered under glimmering electric light and mingled with dusty clouds raised in still-unpaved streets by bare feet, sandals, and the finest European footwear. It was not uncommon for a recent migrant to perish in the path of a streetcar, unaccustomed to the presence of fast-moving menaces made of steel. The flow of information, commerce, and migrants back and forth from the city to the provinces was replicated on a global scale with Mexico now firmly inserted in global circuits of interchange.

Downtown, in a small workshop a few blocks from the city's *zócalo*, an obscure printmaker named José Guadalupe Posada steadily churned out beautiful graphic arts for the entertainment and edification of Mexicans immersed in the modern maelstrom. His broadsheets and chapbooks amused the illiterate, many with thrilling and shocking tales of heroism, violence, and vice.[2] Those broadsheets paralleled the pages of the nation's newspapers, where crime stories elicited both lamentation and titillation, furnishing an increasingly self-aware "Mexican" people with the communal experience of rumor, scandal, and laughter.

Posada's striking imagery spoke clearly to the city's ordinary folk through familiar themes and symbols, providing solace for the uprooted in the urban din while engaging them in a dynamic cultural process. Thomas Gretton has convincingly argued that Posada's work helped to constitute urban identities by providing juxtapositions of typical characters with or against whom the consumers of the artwork could identify: "These varied sorts of people in the capital, like the elite groups from whom they differentiated themselves, were having to work out their relationships to numerous axes of cultural classification and development: to the urban/rural polarity, to ignorance and education, to wealth and poverty, to respectability and disreputability, to national and regional and ethnic identity, and to the pressures of informal imperialism."[3]

Surely Posada's recurring character Don Chepito Mariguano, or Sir Joey Pothead, rarely failed to elicit giggles on street corners throughout the teeming city. Dating to the 1890s, the character owed a debt to precursors in both Mexican literature and French printmaking. Don Chepito was the bourgeois figure enamored with all things foreign, the always ostentatious dandy continually showing off his appreciation for the latest imported fad. Such urban figures were commonly mocked from the print house where Posada worked

FIGURE 7.1. "Don Chepito with a bicycle." (Reprinted in Roberto Berdecio and Stanley Appelbaum, eds., *Posada's Popular Mexican Prints* [New York: Dover, 1972], 92)

and were often contrasted unfavorably with more honorable, "traditional" Mexicans.[4] Posada continually juxtaposed Don Chepito, dressed in the high collar and jacket of the bourgeoisie, with more traditionally attired men and women. Since he was always overzealous in his desire to display his appreciation of foreign imports like bicycles and boxing matches, mishaps never failed to befall the character and prove the error of his ways (Figures 7.1 and 7.2).[5]

By laughing at Don Chepito, Mexico City's ordinary folk could celebrate and to some extent advertise their own honor and intelligence. Marijuana was thus far more than a scientifically discernible element to be measured, judged, and regulated by medical and judicial experts; it was a powerful symbol utilized in a dynamic cultural environment to make meaning, to construct identity, and to establish difference in the practice of everyday life. Though it is notoriously difficult to discern the opinions of illiterate Mexicans from this period, by analyzing this and other aspects of marijuana's cultural history in Mexico, we should be able to get some sense of how ordinary folk viewed this drug.

Among historians there has been much charged debate over the meaning of "cultural history" and how we might study it. I find most useful a definition of culture along the lines proposed by William Sewell Jr., in which "culture"

FIGURE 7.2. "Don Chepito witnessing a boxing match between a black man and a white man." (Reprinted in Roberto Berdecio and Stanley Appelbaum, eds., *Posada's Popular Mexican Prints* [New York: Dover, 1972], 15)

means a semiotic system of oppositions utilized in the practice of everyday life to make meaning. Sewell argues that symbols have meanings to all members of a culture but that those meanings are only "thinly coherent." Thus, while members of a society might not understand a given symbol in identical terms, they will understand it in a similar enough way so that it can be used to convey any number of desired messages. Because the coherence is only "thin," the meaning of a symbol is therefore malleable and gradually altered by its use in practice.[6]

With this understanding of culture, an analysis of Posada—the "printmaker to the Mexican people" and the adopted (postmortem) godfather of Mexico's revolutionary artistic renaissance—and his work becomes especially interesting.[7] Between 1888 and 1913, Posada produced thousands of popular broadsheets in Mexico City, which mobile street vendors sold for a penny. It is believed that Posada tried to produce images that would successfully sell and thus was hardly averse to the same sensationalism that characterized the Mexican press of the period.[8] Furthermore, his idiom, lithography, required allusion to already familiar attitudes and ideas in order to be effective. Thus, his extraordinary work almost certainly reflected popular attitudes toward particular subjects, even if his own production also reinforced these ideas and perhaps even helped to constitute them. With respect to crime, the emphasis of Posada's work certainly suggests a desire to sell through scandal, as he overwhelmingly treated more sensational episodes. Representations of murders, banditry, and boundary-crossing crimes by women far outnumbered those of simple fighting, thievery, or public drunkenness.[9]

Don Chepito Mariguano was one of Posada's best-known characters. Resembling José Joaquín Fernández de Lizardi's Don Catrín de la Fachenda, Don Chepito was a classic example of the urban social climbers who were often mocked by the print house of Vanegas Arroyo where Posada worked. As Posada scholar Patrick Frank writes, "The evidence of the broadsheets suggests that [these bourgeois characters] were regarded as a complete mystery by the members of the urban proletariat. Their ways and fashions are presented in uniformly ridiculous ways, and they are never made to look good or effective. More specifically, at various times they are shown to be socially clumsy or inferior to persons whose culture was more rooted in 'traditional' Mexico."[10] Bulging eyes constituted Don Chepito's signature physical characteristic and indicated that he was always under the influence of marijuana, or perhaps merely demented permanently by its abuse. Because the drug was a decidedly "low-class" substance associated overwhelmingly with Mexico's filthy, violent, and unhygienic prisons and soldiers' barracks, it provided an ironic contrast with Don Chepito's own puffed-up self-image. In these cartoons, the joke was always partially delivered through such ironic details. In some images, for example, Posada provided the character with the additional surnames "Charrasca y Cascarrabias," whose length suggested aristocratic origins but whose meaning evoked a short-fused man given to knife fights. Of course, the latter was precisely the kind of person who was associated with marijuana in the Porfirian press.[11] All of this implies that among Posada's lower-class, mostly illiterate audience, marijuana use was also seen as a "low-class" practice and something to be eschewed.

The character also suggests that the putative link between marijuana and madness was not merely a stereotype of the literate classes. The bulging eyes utilized to indicate Don Chepito's status as a *marihuano* were actually not physiologically accurate portrayals of marijuana intoxication. In reality, marijuana produces photophobia in users. That is, users become sensitive to light and tend to squint while under the influence of the drug.[12] On the other hand, bulging eyes *are* a classic stereotype of madness.[13] At the same time, it's clear that this particular *marihuano* was far from the violent, rampaging menace suggested by most of the newspaper sources. Indeed, Don Chepito's behavior is consistently portrayed as weird but relatively harmless: his appreciation of

FIGURE 7.3. "Don Chepito addressing people in the street from a cart." (Reprinted in Roberto Berdecio and Stanley Appelbaum, eds., *Posada's Popular Mexican Prints* [New York: Dover, 1972], 93)

strange, foreign practices like bicycle riding or boxing matches is often met with befuddled looks by the more traditional Mexicans observing in the background; his effort, for example, to rally the people with apparently unusual or nonsensical ideas is met with a rain of derision from a crowd; and his lack of etiquette when attempting to court a married woman earns him a significant but nonlethal beating (Figures 7.3 and 7.4).[14]

Posada appears to have been playing on popular prejudice against marijuana users, a prejudice that seems to have revolved around the drug's association with "madness." Though in the surviving examples, this was not the violent madness of the Porfirian press, Don Chepito's additional surnames do suggest the knife-wielding, short-fused man who was routinely associated with marijuana violence. All of this indicates that for the ordinary folk who consumed Posada's lithographs, the stereotyped effects of marijuana were not significantly different from those typically reported in the newspapers.

This interpretation is supported by the one other marijuana reference I have found in Posada's work. That broadsheet, produced in 1910, describes a typical marijuana incident: a prisoner in Belén who had smoked marijuana

FIGURE 7.4. "Don Chepito: For loving a married woman." (Reprinted in Roberto Berdecio and Stanley Appelbaum, eds., *Posada's Popular Mexican Prints* [New York: Dover, 1972], 88)

began suffering a "terrible nervous excitation" and then went "totally crazy," rampaged through the prison with a knife, and ultimately stabbed one inmate to death while wounding two others (Figure 7.5). Just like the typical coverage of such incidents in the newspapers, the broadsheet placed the blame for the violence squarely on marijuana and its maddening effects. In fact, in this case it was the oppositionist press that offered a more nuanced view of the incident. Without minimizing the dangers of marijuana, *El Diario del Hogar* nonetheless aimed its criticism more at the corruption and decay of the prison that allowed the marijuana to enter.[15] Again, we see that Posada's view of marijuana, and probably that of his audience, was not significantly different from that found in the mainstream media.

Other sources also suggest that marijuana's reputation was relatively consistent across class lines. During the revolution, Constitutionalist forces often used the term *marihuanos* to smear the followers of Victoriano Huerta. *Marihuano* here fit in with other choice insults like "traitors," "murderers," and "savages."[16] Huerta himself, who, as Michael Meyer points out, "has been singled out for censure and abuse perhaps unparalleled in twentieth-century Latin

FIGURE 7.5.
"Bloody Drama in Belém Jail." (From Patrick Frank, *Posada's Broadsheets: Mexican Popular Imagery, 1890–1910* [Albuquerque: University of New Mexico Press, 1998], 49)

American history," was often called *el marihuano*. For example, in his 1916 *Bajo el terror huertista*, Luis Bustamante referred to Huerta as "El Presidente Mota," that is, "President Marijuana."[17] The label appears to have been used to sum up all of those terrible things with which Huerta was associated—being a traitor, the murderer of Madero, and a scoundrel of the worst kind. Huerta was in fact a famous drunk and eventually died probably from cirrhosis of the liver.[18] Whether or not he ever smoked marijuana, clearly the term was used against him and his followers as an insult of the worst kind.

Consider, for example, the famous song "La Cucaracha," which was often sung during the revolution by Pancho Villa's troops. Popular drug histories have interpreted this song, and its reference to marijuana, to be a celebration of the drug and an indication of its use by Villa's followers.[19] But a contemporary source who spent considerable time with Villa's army, the journalist Wallace Smith, noted that *la cucaracha*, or "the cockroach," was what Villa's soldiers called Huerta.[20] That information facilitates a much more plausible explanation for the tune's famous marijuana reference:

La cucaracha, la cucaracha
Ya no puede caminar
Porque no tiene, porque no tiene
Marihuana que fumar.[21]

[The cockroach, the cockroach
Can no longer walk
Because he lacks, because he lacks
Marijuana to smoke.]

Like so many Mexican folk songs, this one had innumerable versions that were routinely altered by whomever happened to be singing the tune at the time.[22] According to Smith, the song had hundreds of verses among Villa's soldiers: "One by one they take up the major enemies of Don Pancho. Item by item they go over their family history and intimate characteristics; their personal habits and eccentricities. Some of them are boasts for Don Pancho, too. Usually quoting one of Don Pancho's favorite claims, having to do with a real or fancied excess of masculine virility."[23] Given everything else we now know about marijuana in Mexico, it's clear the drug was not being celebrated in "La Cucaracha." Instead, its role there was to humorously and efficiently smear Victoriano Huerta.

Various other sources suggest widespread popular belief in marijuana's propensity to cause madness in its users. In a case examined more thoroughly in chapter 9, during the 1890s an American psychiatrist named Charles Pilgrim made a number of inquiries of Mexican authorities concerning the purported existence of Mexican plants that caused insanity. His search had been inspired by a deranged patient who insisted he had been poisoned by such a substance in Mexico. Pilgrim was eventually informed that two plants in particular were widely believed by Mexicans to have such effects and were thus called "locoweed"—marijuana and toloache (*Datura stramonium*).[24] Pilgrim went on to explain that a number of Mexico's leading physicians denied that either of these substances caused permanent madness (temporary being quite accepted, as we've seen) but that this belief remained strong in the realm of the "popular." For example, it was widely believed among the common folk that that the empress Carlota had been driven mad by a dose of "locoweed" secretly placed in her coffee.[25]

Pilgrim's inquiries eventually inspired an investigation by Fernando Altamirano, one of the Porfiriato's greatest physicians and naturalists. Altamirano also noted the popular belief that various plants could produce such results:

"It is very frequent that Mexican physicians, especially those who practice in the remote and lost little towns, wind up having to give their opinion whether or not this or that case of mental derangement was produced by toxic plants administered by jealous women or some rival." He went on to explain that "among us it is well known" that marijuana and the seeds of *Datura* "produce cerebral effects that can lead ultimately to a violent delirium and madness; these are generally temporary effects but with marihuana they can prolong themselves for a certain time in the form of mania, idiotism [*estupidez*], and a tendency toward homicide." Altamirano described other substances that were used in Mexico and widely believed to cause madness, including ololuihqui and various psychotropic mushrooms.[26]

The period's most direct discussion of lower-class opinion related to marijuana appears in a most unusual source. In July 1908, an individual named José del Moral was arrested for trafficking in large quantities of the weed. The story was covered sensationally by the press, especially *El Imparcial*, and it took a number of curious turns thanks to the idiosyncrasies of the protagonist. Del Moral was quite unusual among those linked to marijuana in that he was highly educated and able to pen a long appeal of his jail sentence. He was also the only person of whom I'm aware that challenged both the legitimacy and wisdom of Mexican marijuana laws of that period, a case he made on both philosophical and legal grounds. He especially took issue with the language in the law that declared marijuana to be "poisonous [*nocivo*]." How, he argued, could this substance be a "poison" if it was recommended as a medicine by countless doctors? How could it be banned if it was sold freely as a medicine in France, the most civilized country in the world? While he admitted that some negative consequences might follow from marijuana *abuse* (though he did not say what those consequences might be), he argued that this was the case with any medicine; in such cases, the blame should be placed squarely on the abuser and not the substance itself. And he claimed, incorrectly, that while alcohol was regularly blamed by medical experts for crimes of blood, such had never been the case with marijuana.[27]

However, despite this fierce repudiation of Mexico's marijuana status quo, del Moral did not suggest that these ideas had their origins in upper-class prejudice against a lower-class practice. On the contrary, he argued that it was the lower classes that tended to be the most fearful of this substance. This was a drug, he contended, that had been brought to Mexico by some "miracle," its secrets passed down for some reason only to the Indians, who "began giving it a role in their idolatrous religious beliefs, attributing to it supernatural effects and virtues."

The witches [*los hechiceros*] of many mountains go into ecstasies by smoking it between prayers and dances, events which only the initiated attend. I don't know for what reason but its use in this form has taken on a mysterious air that has come to horrify distinctly superficial and easily frightened spirits.

The horror that this plant inspires has reached such an extreme that when the common people, having little inclination to research the facts, see even just a single plant, they feel as if in the presence of a demonic spirit. Women and children run frightened and they make the sign of the cross simply upon hearing its name. The friars hurl their excommunications against those who grow and use it and the authorities persecute it with such fury that they order it be uprooted and burnt, imposing cruel penalties on whom they find it. In a word they believe that it is a weed that has come from hell and the ignorant masses curse and scorn it. It is a shame that in the midst of the twentieth century some of us Mexicans are in such a lamentable state of obscurantism that any foreigner who might witness such absurdities with respect to this plant surely would laugh at us, and our ignorance would inspire compassion.[28]

Again, it is striking how elites—even, in this case, one who was defending marijuana—linked Mexico's most fanatical anti-marijuana prejudice to the lower classes.

While no one else so directly discussed popular views of this drug, several researchers of the period worked closely with marijuana-using populations and thus provide some evidence on the question. Carlos Roumagnac interviewed dozens of prisoners around the turn of the century and published the details of that work in 1904. There he described a prisoner named "Manuel T" who had gotten in trouble a number of times for his use of the weed. T had been sent to Belén after stabbing a man to death in a drunken fight over a petty insult. There he had learned to smoke marijuana, and the first time he used the drug "he experienced a heaviness in his body, he had no strength, he had thoughts, imaginations (hallucinations), and he figured that he was free and other things," effects that he continued to experience for some time. "He states in addition, that based on what some of his comrades told him, at the start he must have begun acting crazy." Unfortunately, there is no indication as to what he or his fellow prisoners meant by this.[29]

This was typical of the evidence in Roumagnac's published work in which frustratingly few of his subjects provided any significant detail on the use of marijuana. A female inmate, for example, admitted that some prisoners smoked marijuana but that she had "never seen the effect that this produces."[30] There is nonetheless one other important detail that can be gleaned from Roumagnac's work, for he emphasized that knife fights like the one that landed Manuel T in jail were extremely common. With respect to a similar case, he noted: "Although the press . . . dressed up the facts in the darkest possible colors, unfortunately there is, in truth, nothing in those facts that departs from what is so common among our people: murder during a fight provoked by any insignificance, but which for those people is equivalent to what in other eras inspired Knights to take up arms in defense of their god and their lady."[31] Indeed, Pablo Piccato has demonstrated that such altercations were extremely common during this time period, though he argues that, like duels among elites, these fights were often sparked by an individual's desire to defend his or her honor. "A challenge conferred honor and a fight demonstrated the ability to defend it, regardless of the result. Poverty did not exclude anyone from the claim to that right; to the contrary, it made its defense, as in the Algerian societies observed by Pierre Bourdieu, all the more meritorious."[32] This, as I will argue later, may have been a key aspect of the relationship between marijuana and violent altercations.

There is some reason to believe that novice users of marijuana, like Manuel T, tended to act in a "crazy" manner in Mexico during this period. In his 1886 medical thesis, Genaro Pérez reported something similar that he learned of through interviews with soldiers. "Other soldiers who smoke [marijuana] for the first time, generally on account of the mischievous intentions of their fellow soldiers, *go crazy and run around doing lots of disordered things*, according to the expression employed by the soldiers who have seen such effects: and, in addition, say these same soldiers, some become happy and sing, and others bullies [*valientes*] and quarrelsome."[33] This largely conforms with what we know about marijuana and its effects from the most recent scientific research: that for some, especially novice users, and especially in high doses, the drug can produce unpleasant psychotomimetic effects. The actual manifestation of those effects would of course be a product of expectations and existing behavioral models. What Manuel T's behavior looked like on that first occasion remains a mystery, though he did describe another experience later on where he smoked a very large dose and had some unpleasant results: "On one occasion in which he smoked too much, he began to feel ugly sensations in his brain and spine and later he suffered a great spill of semen which finished with some blood; he does not know what state he was in and he only remembers that he imagined he was having sex with a woman. Since then he thinks that he has lost his procreative powers."[34]

While little user testimony on marijuana's effects has survived, it is none-theless striking that the scientific and medical authorities, even those who worked closely with marijuana users, never completely disavowed popular stereotypes on the subject, even when they sought to temper those stereo-types. In the high-profile 1913 case of Enrique Cepeda, the governor of Mexico City who was thought to have committed murder while under the influence of marijuana, the legal experts brought in to rule on his invocation of the insanity defense denied that long-term madness was a normal consequence of marijuana use in Mexico. They nevertheless supported the idea that it produced short-term manic outbursts:

> First. Marihuana is capable of producing mental derangement when smoked in certain doses, provided always that these be excessive (greater than 30 centigrams of the active principle), with this mental derangement being especially short, the duration becoming shorter the more intense the acute intoxication, and of well defined demented character in chronic and intense intoxication, which is rare and almost exceptional among our customs.
>
> Second. The effects of marihuana on an individual if that person also ingests alcohol are probably more likely to appear and possibly more powerful.
>
> Third. The excitation produced by marihuana is in general of short duration, the stronger the perceived effects the shorter they last, not lasting longer than a few minutes as long as a new dose is not . . . ingested.[35]

Probably the most thorough study of marijuana during these years was performed by the physicians Adolfo Nieto and Eliseo Ramírez, who examined the drug's place in the military. While they did not perform their own experiments with marijuana users, they based their opinions on close observations done by other physicians. They eventually concluded that while the extent to which marijuana produced adverse reactions might have been exaggerated in the popular discourse, those reactions did sometimes occur and in a manner that closely resembled lay stereotype. Thus they claimed that while marijuana intoxication was usually a silent one, it sometimes took on a more frightening hue: "Every once in awhile a smoker surpasses the limits of this silent and hardly discernible intoxication. He becomes agitated, laughs loudly, speaks with an excessively loud voice on various apparently unconnected topics, he insults those who surround him thinking that they make fun of him, he starts quarrels for nothing or for futile reasons that can lead to actions, and in the middle of a great disorder of movements and aggressive words, he winds up being taken to a jail cell by two or more men who with much trouble succeed in overcoming the muscular energy unleashed by him." They also described marijuana's potential to produce terrible "illusions": "The illusions, that is to say, the erroneous perception of real sensations are more common than hallucinations, they are almost always visual or aural, and they consist principally of an exaggeration of the perceptions. A sentry posted on top of a wall that surrounded the Military Hospital in Guadalajara, mistook for a large flowing river a trickle of water that passed by outside and he jumped in head first, diving in order to swim in it and dying as a consequence of the injuries he suffered." But, again, they emphasized that such results were perhaps not as common as generally believed. Dr. Francisco Castillo Nájera, who would later be Mexican ambassador to the United States, had made some similar observations of marijuana users: "A patient of Dr. Castillo Nájera, and a few years ago a soldier interned in the Military Hospital, believing themselves capable of flying, caused themselves serious injuries when they tried it; another insisted that he was a chair that someone was trying to destroy with an ax, and another felt like a pencil that was being sharpened." But he also concluded that "these disorders of the perceptions are less frequent than what is believed" and that they could be made to disappear "through energetic suggestion." The latter point is especially interesting given that, as we saw in chapter 1, a similar claim would be forwarded by Andrew Weil in 1970.[36]

Finally, Nieto and Ramírez argued that with marijuana, "addiction [*toxicomanía*]" was possible but that this was not a typical result and that users were usually able to abandon the drug without much problem. At the same time, they warned that in regular users, over time the symptoms of insanity would grow worse, potentially remaining for the long term.[37] Despite this, there were remarkably few cases of marijuana users who had been institutionalized for madness. In the general insane asylum, Nieto and Ramírez could cite only eight cases between 1911 and 1920. Six of these suffered from multiple drug problems—four alcoholics, one alcoholic/opium addict, and one morphine abuser. Only two of the eight patients had a problem exclusively with marijuana. There were also three recent cases of "chronic *marihuanos* with mental disorders" in the military hospital. "The patient studied by Doctor Ramírez demonstrated as dominant phenomena: a marked decrease in attention, anterograde amnesia, paramnesia of localization, visual illusions and hallucinations, and a tranquil delirium interrupted by crises of excitation which almost always occur at night." But overall, there were fewer such patients than one would expect, given the standard understandings of the drug and its effects. "The previous enumeration makes clear the few *marihuanos* interned at the asylum during the course of ten years, and this fact has its explanation: first, in that hashishism produces in general fewer disorders than alcoholism, as has been proven by the studies done in the Orient and recorded in the work of Meunier, a circumstance to which can be credited the opinion that its use should be tolerated; second, to the little attention that to this date has been given to this issue, as is evidenced by the lack of clinical histories."[38]

Doubt regarding the extent of marijuana madness had clearly begun to creep in, though Nieto and Ramírez were willing to go only so far. They suggested that perhaps sufficient attention had not been given to the problem by physicians, adding that the current director of Mexico City's insane asylum was planning on pushing research toward "a new orientation" that might make more observations of marijuana madness possible. They might have also mentioned exaggerations, if not outright inventions, by the press, which certainly occurred and helped develop existing stereotypes regarding marijuana.[39] Yet it is striking that even here, with physicians who had looked closely at marijuana use in the military and who recognized that perhaps the numbers of such cases had been exaggerated, the basic idea that marijuana produced "mental disturbances" was not challenged.

Other researchers who had significant experience with marijuana-using populations were even less circumspect. Roumagnac had this to say about marijuana in 1904: "Marihuana, as is perfectly understood among all of us, is a weed that when smoked, provokes a delirious intoxication. The person high on marijuana turns into a legitimate mad person, and once they have contracted the vice, they continue to use until they completely succumb to it. It is, along with pulque, another of the great and terrible national threats, and for that reason its sale is vigorously prohibited."[40] Clearly, from Roumagnac's point of view, there was no reason for skepticism, despite the countless hours that he spent with actual prisoners. Echoing Altamirano, the fact of marijuana's murderous effects was "understood among all of us." Similarly, Genaro Pérez spent a year of his medical training in the Military Hospital of Instruction and thus had significant experience with soldiers.[41] For his thesis, he also did experiments with four marijuana-using servicemen, eventually concluding that marijuana produced sufficient mental derangement to make a criminal irresponsible for his crimes. On this point, he did not mince words.

It is certainly striking that while some more serious researchers tried to temper popular stereotype regarding marijuana's effects, none of them, even among those who specifically looked into this question, rejected the basic view that it caused madness and violence. It is nevertheless worth looking more closely at Pérez's work, for while he did not mince words in his conclusion, the evidence he presented suggests a more complex reality that does much to help us tie together these many disparate sources.

Pérez's research was highlighted by experiments with and testimony from four marijuana-using soldiers. These began with twenty-nine-year-old Florencio Gallegos and thirty-year-old Anastasio Campos. Gallegos had been smoking marijuana regularly for fifteen years and Campos for two. Both claimed to smoke one or two marijuana cigarettes a day, and both "denied that the plant produced any effect over them whatsoever. . . . They only experienced, according to their own words, *relaxation, contentment*, and *strength for work*."[42] To test these claims, Pérez had each of the soldiers smoke two marijuana cigarettes consecutively. Upon examination, Campos's only notable symptoms included a small increase in pulse rate, a slight dilation of the pupils, dry mouth and corresponding thirst, and a "greater luster in his gaze and a marked inward concentration." Gallegos manifested the same effects, though in him the inward concentration was more obvious and accompanied by "the air of a certain lack of confidence." Pérez then asked the soldiers to smoke more of the drug, but they refused, contending that "they never smoked more than two [cigarettes] even though if they were to do so, they were sure that they wouldn't feel any of the effects that I had been asking them about. Undoubtedly they were influenced by the fear that they would be taken to be vice-ridden [*viciosos*]."[43]

The experiment was small and unscientific, but it nevertheless suggests a great deal. First, it is clear here that Pérez used leading questions to produce particular answers from his subjects—thus, the soldiers' denial that they would "feel any of the effects that [Pérez] had been asking them about." Second, the experiment demonstrates that these particular soldiers had a far less fantastic idea about the drug's effects than Pérez, a position that was supported by their own comportment while under the drug's influence. They clearly considered marijuana useful to them both as a relaxant and as a stimulant to work, and it appears that they had become adept at controlling their intake to achieve only those desired effects. They did refuse to smoke more than the first two cigarettes, suggesting a recognition that unfavorable results of some kind might be produced by a larger dose. This is especially interesting given the lore that would emerge with respect to users who would "take the three [*darse las tres*]." To "take the three" was, according to the press and other sources, to take just three *puffs* of a marijuana cigarette, the third leading to a frightening delirium. But could that lore perhaps have derived from the belief that more than two *cigarettes* constituted an especially high dose?

Unfortunately, due to Pérez's vague explanation, it is not at all clear what those unfavorable effects might have been in the opinion of these particular soldiers. As we've seen already, Pérez claimed that "other soldiers who smoke [marijuana] for the first time, generally on account of the mischievous intentions of their fellow soldiers, *go crazy and run around doing lots of disordered things*," but it's not clear if that information came from these soldiers with whom Pérez performed the experiments or from other soldiers altogether. Again, the experimental subjects said that "they were sure that they wouldn't feel any of the effects" that Pérez had been asking them about. From the rest of the thesis, it's clear that Pérez was interested in the basic marijuana "madness" described in both Mexican popular literature and the French scientific sources, but he might also have been asking about some very specific symptoms. Perhaps the soldiers did simply fear becoming visibly intoxicated as Pérez surmised, though that seems an odd concern of soldiers participating in a putatively scientific study.

Whatever the case, Pérez was eventually able to produce some clinical evidence of marijuana's effects that more closely paralleled the sinister symptoms described in the popular and scientific literature. This he managed by using the right kind of subjects—those who were already mentally disturbed. For these experiments, he worked with two soldiers who were residents of San Hipólito, Mexico City's mental hospital. Both men were reported to have smoked marijuana "in excess," though no other biographic details were known beyond the fact that both had "alcoholic habits" and had been assigned to the hospital for unknown reasons by the city government. The first soldier, Torribo Ojeda, is described as "young" and as having smoked marijuana "abundantly" for two years prior to his internment in the hospital. He now suffered from visual and aural hallucinations, believed that animals came into his room at night to take his clothes, and was often found stealing the garments of other patients. He also heard voices that commanded him to do various things. On Pérez's request, the patient "gladly agreed" to smoke four cigarettes consecutively of equal parts marijuana and tobacco, and within two hours he had smoked seven of these. At that point, he was behaving in a manner that satisfied the young medical student's expectations:

He manifested a loquacious, incoherent, smiling delirium, characterized primarily by the complete mobility and disorder of ideas. He spoke continuously on diverse topics, especially through words that he randomly plucked from the pronouncements of the other patient, or from someone who passed by in the corridor where we were, or that we ourselves suggested. He didn't hold still for a moment, alternating between standing, walking, or sitting at every step. His hearing had acquired an exquisite sharpness and every sound captured his attention [*le impresionaba*]; his gaze was alive, brilliant, and investigative. Asked about the excitation he was experiencing, he said he didn't feel a thing, he was just happy, and he referred to epigastric sensations, and after Dr. Govantes asked him if he'd be capable of fighting, he answered that he'd do so against anyone, all he needed was a dagger.[44]

A second soldier, a native of Querétaro named Juan Obregón, revealed similar symptoms. Pérez, in a statement that raises further doubt as to the sophistication of his research methods, could not say how long the patient had been at the hospital because the soldier displayed "such a notable loss of memory." In any case, Pérez described the patient's hands as trembling and his features as "revealing indifference and stupor." The soldier was then made to smoke seven of the cigarettes. "The delirium was absolutely incoherent, and for a moment it revolved around erotic ideas, he spoke of beautiful women, strolls, and riches (relative to his social position). . . . We told him to sing and he resisted a little but, we having insisted, he gave in and sang for about twenty minutes, different songs, pieces and *sones*, some in which he invented phrases which he fit into the music, until we told him to be quiet."[45]

From only four cases and some additional testimony collected by a clearly biased researcher, we cannot reach any definitive conclusions. Nevertheless, Pérez's evidence does suggest more or less what we would expect given today's much more controlled and sophisticated research on marijuana. Here it appears that regular users knew how to measure their doses to achieve the pleasurable results they were accustomed to, while for others the drug produced more pronounced and even mostly negative symptoms. This was clearly true for the patients who appear to have already suffered from some sort of psychotic disorder, which is, again, what we would expect. Recent research demonstrates, for example, that cannabis tends to augment the "adverse" symptoms of schizophrenia (see chapter 1). It is also quite interesting that testimony from unnamed soldiers suggested that first-time, reluctant users were said to "go crazy and run around doing lots of disordered things" as a response to their discomfort after smoking the drug.

While Pérez asked leading questions and clearly hoped to confirm his preconceptions regarding the drug's effects, he was also quite willing to present evidence that went against his own bias, as demonstrated by his work with the first two soldiers. That perhaps increases our confidence that, while biased, Pérez was attempting to be honest in his reporting of the facts. Like the other

Mexican physicians and scientists who would eventually look closely at marijuana and its users, Pérez ultimately concluded that marijuana produced effects very much like those stereotyped in the press during these years:

> The acute intoxication is characterized by a mental perturbation noted by a sensation of well being, a brightness of memory, a multiplicity and facility of conceptions, an incoherence of words and actions, at first the need for repose and isolation, and later the need for movement. There is a disassociation of ideas, delirious conceptions, illusions and hallucinations, and damage to the emotions, etc.
>
> This acute, temporary mental perturbation is a true madness, fleeting and artificial if one prefers, but always a kind of madness.[46]

Pérez, like Roumagnac, Nieto, Ramírez, and Heriberto Frías, had considerable experience with actual marijuana-using populations, having worked in a military hospital during his medical training, yet he had little doubt that the reported violent effects of marijuana among soldiers and others were legitimate. Pérez was ultimately convinced that marijuana produced mania in its users, and the symptoms of that disorder provoked a host of different crimes. Thus, he concluded that "the criminal responsibility of an individual in a state of acute marijuana intoxication should be exactly the same as that of the maniac."[47]

That conclusion provides an excellent segue to one final, complicating factor: that criminals and defense lawyers cynically used marijuana's purported effects as a means of invoking the insanity defense during criminal trials. Both soldiers and civilians routinely sought exoneration for crimes based on the premise that they were either drunk on alcohol or, less commonly, high on marijuana.[48] This was a practice that dated to the colonial era. A revised military Code of Justice in 1879 specifically addressed this problem, noting that most soldiers were under the very false impression that "drunkenness" was an extenuating circumstance in the commission of a crime. Though such had actually not been the case in Mexico's military Code of Justice since at least the eighteenth century, "despite this antique prescription that has always been followed, we repeatedly see occur that they intoxicate themselves in order to commit a crime, attempting later to excuse themselves with the drunkenness that they voluntarily contracted."[49] Article 308 of that code specifically forbade soldiers from seeking recourse in the insanity defense as long as their intoxication had been acquired voluntarily. In a later manifestation of the code, and perhaps reflecting the growing profile of marijuana use in Mexico, Article 970 would ensure that *embriaguez* was not simply understood to be caused by alcohol, redefining it as "any temporary perturbation of the mental faculties procured voluntarily."[50]

Civilians also sought refuge in the insanity by intoxication defense, though these efforts were well justified by the criminal law. The Federal Penal Code of 1871, which was copied almost verbatim by most of the states, specifically cited intoxication as an exculpatory circumstance:

> Art. 34: The circumstances that exclude criminal responsibility for the infraction of the law are:
>
> 1) The accused violates a law while in a state of mental derangement that removes his liberty or which totally impedes his ability to understand the illicit nature of the act or omission of which he is accused.
> 2) There is well-founded doubt, in the judgment of medical experts, whether an accused person who suffers from intermittent madness had a clear head when he violated a law during an intermittence.
> 3) Complete drunkenness that completely deprives one of reason, if it is not habitual, nor has the accused before committed a punishable infraction while drunk; but even then he does not remain free from the punishment for drunkenness, nor from civil responsibility.

These provisions obviously provided significant opportunity for abuse by criminals and lawyers, something that other aspects of the code tried to prevent. For example, Article 11, Fraction 4, specifically made those who had previously committed crimes while intoxicated, or who were habitually drunk, culpable for their actions. Article 923 punished "habitual drunkenness that might cause serious scandal," while Article 924 aimed to punish those who more than once had committed a crime while intoxicated.[51] The authors of the code had in fact specifically considered the potential ambiguity of the insanity defense given contemporary understandings of drunkenness and had therefore addressed the question directly. But in its final form, the code stated that in order to invoke the insanity defense, such intoxication must be "complete," a definition that simply opened the door to legal challenge.[52] This was further complicated by Article 41, which made incomplete intoxication a third-class (meaning two grades more significant than first-class) attenuating circumstance.[53] Thus, there was much incentive to invoke the intoxication defense, or, as military officials had lamented, to become intoxicated in order to commit a crime.

Not surprisingly, then, civilian and military criminals invoked the insanity defense with frequency during this period.[54] In 1899, *El País* bemoaned that "in effect it is a belief of men from the lower class and even among many from the higher social strata that it constitutes an exculpatory defense or at the minimum a weighty excuse to say: I did it because I was crazy due to drunkenness."[55] The currency of this defense in both civilian and military situations was indicated by *El Diario* with biting sarcasm in 1913 when, after a soldier had shot two others, it noted, "The murderer excuses himself with the really novel palliative that he was under the influence of the pernicious weed of which there is so much consumption in the barracks."[56] Maybe the most famous invocation of the intoxication defense occurred in the 1913 trial of Enrique Cepeda, who, shortly after Victoriano Huerta's coup, went to Belén in a fit of pique and murdered Gabriel Hernández, a prominent Maderista, and then burned the corpse. The press covered the twists and turns of the story in detail for months. It was initially reported that Cepeda had been suffering "alcoholic madness," but soon the defense's strategy turned to the notion that he had been high on marijuana, which had been given to him without his knowledge. This was later rejected by the medical experts, but Cepeda's crack defense team simply called for more medical witnesses until they received a more favorable ruling. In the end, the intoxication defense was accepted, and Cepeda was acquitted for having been high on marijuana, leading to very plausible claims that the judge had been pressured by Huerta and his henchmen to come to that conclusion.[57]

The intoxication defense had nonetheless been controversial for some time prior to Cepeda's acquittal. In 1903, the governor of Puebla, Mucio Martínez, proposed a reform to the state's penal code that transformed intoxication from a potentially exculpatory circumstance to an aggravating one. To justify the law, Martínez argued that the typical efforts to fight drunkenness were in general useless because they attacked the results rather than the causes of the problem. One of these causes was the favor with which the penal law treated those who committed crimes while drunk.

Since the state of mental perturbation caused by drunkenness, strictly speaking, [which] predisposes one to impulsive and criminal acts, is not simply an effect of alcohol, but rather, occurs very often as a result of many other psychoses originating in the abuse of morphine, ether, mariguana, etc. there is no doubt that, in the noteworthy persecution of the social evil with which we deal, it is necessary not to limit ourselves to intoxication by alcohol, but rather to deal with all temporary cerebral derangements, whatever their nature, if they result from the voluntary act of the sufferer, something the degeneration of life habits [*costumbres*] is bringing to light.[58]

The actual changes in Puebla, which were approved and put into law on April 1, 1903, were quite telling with respect to Mexican thinking on drugs and their effects. The original language, which was the same as that noted above in the Federal Penal Code, had simply referred to *embriaguez* (normally meaning "drunkenness") as an extenuating circumstance. To account for non-alcoholic substances that should also be covered by the law, the new language excluded reference to *embriaguez* altogether and simply referred to temporary *enajenación mental*, which can be translated as either "mental derangement" or, simply, "insanity." In short, Fraction 3 of the old code (cited above in the federal version) was simply eliminated and Fraction 1 was revised to read: "To violate a law, when the accused finds himself in a state of mental derangement that denies him liberty or that impedes his understanding of the illicit nature of the act or omission of which he is accused. This circumstance will not be exculpatory when said derangement consists of a temporary disorder of the mental faculties resulting from a voluntary act of the accused." At the same time, Article 47, Fraction 15, declared that the commission of a crime while in a state of "transitory mental derangement resulting from a voluntary act" would serve as a fourth class (the most severe) aggravating circumstance.[59] In short, the increasingly problematic use of the term *embriaguez*, which had always meant drunkenness, could be easily avoided by simply cutting to the chase and speaking of voluntarily acquired temporary insanity. This was the essence of the discourse on intoxication in turn-of-the-century Mexico.

All of this significantly complicates the issues under discussion here. Clearly there was considerable incentive among ordinary criminals to play up the effects that marijuana and other drugs had on them. Military authorities quite specifically stated that intoxication must *not* be an exculpatory factor; otherwise, soldiers would get intoxicated to commit a crime. And since soldiers, prisoners, and common criminals were clearly aware of these laws, would it not behoove them to smoke some marijuana and then commit their violent crime in a stereotyped manner that suggested insanity? Clearly there was a stereotyped "marijuana madness" that could be easily mimicked. At the same time, the evidence also indicates that such stereotyped effects did not merely result when crimes were being committed. Pérez's military testimony claiming that novice users ran around doing disordered things is especially compelling evidence on this point.

One cannot help but be reminded here of the "running amok" phenomenon, that "culture-bound syndrome" discussed in chapter 1. As noted there, recent scholarship has defined amok as "a sudden mass assault" and "a variant of a worldwide, biological disorder on which cultural trappings are layered."

The phenomenon looks remarkably like one especially prominent version of "marijuana madness" in late-nineteenth- and early-twentieth-century Mexico: an individual, after a period of brooding, would attack those around him or her in an outpouring of more or less random violence. This was generally followed by claims of amnesia. There is considerable debate over whether such behaviors should be classified as psychiatric disorders or as a "socially learned, culturally channeled and sanctioned means of expressing normally forbidden emotions." But either explanation would neatly fit the Mexican cases explored here, with marijuana, and perhaps the insanity defense, serving as additional catalysts.[60]

A particularly interesting piece of evidence on this was offered in 1908 by an American physician working in a Durango mining camp. In a paper published in the *Boston Medical and Surgical Journal* and the *New England Journal of Medicine*, Dr. I. S. Kahn argued that cases of hysteria and mania were extremely common around the camp.

One particular set of specialists ought to visit this section of the world,—I mean the "nerve-men." My little camp of 700 or 800 is a perfect clinic of hysteria; I see it in all its phases. It is the bane of a doctor's life, hereabouts; there is scarcely a day that I do not get a call to see a woman having an "attaqué" [*sic*] as they call it, an hysterical fit or convulsion. I see it even in children of nine or ten, probably imitative, as an attack usually attracts most of the neighborhood. Even acute mania lasting two or three days is not uncommon. Much of this mania is not real hysteria, but is caused by smoking a weed, growing abundantly in the hills, called "*marihuana*," a vice rather common in Mexico. Its use is, of course, vigorously denied. Usually the women are the ones affected, as they all smoke more than the men. I can't blame them as Mexican tobacco is cheap, and far and away superior to the American article. This "*marihuana*" mania is extremely violent for two or three days, requiring enforced restraint; it is accompanied by hallucinations of sight and hearing, cyanosis, rapid, weak pulse with occasional vomiting, followed by exhaustion and mental confusion lasting two or three days longer. I have not seen a death and understand that it is seldom fatal. I give all my hysteria cases the same treatment—apomorphine subcutaneously, followed later by salts and later by bromides if necessary. If it is "*marihuana*," it certainly helps; if it is hysteria, the apomorphine usually gives them something to think about for a while. I recently found a new arrival in camp, a man of forty-five, carried here, sick several months with spastic hemiplegia, completely bed-ridden, resisting all handling and even interfering with speech. Suspecting the usual, I told him I could cure him, rubbed his legs and arms with a common gargle, and next day he was working in the mines, making my reputation solid forever in this community. Such "cures" are common.[61]

Kahn's description is in some ways confusing. He notes that the use of marijuana is "of course" always denied, though it is not at all clear why. Perhaps because people wanted their "hysteria" to be taken seriously? Or because they did not want others to know they had smoked marijuana? Nor is there any explanation for what the quality of tobacco had to do with the smoking of marijuana or why a dose of apomorphine would give the truly hysterical patients "something to think about." But I am struck in this description by Kahn's suggestion that these episodes were extremely common, that even children experienced them, probably in imitation of their elders since attacks usually attracted the whole neighborhood, and that they could be cured essentially through suggestion. The description has all the hallmarks of a "culture-bound syndrome."

While the patchy judicial archives have not produced much evidence of violent marijuana outbursts, some arrest records do suggest that the wild behaviors often associated with marijuana and alcohol intoxication were not especially unusual, nor were they understood as surprising. Witnesses sometimes noted that individuals acted "crazy" or lost consciousness when intoxicated. In one case, for example, a man named Nicolás Chaves tried to steal the shawl of another man's wife. When confronted by the husband, Chaves proceeded to attack the man, scratching his face and kicking him on the ground after he'd fallen down. Chaves eventually claimed that a coworker had given him some tequila to drink and a cigarette; the latter "he assumed" had been of marijuana because he completely lost consciousness of his actions for a few moments. Various witnesses confirmed his state of intoxication that day and the fact that he was normally a quite sober and honorable man but that when he was drunk, he became totally unaware of his actions. Medical witnesses ruled that given his normal sobriety and the amount of tequila imbibed, he very well could have been too intoxicated to understand his own actions. He was thus acquitted on those grounds.[62] In another case reported by the *Mexican Herald* on October 16, 1900, a man named Leocadio Gaspar had gone to his estranged wife's house in a jealous rage, fueled by alcohol and marijuana, with the intention of murdering her. She escaped, but he ended up murdering his stepson during the incident. He then ran into the street and attacked the police who tried to apprehend him. Two weeks later, *El País* reported that the initial explanations of the case were wrong and that Gaspar had not been drinking or smoking marijuana on that day, though the other details of the case were confirmed. Gaspar eventually filed an appeal, which has survived. That record also confirmed most of the details as reported by the press. Gaspar's defense team argued that he had been suffering intermittent madness from delirium tremens, but this defense was rejected as improvable and a death sentence was confirmed.[63] The case is especially interesting because it produced significant testimony from various individuals who claimed that whenever Gaspar drank, he became "completely crazy," though he hadn't actually been drinking during this particular incident. Gaspar himself explained his "running amok" type behavior: he had attacked the police in order to provoke them into killing him.[64]

One final example is worth noting. In 1909, a certain Juan Hernández was reported to have attacked two women and then a plainclothes police officer. The story was a classic example of a "running amok" type incident in that the man attacked the police officer with a furious and absolutely reckless abandon. Here the newspapers only implied that the violence was caused by marijuana, stating that Hernández was a regular marijuana smoker who went wild anytime he smoked it but not actually saying that in this case the marijuana had caused the incident.[65] The case file itself says nothing of marijuana specifically. The suspect's brother claimed that his sibling was *muy ebrio* that day, which usually meant "really drunk," but it could also mean simply "very intoxicated." Typical of the incomplete nature of these files, testimony was either not taken or did not survive from the two women with whom the suspect had spent most of the day. These were the two people most likely to know if he had been smoking marijuana. Nevertheless, most of the details of the case as reported in the press were in fact confirmed. All of the witnesses who actually saw the incident described the wild, "running amok" type behavior. The man was seen charging down the street with a knife; then, when confronted by the police officer, Hernández attacked him relentlessly despite his firing two warning shots in the air. The police officer then shot and killed Hernández. Even the suspect's brother confirmed this detail, noting that when the officer fired shots into the air, this just led his brother to redouble his attack "with more fury." Another witness noted that the suspect demanded that the police officer shoot him.[66]

Given what we know about the "psychoactive riddle" and the propensity of drugs to have effects based on the expectations of users and the setting of the drug use, it seems quite plausible that violent outbursts related to marijuana manifested themselves in nineteenth- and early-twentieth-century Mexico as a kind of "culture-bound syndrome," whether fueled by the realities of the insanity defense, by fears of witchcraft and poisoning by psychotomimetic drugs, or simply in a kind of feedback relationship with the widespread belief that marijuana caused madness. As Andrew Weil argued in 1970, panic attacks are among the most common adverse reactions to marijuana. Weil claimed that such a condition significantly worsened when clinicians treated it as "acute toxic psychosis," an approach that convinced patients that their condition was "psychotic." On the other hand, patients who were simply reassured that they would be fine improved rapidly. Could not the widespread belief in "marijuana madness" evidenced in the newspapers, the penny press, and other sources have elicited the reinforcement of panic reactions due to marijuana, worsening those symptoms and provoking a stereotyped response to them, particularly in a context where knife fights were common and where the insanity defense made such responses useful to deviants?

We should also keep in mind the frequency with which knife fights broke out in disputes over honor during this period. As Piccato has argued, "Honor was a right that had to be defended daily, against many threats, and at a very high cost."[67] Marijuana, a psychotomimetic substance well known to produce paranoid reactions in users, would have been a very dangerous drug under these circumstances, especially in the often highly stressful environments of prisons and soldiers' barracks. Here a prisoner's or soldier's paranoia that his comrades were disrespecting him could have easily turned violent, with an individual feeling compelled to respond to a perceived slight with aggression even if vastly outnumbered (thus reinforcing the perceived "irrationality" of the act). We therefore might also presume that marijuana use "caused" violence in such scenarios, though only because its use occurred in this very specific cultural setting.[68]

This appears to be the most plausible explanation for the hundreds of reports that marijuana produced "mad" behavior and violence in Mexico a century ago. There were simply too many reports, from too many different sources, with virtually no counterdiscourse, to believe that they were all fabricated. At the same time, exaggeration and sensationalism were clearly also part of the equation, fueled by prejudice and fear of the highly marginal people who smoked (and sold) marijuana. Ultimately, reality and myth surely fueled each other. Sensationalism and expediency (that is, the insanity defense) likely reinforced beliefs that themselves fueled stereotyped responses to marijuana's pharmacological properties, thus fueling more sensationalism.

All of this helped to thoroughly demonize marijuana and facilitate its eventual prohibition nationwide. To that prohibition we now turn.

*Chapter 8*

NATIONAL LEGISLATION
AND THE BIRTH OF MEXICO'S
WAR ON DRUGS

On March 2, 1920, Mexico's Department of Public Sanitation promulgated its "Dispositions on the Cultivation and Commerce of Products that Degenerate the Race." This was the first law in Mexican history to ban the cultivation and commerce in marijuana nationwide. It also imposed significant restrictions on the sale and distribution of the opiates and cocaine. It was, in short, a landmark in Mexican drug history and the true starting point of Mexico's nationwide war on drugs.

As has been thoroughly illustrated in the historical literature, the origins of international drug control regimes lie in the early twentieth century and, more specifically, in the Hague International Opium Convention of 1912. Knowing that history, one could easily assume that Mexico's 1920 legislation had been inspired by those recent international happenings or hypothesize, as some scholars have, that the United States pressured Mexico into adopting policies like those already enacted north of the border.[1] But, in fact, when we trace the roots of this legislation, we find that they run extraordinarily deep in Mexican history.

This chapter explores those deep and tangled roots, demonstrating not only that Mexican drug laws and ideology were fully in step with the emerging standards being dictated at international conferences by the Great Powers, principally the United States and Great Britain, but also that in most ways Mexico was ahead of these nations on the road to prohibitory regimes and modern drug wars.

■ Drafted in the midst of revolution, the Constitution of 1917 created the Department of Public Sanitation and gave it unprecedented power to legislate nationwide on all matters relating to "alcohol and other substances that poison the individual and degenerate the race."[2] This was a watershed not because it signaled a radically different attitude toward drugs in Mexico but rather because it demonstrated how drugs were helping to justify a new, more centralized approach to governance. In truth, the Department of Public Sanitation was just the most recent and most powerful incarnation of a centuries-old institution in Mexico.

Spanish regulation of medicine and pharmacy produced the blueprint for later Mexican approaches in these matters. Though during the Middle Ages the practice of medicine had become a stagnant and backward field in most of Europe, Iberia had managed to avoid this general malaise thanks to the influence of its Muslim conquerors. The Moors preserved and studied the classic medical texts of the Mediterranean basin, and their own great thinkers advanced medical knowledge. While most Europeans were lost in those "dark" times, the Christians who would eventually reconquer Spain were benefiting from "Eastern" learning. By the sixteenth century, Spanish medicine had become Europe's most advanced.[3]

Early modern Spanish history saw significant innovations in the regulation of medicine and pharmacy, but these had their roots in the very tail end of the Middle Ages when, in 1420, Alfonso V of Aragón established a four-man tribunal to examine medical practitioners, issue licenses, and monitor medical credentials. Because his personal doctor, the "first physician" or *proto-médico*, was on that tribunal, he dubbed the whole board the *protomedicato*, the name that similar bodies would carry for the next four centuries throughout the Spanish Empire. In 1477, the Catholic kings created a central *proto-medicato* charged with examining not only the various medical practitioners of the day (from midwives to surgeons) but also apothecaries and spice merchants. Furthermore, they deemed that the tribunal should have judicial responsibilities. Soon after, judges and law enforcement agents were serving on the board.[4] This bears repeating: already in the fifteenth century, the Spanish kingdoms had begun using law enforcement and judicial officials to monitor the practice of medicine and the distribution of drugs in their realms.

Shortly thereafter, similar institutions were created in the Americas. The first *protomedicato* was appointed during the island phase of conquest—on Hispaniola—though that appointment was short-lived. The local colonists, citing disruptions to the island's very tenuous state of order, protested the appointments, leading Charles I to reverse them. But the two members of that original American *protomedicato* were able to flee to more hospitable Mexico City, where, in the late 1520s, each was appointed in succession to serve as *protomédico* by municipal authorities. While they did not form a full-fledged *protomedicato*, these first physicians were given the power to levy fines and ban repeat offenders from the colony.

Over the coming decades, more steps to control the distribution of drugs were taken in New Spain. Regulations in 1528 and 1529 ordered the inspection of pharmacies and the examination of their wares to ensure that they conformed to the reigning standards.[5] Then, in 1538, Charles I ordered that the viceroys, municipal presidents, and governors in the Americas regularly visit the apothecaries of their districts to inspect their medicines and ensure that these had not become corrupted and thus dangerous to the public.[6] Gradually, city officials began appointing full-fledged boards to carry out these tasks, a development that has led scholars to label this the "municipal phase" of medical regulation in New Spain. Because the Spanish kings did not choose to appoint *protomedicato*s during this period, the municipal authorities did it themselves, perhaps revealing that medical regulation was increasingly becoming an issue of common governance even for local Spanish authorities.[7] Finally, in 1628, New Spain's first royal *protomedicato* was created. After further expansion into the area of public sanitation, the tribunal would function, in the opinion of Gordon Schendel, "as a Public Health Department in virtually every modern respect."[8]

Over time, the *protomedicato*'s regulations relating to pharmacy advanced in terms of their specificity and detail. Consider those in place at the end of the colonial period. For an apothecary to begin practicing, he was first required to demonstrate four years of study under an approved professor and certification of having attended a course on pharmaceutical botany. He then had to undergo a series of exams to prove his competence. Once approved, his practice was to be governed by a number of regulations: he could not dispense prescriptions without the signature of a physician; he had to always furnish the drugs that he claimed to be providing and not substitutions; medicines prepared from a combination of substances required a label indicating the date of their preparation; if he were to sell a deadly medicine with malicious intent, he would receive the death penalty; poisonous medicines could be sold only under the reigning standards of the profession (*las reglas del arte*); any apothecary who sold or dispensed a poisonous medicine without a prescription would be subject to a fine and penalty; secret medicines could be sold only with authorization from the board; the sale of adulterated medicines would be met with a fine; all potentially noxious drugs had to be kept under lock and key; and, finally, apothecaries were required to have on hand the necessary tools and medicines to properly do their job, and those items were enumerated in lists provided by the *protomedicato*.[9] All of these regulations were to be enforced by official inspection every two years and any other time complaints were received. This was the *protomedicato* model at the height of its development, and it was probably applied with greater success in Mexico than anywhere else in Spanish America.[10] It also served as the blueprint for medical and pharmaceutical regulation in independent Mexico.

■ In the 1820s, as the dust settled from a decade of independence wars, medical reformers in Mexico began contemplating reforms to the *protomedicato* system. In 1831, these efforts bore fruit when President Anastasio Bustamante dissolved the *protomedicato* and replaced it with the Facultad Médica del Distrito Federal (Medical Faculty of the Federal District). Though bearing a new title, the Facultad Médica looked and acted just like its predecessor, granting professional titles, regulating and approving specific medical practices, and indicating pharmacopoeias whose guidelines should be followed. A decade later, in January 1841, a new ordinance regulating medical studies, professorial exams, and sanitary matters was promulgated, and Bustamante's Facultad Médica was replaced by the Consejo Superior de Salubridad, or the Superior Sanitary Council of the Department of Mexico.[11]

The birth of that institution, which I will now refer to simply as the sanitary council, may have augured a new era of modern "public health" in Mexico, but it was far from the bureaucratic fortresses that represent such authorities today. It comprised an august body of three councilmen charged with monitoring the whole of the Department of Mexico's medical practice. The Department of Mexico, recently created by the centralist Constitution of 1836, included Mexico City, Mexico State, Morelos, Guerrero, and Tlaxcala. Badly underfunded, created in the midst of Mexico's midcentury political upheavals, and equipped with the funding and bureaucratic firepower to perhaps effectively govern medical practice in one medium-sized town, the sanitary council fought an uphill battle against quackery and disease.[12]

But my focus here is on the intellectual and legislative precedents for future drug policy. In the folded and battered remains of 1840s sanitary mandates, those precedents are clearly visible. The council was charged with ensuring that in the Department of Mexico, only legally authorized and law-abiding professionals practiced in the medical fields. To ensure compliance, fines were to be imposed based on the standards created in 1831 under Bustamante's Facultad Médica. The council was also to ensure that warehouses (*almacenes*) sold only medicinal products to pharmacists, who, in turn, were the only vendors legally authorized to distribute them. The council was to annually visit the establishments where drugs were manufactured, the warehouses where they were distributed, and the pharmacies where they were sold in order to ensure compliance with all existing regulations. Among other things, those regulations prohibited the sale of secret medicinal preparations that had not been examined, approved, and licensed by the council.[13] A new regulation of November 26, 1846, then further detailed these procedures. "Extraordinary" visits to pharmacies, that is, those that occurred more than yearly, would precede the opening of new establishments, in situations of complaints against particular firms, and whenever they otherwise might be necessary based on the judgment of the council's members. During the visit, the pharmacy's license and equipment would be reviewed, as would the stock of "typical elemental and compound medicines" and those secret remedies approved by the council. Violations of the law, if not exceeding ten in number, would result in a fine of one to ten pesos for each and the temporary closing of the establishment until the problems had been remedied. More than ten violations would result in the permanent closure of the pharmacy.[14]

It was at this point that marijuana began to enter into this regulatory system for the first time, being listed among the "typical elemental medicines" of the period.[15] The list also included other intoxicating plants that grew wild in the Mexican countryside like belladonna, henbane (*beleño*), hemlock (*cicuta*), digitalis, jimsonweed (*toloache*), tobacco, and coffee, as well as more exotic substances like opium. All of these drugs *except* marijuana were also listed among those substances that pharmacists must have on hand at all times to avoid penalties from the sanitary council. Similarly, marijuana was excluded from a list of appropriate doses to which pharmacists should adhere when prescribing more dangerous drugs. These absences are interesting, but too much should not be made of them, for they probably just reflected the relatively recent emergence of this substance within European-style medical practice.[16]

Through the foreign invasions, civil war, and rebellions that defined Mexican history during the middle of the nineteenth century, the sanitary council, in various incarnations, nonetheless continued to promulgate restrictions of this kind. In 1883, the distribution of marijuana was for the first time targeted for significant regulation. An 1866 listing of restricted medicines had not included it, nor had an 1878 list of "dangerous substances that can be employed exclusively with a medical prescription . . . and which should only be sold to pharmacies or pharmacists."[17] The latter absence is conspicuous given that marijuana had already been banned by the Federal District in 1869. Furthermore, many other drugs typically found in the collections of *herbolarias* were restricted by the 1878 *reglamento*, including belladonna, henbane, hemlock, digitalis, and others, while common drugs like opium, morphine, and, somewhat surprisingly, caffeine, were included as well.[18] Whatever the reason for those omissions, the new regulation of 1883 did include marijuana in two separate lists. First, it was among two dozen drugs that could be sold only by prescription. That list also included belladonna, henbane, hemlock, digitalis, jimsonweed, opium, and *zoapatle* (*Montanoa tormentosa*). Second, it appeared in a list of substances that *herbolarias* could sell only to pharmacists.[19] There it shared space with *cabalongas* (*Thevetia peruviana*), *codos de fraile* (*Thevetia yccotli*), hemlock, *cintul* (*Veratrum frigidum*), *cebolleja* (*Veratrum officinale*), henbane, belladonna, jimsonweed, *yerba de la puebla* (*Senecio canicida*), black nightshade (*yerba mora* or *Solanum nigrum*), and, again, *zoapatle*.[20]

While these early restrictions certainly were the precursors to formal drug prohibition in Mexico, they were not aimed primarily at the recreational use of these drugs. In a long introduction to the 1883 guidelines, the council argued for their approval on the grounds that unregulated medical practice, particularly in the use of certain harmful substances, "had occasioned numerous accidents," sometimes even resulting in loss of life.[21] "For similar reasons," the council continued, it was also imperative to "take note of the sale of every type of plant and other medicinal product, many of which are toxic or abortive, and which the merchants who dedicate themselves to this business, known commonly as 'Herbolarias,' sell without any restriction whatsoever."[22] The council did refer to the most dangerous substances as "terrible arms when in criminal hands," but this language almost certainly referred to poisonings, for the same reference to criminal ends is made with respect to the many industrial products that were also deemed dangerous. Furthermore, poisoning and suicide by means of these substances were major concerns of the sanitary council during this period. In one case, for example, the council's legal medicine department had analyzed some small folded papers containing a substance that turned out to be morphine. The council argued that the "substance should be analyzed in order to determine what baleful ends it could have served if it were put in someone's food, for it has been found that the person to whom it belonged intended to narcoticize a relative of the person who has reported the incident."[23]

There was nothing remotely new about those concerns or law enforcement responses to them in Mexico. Consider Article 842 of Mexico's first Federal Penal Code, which was published in 1871 and remained in force until 1929:

The person who without legal authorization manufactures for sale harmful substances [*nocivas a la salud*] or chemicals that can cause great havoc [*grandes estragos*]; will suffer the penalty of four months of arrest and a fine of 25 to 500 pesos.

The same penalty will be imposed on the person who trades in those substances without the corresponding authorization, and on the person that having such authorization dispenses them without observing the steps established [*formalidades*] in the corresponding regulations.

This was one of several articles in the code's section on "Crimes against Public Health." Remarkably, the direct precedent for this article was the thirteenth-century Castillian legal code known as the Siete Partidas:[24]

*PHYSICIANS AND SURGEONS WHO CLAIM TO BE LEARNED IN THEIR PROFESSIONS AND ARE NOT SO, DESERVE TO SUFFER PUNISHMENT IF ANYONE DIES THROUGH THEIR FAULT*

Some men profess to be more learned in medicine and surgery than they are, and it happens at times, for that reason that they are not so well informed as they say they are, sick or wounded persons die through their fault. Wherefore we decree that if any physician gives medicine which is too strong, or such as he should not give, to any man or woman under his care, and the sick person dies, or if any surgeon uses a knife upon a wounded person, or a saw upon his head, or burns his nerves or bones in such a way that he dies on account of it; or if any man or woman gives herbs or medicines to any other woman in order that she may become pregnant and she by reason of their administration dies; he who commits an offense of this kind shall be banished to some island for five years, because he was greatly to blame for practicing what he did not positively know, as was necessary, and which he professed to be familiar with, and he shall afterwards be forbidden to practice said profession.

Where the part who dies through the fault of the physician or surgeon is a slave, the former shall pay his master an amount fixed by the judgment of reliable men. Where, however, a physician or surgeon knowingly and maliciously commits any of the aforesaid offenses, he shall be put to death on this account. Moreover, we decree that if an apothecary gives a man scammony, or any other powerful medicine, to eat or drink, without the order of a physician, and the person who takes it dies in consequence, he who administered it shall suffer the penalty for homicide.[25]

Though clearly some of the concerns here were from another era, the basic link between harmful substances and malpractice obviously remained. Article 843 of the 1871 Penal Code expanded further on this concept: "The sale of any other goods that are necessarily noxious [*nocivos a la salud*], done without legal authorization, and without the requirements indicated in the corresponding regulations, will be punished with major arrest [*arresto mayor*] and a second class fine."[26] Though the primary object of these laws was not to stem "recreational drug use," as we would call it today, the laws that these earlier motivations left in place provided a perfectly reasonable justification for prosecuting the distributors of recreational drugs. This was especially clear with marijuana, which was almost never lamented as a problem because it caused "addiction" but rather because it was believed to cause damage to the brain and, hence, madness.

Eventually the sanitary council would gain sufficient power to ban the sale and cultivation of marijuana altogether. But before then, a number of obstacles had to be overcome. Mexico's chronic instability during most of the nineteenth century had greatly affected the council's ability to carry out its mission. In no way was this more visible than in the jurisdictional issues that plagued the council from the very beginning. The main source of these problems were the frequent changes between the centralist and federalist political systems. The sanitary council itself had been inspired by one of these jurisdictional snafus. Bustamante's Facultad Médica had been created within a federalist system in 1832, but the return to a centralist constitution in 1836 forced a remaking of that institution. The result was the Consejo Superior de Salubridad.[27] The Constitution of 1857 then brought into question the constitutionality of that entity. But before any challenges might be raised, the French invaded, installed Emperor Maximilian, and reorganized the sanitary council again.[28]

All of this created significant confusion regarding the state of sanitary law in Mexico City. In 1868, shortly after the fall of the Second Empire and Maximilian's execution, Federal District governor Francisco Montes de Oca posted double-sized, machine-printed advisories announcing that the 1840s sanitary laws were still in effect, and "so that no one claims ignorance" of them, he reprinted their most important enduring provisions. Two years later, the city government sent drugstores handwritten reminders of the same.[29] But ignorance was hardly the greatest impediment to their continued relevance, for Articles 3 and 4 of the 1857 constitution had made them, apparently, unconstitutional. Those articles gave the legislature the *exclusive* privilege of regulating the professions while granting Mexicans the right to take up any "useful and honest profession" as long as the rights of others were not compromised in the process. Thus, on January 30, 1872, Federal District governor Tiburcio Montiel posted another advisory, this time declaring the old laws officially dead and a new, constitutionally sound mandate for the council in effect.[30] The new law appears to have skirted the constitutional questions by means of ambiguity. Thus, while the 1842 statute had specifically charged the council with "ensuring that drugstores only sell medicinal substances to pharmacists, and that medical preparations are not sold outside of the offices of pharmacists," the same mission was only implied in the new regulation. Article 5, Section 1, vaguely ordered the council to "dictate through the respective authorities all those measures relating to public health, both in times of epidemic and in normal times," while Section 2 required that it "visit when it believes it necessary or it is ordered to do so by the District government, hospitals, jails, cemeteries, establishments either commercial, industrial, or public, and at the same time ensure that foodstuffs are not adulterated and are appropriate for consumption, proposing to the District government the measures that it deems necessary, only with respect to that which refers to public hygiene."[31] In contrast with earlier statutes, a provision calling for the inspection of new pharmacies (Article 5, Section 4) stood as the only specific mention of that profession in the new regulation.

The law's ambiguity in some ways avoided the immediate violation of the constitutional articles, for it aimed neither to significantly regulate any professions (which was the domain of the legislature) nor to impede the rights of Mexicans to make a legitimate living. But the vagueness also left the door open for a more aggressive interpretation. Indeed, using the mandate suggested by Article 5, Section 1, the council, in 1878, published much more specific guidelines for the practice of pharmacy in Mexico City, including restrictions on the sale of certain substances, requirements regarding the organization of specific establishments, and lists of products and equipment that were required to be on hand at all times.[32]

Yet this new regulation still reflected the uncertainty of the council's mandate by not specifying any penalties for violators of its provisions, a fact that provoked controversy when an 1880 pharmacy inspection revealed numerous violations of the new rules. The lack of sentencing guidelines prompted Federal District governor Luis Curiel to propose the appropriate penalties to Gobernación (the Interior Ministry), which was the agency officially charged with approving the council's enforcement activities. This in turn forced a reevaluation of the constitutional issues by Gobernación's Ramón Monterola, who, predictably, opined that these penalties likely violated Articles 3 and 4 of the constitution. Monterola argued that only professions that might prejudice the rights of others could be restricted, and such "prejudices" could be determined only by "the law," that is, by specific legislation relating to that particular profession promulgated by the federal legislature. Since regulations promulgated by the council could not constitute "legislation," even if approved by Gobernación, anyone penalized under the provisions could likely take successful refuge behind an *amparo* (appeal). As Monterola concluded: "The difficulties that arise every moment for lack of organic laws relating to Articles 3 and 4 of the Constitution, and the prejudices which, because of this, the most sacred interests of society suffer, are made every day more clear, and for that reason the undersigned suggests that [Gobernación] request of Congress that it pass related laws as quickly as possible."[33] With the approval of President Porfirio Díaz, this opinion as well as the letter and recommendations from the governor of the Federal District were then forwarded to the Chamber of Deputies for consideration.

The incident is illustrative of the centralizing impulses coursing through Mexican politics during this period. Though the liberal authors of the highly federalist Constitution of 1857 had won the War of the Reform and, thanks to conservative aid to the French Empire, had succeeded in totally discrediting their centralist enemies, the lessons of foreign invasion and civil war had guaranteed the permanence of a strong centralizing impulse below the solemnized liberal doctrines of individualism and equality before the law.[34] Mexico, it was often argued, could not afford disunity. With the aid of Auguste Comte's positivism, the late nineteenth century would thus see a gradual "transformation of liberalism" toward a more centralist approach to government.[35] The activities of the sanitary council, though still highly restricted by the constitution, helped this process along by setting into motion challenges to the reigning federalist charter.

With respect to the constitutionality of the 1878 restrictions, the legislature did not act. Thus, the same issue once again arose after the sanitary council sent a far more detailed "Regulation of Pharmacies" to Gobernación in 1883. As noted above, that regulation continued in the tradition of those promulgated since the 1840s, with lists of drugs and materials that all establishments must have on hand and a slate of restricted substances that could be sold only with a doctor's prescription. Ramón Monterola once again wrote Gobernación's opinion on the new *reglamento*, beginning with a brief history of these regulations and the constitutional questions relating to them. He noted that "various well respected constitutional authorities" had long maintained that any law that restricted the exercise of a profession under the authority of Article 3 of the constitution must be one that could be generalized to the entire Republic. Since no such law had yet been passed, a number of *amparos* had been claimed with success regarding attempts by the Federal District government to restrict the practice of medicine. The same was said to be the case with Article 4.

However, recent decisions by Supreme Court president Ignacio Luis Vallarta had altered this situation considerably. Vallarta had argued convincingly that many of the constitutional articles referring to the rights of citizens involved matters that corresponded to the jurisdiction of the states rather than to that of the federal government. That is, certain protections—for instance, against unlawful detention or retroactive law enforcement—were indeed guaranteed by the constitution, but, at the same time, these were matters over which only the individual states would normally have jurisdiction. In such matters, any "legislation" referred to in these articles had to be promulgated by necessity by the state legislatures, or in the case of the Federal District, by the local authorities. Therefore, any laws that had been passed within the states or the Federal District with reference to the guarantees outlined in these particular articles were to be considered valid even without the existence of "organic" federal legislation applicable to the Republic at large. The articles said to fall within these parameters included 14, 19, 21, and 26, and, according to Monterola, the same logic could be applied to Articles 3 and 4 as well.[36] Thus, the provisions relating to the practice of medicine in the penal code of the Federal District constituted sufficient authority to approve the new Regulation of Pharmacies. However, because the new regulation, like that of 1878, had not come with any proposed penalties for violators, Monterola recommended putting aside the proposal until sentencing guidelines could be added. That step was then superseded by the promulgation of Mexico's first Federal Sanitary Code in 1891.

These episodes, and the many *amparos* filed before the Supreme Court relating to the exercise of medicine, demonstrate how the sanitary council had become an active agent in the shaping of the state's jurisdiction with respect to individual rights under the Constitution of 1857. While the six separate regulations published between 1842 and 1883 appear to have had only a marginal impact on the distribution of drugs in Mexico, those that followed the French Intervention (along with the revised National Farmacopeas of 1874 and 1884) did categorize certain substances as sufficiently dangerous to necessitate significant restriction. These regulations and the court challenges that they inspired thus forced reevaluations of the state's jurisdictional limits by providing new justifications for interventions into the activities of the public.

All of this culminated in "The Sale of Medicines and Other Substances of Industrial Use in Drug Stores and Apothecaries and Analogous Establishments," an entire chapter in Mexico's first Federal Sanitary Code (1891). The chapter was derived, in many cases word for word, from the aborted pharmacy regulations of 1883, and several articles are of particular significance for our purposes here. Article 201 set forth that in every establishment where medicinal substances were sold, there must be a legally authorized pharmacist who would be responsible in both criminal and civil cases for their purity and quality (*buen estado*). Article 202 required that there be a pharmacist on hand at all times in such establishments, while Article 205 mandated that the name of that pharmacist be posted clearly on the establishment's facade. Article 206 dictated that all substances sold as medicines be dispensed in the dosage strictly requested and with a label on the container indicating "medicinal use." Article 208 stated that "dangerous medicines, whether in elemental or compound form [*simples o compuestos*], for use in either human or veterinary medicine, and which appear in the [sanitary] regulations, could only be sold with a prescription written and signed by a doctor, or at the request of, or with the stamp of the apothecary or of the office of a doctor (physician, pharmacist, veterinarian)." And, equally critical, Article 209 required that "the persons dedicated to the collection and sale of medicinal plants and animals, may not sell those items that in the regulations are declared poisonous except to pharmacists and druggists."[37]

Other articles had important consequences for the distribution of drugs. Article 212 indicated that when receiving requests for medicines in unusually high doses, pharmacists were not to dispense the medicine until consulting with the prescribing physician to ensure that no mistakes had been made. Article 214 mandated that in all of these establishments, there should be a book indicating all of the medicines that had been dispensed, including the name of the physician or pharmacist who had prescribed them and the name of the employee who had released them. Article 216 stated that "secret medicines or cosmetics that in the judgment of the Superior Sanitary Council are essentially harmful or that may be used for criminal ends, will be removed from public consumption and their sale will remain thereafter prohibited." And, finally, Article 219 noted that no establishment for the distribution of medicines could be opened without the permission of the government of the Federal District, that permission to be offered only after a recommendation by the sanitary council. The penalties for violations of any of these rules ranged from one to one hundred pesos (Articles 335, 292, respectively), as long as the violation was not already covered by Articles 842, 844, 845, or 1,150

(Fraction 2a) of the penal code. In 1903 (Article 363), that fine was raised to a range of twenty-five to five hundred pesos.[38]

The two most important provisions for our purposes were those that restricted access to substances that were gradually becoming controversial as "recreational drugs"—that is, Article 208, which required that "dangerous" medicines be sold only with a medical prescription, and Article 209, which declared that *herbolarias* could sell "poisonous" plant and animal matter only to pharmacists. What constituted "dangerous" and "poisonous"? The former list was extremely long and contained, among many other drugs, opium, morphine, cocaine, and "canabina," which at the time was thought to be the active component in marijuana.[39] Curiously, the word "marijuana" appears only among those "harmful [*nocivas*]" substances that *herbolarias* could sell exclusively to pharmacists. There it appears in a list nearly identical to that of 1883, among *cabalongas*, cicuta, *beleño*, belladonna, toloache, *zoapatle*, and a few others.[40]

These restrictions were ahead of their time. Consider, for example, the Hague International Opium Convention of 1912, which became the foundation of international drug control in the early twentieth century. One of the main objectives of the convention, as outlined in Article 9, was to encourage contracting powers to "enact pharmacy laws or regulations to confine to medical and legitimate purposes the manufacture, sale, and use of morphine, cocaine, and their respective salts unless laws or regulations on the subject are already in existence."[41] These were precisely the kind of regulations that had existed in Mexico since the colonial era, though, of course, in those days cocaine and most of the opiates (for example, morphine, codeine, and heroin) had yet to be discovered, much less fetishized as especially pernicious. Even in the United States, similar regulations did not begin to emerge until the 1860s, and then only on a gradual, state-by-state basis.[42]

The major limitation of the sanitary code was, once again, jurisdictional—under the Constitution of 1857, a federal code of this kind could apply only to Mexico City, the federal territories of Baja California and Tepic, and the nation's ports. The same, of course, was true for the penal code and its provisions on drugs and their distribution. However, this was overcome to a certain extent by the adoption of these codes, in part or in full, by the individual states.[43] Thus, by 1891, at the very latest, there was considerable if not overwhelming support in Mexico for prohibitionist drug policies.

This was reflected in the passage of many state and local statutes prohibiting the distribution and sometimes even the use of marijuana. In 1869, Mexico City banned its sale.[44] In 1882, Porfirio Díaz, in the brief interregnum during which he served as the governor of Oaxaca, prohibited the sale of "Rosa María, known by the common name mariguana," using Articles 842 and 843 of the state's penal code (which were identical to the same articles in the federal version cited above).[45] In 1888, the city of Cosalá, Sinaloa, prohibited the sale and use of marijuana, with distributors to pay a fine of five to twenty-five pesos and users to be given a penalty "that the public authority deems appropriate."[46] In 1891, the State of Mexico prohibited its sale.[47] In 1896, Mexico City's municipal government reemphasized the prohibition on the sale of marijuana to anyone but pharmacists as mandated by the sanitary code.[48] In the same year, the state of Querétaro prohibited the commerce and cultivation of marijuana and toloache (jimsonweed).[49] Also in 1896, the district of Culiacán, Sinaloa, banned the sale or use of marijuana without a prescription, instituting a fine of two to ten pesos and arrest of three to ten days.[50] And in 1908, Mexico City's governor, Guillermo de Landa y Escandón, reemphasized the ban on marijuana and increased penalties to a mandatory thirty days in jail for violators with no chance for commutation through the payment of a fine.[51]

There appears to have been virtually no resistance to these laws within the political class, despite them being somewhat contrary to the liberal principles enshrined in the 1857 constitution. In 1878, prior to the Supreme Court's more friendly stance on the regulation of medical practice and drug distribution, an article in the liberal newspaper *El Monitor Republicano* took on the question of drug prohibition versus freedom of commerce. Here it used a recent marijuana prohibition in Guanajuato as an example of legislation that appropriately trumped a person's right to make a living:

> The freedom to make a living in trade is one of the rights of the individual; but if he utilizes this liberty to sell what continuously results in harm to the public, destroying the moral, intellectual, and physical health of a large number of the citizens, the government, with the same right cited above, has the privilege and the responsibility to take away from him his absolute liberty with respect to this trade. The government has used this right to prohibit the free commerce in poisons of various kinds, and notably with respect to mariguana. Nonetheless, it is well known that the sale of intoxicating liquors produces the misery and ruin of more families than all of the other poisons combined.[52]

*El Imparcial* would make precisely the same argument in 1903 when new restrictions on the sale of alcohol were being attacked as an assault on freedom of commerce:

The freedom of commerce argument is by now so discredited that it shouldn't even be raised. By now all of us know that individual liberty is limited by the society's [best] interests: it doesn't occur to anyone to protest because the law regulates the carrying of arms, or that it prohibits the sale of poisonous substances, or explosives, which in inexperienced hands can cause very serious accidents. To date no one has wanted to invoke freedom of commerce in order to request the repeal of the disposition which prohibits the sale of marihuana and other noxious herbs in the city's markets.

But it is true that the "herbolarias" do not represent assets like those that are controlled, as a whole, by the owners of taverns.

Could it be that because it deals with capitalists the restriction ceases to be beneficial? Surely not.[53]

But even this was not enough for the more prohibitionist elements in the press. In 1908, *El País* would criticize *El Imparcial* for applauding marijuana's proscription while being against the total prohibition of alcohol. "Why isn't the same thing that is done with marihuana done with alcohol; instead with the latter taxes are imposed, its sale is left free, absolutely free without any other restriction beyond prohibiting its sale at certain hours and on certain days?"[54] The newspapers also routinely called for the authorities to crack down on the sale of marijuana more vigorously.[55]

Violators of marijuana law were arrested and imprisoned throughout this period.[56] But many of these laws offered a loophole for violators: they punished only commerce and/or cultivation intended for sale but not the possession or the giving away of the weed. This appears to have been understood by some of the individuals arrested with marijuana. For example, on February 25, 1900, *La Voz de México* reported that several *soldaderas* had been stopped coming into the barracks carrying marijuana. The women sought to absolve themselves by insisting that the weed was for personal use.[57] An especially interesting case of this kind occurred at Belén in 1907 when a corporal from the Twenty-Fourth Battalion named Benigno Cano was caught in the act of giving a marijuana cigarette to an inmate named J. Ascención Ramírez. According to the latter, the cigarette had been given in exchange for a ring. Cano admitted that he gave away the cigarette but denied having traded it for the ring. The judge explained that he could not be convicted, for it could not be proven that he had actually *exchanged* the ring for the marijuana.[58]

In another case, José Refugio Serrano and his sister María were arrested with over a kilogram of marijuana in their possession. They had turned a small room on the ground floor of their house into a store from which they ostensibly sold fruit, though they called the store "La Seductora" and distributed marijuana from it. A customer who had just purchased three cigarettes from them tipped off the police. Serrano claimed that they used the drug only for medicine, though the police clearly didn't believe his story given the huge quantity of marijuana on the premises. His sister also claimed that it was medicinal and explained the quantity saying that they rarely had a chance to go to "the interior" to pick some up, so, when they did, they brought home a lot. But she also admitted to selling three cigarettes to the man who had turned them in. The judge convicted her while absolving her brother, though he too had been in possession of more than a kilogram of the weed.[59]

There were nonetheless other ways to punish those simply intoxicated with marijuana if the authorities so desired. Article 903 of the penal code was dedicated to "habitual drunkenness [*la embriaguez habitual*]" and laid out penalties for scandalous drunken behavior. While the article was a descendant of edicts promulgated in 1796, 1810, and 1856 and was clearly aimed at "drunkenness," we've seen how the emergence of other intoxicants like marijuana had begun to expand that definition.[60] Presumably, violation of this article could have provided justification for the arrest of some marijuana users.

Whatever the case, these regulatory laws provided important precedents and procedures. If nothing else, policymakers, professionals, and even the ordinary public were surely conditioned by the presence of such laws over decades and to some extent centuries to eventually recognize them as commonplace and even commonsensical. In short, by the 1910s Mexico had developed a patchwork of state, local, and federal laws that placed significant restrictions on marijuana's cultivation and commerce, and there was virtually no resistance to these laws, even on constitutional grounds. But modern drug control regimes could not truly emerge until they were implemented on a national scale, and that required significant change to the constitution.[61] There were, as we've seen, a number of factors working in favor of such a change. A general centralizing tendency had been present in Mexican politics almost from the moment the ink had dried on the Constitution of 1857. Furthermore, notions of "degeneration" had become a kind of common sense of the times, and one of the hallmarks of degeneration theory was its tendency to transform even individual or isolated maladies into threats to the entire nation. The stage was thus set for a change. The Mexican Revolution provided the opportunity.

■ In December 1916, as the forces supporting Venustiano Carranza were consolidating their revolutionary triumph, delegates convened in Querétaro to revise the Constitution of 1857. The meetings would carry into the next year and would eventually produce a quite radical revision of that charter. In the process, the discourses on drugs and degeneration would play a major part in that overhaul, helping to justify a new, more centralized and nationwide approach to the drug problem.

On the night of January 18, 1917, Brigadier General José María Rodríguez, the acting head of the Federal District's Superior Sanitary Council and personal physician of Venustiano Carranza, rose before the delegates to the Constituent Convention at Querétaro and argued passionately that, for the sake of Mexico's national survival, a certain "tyranny" of a newly constituted sanitary council should be written into the revolutionary charter.[62] In a speech that drew on a constellation of associations that had dominated discourses on vice for decades in newspapers, novels, scientific publications, and, surely, everyday conversation in Mexico, Rodríguez gained almost unanimous approval for a measure that gave the sanitary council unprecedented policymaking power under the new constitution.

According to Rodríguez, by any standard of measure, Mexico's position was perilous in the "competition of nations." One need only visit the towns on each side of the Rio Bravo (aka Rio Grande) to see "with discouragement our pitiful standard of living in comparison with our neighbors on the other side." The Mexican race, he argued, was "infirm" and "degenerated," raising issues of "transcendent importance" for the future of Mexico.[63] "The strength of our nation will be determined by means of the number of its inhabitants and its individual and collective wealth; but if the components of our race, in their immense majority, are degenerated by alcohol, or are descendants of alcoholics, or degenerated by illnesses and, on top of all of that, poor and miserable so that they cannot work or fight successfully for their lives due to their physical and, naturally, moral inability, the nation's strength will therefore be diminished in . . . proportion to the numbers of physically incapacitated members, of the sick and the poor."[64]

Improved hygiene could nevertheless alter this trend. But to achieve such change, "despotic" intervention was necessary. "Experience has shown that positive results can only be obtained when directly organized personnel, that is, armed, supplied, and guided by the sanitary council, are put in charge of the campaign. In all campaigns, military or otherwise, the unity of command and instruction is the foundation of success." Such direction, he argued, should naturally come from Mexico City in the form of a newly organized Department of Public Sanitation benefiting from executive power, a department whose recommendations on the most critical issues of hygiene would immediately become law. While the states, being free, would retain some power over local sanitary issues, with respect to problems of "the general health of the Republic and care of the race," they would be subordinate to Mexico City. Furthermore, that department should have the unprecedented power to dictate all laws and campaigns against alcoholism "and the sale of substances that poison individuals and degenerate the race," with Congress retaining only the right to overturn department dictates after their implementation. To justify this final measure, Rodríguez forwarded a battery of statistics, noting that "criminality" in Mexico City outpaced that of Paris, Vienna, and Berlin combined and that 80 percent of "crimes of blood" in Mexico were caused by drunkenness.[65]

The proposal was radical but not completely surprising. While an all-powerful Department of Public Sanitation would be a government agency of unprecedented force and one that would help undermine the liberal principles originally enshrined in the hallowed 1857 constitution then under revision, the measure was for the most part textbook Carrancismo—a strong, centralized state agency designed to "govern, control, repress, purge, guide, educate, uplift," conceived from ideas developed and popularized during the Porfiriato and ultimately driven to the fore by revolutionary upheaval.[66] Despite the extraordinary power it would grant the sanitary council, the proposal itself received little opposition from the delegates, and after a few tepid counterarguments, the debate was ended with José Alvarez's famous injunction that "if the laws of Moses were written on two stones, the Mexican Constitution should be written on two bars of soap," drawing roars of laughter from the delegates. The measure then passed by 143 votes to 3.[67]

The new constitution was eventually approved, and on February 5, 1917, it was published in the *Diario Oficial* and thus formally became the law of the land.[68] Like the delegates in 1916–17, over the next few years the newly empowered sanitary council would demonstrate almost unanimous support for significant, sometimes even draconian, measures with respect to drugs. In the summer of 1919, for example, Rodríguez, who still headed the council, proposed that a letter of commendation be sent to Governor Plutarco Elías Calles of Sonora, who had recently instituted the death penalty for violations of his statewide prohibition of alcohol. The proposal was approved with only one dissenting vote.[69]

Nonetheless, taking real action was a somewhat more complicated proposition. With respect to alcohol, by far Mexico's most widely abused drug, fiscal considerations precluded any radical measures by the council. President Carranza had specifically instructed Rodríguez to carry out measures against alcoholism, but he also emphasized that those measures should under no circumstances reduce receipts at the federal treasury. The same argument had in fact prevented total alcohol prohibition at Querétaro three years earlier.[70]

On the other hand, with respect to marijuana, cocaine, and the opiates, there was no debate regarding the basic wisdom of new regulatory measures. Since 1917, the newly created sanitary council had been inundated with requests from legitimate pharmacists to legally import opiates, a circumstance that repeatedly reminded the council that it had yet to act on its new mandate to control the distribution of drugs. As it was argued in the council's meeting of July 1, 1919, any day critics might demand to know what had been done with respect to "substances that poison the organism," and the council would have no answer.[71] In fact, congressional members of the so-called medical bloc had been looking for ways to prohibit alcohol nationwide but had been frustrated because the new constitution had specifically granted the sanitary council the lawmaking power in that area.[72]

Yet despite that obvious mandate and general council support for new regulations, some council members were reluctant to take advantage of so much power when actual drug control measures were first proposed by the council's Apothecary Commission on April 25, 1919. Their reluctance, and the debates that resulted, reiterate just how radical that new mandate was. The issue came to a head in December 1919 when the council's lawyer, Fernando Breña Alvírez, made a long statement clarifying the basis of these extraordinary powers. Here he turned back to 1917, quoting at length from Rodríguez's speech at Querétaro: "The first condition required so that a nation is strong and can fight with energy in the general competition of nations, IS THE CARE OF INDIVIDUAL AND COLLECTIVE HEALTH, that is the improvement of the race taken to its highest level; and seeing as some corporation or authority should take it upon itself to put into practice all of the [necessary] procedures in order to ensure the happy success of these determinations, IT IS INDISPENSABLE THAT THE SANITARY AUTHORITY BE THAT ONE WHICH TAKES UPON ITS SHOULDERS THIS JOB." Breña Alvírez stressed that the Constituent Convention had *obligated* the council to act on such measures. Here he again turned to Rodríguez's words from 1917: "It is indispensable that the dispositions dictated to correct this sickness of the race (degeneration), stemming principally from alcoholism and the poisoning by medicinal substances like opium, morphine, ether, cocaine, and marihuana, etc., be dictated with such energy that they may offset in an effective and efficacious manner, the abuse from the commerce in these substances that are so poisonous to health, that today have occasioned disasters of such a nature, that they have multiplied mortality to levels among the highest in the world." Debate on these points then ensued and Rodríguez, still council president, once again triumphed. He acknowledged the relatively radical nature of Article 73, which, he noted, had drawn some significant, even justified opposition from a few delegates at the Constituent Convention. Those detractors had argued that the sanitary council was in effect being given even more power than the president of the Republic with respect to drugs. But, he had maintained, given the severity of the problem, "this sacrifice was necessary," and in the end, "all of the deputies agreed." Breña Alvírez's statement, which had confirmed the council's extraordinary power, was then approved unanimously.[73]

In January 1920, the final version of the legislation was tweaked by the council. In those discussions, marijuana was slated for total prohibition, "one of the most pernicious manias of our people [*nuestro pueblo*]" and "not a medicine."[74] On March 2, the council proclaimed its "Dispositions on the Cultivation and Commerce of Products that Degenerate the Race." The legislation banned the cultivation of and commerce in marijuana completely. It also required drug wholesalers to obtain special permission from the sanitary council in order to import opiates or cocaine; it mandated that importers could sell those drugs only to licensed medical distributors and doctors who had also received specific permission to receive them; it required that special bookkeeping measures be taken by distributors to document the commerce in these products; and it banned the cultivation of opium and the extraction of its narcotic latex without special permission.[75]

There was little in the legislation that was absolutely new. As we've seen, bookkeeping requirements and bans on marijuana had existed in Mexico for some time in the patchwork of legislation described above. But here, for the first time, the sanitary council could now utilize its executive power to make uniform laws for the entire nation on these matters. The law also, for the first time, specifically fetishized marijuana, cocaine, and the opiates as especially pernicious. The latter two had emerged as the bêtes noires of international drug control, and their inclusion in this legislation reflected, to a certain extent, Mexico's participation in those incipient international regimes. In 1912, Francisco Madero had sent Federico Gamboa, author of works on degeneration and vice, to sign the Hague Convention, which he did in May of that year.[76] And though that treaty would not be ratified in Mexico until 1925, its basic precepts were hardly controversial among Mexican policymakers.[77] But marijuana's inclusion was clearly Mexico's own contribution, for that drug would not become a target of international anti-drug efforts until 1925.[78]

In this manner, the foundation of Mexico's modern War on Drugs was laid. Though it had been in the making for decades and even centuries, the full title of the 1920 "Dispositions" very much reflected the intellectual climate of the period. The concept of degeneration had helped to turn "drugs" into a national threat in Mexico, a problem against which a "war," with all of the inevitable violations of peacetime principles and rights, had to be waged.

*Chapter 9*

POSTSCRIPT

MEXICAN IDEAS MOVE NORTH

Mexico's prohibition of marijuana in 1920 was largely a domestic affair. None-theless, as discussed earlier, global historical factors played a role throughout this drug's Mexican history, from the emergence of "degeneration" as a kind of modern common sense, to the global outlook of Mexican thinkers concerned with their country's place in "the competition of nations." This is hardly sur-prising. Scholars have long recognized the influence of the outside world on Mexico, especially in the late nineteenth and early twentieth centuries, when European models were a prominent source of inspiration and aspiration for Mexican elites. José Guadalupe Posada consistently lampooned such thinking in his penny-press lithographs and particularly in his character Don Chepito Mariguano (see chapter 7), though, ironically, that character itself owed a debt to French graphic influences. Such ironies are typical of a globalizing en-vironment where the flow of ideas and influence is often subtle and complex.

This final chapter examines the outbound trajectory of these discursive flows. Here I offer an important revision to existing scholarship by demon-strating that, beginning in the 1890s, Mexican ideas formed a crucial founda-tion for developing anti-marijuana sentiment in the United States. Yet this is also a story of transformation, for once these ideas entered a new historical context north of the border, they were subtly remolded by already established notions about Mexicans and drugs and by the specific political and material interests of a rising American empire.

■ Professional historians have given relatively little attention to the early his-tory of marijuana in the United States. Two excellent books of the early 1970s, *The Marihuana Conviction* by Richard Bonnie and Charles Whitebread and *The American Disease* by David Musto, remain the standard academic texts on marijuana's U.S. history, though Musto's work deals with other illicit drugs as well. Jerome Himmelstein's *The Strange Career of Marihuana*, published in 1983, and a recent short article by Dale Gieringer have provided some nuance to the original paradigm.[1] But in the countless books that raise the question of marijuana's early history and prohibition in the United States, the vast majority simply cite Bonnie and Whitebread, Musto, or Himmelstein.

A critical aspect of this drug's early U.S. history, and especially its prohibition, was one that has been central to this book: the idea that marijuana caused crime, violence, and madness. That idea was famously espoused by the Federal Bureau of Narcotics (FBN) and its infamous longtime chief, Harry Anslinger, during the 1930s. Bonnie and Whitebread give the most detailed account of that notion and its origins in the United States in a chapter titled "What Was the Marihuana Menace?" There they argue that the link between marijuana and insanity was primarily an import from Egypt and India, where such a belief was already well developed. With respect to the connection between marijuana and crime so touted by Anslinger and the FBN, they argue that this was "primarily a contribution of the American experience" and developed mostly after about 1930. But their argument is at times inconsistent. Earlier in the book, for example, they claim that any drug that was labeled a "narcotic" by medical or law enforcement personnel became a substance that was assumed to cause "addiction, lethargy, crime, insanity, and death" and that any drug that became associated with "street use" inevitably came to be labeled a "narcotic." In other words, as soon as marijuana was associated with such street use, its connection to crime and insanity was inevitable. Also early in the text, and more significant given my argument here, the authors note that, in the 1910s, Mexican "patricians" along the border espoused a frightening "Mexican marijuana folklore" in which violence and madness played a prominent role: "The Mexican marihuana folklore apparently made a deep impression on any American who came in contact with the drug or its alien users." The authors explain this folklore in class terms. It was class-consciousness that resulted in Mexican "patricians" being even more fanatically anti-marijuana than their U.S. counterparts. But this argument is abandoned after a short section on Texas and totally excluded from the subsequent "Marijuana Menace" chapter cited above.[2]

Though Musto did not take on the question directly, he clearly implied that the marijuana-violence discourse had emerged from the drug's association with Mexican users who, in general, were "feared as a source of crime and deviant social behavior." This was an argument also forwarded by Bonnie and Whitebread: "Since its users—Mexicans, West Indians, blacks, and underworld whites—were associated in the public mind with crime, particularly of a violent nature, the association applied also to marihuana, which had a similar reputation in Mexican folklore." As Musto demonstrates, by 1919 prison officials in the Southwest were attributing violence to marijuana-using inmates, and by the mid-1920s "horrible crimes were attributed to marihuana and its Mexican purveyors."[3] Perhaps because of its parsimony, and because it dovetails nicely with Bonnie and Whitebread's broader narrative emphasizing the role of anti-Mexican sentiment in the genesis of state-level marijuana laws, most subsequent authors have simply followed Musto's lead and implied that these ideas were a product of anti-Mexican racism.[4] This view has been buttressed by the notion that marijuana was "a casual adjunct to life" in the Mexican community or a manifestation of "historically persistent tradition" akin to coca chewing in the Andes, something that appears to have been assumed by most of the authors who have written on the subject.[5] That, of course, was a reasonable assumption given late-twentieth-century notions of marijuana's effects and use patterns throughout North America. But, as we have already seen, the story was considerably more complicated than that.

It is important to recognize that widespread knowledge of cannabis and its intoxicating effects dates back to the mid-nineteenth century in the United States. As noted earlier, it was during that period when the intoxicating properties of this drug, usually referred to as "hashish" or "Indian hemp" in the United States, began to be widely recognized in much of the Western world. At that time, its commonly described effects varied tremendously, with some sources even linking it to madness and violence. But the latter effects would begin to dominate the drug's reputation in the United States only when Mexican ideas about "marijuana" began to cross the border at the end of the century.

As I have already demonstrated, by the 1890s marijuana's reputation for causing madness and violence was well established in Mexico, and over the next two decades that reputation would be reinforced with sensational detail by a flourishing yellow press. It was from this atmosphere that the U.S. media began to pluck exotic, sensational stories of a new drug menace south of the border. These stories, appearing in dailies across the United States, introduced readers to a substance that, importantly, was not usually recognized as simply another form of cannabis. The word *mariguana* was the key here, for until that point it had been known in the United States only as the name of an island in the Bahamas (today's Mayaguana).[6] Thus, as these reports arrived from Mexico, they suggested a substance distinct from cannabis, sometimes left unidentified, and sometimes erroneously classified as something else altogether. In other words, older ideas about hashish or Indian hemp were not simply being grafted onto emerging marijuana discourses in the United States.

Perhaps the most significant development for the spread of these Mexican discourses into the United States was the founding of the *Mexican Herald*, an English-language newspaper based primarily in Mexico City that began publishing in 1895.[7] The *Herald*'s circulation in Mexico at the turn of the century was only a few thousand issues a day, but it was linked closely to the United States because it owned the Associated Press franchise for the Mexican capital. Thus, its stories were easily picked up by papers in the United States for consumption by audiences far removed from the streets of Mexico City. As the identity of marijuana was uncertain, it was not infrequently confused in these stories with other substances such as jimsonweed (*Datura stramonium*) and locoweed (any one of several varieties of *Astragalus*). It was also common for a single story to enter the wire service and then make its way through newspapers across the country over the course of many years, with the story's details gradually being transformed along the way. As a result, marijuana's reputation took a journey that left all of its most important elements intact but that gradually altered its outward hue in ways particular to the U.S. environment.

The process began in March 1896 when the *Mexican Herald* reported that the pulque sold in Mexico City's shops was often adulterated with "marihuana," a drug that, the paper reported, caused "temporary madness" in its users. Here, marijuana was identified as jimsonweed, but its general symptoms held true to stereotype. "Those who are two [*sic*] strong to be prostrated are maddened by it, and pull out knives and stab their comrades upon the slightest provocation." The author of this particular story claimed to have himself come under the drug's influence thanks to some adulterated pulque. "I am certain that if anyone had been with me, I should have quarreled with him and tried to fling him down the *barranca* [ravine], not from bloodthirstiness, but because the effect of the horrible drug upon the nerves was to incite to a struggle." The vendors believed such adulterations necessary, the author claimed, "for the lowest classes of the capital drink that they may be intoxicated. Like the Indians of our own land they 'like to feel drunk come.'"[8] The story's most important details were picked up shortly thereafter by U.S. consul general Thomas Crittenden, who repeated them in an article of his own that appeared in the *Herald* and in various other publications, including *Current Literature* and *Monthly Trade and Consular Reports*: "The effect upon the nerves is singular, and it almost forces men into physical struggles of which they are unconscious at the time."[9]

Over the coming years, the *Herald*'s reporting on marijuana continued, as did the adoption of these stories by U.S. media outlets. Marijuana could serve as an exotic curiosity that was sometimes slipped into humorous stories for effect, but mostly it was written about in frightening tones and as a mysterious new drug menace.[10] This was the case in a *Herald* story picked up by the *Broad Ax* of Salt Lake City in October 1898 that identified marijuana as a lower-class drug in Mexico and warned that the use of this "maddening weed" was increasing alarmingly among young people: "An illustration of this was given yesterday afternoon . . . where a young boy not much over twelve years of age, who had been crazed by smoking marihuana, was running wildly down the center of the thoroughfare, tearing his clothes and attacking all who crossed his path."[11]

Though the *Herald* was the most common source of such stories, there were sometimes reports from other parts of Mexico or the border region as well. One widely published story appeared under various headlines ranging from "A Seductive Weed" to "New Opiate" to "Along the Border, Curious and Interesting Things on the Mexican Frontier." The first version of which I am aware appeared on November 18, 1897, in the New Philadelphia *Ohio Democrat* and reported that the "seductive mariguana" was being smuggled into the prisons of southern Arizona. "This is a kind of 'loco' weed, more powerful than opium. . . . It is a dangerous thing for the uninitiated to handle, but those who know its uses say it produces more ravishing dreams than opium."[12] Though the original version of this story did not include specific reference to the violent effects so often reported in the Mexican press at the time, more sinister details would be added later. The *Spirit Lake (IA) Beacon*, which had reprinted the story above almost verbatim on January 21, 1898, ran it again a month later but provided this troubling addition: "Under its influence the sedate Mexican becomes noisy as a cowboy and has to be lassoed and put in the calaboose."[13] Similarly, the *Marysville (OH) Tribune* added its own wrinkle: "Mixed with tobacco the Mexicans revel in it. . . . Saturated with this drug they forget all of the ills and cares of life, are reckless and pugnacious, and will fight on the smallest provocation, or no provocation at all."[14]

The story also illustrates one of the key elements in the shaping of marijuana's reputation in the United States—its putative identity as "locoweed." Locoweed is an actual species of plant (*Astragalus* of several varieties) that grows in the southwest United States and northern Mexico and is often ingested by horses and livestock, resulting in an actual neurological disease now known as "locoism." The results of locoism are quite disturbing. An 1885 article published by Henry M. Hurd in the *Journal of Insanity* accurately described the action of locoweed or "rattle weed" upon animals that ingest it:

> The brain as well as the cord becomes affected and it is said that the animal acts as if absolutely crazy. He cannot be coerced or driven and becomes exceedingly dangerous. He loses his shining coat, falls away in flesh, refuses to eat even when food is placed in his mouth, and finally dies of exhaustion. Although tormented by a persistent thirst which impels him to seek water, when it is found he does not drink, but lies down in it and frequently drowns in a very shallow stream. . . . When it once has been tasted it seems to possess for them the same fatal attraction that opium does for too many human beings and they will then refuse all other forage and wander for miles in search of the plant.[15]

By the turn of the century, a significant discourse on the effects of the real locoweed was already developing in the United States. The fact that news of marijuana's effects would begin to enter the public consciousness around the same time as the locoweed of range animals, a substance with a Spanish-derived name meaning "crazy" and that actually produced a disturbing kind of neurological damage, surely helped cultivate in the public mind both the "Mexicanness" of marijuana and its reported tendency to produce madness. It was a perfect coincidence that helped stoke a growing marijuana mythology in the United States.

The development of the marijuana/locoweed confusion also richly illustrates how previously existing perceptions in the United States came to shape views of this drug north of the border. That confusion began with a fictional story that appeared in an 1887 issue of *Scribner's Magazine*. The story, authored by Thomas Janvier, did not actually mention marijuana, but it did describe the plight of a man who had been poisoned with "locoweed" by a spurned lover, a plant that Janvier termed the "flower of death." Janvier was referring to toloache, a plant today identified as any one of several varieties of *Datura* and, as noted previously, occasionally confused with marijuana in the U.S. press. In fact, doses of *Datura* can produce bouts of psychotomimetic symptoms for extended periods and even permanent insanity in very high doses.[16] Janvier's story was fictional but based on the widely held belief in Mexico that poisoning by this substance caused permanent madness. As Janvier would later clarify, marijuana was understood in much the same way in Mexico and sometimes called "locoweed" as well. However, Janvier's toloache story deserves a few more moments of attention because it so elegantly demonstrates the lens through which many Americans likely viewed Mexicans and puta-tively "Mexican" drugs of this kind.[17]

Janvier's tale involves a man named George Rand who is of "tough New England stock" but within whose "cool, practical Yankee blood ran another strain." That strain is a product of his grandfather's world travels. Many years before, his grandfather had returned from these journeys and "vexed sorely the Puritan prejudices of his family by bringing home a Papist wife." No one knew exactly where he'd found her, but an old portrait "was proof enough that she came from a southern land: a gentle, gracious face of clear olive brown; dark eyes, all fire and tenderness; lips soft and full, on which warm kisses seemed to wait." Rand's blood carries that foreign strain, and as a child, seemingly by instinct, he would worship his grandmother's portrait, kneeling before it to say prayers. One day he was caught in this position by his mother, who, "being fair herself, and holding to sound Congregational doctrine, hated black-haired Papistical women as she hated the personal devil who was an im-portant part of her rigid creed." From that moment he was forbidden to kneel before the portrait in such a way.

Rand eventually grows to become an engineer and marries a proper New England Protestant girl, a woman in the image of his stern mother. But just before their first child is born, an unparalleled and singular business oppor-tunity presents itself in Mexico. Thus, he makes his way south of the border. There he finds the slow pace of life surprisingly comforting: "Custom could not stale for him the charm of this easy-going languorous life; that yet had underlying it lava seas of passionate energy—whence, at any moment, might burst forth storms of raging hatred, or not less raging storms of love." Though without specific mention of the "atavisms" with which we have become famil-iar in this book, Janvier's description of Rand clearly drew on related notions. He explained that Rand felt but could not understand his affinity for the Mexican way of life. It was as if he had been on a long journey but finally come home. At first he humors these feelings by fully immersing himself in local life, but he soon finds that it is difficult to turn back: "He knew that he was losing his old-time fighting power; that his moral strength was slipping away from him; that he was dropping each day more and more into the very Mexican habit of drifting with the stream." But Rand is still tied by his wife and child back in New England to that "sterner, higher civilization of which he had been a part." He struggles with the competing impulses.

He is soon overcome with desire for a Mexican woman named Josefa, whose "dark beauty entreated him, and whose Latin-Indian blood was flame." The girl is the daughter of a dissipated old man whose love of drink and gambling, along with profligate spending on "fiestas" of various kinds, had virtually wrecked the family. Temptation severely tests Rand.

> He called to his aid the steadfast honesty and the love of honor for honor's sake that belonged to him by right of his Saxon blood; and with these he fought the weakness that his Latin blood had brought him. But his weakness had many strong allies. The strangeness of his life, that was all the stranger because it seemed so familiar to him; the absence of the bracing moral atmosphere, out of which—even in the roughest of his frontier life in the States—he had never lived; a climate that filled him with a fuller, richer sense of life than he had ever known: all these forces were allies to his weakness; all were united to arouse that portion of his nature which had slumbered ever since he was a boy.

Eventually the two become romantically involved and make a home together. Within six months, Rand is completely changed. His friends would not have recognized him. His former "brisk" and "erect" manner has been replaced by "a slouching slowness," while "grim taciturnity had taken the place of his habit of frank, cheery speech." Perhaps most telling of all are his eyes, which before had always looked straight into other men's eyes but now "were cast downward or raised only in quick, furtive glances; and in his eyes, and over all his face and form, there was an unlifting weight of melancholy." Rand has been turned from a tall, erect New Englander into a taciturn and shifty Latin.

As time goes on, Rand's two natures continue to battle for his allegiance. Letters from his wife in New England exacerbate his confusion while arousing murderous jealousy in Josefa. He then receives word that his son has died and that his wife is gravely ill. He informs Josefa that he must return to the north, to which she responds with alternating fits of tender sobbing and murderous rage. Within hours of his decision, "the decisive step . . . had told upon his moral tone. He was beginning to be a man again; and a feeling not only of horror, but of disgust, was coming over him as he began to realize what his life for the past six months had been. This feeling was intensified as he looked about him at the dwelling in which, for a good part of the time, he had been content to live. It was a hole not fit, even, to be the abiding place of brutes. . . . Of a truth, Rand thought, as his eyes were opened and he perceived the loathsomeness of his surroundings, he had indeed come to feed upon husks and live among swine."

Josefa considers murdering him but decides on a worse fate: she will poison him with toloache, which, according to Janvier, was a plant used by vengeful women since before the conquest to strike their enemies with madness. Called the "flower of death," toloache produced violent headaches, frightening hallucinations, painful thirst, and permanent insanity. Before Rand's departure, Josefa feigns forgiveness and offers him a cup of coffee in which she has placed the toloache. Within an hour, he begins raving.

The story makes clear the extraordinary compatibility between Yankee and Mexican worldviews at this point in time, though these were obviously derived from different frames of analysis. For Mexican observers, frightening atavisms lurked within their people thanks to Indian and conquistador bloodlines. For Americans like Janvier, the threat was miscegenation with any member of the "southern races," for these were Oriental peoples given to sloth and passion. Josefa was the dangerous forbidden fruit whose emotions alternated violently between fits of love and hatred. One can see in her figure a metaphor not only for the "southern races" in general but for the irrationality that was supposedly produced by a "Mexican" drug like marijuana.

Though fictional, this tale would play a crucial role in the marijuana/locoweed confusion thanks to a similar but true-to-life incident that occurred shortly after its publication. That incident began when, in the late 1890s, a doctor named Charles Pilgrim at the Hudson River State Hospital in New York received a patient who told a remarkably similar story. Like Janvier's main character, the man had been drawn to Mexico, like so many other American professionals, by the economic boom there. He had been working in Oaxaca as a civil engineer on a coffee plantation in a rather intense atmosphere of conflict between neighboring coffee producers. There were also constant disturbances from "marauding Indians." A work stoppage was forced by the chaos, the man's "habits grew worse," and he wound up falling ill with a fever. While lying in bed, he had been brought some food by an Indian with whom he had had some conflict. Though another Indian had warned him not to touch the food, he did so anyway, only to find himself suddenly overcome by a remarkable thirst, illusions, hallucinations, and depersonalization. He came to believe that he had become one of the characters in a book he had been reading. Soon after, as tensions reached a boiling point on the plantation, his friends decided to take him to Mexico City for medical care. The journey was nightmarish, as he was bound by his companions and forced to travel on horseback or in a litter, at one point being left to rest so close to a campfire that his feet were blistered and burned. At another point he was once again served food by an Indian, warned by another not to eat it, but again, ignoring the advice, partook of the sustenance and like before became "crazy with thirst." Once in Mexico City he was taken to the American hospital, where he was bound to a bed to prevent him from committing suicide or escaping. His condition and treatment remained the same on the return journey by ship to the United States. When examined by Pilgrim, the patient displayed incoherent speech, a feeble gait, and a confused sense of time and space and was experiencing auditory and visual hallucinations. He also exhibited the symptoms of secondary syphilis. After nearly six months of treatment, he recovered.

Pilgrim was convinced that the root cause of the problem was syphilis and not poisoning, but the patient's friends, along with a doctor in Mexico City, were steadfast that "loco-weed" was to blame. To prove them wrong, Pilgrim undertook a follow-up investigation. He began a correspondence with Janvier, whose story he recalled reading. Janvier informed him that "'the loco-weed' of Northern Mexico is the *Datura stramonium* of our pharmacopeia; the plant is known also in Southern Mexico together with another 'loco-weed'— mariguana—our *Cannabis sativa*." According to Janvier, doses of these loco-weeds were said to cause confusion of thought and disturbing sensations of suffocation, nausea, and thirst as well as a delirium, "sometimes of a furious, sometimes of a whimsical character. . . . It is the popular belief (of which I made use in my story, by reference) that a permanent madness can be induced by the 'loco-weed.' Dr. Eduardo Liceaga, the leading physician of the City of Mexico, and the eminent Dr. Elenterio Jose Gonzales, late of Monterey [sic], have denied this positively. I have known of one case of insanity that was attributed to this weed, but not certainly traced to that cause, in which the madness lasted for three months and was ended by death."[18]

Further correspondence between Pilgrim and informants in Mexico demonstrated how the real locoweed (*Astragalus*) was beginning to be confused with the locoweed of legend in Mexico (either *Datura* or marijuana). Dr. Isaac Ott, who had studied a variety of *Astragalus mollissimus*, said that while the plant produced some strange phenomena in horses, he had never seen it produce insanity in men. Dr. Edmond Goldmann, who practiced for several years in Monterrey, wrote that despite his personal lack of experience with "loco-weed," he was aware of hearsay on the subject and went on to explain that "the name 'loco-weed' signifies an herb that produces mental disease. In Mexico, however, people attribute this effect not so much to the 'loco-weed,' which is a species of astragalus, as to the stramony leaves and seeds (*Datura stramonium*)." During his days in Monterrey, he'd seen a number of cases of madness that had been attributed to locoweed, but each time he requested a sample, it turned out to be *Datura* rather than *Astragalus*. He was also doubtful that the plant had actually caused the insanity, for there were plenty of other common and more likely causes of mental disturbances in Mexico, from syphilis to malaria.[19] A certain Dr. Benavides responded in similar fashion, noting that "the Aztec Indians use the dried leaves of Stramonium and Cannabis sativa for smoking by mixing them in small quantities with tobacco" and that "when they wish to poison a person they either mix the dried leaves very strongly with tobacco or make a decoction and administer it in some drink." Nevertheless, he concluded that "he knew of no case of insanity due to the use of these plants." From all of this, Pilgrim concluded the following: "While it is well known that Stramonium, Cannabis sativa and kindred plants, produce temporary delirium, and even death when given in excessive doses, and that their long continued use will result in marked mental disturbance, my investigations have convinced me that there is no 'loco-weed' which will, in single doses, produce permanent insanity." The key distinction here was between temporary and permanent madness and pitted "popular" belief against that of physicians, a fact briefly considered already in chapter 7. Physicians readily admitted that these drugs produced temporary delirium but rejected claims of permanent madness resulting from their use. The public, however, was convinced otherwise, as Pilgrim explained:

> The contrary belief . . . is so firmly established in the minds of Mexicans that a bill has recently been introduced in the legislature in the State of Queretaro . . . forbidding the cultivation of Stramonium and Cannabis sativa on account of the evil uses to which such plants are put by the native Indians. Indeed it is a common belief in Mexico that a decoction of the "loco-weed" was administered to the Empress Carlotta [*sic*] just before her departure to seek assistance from Napoleon, and that it was the cause of her insanity and subsequent seclusion at Miramar. Mme. del Barrio, who accompanied the Empress from Mexico, and who for more than thirty years has been the faithful companion of her lonely life, clings tenaciously to this belief. To the alienist, of course, no such explanation is needed, as her father's death, to whom she was devotedly attached, the loss of the crown, which was more to her than life, and the knowledge of the futility of her efforts to save Maximilian from the fate which later befell him on the "Hill of the Bells," were more than enough to upset even a stronger brain than hers; but the average Mexican brushes aside all such causes as trivial and remains firm in his belief that sometime the secrets of State will show that this dread weed was the sole cause of the hopeless madness of the unhappy Empress.[20]

As noted in chapter 7, Pilgrim's inquiries helped inspire an investigation into the subject by Fernando Altamirano, who had also noted how doctors, especially in rural areas, were routinely confronted with claims of malicious poisonings by such "locoweeds." Similarly, in a 1902 issue of *Science*, Dr. V. K. Chestnut noted the tendency in Mexico to refer to several different substances as "locoweeds" because they were thought to cause madness, though he clarified that the actual "locoweed" of the Southwest was in fact *Astragalus mollissimus*. Among the commonly cited locoweeds in Mexico stood marijuana: "It is not uncommonly asserted by Mexicans that sometimes a single dose of hemp will cause long-lasting insanity." But he too was skeptical, "especially in regard to the crazing effect of single doses." Chestnut also noted that while the word "mariguana" usually referred to cannabis in Mexico, it could be used for *Datura*, though beyond the 1896 *Mexican Herald* article cited above, I'm not aware that anyone else ever made this claim.[21]

In any case, the similarities between the purported effects of both locoweed and intoxicating drugs like marijuana were not lost on observers both far away from and near to locoweed's natural habitat in the borderlands. As the *Marshall (MI) Daily News* put it: "The effect of the loco poison on animals appears to be something like that of the drug habit on human beings. After an animal has eaten loco it will eat nothing else, but will wander about in a stupor not unlike that of a 'dope fiend,' looking for the poisonous weed." In 1905, the *Laredo Times* identified marijuana as both "locoweed" and "that narcotic Mexican weed of 'bughouse' propensities." And in 1906, the *Denton (MD) Journal* contributed to the confusion with this tidbit: "Various states have attempted to adopt measures for the eradication of the loco weed, but so far these attempts have not met with much success. Colorado, a number of years ago, offered a reward of so much per ton for quantities of the loco weed brought in for extermination. The Mexican greasers, with great thrift, started in to farm and raise loco weeds."[22] The paper here referred to the actual locoweed consumed by range animals, but one can see how the distinction between the weed linked to animals and that linked to Mexicans was becoming somewhat murky. A 1911 *Washington Post* story titled "Loco Weed Hoodoos Horses" perhaps best represents the growing marriage of the discourses on *Astragalus* and "narcotic" drugs during this period:

> To ride a horse of this sort is dangerous. His mind is apparently filled with all the demons that can frighten horses. On a plain that is absolutely desolate he will shy at a thousand imaginary terrors. He sees things that his master or his rider cannot see. Doubtless these are the imaginary terrors that his diseased brain is picturing. He seems to have more horrors around him than a hasheesh eater or a coke fiend.
>
> Whatever it is that a horse sees in the place of the snakes, worms and

kind-faced purple cows of the human inebriate must haunt the "locoed" horse. He seems to have all the "horrors" that can be packed into his skull.[23]

Even at the retail level in the United States, where cannabis could still be sold over the counter without a prescription, the nomenclature was confused. The proprietor of the International Drug Store in El Paso, Texas, noted to investigators in 1917 that he had sold cannabis to about twenty soldiers on their return from General Pershing's expedition to Mexico. "Sometimes they ask for Marihuana and sometimes for 'Loco Weed.'"[24]

While the locoweed discourse was mixing confusingly with that of marijuana during these years, the *Mexican Herald* continued to publish stories from Mexico City that were picked up by newspapers across the United States. One story, which first began to appear in U.S. papers around 1905, was especially influential. It also clearly drew on the investigations done by either Pilgrim or Altamirano or both. As the story ran in the United States, it included the classic elements of the marijuana discourse in Mexico—it was used by the lower classes and especially prisoners sentenced to long terms, and its effects were terrifying:

> The dry leaves of marihuana, alone or mixed with tobacco, make the smoker wilder than a wild beast. It is said that immediately after the first three or four drafts of smoke smokers begin to feel a slight headache: then they see everything moving, and finally they lose all control of their mental faculties. Everything, the smokers say, takes the shape of a monster, and men look like devils. They begin to fight, and of course everything smashed is a monster "killed." But there are imaginary beings whom the wild man cannot kill, and these inspire fear until the man is panic stricken and runs.
>
> Not long ago a man who had smoked a marihuana cigarette attacked and killed a policeman and badly wounded three others. Six policemen were needed to disarm him and march him to the police station where he had to be put into a straitjacket. Such occurrences are frequent.

The article, which went on to cite Empress Carlota's apparent poisoning by toloache, appeared in papers around the United States over the next decade under various titles, including "Madness in Plants," "Smoking That Maddens," "Dangerous Mexican Weeds," and "Evil Mexican Plants That Drive You Insane."[25] Other similarly sensational stories from the *Herald* also hit the wires during this period, making the rounds for months and even years.[26]

As noted already, almost none of the newspaper articles appearing prior to 1910 recognized the word "marihuana" as a synonym for cannabis or "Indian hemp," as it was commonly called in the United States at the time. For example, in 1909 it was widely reported that a researcher in Texas named James Love had been granted permission to import "the deadly marihuana plant" for research on its medicinal properties, though research on cannabis had been ongoing in the United States and Europe for nearly seventy years.[27] Again, this is important because it further demonstrates that U.S. sources were not merely grafting older ideas regarding hashish onto the emerging marijuana discourse.

Nonetheless, clearly a kind of Orientalism was at work in all of this. This was an Orientalism in the true sense described by Edward Said, one that helped "other" Latin America in a manner conducive to imperial ambition. And this was precisely the moment, of course, when the United States was experimenting with formal colonialism for the first time. Perhaps the most glaring example of this came in a 1905 *Washington Post* article on the research of Frederick Starr, the well-known founder of anthropological study at the University of Chicago. As the *Post* put it:

> Curiosity has often been expressed as to the peculiar mental traits of Latin-American warriors and revolutionists which lead them to view "North America" as a monster of hideous shape and ungovernable appetite, and at the same time endow them with a super-human, soul-bursting valor, and defiance of the monster their imagination has conjured up. The recent inexplicable maneuvers of our busy little friend, Cipriano Castro, of Venezuela, in seeking trouble with the United States are a manifestation of this mysterious trait. So, too, is the manifesto of Castro's adviser, Col. John the Baptist Lamedo, whose threat to invade the Mississippi Valley with 30,000 sons of Bolivar is still shaking New Orleans like an earthquake.

The *Post* argued that Castro's valor might be explained by a "strange weed" called "marihuana," which, the article claimed, Starr had "discovered" and which happened to flourish in Venezuela:

> The Celestial smoker of the poppy draws visions of comfort and opulence from his thick tube and little pill. The hasheesh eater builds him an airy palace, and beholds fat hours dancing to the music of shawm and cimbalom. But the smoker of marihuana meets a different fate:
> The first effect of smoking marihuana is a slight headache. It comes after the first three or four draughts of smoke. A marked dizziness then sets in. Everything seems to move around the smoker, this whirl becoming faster and faster, until all sense of his surroundings is lost.

The next stage of the intoxication is full of terrors. Troops of ferocious wild animals march before the vision of the smoker. Lions, tigers, panthers, and other wild beasts occupy his vision. The wild animals are then attacked by hosts of devils and monsters of unheard of shapes. The smoker becomes brave and possessed of superhuman strength. It is at this stage of the debauch that murders are committed by the smoker.

We have heard, in a dim way, of the "pipe dreams" which cause ordinarily sedate and meritorious persons to scandalize their neighborhood. Their effect, however, is usually transitory, and the dreamer returns to his daily grind, like a horse that has partaken lightly of the loco weed. On the other hand, the marihuana dreams that come to Castro and his ancient Col. John the Baptist Lamedo, are of the most violent, enduring, and provocative character. If they do not break themselves of the habit, their visions may materialize in the shape of ironclad monsters belching fire and nickel-nosed balls in the heavily mortgaged harbors of the sons of Bolivar. They must forswear marihuana, and live cleanly, as patriots should.[28]

The article is so ridiculous that I considered the possibility that it might have been written tongue-in-cheek. But in fact it appears on a page surrounded by mostly sober news of domestic and international events and is evidently quite serious. It is nonetheless fascinating in that it demonstrates how multiple flows of information within a transnational environment swirled together to produce an emerging U.S. discourse on marijuana: a core of Mexican ideas regarding marijuana's effects, seasoned with notions of "locoweed," drawn into a comparative framework where the character of opium and hashish users was well established, and punctuated by the racism and imperial ambition that were so prominent a feature of early-twentieth-century American history. The article also makes clear what most other sources of the period simply implied through omission—that marijuana and hashish were widely viewed as distinct drugs at this early, critical juncture. The link to Venezuela is curious. To my knowledge, this is the only reference of the period to link marijuana to that country, and Starr's Latin American fieldwork at the time was mostly in Mexico.[29] It may simply be that, among the various absurdities and exaggerations captured here, the *Washington Post* decided also to fit Starr's work into the more pressing political framework of the issues with Venezuela, which had, of course, recently inspired the Roosevelt Corollary to the Monroe Doctrine. Mexico, after all, provided few signs of defying Uncle Sam, as it was still the calm model of Porfirian stability championed by much of the U.S. press.

In any case, articles resembling the various examples cited above continued to be published in newspapers throughout the second decade of the twentieth century in the United States, often with the same details repeated from stories of a decade before.[30] While many sources continued to present marijuana as a kind of mysterious plant from south of the border, the link to cannabis does appear to have gradually become more widely recognized. For example, under the headline "Crazed with Dope Two Men Attacked," the *Abilene Daily Reporter* explained that "'marihuana' is commonly used in many parts of Mexico. It is a form of 'cannabis indica,' producing peculiar ocular illusions, and by frequent use, a fiendish desire to slaughter animals or men." Yet in other stories, the identity of the plant remained largely mysterious, even when its effects were compared to hashish, as in this *San Antonio Light* story titled "Marihuana, Mind-Destroyer Is Grown in San Antonio": "Marihuana, a Mexican plant whose leaf produces effects similar to those of the hasheesh of India or the opium of China, causing mental delusions and hallucinations that frequently end in homicidal or suicidal mania, is grown, cured and smoked right here in San Antonio."[31]

The growing dissemination of marijuana's reputation is also evident in its more frequent appearance in novels and traveler's accounts and even as a simple synonym for insanity in environments far removed from Mexico. Thus Phillip Terry's Mexican travel handbook recounted the story of Empress Carlota's supposed poisoning and noted that "there are Mexicans who say the Empress was secretly poisoned with Marihuana (a deadly native drug) before she departed from Mexico." A short story by Alfred Henry Lewis in *Cosmopolitan* featured the following description from an old sage on the western range: "No; marihuana ain't loco. Marihuana comes from 'way off yonder in the south country, down some'ers about Yucatan. Loco you finds as far no'th as the Arkansaw, an' farther. Moreover, what Mexican's got it in for you hands you loco in the shape of tea, while as to marihuana — they dries the leaves an' saws it off on you in a cigarette. You drinks one, an' you smokes the other. Both is a dead shot, only with loco you bogs down mental all quiet an' slow; while, once the old marihuana wrops its tail about your intellects, you become voylent an' blood-hungry, an' goes on the onaccountable war-path, mighty deemoniac." Similarly, a character in the novel *Connie Morgan in Alaska* by James B. Hendryx drily concluded from the strange ramblings in a dead man's diary that he had "gone marihuana," that is, gone crazy, out alone in the Alaskan forests looking for gold.[32] Use of marijuana was even used in a California courtroom in 1919 to bolster an insanity defense.[33]

These ideas also moved to the United States through direct word of mouth.

In 1917, the Agriculture Department conducted a large survey of marijuana use along the border area and there interviewed a number of Mexicans or other individuals with significant experience in that country. These informants (the "patricians" cited by Bonnie and Whitebread) confirmed marijuana's pernicious reputation. A certain Colonel F. A. Chapa, "a Mexican by birth, born in San Antonio, and at present a member of the Governor's Staff of the State of Texas," owned a drugstore in that city and explained the following to investigators: "Marihuana smoking, although prohibited by the Mexican government, is common among the soldiers in the Mexican army. Continued smoking of Marihuana produces imbecility. In Mexico a 'Marihuana fiend' is ostracised from all society. No one will have anything to do with him or trust him. He is absolutely unreliable and irresponsible." Dr. Francisco de Ganseca of Laredo, Texas, who graduated from the National School of Medicine in Mexico City and who practiced medicine in Mexico for twelve years, testified that marijuana made people hear and see things that didn't exist, that they imagined others were making faces at them, and that they were driven to commit crimes by the sensations in their eyes and ears. "In fact I knew of a case in Mexico where a soldier under the influence of the drug shot down one of his comrades. He was sentenced to be hanged immediately in the Military Hospital at Monterey [sic], where the killing had taken place. Instead of shrinking from the death penalty he was laughing and happy because he had succeeded in killing the man. . . . It is worse than opium as it not only destroys the life of the person who smokes it, but it causes him to take the lives of others. Continued use of the drug slowly wears the body away." Also in Laredo, a doctor named Juan de la Garza who had practiced medicine in the Mexican military for four years offered that, in addition to certain medicinal uses, marijuana was smoked in Mexico and produced hallucinations. "A person under the influence may see a friend and imagine that he is an enemy and kill him. The worst effects begin in about four hours after the person has been smoking." Similarly, the proprietor of Warner Drug in El Paso, who had worked in Mexico for several years, explained that "it is used by the Mexicans and smoked in the form of cigarettes. It drives the person using it crazy and makes him irresponsible and absolutely fearless of any danger. Even one cigarette may cause this effect. It is an exceedingly dangerous drug and only used for smoking purposes. Its use should be prohibited by law." Finally, Mr. F. Ramos of the Botica Economical Store claimed to have actually served in the Mexican military during the Díaz years. "We used to shoot sometimes as many as 8 or 10 soldiers in our regiment a week when they went crazy from Marihuana. We had orders to do so."[34]

These and other reports often emphasized how the drug's use was already "strictly prohibited" in Mexico. On December 28, 1905, for example, the *Christian Advocate* claimed, incorrectly, that "the Superior Board of Health of Mexico prohibits the sale throughout the country of marihuana, a drug the use of which soon causes insanity." In 1907, the *Chillicothe (MO) Constitution* claimed that Mexican authorities had declared "war" on marijuana. "Heavy penalties are imposed upon those who violate this order. Marihuana still finds its way into the barracks of the soldiers and many cases of insanity are produced each year by its secret use. The law against its gathering and sale has been extended to apply to all classes of people as the marihuana smoking habit was becoming quite general among the lower classes." By this means, not only did marijuana's reputation reach the United States, but so did news of Mexico's prohibitionist approach to its sale and use.[35]

There were also a number of specific, especially sensational incidents that drew the attention of the U.S. press to the role of marijuana in Mexico, especially after the onset of the Mexican Revolution. As we've seen, shortly after the Huerta putsch of February 1913, the general's brother-in-law and governor of the Federal District, Enrique Cepeda, was arrested for summarily executing Gabriel Hernández, an ex-Maderista who was in jail. The *New York Times* reported, as did the Mexican press, that "crazed" by marijuana, Cepeda had gone to the federal penitentiary and ordered the release of Hernández so that he could shoot him. It was later reported that, thanks to the marijuana, Cepeda was declared to have been temporarily insane when committing the crime and escaped Mexico without trial.[36] The story was widely publicized and offered yet another opportunity for newspapers to introduce marijuana to their readers. The *Naugatuck (CT) Daily News*, which had run the "Madness in Plants" story back in 1905, explained that Cepeda's "condition arose mainly from the smoking of cigarettes made of marihuana, a weed gathered by the Indians, and having the effect of always crazing its smokers with homicidal mania. . . . An overwhelming desire to kill is aroused in the brain of the smokers of these cigarettes. Indians smoke them before going to war."[37]

A second incident of some controversy was the murder of an American soldier named Sam Parks after the occupation of Veracruz in the spring of 1914. Parks had apparently become insane and had wandered over enemy lines only to be captured, interrogated, and then shot. Though some early reports linked his insanity to sunstroke, a story in the May 9 edition of the *New York Times* cited a Mexican officer's suggestion that perhaps Parks had been given a poisoned cigarette. As the officer explained to the American lieutenant general Elmore F. Taggart, "Mexican women in Vera Cruz give them to men and they always go crazy."[38] The *Times* decided to investigate the claim and found a doctor in Brownsville, Texas, named F. Leroy Silvey with some experience in Mexico. Silvey claimed to have seen several American soldiers in a similarly demented condition. "It is the result of smoking marajuana [*sic*], one of the most mysterious and deadly drugs I have ever seen. The Mexican women mix the weed with tobacco and make cigarettes of the combination. It only takes a few to affect a man's brain seriously." He went on to recount the case of an oil driller who had become infatuated with a girl but then lost interest, much like Janvier's locoweed story of 1887. The girl had consulted some older women who suggested she give him some marijuana cigarettes. "The native tobacco is bitter and one cannot notice the taste of the marajuana [*sic*]. I ran across the man after he had smoked the drug and the change was awful. I treated him with everything I knew for some time, but it was hopeless." He also claimed to have puffed on one of these cigarettes before as an experiment and found that "it acted on me like the strongest narcotic and I could feel it in my head for a week."[39]

A few days later, the *Times* received a letter from a certain William B. Hale refuting Spivey's claims. This was surely William Bayard Hale, the American journalist who had written on the Huerta coup, among various other issues of international affairs over the years. Hale stated unequivocally that Spivey was wrong. Marijuana was in fact a "species of wild hemp" and that the dried leaves were mixed with tobacco and only smoked alone by the real "aficionados of long use. . . . It is used in the Orient, as hasheesh, bhang and gunga, &c., and is not poisonous, though the fascinations of its dreams are such that it may lead in the end to immoderate indulgence, and thus, through long-continued abuse, end in imbecility and death." He claimed that Mexicans set up clubs along the border to smoke the substance and, perhaps because of temperament or diluted doses, rarely abused the weed. Interestingly, despite this, he did note that "on the other hand, this drug seems to arouse their worst passions, lust and blood shedding, and the county authorities on the Rio Grande border are very active in checking the use of mariguana." Instead, Hale offered that, if Parks had been driven mad by a poisoned cigarette, the culprit was instead toloache, again identified as "a species of *Datura stramonium*." He noted that this was an especially powerful drug that could cause "melancholic idiocy" and "violent insanity." He also noted that, "curiously enough, [*Datura stramonium*] is used in Hindostan by jealous women for the same purposes as their Mexican sisters, viz., to cause their lovers to lose their minds."[40] The story was then picked up by the wire service and given some local color. The *Logansport (IN) Pharos-Reporter*, for example, added that "the report that Private Parker was temporarily insane from a poisoned cigarette given him by a Mexican girl . . . is highly creditable to those who have traveled in the 'land of the greasers.'"[41]

Here marijuana had explained the folly of an American soldier that ended up getting him killed, but the story had also highlighted a perceived Mexican "defiance" of the United States that would be punctuated by Pancho Villa's attack on Columbus, New Mexico, in March 1916. Such "defiance" provided an opportunity for marijuana to again appear as an explanatory factor, as it did in the *Ogden City (UT) Standard* in September 1915. Clearly drawing on the many stories that had been in circulation since the turn of the century, the *Standard* asked, "Is the Mexican Nation Locoed by Peculiar Weed?" The story's focus and evidence paralleled that of the 1905 *Washington Post* story detailed above. It noted that the "'bravery' of 'Greaser' Bandits who defy the United States" might be found in the same substance that was reputed to have driven "Queen Carlota" mad.

> General Villa tells the United States it can "go to h———," Mexican troops cross the border and shoot down American ranchers and all in all it seems that the nation south of the Rio Grande would just as soon defy and fight the mighty Uncle Sam as to continue its own internal warfare.
> And why?
> Are the Mexicans becoming a mightier and braver race, or in the language of Texas, are they becoming "locoed"?

The paper reported that Mexicans under the influence of marijuana believed they could "single handed whip the entire regular United States army" and that if reinforced by several more Mexicans,

> he might include a few European nations in his dream conquests. . . . In fact, the marihuana seems to be nothing less than the loco-weed that causes insanity to both men and beast. If the devastation of the drug is so great on this side of the Rio Grande, with our jails filled with men who have committed crimes while under the influence of the drug, and with our insane asylums filled with those who have lost their minds through the use of the marihuana, imagine the terrible effect of its indulgence on the people of Mexico and then ask the question: Where do the Mexican bandits get their nerve to commit their attacks on the Americans and . . . [how do] leaders summon courage to defy the government of Washington?[42]

Perhaps the most cynical use of the purported connection between Mexican revolutionaries and cannabis was perpetrated by Dr. Paul Bernardo Altendorf, a former U.S. intelligence officer who in 1919 was working for the National Association for the Protection of American Rights in Mexico. That organization had been founded by oil and other interests to lobby for U.S. intervention to prevent the implementation of Article 27 of the Mexican Constitution, an article that opened the door to Mexican government intervention in foreign concerns on Mexican soil. Altendorf helped take the organization's case to Congress, arguing that the country was disintegrating, that Venustiano Carranza was a Bolshevik, and that a "large proportion of Mexicans, officers as well as men, are dope fiends. They smoke mariguana, which is made from the loco weed familiar to cattle men in the Southwest, which has an effect like hasheesh. They will not go into battle without a dose of mariguana which imparts a sort of false courage."[43]

■ According to scholars of U.S. drug history, Mexicans played a prominent role in the prohibition of marijuana in this country but mostly as passive victims of American prejudice. These scholars have described marijuana as having been a "casual adjunct to life" in Mexican immigrant communities, and some have hypothesized that marijuana gained a violent reputation simply through its association with Mexicans. But as we've seen here, Mexicans played a much more active role in this story. Though Americans would quickly turn marijuana lore against Mexican immigrants, that lore was based primarily on Mexican ideas transported earlier by transnational circuits of information interchange. Certainly racism played a significant role here—just as Mexican elites orientalized their own country's lower classes, Americans stereotyped Mexicans as irresponsible and given to irrational outbursts of violence. But marijuana did not become a victim of such ideas as much as it served as an ideological adhesive, bonding related but in some ways contradictory modes of thought.

Over time, the many threads of this globalizing process gradually crisscrossed to form the stitching of a strong and ultimately extremely resilient transnational political and ideological fabric. The result was a powerful, international prohibitionist alliance between Mexico and the United States. We are still living with the consequences.

# Conclusion

In October 1938, Dr. Leopoldo Salazar Viniegra, director of the Anti-alcohol Division of Mexico City's Hospital for Drug Addicts, scandalized the public with a paper titled "The Myth of Marijuana." There, Salazar argued that the common assumptions of both public and scientific opinion pertaining to this drug were based in fantasy. Marijuana was a relatively innocuous substance, he claimed, whose symptoms included little more than a reddening of the eyes and a drying of the mouth's mucous membranes. Furthermore, stories linking this substance with madness, violence, and crime were based in myth propagated by a sensational press and, above all, the drug enforcement authorities of the United States. According to Salazar, those ideas anchored policies that had turned marijuana users into over 80 percent of Mexico's drug-law violators. Ultimately, he argued, Mexico should repeal the prohibition of marijuana both to undermine the illicit traffic in the substance and to facilitate action on the more serious drug problems of alcohol and the opiates.[1]

Though they were based on experiments with patients, doctors, and other functionaries at La Castañeda, the insane asylum within which the Hospital for Drug Addicts was housed, Salazar's highly controversial views elicited a rapid and emotional response from other physicians, private citizens, and the press. In November, *Excelsior* reported that Salazar had forced patients to sign contracts obliging them to smoke marijuana for months on end for the sake of his experiments. The results, the paper reported, had been ruin for patients who might otherwise have been regenerated. The same article commented on the doctor's strange mannerisms and suggested that Salazar himself might have lost his mind from smoking the drug.[2] A month later, the highly respected criminological journal *Criminalia* republished Salazar's article in tandem with a 1931 piece by Gregorio Oneto Barenque, a prominent doctor who had drawn a far more mainstream, and menacing, picture of marijuana.[3] The impact of Salazar's pronouncements were then summed up by *Excelsior* in a New Year's Day special feature on the greatest "scandals and polemics" of 1938: "It would be difficult to imagine in the history of medical doctrines, and especially those of psychiatry, that such a dust up could have occurred like the one created by [Dr. Salazar Viniegra] when he asserted that marijuana does not bring about the dangers that have been attributed to it, and that those who doubt this can smoke it and see for themselves that it is not the dangerous weed about which so much has been said, even among some of the decent people who enjoy it."[4]

■ By the end of the 1930s, most of the elements necessary for the North American "War on Drugs" were in place in Mexico and the United States. In 1937, the United States prohibited marijuana on the federal level, thus providing the impetus for a major international market in a product that both grew wild and could be easily cultivated in Mexico. As a result, a Mexican-grown product would soon account for most of the marijuana available on the U.S. market.[5] U.S. drug enforcement agents had also begun operating on Mexican soil during that decade—sometimes with permission, sometimes clandestinely—with the perceived urgency of the issue in both countries as justification.[6] Finally, it was also at the end of this decade that the United States would intervene to crush an alternative approach to opiate addiction conceived of by Salazar and approved by Mexico's public health authorities. The plan had sought to supply addicts with "maintenance" doses of opiates in order to keep them off the black market.[7] That episode signaled what would become increasingly clear over the course of the century—that in the event of disagreements over drugs, the United States would be very willing to force its drug-fighting vision on Mexico.

But Salazar's "Myth of Marijuana" and the controversy it ignited illustrate that while U.S. hegemony on the issue of drugs in North America would be an obvious fact of subsequent decades, by the 1930s Mexico's drug-control options had already become severely limited—by the force of public and scientific opinion—to approaches that for the most part coincided harmoniously with U.S. initiatives. Attitudes toward marijuana were critical here. The Salazar controversy revealed that within mainstream Mexican opinion, arguments deviating from the traditional orthodoxy on marijuana would be deemed beyond the pale of rational discourse and could threaten the professional reputation of otherwise respected authorities. Indeed, the controversy helped to discredit Salazar and his desire to reform the way Mexico dealt with opiate addicts. In short, Mexican public and scientific opinion was strongly in favor of what are now often called "U.S.-style" drug-control strategies, and this circumstance left Mexico little room for negotiation, even when an iconoclast like Salazar briefly took the reins of Mexican drug policy.

Yet while Salazar was quick to blame these ideas on the powerful propaganda being emitted by Harry Anslinger's office at the Federal Bureau of Narcotics in Washington, the association between madness and marijuana, as I have demonstrated, dated to the 1850s in Mexico and had begun to form a century before. Furthermore, it had been from Mexican sources that the U.S. government and press first heard that marijuana turned ordinary people into ferocious maniacs. It was during that earlier era, through the work of Mexican scientists, novelists, journalists, and artists, that these ideas became sufficiently entrenched as to make any deviation from them appear, appropriately, "crazy" decades later. These were the ideas that had facilitated marijuana's proscription in Mexico on March 2, 1920. They were also the ideas that, as the United States began putting its growing power behind the War on Drugs, made any serious deviation from U.S. drug policy ideologically indefensible *in Mexico*. Thus, while the drug war would not become a central political concern until later in the century, it was during this earlier era, when marijuana was a far less obvious presence in Mexican life, that its central role in that future war was determined.

As I've tried to demonstrate here, this was never a simple or linear process. From the beginning, Mexico was inserted in global circuits of communication, initially as a Spanish colony and later as an independent nation in a rapidly globalizing world. Thus, the lines of perspective and potential influence were wide-ranging. Yet they also ran deep, for attitudes about this substance, in part because of their meaning on a broader scale (for example, cannabis's link to the Orient or "Indian" Mexico or prisons), cut into some of the most sensitive and intimate dilemmas on the minds of Mexicans of all classes, from the definition of Mexico as a nation to the meaning of respectability in urban neighborhoods. All the while, these factors were complicated by the rush of information so typical of the modern world and, above all, by the extraordinary complexity of drugs and their effects. The psychoactive riddle ensured that these many factors would gradually become imbued in the meaning of the drug itself and would probably manifest themselves in the actual behavior of individuals.

Surely the same general dynamics are still at work. Today, drug control authorities claim that marijuana provides the single greatest source of income for Mexico's extraordinarily powerful and brutal drug "cartels."[8] As I write this, the body count continues to mount in Mexico. Nearly 35,000 people have been killed in the last four years alone as a result of what the press usually refers to as "drug-related violence."[9] This is a misnomer. If not for its clumsiness, the phrase "drug-policy-related violence" would be a much more useful and accurate description of this situation. There is little doubt that it is the *policy* and not the drugs that has produced the extraordinary profits that inspire drug trafficking gangs to engage in horrific acts of violence, acts that now threaten to destabilize Mexico.

Scholars and commentators have blamed the recent upsurge in violence on the breakdown of the old means by which the Institutional Revolutionary Party (PRI), which ruled Mexico from 1929 to 2000, kept the drug traffickers under control. Security forces created in the 1940s made deals with the strongest traffickers, allowing them to control certain transshipment routes in exchange for payoffs and an understanding that they would mostly stay out of politics.[10] That corrupt system mostly "worked," at least in comparison to the carnage that the present state of "war" has produced in Mexico. But if this theory is accurate, it must nonetheless be recognized that the architects of that system surely did not anticipate just how massive the market for illicit drugs would become, and therefore just how formidable a challenge those trafficking organizations would eventually present.

The 1960s famously saw a massive boom in recreational drug use in Western nations, especially the United States, and the market for these substances grew exponentially. Those of the so-called counterculture adopted marijuana as a consumable symbol of their movement. This was highly appropriate, given that marijuana had long been characterized in the West as a quintessentially "Oriental" substance and therefore antithetical to Western civilization. It was, in short, a perfect accessory for Western *counter*cultures. Mexico appears to have once again served as a quasi-Orient during this period. It was the place from which most of the counterculture's marijuana came, and it was a country uniquely stocked with the powerful, natural hallucinogens that would also become a hallmark of the movement. In fact, it was a 1957 *Life* magazine article by R. Gordon Wasson on Mexico's "magic mushrooms" that gave critical fuel to what would eventually be termed the "psychedelic" movement during these years.[11] There is a rich, transnational cultural history here that has yet to be told, but it seems clear to me that Mexico's traditional role as a convenient and nearby Orient contributed importantly to the development of "the Sixties" as we now understand that decade.

But traditional Mexican ideas about marijuana would also play an important role in this later history. This was richly illustrated by a curious pop cultural phenomenon in the United States during the 1970s. At the start of that decade, a patron of the Library of Congress in Washington, D.C., named Keith Stroup would stumble upon a dusty reel-to-reel titled *Reefer Madness*, a 1930s film documenting the supposed dangers of marijuana. Stroup was there looking for old-fashioned portrayals of that controversial drug, and with *Reefer Madness* he struck gold. The movie was a classic example of what buffs term the "exploitation" genre, flicks that trafficked in the forbidden—in sex, drugs, and violence. During an era of significant censorship, filmmakers successfully delivered such content behind the facade of a public health message. *Reefer Madness* (aka *Doped Youth, The Burning Question, Tell Your Children*) sensationally portrayed the dangers of marijuana use, including unleashed sexual passions, fits of madness, and violence. Thanks to a quirk in copyright law, *Reefer Madness* had already entered the public domain, and for the nominal fee of $297, Stroup was able to purchase a copy.[12]

He soon began showing the film at rallies for his new organization, the National Organization for the Reform of Marijuana Laws, or NORML. The group's acronym directly confronted mainstream opinion that pegged drug users as weird, defective, and criminal. The name also conveyed a sense of humor and an appreciation for the absurd. For many Americans, particularly those of the so-called youth culture, the idea that marijuana could suddenly make an individual "abnormal" was ludicrous. That helped to reinforce marijuana's role as a powerful symbol for the counterculture and its use as a rite of passage for many college students.[13]

Soon after Stroup introduced the film at his rallies, other entrepreneurs recognized opportunity and began showing the film at "midnight movies" in cities and college campuses. Half a million people reportedly saw the film in 1972. Over the next three years, *Reefer Madness* became a late-night staple, eventually being distributed by New Line and drawing droves of bell-bottomed, pot-smoking moviegoers to the theater. As Stuart Samuels has argued, "To the tens of thousands of young students, going to the film became a public act that symbolized a widely held private belief."[14] The *Reefer Madness* phenomenon demonstrated what was already becoming clear to anyone who was paying attention: marijuana had become a powerful symbol in the emerging American "culture wars."

In part, we can credit this development to those original Mexican ideas that served as a foundation for notions of "reefer madness" in the United States, though by the 1930s those ideas had taken on some specifically American characteristics (the emphasis in the film, for example, on sexual promiscuity as a result of marijuana use). Thus it was appropriate that as American marijuana use boomed in the 1970s, the great beneficiaries should be drug traffickers in Mexico. These entrepreneurs began accumulating fortunes with which they could purchase not only luxury items but also increasingly formidable stocks of weaponry. Meanwhile, thanks largely to the culture war aspects of marijuana and other drug use, in 1971 Richard Nixon declared drugs "public enemy #1," a fact that probably only increased their appeal to the counterculture.[15] It certainly increased the funding being pumped into the War on Drugs. That escalation received more fuel toward the end of the decade as a grassroots movement emerged in American suburbs demanding a crackdown on the period's relatively permissive cultural atmosphere toward drugs, especially marijuana.[16] This served as the impetus for Ronald Reagan's War on Drugs after his election in 1980. Ironically, the death of the young black basketball star Len Bias from a cocaine overdose in 1986 justified an even more fanatical "war" against crack cocaine, a campaign that for all intents and purposes meant a war on African Americans. Prisons in the United States have since bulged.[17]

Yet economic logic would not be denied. In what scholar Eva Bertram and her collaborators have termed the "profit paradox," increasing efforts to fight the War on Drugs simply make the illicit drug industry more attractive to potential participants. Increased interdiction and eradication of drug supplies produce a rise in the price of these substances, and while theoretically price increases should have a downward effect on demand, they also have an upward effect on supply as new producers get into the market to benefit from the greater potential for profit. Increased production then decreases prices. These fundamental economic facts are exacerbated by the transnational nature of the illicit drugs industry, by the great disparities in wealth between American consumers and peasant producers of these substances in Latin America, and by the fact that 90 percent of the value added in the market occurs on the U.S. side of the border. By raising prices only slightly at the retail level, trafficking organizations can thus double and triple the financial incentives for peasant producers and others along the commodity chain. As countless scholars have demonstrated, the fundamental economic realities make this an unwinnable war that results in massive collateral damage.[18]

Yet the "war" marches on, even as the drug-policy-related violence becomes increasingly grotesque. As I write this, the newspapers are filled with reports on the latest grizzly incident—fifteen decapitated bodies left in a shopping center in the once glitzy resort town of Acapulco.[19] Why do policymakers, despite the enormous evidence that the drug war cannot succeed, continue to insist that the fight must go on? Though the answers to that question are complex, it is clear that the War on Drugs is anchored by a strong, transnational ideological foundation that developed long before governments were spending billions to root out certain fetishized illicit intoxicants and their users. While opinion in favor of all-out prohibition seems to be declining somewhat, especially in the United States, where 46 percent of Americans now support marijuana legalization, Mexicans remain overwhelmingly opposed to that course of action, with only about 15 percent in favor.[20] Further delaying any significant reform is the fact that most people fundamentally misunderstand how drugs work and continue to treat them as if their effects were governed by almost magically consistent pharmacological processes. In reality, they are complex substances whose effects are determined by "set" and "setting" as much as by anything else.[21] With commentators warning of the destabilization of Mexico by powerful drug trafficking gangs, the historian cannot help but wonder, with the centennial of the Mexican Revolution having just passed, if today's violence will not lead to something still more tragic.

Whatever the future holds, over the last century it has become clear that this history has long been governed by complex transnational cultural, political, and economic factors. To understand those factors, we must take into account the critical role that Mexico has played in all of this from the very beginning, not merely as a source of drugs for the United States but as a generator of the ideas and policies that constitute the foundation of the tragic and quixotic War on Drugs.

# *Appendix* NEWSPAPER ANALYSIS

In this appendix, I provide additional methodological information for the newspaper analysis in chapter 4. Some of the charts in that chapter are relatively self-explanatory and thus have not been elaborated upon here. For the rest, the information is organized by the order in which the charts appear in the text.

## BASIC DATA ON THE NEWSPAPERS ANALYZED

As noted in the chapter, this analysis drew on a database organized by Readex in partnership with the Center for Research Libraries. Table A.1 provides a list of the newspapers used for the chapter and some key data for each at the time of my analysis. As noted in the chapter, two major eras were covered here, one dominated by highly political publications dedicated above all to serious news analysis, and a second, much more "yellow" era that began around 1880. *El Diario de México, La Mosca Parlera, El Siglo Diez y Nueve*, and *El Universal* all fit firmly in the earlier era and together produced only four total references to marijuana. They thus did not figure significantly in the analysis.

TABLE A.1. AVAILABLE MEXICAN NEWSPAPERS IN THE READEX/CRL: WORLD NEWSPAPER ARCHIVE

| Title | # of Issues | Dates | Location |
|---|---|---|---|
| *El Diario de México* | 3,568 | 1805–16 | Mexico City |
| *La Mosca Parlera* | 16 | 1823 | Mexico City |
| *El Monitor Republicano* | 4,210 | 1833–95 | Mexico City |
| *El Siglo Diez y Nueve* | 4,062 | 1841–62 | Mexico City |
| *El Universal* | 2,457 | 1848–55 | Mexico City |
| *Two Republics* | 233 | 1867–1900 | Mexico City |
| *El Dictamen* | 3,733 | 1880–1922 | Veracruz |
| *La Patria* | 803 | 1881–1913 | Mexico City |
| *El Diario* | 1,428 | 1882–1920 | Mexico City |
| *La Voz de México* | 6,788 | 1886–1909 | Mexico City |
| *Mexican Herald* | 6,896 | 1895–1915 | Mexico City |
| *El Imparcial* | 5,653 | 1897–1914 | Mexico City |
| *El País* | 5,433 | 1899–1915 | Mexico City |
| *Nueva Era* | 562 | 1911–13 | Mexico City |
| *La Revista de Yucatán* | 319 | 1913–22 | Mérida |
| *Excelsior* | 1,686 | 1917–22 | Mexico City |

## CHART 4.1: REFERENCES TO VICE IN THE MEDIA ("RAW HITS"), 1880–1922

Chart 4.1 analyzes the "raw hits" when searching particular keywords. Raw hits are not the same as articles because when a particular keyword is searched, the database actually identifies articles *per page* in the collection that include that keyword. Thus, if I were searching for the word "alcohol" and *El Imparcial* had published an article that began on page 1 and concluded on page 2 with the word "alcohol" appearing on both pages, the database would cite two separate "articles," though there was actually only one. At the same time, if there were two different articles that mentioned "alcohol" on the same page, then the database would, appropriately, count them separately. The database also includes some duplicate issues that were added to provide better digital images of some select pages. Thus, the number of raw hits listed in the text represents, in most cases, a number somewhat higher than the actual number of distinct articles on each subject. Since in this section I am merely seeking to gain a general sense of the relative frequency of references to different subjects, these slight imperfections in the database are of little concern. In any case, there is no reason that the rate of inflation for one category should necessarily be higher than that for another.

The specific keywords used for this search and the associated results were as follows:

Pre-yellow press era (1805–79): *embriaguez*—635; *ebriedad*—124; drunkenness—2; *el opio*—61; opium—7; *morfina*—18; morphine—2; *marihuana*—2; *mariguana*—6; peyote—3; peyotl—0; *cocaína*—0; cocaine—1

Yellow press era (1880–1922): *embriaguez*—6,068; *ebriedad*—3,765; drunkenness—108; *morfina*—2,677; morphine—105; *marihuana*—664; *mariguana*—80; *el opio*—390; opium—195; *cocaína*—45; cocaine—48; peyote—11; peyotl—1

## CHART 4.2: VARIANCE IN MARIJUANA NEWS COVERAGE IN RAW NUMBERS, 1878–1920

Only those newspapers that had two or more articles on marijuana were included in this analysis. A small number of the articles were excluded for being illegible, and others were not really relevant to the analysis. For example, in 1919 there was a series of advertisements in *Excelsior* marketing a cure for drug addiction, including marijuana. That ad was repeated many times, and none of those issues were included. Furthermore, I excluded any "repeat" stories—that is, stories that re-reported an event already covered by the same or a different newspaper. By excluding repeats, I avoided the inevitable anomalies produced in the data by a single especially scandalous and widely covered event. It should nonetheless be noted that some high-profile, repeated stories were likely disproportionately influential in shaping the discourse, since they surely garnered more interest from the reading public.

## CHART 4.3: VARIANCE IN MARIJUANA NEWS COVERAGE BY PERCENTAGE, 1878–1920

To establish these numbers, I sorted through all of the marijuana references for the actual number of legible articles that referred to it in some way (thus duplicate issues, multiple page stories, or advertisements repeated daily were excluded and did not distort this number). That number, for each paper and each year, was divided by the actual number of issues of that paper available in each year. The latter number was arrived at through a manual count of the database. For this chart, repeat stories (see explanation for Chart 4.2) were also excluded.

## CHART 4.4: DEMOGRAPHIC CHARACTERISTICS OF MARIJUANA USERS AS REPORTED IN THE PRESS, 1854–1920

For this chart, I read each newspaper story for demographic information. Some stories spoke generally about demographics; for example, "Marijuana is smoked by prisoners and soldiers." Other stories involved an individual; for example, "Jorge Pérez was a cook who smoked marijuana." Each time a particular demographic category was mentioned, I marked it down. Thus, the first example would count as one soldier reference and one prisoner reference, even though it was obviously referring to many soldiers and prisoners. The second example would have counted as one reference to "laborers."

Most of the categories included in the analysis are relatively self-explanatory and therefore have not been elaborated upon below. As a basic rule, a reference was counted toward a particular demographic category only if the article in question *specifically* referred to that category. Thus, for example, while there were many stories that described individuals with obviously "degenerated" characteristics (in the social-scientific parlance of the day), those individuals counted toward the "degenerated" category only if some form of the word "degeneration" was specifically used. The exceptions to that basic rule, or categories that might be open to interpretation, are elaborated upon below. Note that some articles mentioned multiple demographic categories (the same is true for the analysis of "effects"). Thus, while there were 424 articles that mentioned demographics, there were 481 total demographic descriptions.

Children: Individuals under the age of eighteen, whether small children or teenagers.
Countryfolk: Individuals referred to as *campesinos*.
Laborers: Working-class people of any kind. Barbers, bakers, street vendors, drivers, and so on were all included here.
Middle class: This was a difficult category to isolate because the dividing line between middle and upper class was not always clear. A good example of middle class was provided in one story in which a young man was described as being of "good habits and irreproachable antecedents" but was not said to be either wealthy or "elegant," as was common for the truly rich.
Tough guys: One story stated that marijuana was smoked by the kind of men who had "hair on their chest." While there was only one reference of this kind, I included the category because the absence of other similar references struck me as noteworthy—this was not a substance that was normally associated with "manly men."

Upper class: Like the middle class, this category was sometimes difficult to isolate. It was used when either significant wealth or something similar was noted — for example, when people were referred to as *elegantes*.

*Viciosos*: In the language of late-nineteenth- and early-twentieth-century Mexico, *vicioso* meant something like "vice-ridden" and suggested a predilection to vice of various kinds. A *vicioso* was a person who bordered on what we would today call an "addict," but he or she wasn't exactly that. Such a person was given to vice but not because a powerful withdrawal syndrome compelled him or her to take drugs.

### CHART 4.6: SEX OF INDIVIDUALS LINKED TO MARIJUANA IN THE PRESS

Articles that repeated a story already covered either in the same or another paper were included for this chart. Cases only received a sex designation if a person was specifically mentioned, with the following two exceptions: 1) when an article mentioned the use of marijuana by soldiers, it was counted toward the "male" category since all soldiers were men at this time; and 2) when an article mentioned the sale of marijuana by *herbolarias*, it was counted toward the "female" category since *herbolarias* were almost universally presumed to be female. Use by prisoners was counted toward either category only if an individual was specifically mentioned since prisoners were both male and female, though most prisoners were male. Eleven cases (seven male, four female) specifically mentioned individuals but did not indicate if they were users or sellers. These cases were excluded from this chart.

### CHART 4.8: EFFECTS OF MARIJUANA AS REPRESENTED BY THE MEXICAN PRESS, 1854–1920

As with the demographics question, for this chart I read each newspaper story for information on the purported effects of marijuana. Some stories spoke generally about effects (for example, "Marijuana has driven hundreds of people crazy"), while other stories involved individuals who displayed certain symptoms after smoking marijuana (for example, "Jorge Pérez ran amok after smoking a marijuana cigarette"). Each time a particular effect was mentioned, I marked it down. Thus, in the first example above, while the story may have been referring to hundreds of cases of madness, the story would have counted only once toward that category.

Unlike the demographic categories used in the analysis (see above), most of the effects and how they were defined require some further elaboration. However, just as with the demographics, those that are relatively self-explanatory are not included below. Also like demographics, because some articles mentioned multiple effects, there were more total effects mentioned than articles analyzed.

Accidents: When an accident, like falling in front of a train or crashing a car, was blamed on the use of marijuana.

Addiction: When marijuana was reported to produce a habit that was difficult to break. References to *marihuanos*, for example, were not included here because that word was sometimes used simply to describe someone high on marijuana.

Ages: When marijuana was said to make users grow old faster than normal.

Crime: When a story specifically stated that marijuana generally caused "crime." Specific crimes like murder were not included here.

Crime implied: When criminals were captured and in passing the report noted that they had been carrying marijuana. The implication of such articles was that the marijuana had something to do with their status as criminals, but the text didn't actually come out and say that.

Death: When an article specifically cited death as a likely result of marijuana use. Those cases where a user committed suicide or someone was killed by a marijuana smoker were not included here.

Degeneration: When an article specifically mentioned degeneration. Many articles had features that would have fit them snugly into the larger discourse on degeneration that was so prominent during this era, but an article received this classification only if some form of the word "degeneration" was specifically mentioned.

*Endemoniado*: When papers specifically referred to a user as having been "possessed by the devil," which figuratively meant to be especially perverse or dangerous. The 1899 dictionary of the Real Academia Española defined *endemoniado* as either "possessed by the devil" or "extremely perverse, bad, or harmful." The latter was the most common connotation around the turn of the twentieth century. However, given the long history of links between drugs like marijuana and the devil in Mexico, the language was, in my opinion, worth noting.

*Escandaloso*: A term that denoted loud, rude, or antisocial public behavior. To be *escandaloso* was a step below actual violence but certainly moving in that direction.

*Excitación*: A kind of hyper and out-of-control intoxication. This term was closely related to the kind of "madness" that was usually described in relation to marijuana use.

Exploitation: When marijuana was used in order to drug someone and then take advantage of him or her in some way.

*Fiera*: A word often used to describe wild fits of violence. A *fiera* is a wild animal. The term thus likened people to animals, namely, irrational beings. The word was therefore closely linked to madness.

*Furia*: This meant something very close to *fiera*. In fact, sometimes both *furia* and *fiera* were used in the same article to describe a marijuana user. The 1899 version of the Real Academia's dictionary describes a *furia* as an "access of insanity."

Hallucinations: Sometimes descriptions of "marijuana madness" included hallucinations as a basic feature, but sometimes hallucinations were described without the word "madness" being used. This category was marked in the latter circumstance. Of course this category, like *fiera* and *furia*, could have easily been rolled into the madness category as well.

Insubordination: When soldiers attacked or severely disrespected superior officers. Insubordination often overlapped with violence but deserved its own category because this kind of disrespect was treated with extraordinary severity by the military.

Madness: When the word "madness" or its cognates were used to describe marijuana's effects. These words included *loco, delirio, loco furioso, locura,* maniac, and the like.

Madness implied: When an insane person was described as having smoked marijuana, though the marijuana was not directly blamed for his or her condition. This category was also used for vague descriptions that clearly suggested a kind of madness but did not specifically label it as such.

Pernicious: A catchall category used when marijuana was vaguely described as a bad thing. The most common word of this kind used to describe marijuana was *pernicioso,* but there were many others, such as *peligroso, desastroso, malísima yerba, funesto,* and so on. This category was marked only when the article could not be more specifically classified in one of the other categories listed here.

Poisons: When an article specifically used the word "poison" to describe marijuana's effects. In most of these cases, the word was used in a somewhat figurative sense—for example, "the poisonous weed." There were a couple of cases of actual claims of purposeful poisoning, but those were exceptions to the rule. Most of these cases would have fit comfortably under the "pernicious" label, but they were given their own category because the word "poison" was a critical aspect of Mexican criminal law on marijuana.

Run amok: This phrase was used by the *Mexican Herald* on a number of occasions but has no real cognate in Spanish. However, the action of running amok—a mad rush through the streets or within an institution, which threatened the safety of all those in the marijuana smoker's path—was often described by the Spanish-language papers. Such cases were thus cited in this category. It was a symptom that clearly threatened violence but did not necessarily result in it. I was extremely conservative with this category and included only those articles that blatantly described the running amok phenomenon.

Suggestibility: When individuals who had smoked marijuana were described as becoming vulnerable to suggestion by others. An individual might, for example, be told to commit a crime and go through with it, thanks to marijuana.

*Trastornado*: This category included descriptions that did not specifically cite madness but did mention something very close to it—for example, *trastornado* or *perturbaciones mentales.*

Unreality: When marijuana was described as providing an escape from reality without specifically mentioning hallucinations or delusions.

Vague intoxication: When a marijuana smoker was vaguely described as having become very confused and disoriented.

Violence: Whenever marijuana use produced violence of any kind.

Violence implied: When a violent incident was described and marijuana was mentioned, though the marijuana was not directly blamed for the incident.

CHART 4.9: EFFECTS OF MARIJUANA WITH CONSOLIDATED CATEGORIES

As explained in the text, this chart consolidated the various effects that were closely related to madness and violence but that did not specifically cite those two phenomena. Violence here includes the following categories: violence, violence implied, and *escandaloso*. Madness here includes madness, *furia*, run amok, *excitación*, hallucinations, *fiera*, *trastornado*, madness implied, unreality, and *endemoniado*. For these numbers, I controlled for "double dipping" between the subcategories of both violence and madness respectively. So, for example, some articles were initially categorized as having references to both madness and *furia*. I subtracted all such cases for this chart.

Because there was no significant difference in the proportions between categories after excluding repeat articles, for this chart I simply used the raw data, repeats included. In the original count, for example, excluding repeat articles reduced all of the top four categories between 23 percent and 29 percent. A few of the minor categories showed less change. For example, hallucinations were reduced only by 10 percent. But that did not significantly alter the main point: that references to madness and violence vastly outnumbered all other categories. Thus, though hallucinations were reduced only by 10 percent in the second data set, the ratio of hallucinations to violence changed only by 1 percent: from being 5 percent as common as violence to 6 percent as common. The one significant change occurred in the category of amnesia, which, like the professional category in the demographic chart, was distorted by the high-profile case of Enrique Cepeda in 1913.

# Notes

ABBREVIATIONS

AGN      Archivo General de la Nación, México, D.F.

AHH      Archivo Histórico de Hacienda, Archivo General de la Nación, México, D.F.

AS      Actas de Sesión, Archivo Histórico de la Secretaría de Salubridad y Asistencia, México, D.F.

Bandos      Bandos, Archivo General de la Nación, Mexico, D.F.

CV      Correspondencia de Virreyes, Archivo General de la Nación, Mexico, D.F.

ECG      Serie Empleados de Cárcel General, Archivo Histórico del Antiguo Ayuntamiento, México, D.F.

EM      Ejercicio de la Medicina, Archivo Histórico de la Secretaría de Salubridad y Asistencia, México, D.F.

FEMyA      Fondo Escuela de Medicina y Alumnos, Archivo Histórico de la Facultad de Medicina de la UNAM, México, D.F.

FR      Fondo Reservado, Biblioteca Nacional de México, Mexico D.F.

GdP      General de Parte, Archivo General de la Nación, México, D.F.

GyM      Guerra y Marina, Archivo General de la Nación, México, D.F.

IF      Inspección de Farmacias, Archivo Histórico de la Secretaría de Salubridad y Asistencia, México, D.F.

INQ      Inquisición, Archivo General de la Nación, México, D.F.

IyC      Industria y Comercio, Archivo General de la Nación, Mexico, D.F.

ML      Medicina Legal, Archivo Histórico de la Secretaría de Salubridad y Asistencia, México, D.F.

SEC      Secretaria, Archivo Histórico de la Secretaría de Salubridad y Asistencia, México, D.F.

SEDENA      Archivo Histórico de la Secretaría de la Defensa Nacional, México, D.F.

SRE      Acervo Histórico Diplomático de la Secretaría de Relaciones Exteriores, México, D.F.

Tierras      Tierras, Archivo General de la Nación, México, D.F.

TSJDF      Tribunal Superior de Justicia del Distrito Federal, Archivo General de la Nación, México, D.F.

INTRODUCTION

1. Icaza, *Conquistadores y pobladores*, 1:114.

2. *Recopilación de leyes de los reynos de las Indias* (1973), 117.

3. *Diccionario de la lengua española* (1729), http://buscon.rae.es/ntlle/SrvltGUIMenu Ntlle?cmd=Lema&sec=1.0.0.0.0. (June 7, 2011).

4. Pérez, "La marihuana," 57, 58. "La marihuana y la criminalidad," *El Imparcial*, July 23, 1898, 1.

5. *El País*, Mar. 30, 1909, 5.

6. José del Moral, Oct. 27, 1908, c. 0729, exp. 128284, TSJDF.

7. Departamento de Salubridad Pública, "Disposiciones sobre el cultivo y comercio de productos."

8. Benavie, *Drugs*; Duke and Gross, *America's Longest War*; Weir, *In the Shadow of the Dope Fiend*; Musto, *American Disease*; Gerber and Jensen, "Internationalization of U.S. Policy," 1–2; Friman, *Narcodiplomacy*, 4. Britain too has received a significant amount of credit/blame for early international drug control efforts. See McAllister, *Drug Diplomacy*; A. Taylor, *American Diplomacy and the Narcotics Traffic*; and Lowes, *Genesis of International Narcotics Control*. There is no doubt that at particular moments, the United States has come to exert enormous pressure on Mexico to fight drugs in a particular fashion. However, a lack of research into Mexico's early history with drugs and prohibition has led scholars to assume that such pressure must have been the key from the beginning. See, for example, Toro, *Mexico's "War" on Drugs*, 6–8; Astorga, *Drogas sin fronteras*, 353; and G. González, "The Drug Connection," 2. For the view that, along with U.S. pressure, increasing drug abuse inspired prohibition in Mexico, see Martínez Cortés and Martínez Barbosa, *Del Consejo Superior*, 231–32. See also Valero Palacios, "Formación," 24; and Gutiérrez Ramos, "La prohibición," 38. Ricardo Pérez Montfort argues that "international pressures and tendencies" combined with the self-interest of Mexican politicians to produce drug prohibition there. See his "Fragmentos de historia de las 'drogas' en México," 163. Richard Craig argues that U.S. pressure was "belated" since "unofficial Mexican efforts against illicit opium cultivation began early in [the twentieth century]." See his "U.S. Narcotics Policy," 72. William Walker argues that at the turn of the twentieth century, "the attitude toward antidrug activity in the United States was far different from that in Latin America," but that by the 1920s, Mexico's leaders were as opposed to drug use as those in the United States, thanks largely to increased drug use there. See his *Drug Control in the Americas*, 1–2, 48–49, 59.

9. Davenport-Hines, *Pursuit of Oblivion*, xi–xii; Walker, *Drug Control in the Americas*, 1–2. Marijuana has also been portrayed as a "casual adjunct to life" within Mexican immigrant communities in the United States during the early twentieth century. See Bonnie and Whitebread, *Marihuana Conviction*, 33–34. See also Musto, *American Disease*, 218. Miguel Ruiz-Cabañas has argued that in the first decades of the twentieth century, marijuana was understood in Mexico "more as a useful substance with medical and other applications than as a drug." See his "Mexico's Changing Illicit Drug Supply Role," 47.

10. A number of shorter or broader works that deal in some way with the topic do exist. See Pérez Montfort, "Fragmentos de historia de las 'drogas' en México"; Astorga, *El siglo de las drogas*; González and Tienda, *Drug Connection*; Toro, *Mexico's "War" on Drugs*; Astorga, *Drogas sin fronteras*; Walker, *Drug Control in the Americas*; Valero Palacios, "Formación"; Gutiérrez Ramos, "La prohibición"; and Martínez Cortés and Martínez Barbosa, *Del Consejo Superior*.

11. The best book on the prohibitionist foundations of the War on Drugs is Bertram et al., *Drug War Politics*. For an economist's case against drug prohibition, see Benavie, *Drugs*.

12. The two moments most commonly cited for the declaration of the War on Drugs

are a June 1971 speech by Richard Nixon and an October 1982 speech by Ronald Reagan. See Wisotsky, *Beyond the War on Drugs*, 3. Other dates have been cited, including 1969 and 1986. For 1969, see Tony Payan, *Three U.S.-Mexico Border Wars*, 23. For 1986, see Denq and Wang, "The War on Drugs in Taiwan," 149. Preston Peet points out that Nixon did not actually utter the phrase "war on drugs" but merely declared narcotics to be "public enemy #1." *Under the Influence*, 244. In fact, if one cares to pursue that decidedly pedantic approach to the question, the phrase "war on drugs" or "drug war" can be found in sources dating back to the early twentieth century. See, for example, "Labor Secretary Backs New War on Drug Traffic," *New York Times*, Jan. 10, 1923, 1; "Our War on Drugs Told," *New York Times*, June 14, 1926, 5; and "President Launches Drive on Narcotics," *New York Times*, Nov. 28, 1954, 1. This final article notes that "President Eisenhower called today for a new war on narcotic addiction." In 1926, the *Times* reported that Mexican president Plutarco Elías Calles had made a similar declaration. "Calles Declares Drug War," *New York Times*, Feb. 7, 1925, 3.

13. Astorga, *Drogas sin fronteras*, 355.

14. A "Schedule 1" drug is defined in the following terms: "(A) The drug or other substance has a high potential for abuse. (B) The drug or other substance has no currently accepted medical use in treatment in the United States. (C) There is a lack of accepted safety for use of the drug or other substance under medical supervision." See http://www.law.cornell.edu/uscode/html/uscode21/usc_sec_21_00000812——000-.html (June 7, 2011).

15. For an excellent and dispassionate survey of the scientific research on cannabis, see Earleywine, *Understanding Marijuana*. The designation also fails in the face of twenty-first-century common sense, when many, if not most, Americans have either used or known users of the drug. These facts have inspired a significant popular literature on the subject complete with conspiracy theories to explain marijuana's prohibition in the United States. The most famous of such works is Herer, *Hemp and the Marijuana Conspiracy*. For a more academic investigation into some of Herer's claims, see Lupien, *Unraveling an American Dilemma*.

CHAPTER ONE

1. Li, "Origin and Use of Cannabis," 56.

2. Rosenthal, *Herb*, 86–87. On cannabis's reputation for producing madness among Indian Muslims, see Chopra and Chopra, "Use of the Cannabis Drugs in India," 11–12.

3. Marzolph, "Preface," ix.

4. *Book of the Thousand Nights*, 11:14–30. Also typical in the *Nights* were hallucinations of status, with cannabis users routinely imagining themselves to be of a higher social station than they actually were. See, for example, "The Tale of the Hashish Eater," in which a poor man eats hashish and dreams he is rich, only to be ridiculed. Ibid., 2:315–17. The story of "The Sleeper and the Waker" sees a Caliph trick an ordinary young man by spiking his drink with bhang so that he falls unconscious. The young man is then transported into sumptuous quarters and surrounded by slaves and a harem. Thoroughly hoodwinked, in the morning he exclaims: "By Allah, either I am dreaming a dream, or this is Paradise and the Abode of Peace." Ibid., 9:1–28. See also "Khalifah, the Fisherman of Baghdad," in which the title character winds up whip-

ping himself and being ridiculed by the townspeople. Ibid., 6:305–7. "The Story of the Three Sharpers" describes several con artists eating hashish and enjoying great merriment. Ibid., 10:361. "The Tale of the Ensorcelled Prince" describes a wife who drugs her husband with bhang so that she may commit adultery. Ibid., 1:64–68. The *Nights* was first translated into a European language (French) by Antoine Galland in 1704 and would probably play as significant a role as any other source in shaping Western discourses on cannabis drugs in the modern era. Galland's translation was followed by countless editions in dozens of languages, eventually inspiring an enormous artistic vogue for storytelling in the "Oriental" style, whether in fiction, dance, music, or even architecture. See Marzolph, "Preface," ix.

5. As quoted in Mills, *Cannabis Britannica*, 21.

6. Grose, *Voyage to the East Indies*, 1:123. The same passage is quoted by Mills, *Cannabis Britannica*, 21, as cited (slightly altered) in the *Portable Instructions*.

7. Mills, *Cannabis Britannica*, 21–22. Mills questions this description's veracity:

It is difficult . . . to claim that Grose's account of cannabis, or indeed of India, is reliable or accurate and much easier to conclude that it was never his intention to produce information that was any of these things. The book seems to be written in order to appeal to his audience and the List of Subscribers that bought the first edition suggests that this was a fairly representative slice of eighteenth century, middle-class England. . . . Such an audience's predilection for titillating tales of oriental excess and for reassuring paragraphs on "the mildness and tolerance of the English government" suggests that John Henry Grose would have carefully selected and embellished his stories rather than simply presented a balanced view of all that he witnessed in Asia. Grose made an association between cannabis drugs, violence, madness, and death which had these questionable origins. Nevertheless, this association remained the basis of the information available to British officers and other merchants on cannabis in the *Portable Instructions* that continued to be used into the twentieth century.

Ibid., 24.

8. Johnston, *Chemistry of Common Life*, 88–90.

9. Daftary, *Assassin Legends*, 5.

10. Ibid., 34.

11. Ibid., 23–24, 89.

12. Rosenthal, *Herb*, 142.

13. Daftary, *Assassin Legends*, 93.

14. Ibid., 117.

15. Sacy, "Memoir on the Dynasty of the Assassins," 168.

16. B. Taylor, "The Visions of Hasheesh," 402.

17. Johnston, *Chemistry of Common Life*, 99.

18. Anslinger, "Marihuana: Assassin of Youth," 150.

19. Bibra, *Plant Intoxicants*, 151.

20. Dumas, *The Count of Monte Cristo*, 382–88, 517, 739–40.

21. Boon, *Road of Excess*, 132–44; Baudelaire, *Artificial Paradise*.

22. W. O'Shaughnessy, "On the Preparations of the Indian Hemp," 345.

23. Ibid., 368.

24. Ibid., 344.

25. Holmstedt, "Introduction to Moreau de Tours," ix–xxii.

26. Moreau, *Hashish and Mental Illness*, 17.

27. Ibid., 18.

28. Ibid., 19. Holmstedt makes the connection to Aristotle in "Introduction to Moreau de Tours," xvii.

29. Moreau, *Hashish and Mental Illness*, 19.

30. Moreau, "Recherches sur les Aliénés en Orient." Quoted in Holmstedt, "Introduction to Moreau de Tours," xviii–xix. Emphasis in both cases in the original.

31. Moreau, *Hashish and Mental Illness*, 38–40.

32. Ibid., 64–67.

33. Ibid., 68–86.

34. Ibid., 3.

35. See, for example, *Book of the Thousand Nights and a Night*, 3:159 n. 1.

36. Dumas, *Count of Monte Cristo*, 541.

37. Mills, *Cannabis Britannica*, 93–105.

38. The National Organization for the Reform of Marijuana Laws celebrated the report on the occasion of its centennial, declaring that the report's conclusions "in no way justify the current War Against Marijuana." NORML's press release is available at http://www.erowid.org/plants/cannabis/cannabis_history1.shtml (June 7, 2011). See also Mikuriya, *Excerpts from the Indian Hemp Drugs Commission Report*.

39. Indian Hemp Drugs Commission, *Report*, 1:199–201, 257–58, 225–26.

40. Ibid., 264.

41. Ibid.

42. Ibid., 266–67, 363–477.

43. Ewens, "Insanity Following the Use of Indian Hemp," 403.

44. Ibid., 407–13. On delusions of grandeur in the *Nights*, see n. 4 above.

45. Robertson-Milne, "Notes on Insanity"; Peebles and Mann, "Ganja as a Cause of Insanity"; Bournhill, "Smoking of Dagga"; Oneto Barenque, "La marihuana ante la psiquiatría."

46. "Report of Committee Appointed by the [Canal Zone] Governor," 135.

47. Bonnie and Whitebread, *Marihuana Conviction*, 142. See also Salazar Viniegra, "El mito de la marihuana."

48. Anslinger, "Marihuana: Assassin of Youth," 150.

49. Bonnie and Whitebread, *Marihuana Conviction*, 200–202; Musto, *American Disease*, 228–29.

50. Bonnie and Whitebread, *Marihuana Conviction*, 218–20; Earleywine, *Understanding Marijuana*, 49–50.

51. Talbott and Teague, "Marihuana Psychosis," 302.

52. Weil, "Adverse Reactions to Marihuana," 998. Howard Becker made very similar arguments a few years earlier with respect to both marijuana and LSD. See his "History, Culture and Subjective Experience."

53. Weil, "Adverse Reactions to Marihuana," 998.

54. Ibid., 998–99.

55. Ibid.

56. DeGrandpre, *Cult of Pharmacology*, 120–21. For an excellent discussion of the scientific research into placebo effects in general, see Kirsch, *Emperor's New Drugs*, especially chapters 5 and 6.

57. Ibid., 120.

58. Ibid., 185–86.

59. Falk, "Discriminative Stimulus." The study is also summarized in DeGrandpre, *Cult of Pharmacology*, 203–4.

60. DeGrandpre, *Cult of Pharmacology*, 200–201.

61. Grose, *Voyage to the East Indies*, 1:123.

62. Browne, "(Ng)amuk Revisited," 147–48. See also Simons, "Introduction: The Sudden Mass Assault Taxon."

63. Simons, "Introduction: The Sudden Mass Assault Taxon," 197; Carr, "Ethno-Behaviorism," 201–2.

64. Kaempfer and Carrubba, *Exotic Pleasures*, 191–92.

65. DeGrandpre, *Cult of Pharmacology*, 62.

66. Keeler, "Adverse Reaction to Marihuana," 675–76. Keeler's study very much represents that historical moment. More than once he notes that these subjects were "not delinquents" and of "high intelligence," reflecting the belief going back decades in the United States that marijuana abuse was a consequence of the premorbid delinquency of its users. It was this traditional association between marijuana and the undesirable classes, coupled with the drug's sudden adoption by middle-class youth, that had stirred up so much controversy during the 1960s. Keeler at one point even suggested that rejection of bourgeois norms by marijuana smokers might be considered an "adverse effect" if not a sign of psychopathology. It was not just that marijuana was a health risk; it was that it was a threat to the conventional American way of life, especially if it could turn an otherwise highly intelligent, nondelinquent college student into an underachiever with a nonconformist wardrobe.

67. Ibid., 677.

68. Isbell et al., "Effects of delta-9-trans-tetrahydrocannabinol."

69. Weil, Zinberg, and Nelsen, "Clinical and Psychological Effects," 1241–42.

70. Earleywine, *Understanding Marijuana*, 121–26.

71. Ibid., 125–26.

72. Zuardi et al., "Effects of Ipsapirone and Cannabidiol."

73. Earleywine, *Understanding Marijuana*, 136–37.

74. Ibid., 137–38.

75. Lyons et al., "How Do Genes Influence Marijuana Use?" 412.

76. For a summary of various other studies of this kind, see Castle and Solowij, "Acute and Subacute Psychotomimetic Effects," 42–43. See also Earleywine, *Understanding Marijuana*, 102–17; Halikas, Goodwin, and Guze, "Marijuana Effects"; and Tart, *On Being Stoned*.

77. McLaren et al., "Assessing Evidence"; "Substance-Induced Psychotic Disorder," accessed through STAT!Ref Online Electronic Medical Library.

78. Earleywine, *Understanding Marijuana*, 144–45; Castle and Solowij, "Acute and Subacute Psychotomimetic Effects." According to Earleywine, a 160-pound person

would have to ingest approximately 900 consecutive marijuana cigarettes to achieve a fatal dose.

79. Chopra and Smith, "Psychotic Reactions," 24–25.

80. Ibid., 25.

81. Ibid., 25–27.

82. Proving causality in such cases is notoriously difficult. To prove causality, researchers must demonstrate that the symptoms would not have occurred without the use of cannabis, that the use of cannabis definitely preceded the outbreak of symptoms, that all other plausible alternative sources of the psychosis can be excluded, and that "cannabis psychosis" displays symptoms distinct from those of other brands of psychosis. Hall and Degenhardt, "Is There a Specific 'Cannabis Psychosis'?"; McLaren et al., "Assessing Evidence."

83. Hall and Degenhardt, "Is There a Specific 'Cannabis Psychosis'?" 97.

84. Earleywine, *Understanding Marijuana*, 145–46; McLaren et al., "Assessing Evidence."

85. Andréasson et al., "Cannabis and Schizophrenia."

86. Ibid. For the similar hypotheses from the earlier Indian studies, see Indian Hemp Drugs Commission, *Report*, 1:264; and Ewens, "Insanity Following the Use of Indian Hemp," 403.

87. McLaren et al., "Assessing Evidence," 17.

88. Hides et al., "Psychotic Symptoms."

89. Francoeur and Baker, "Attraction to Cannabis," 133–34.

90. Costain, "Effects of Cannabis Abuse"; Francoeur and Baker, "Attraction to Cannabis."

91. Costain, "Effects of Cannabis Abuse," 229–30.

92. Francoeur and Baker, "Attraction to Cannabis."

93. Hall and Degenhardt, "Is There a Specific 'Cannabis Psychosis'?" 96.

94. Andréasson et al., "Cannabis and Schizophrenia," 1484; Hall and Degenhardt, "What Are the Policy Implications of the Evidence on Cannabis and Psychosis?" 570.

95. Hall and Degenhardt, "What Are the Policy Implications of the Evidence on Cannabis and Psychosis?" 38–40.

96. Castle and Solowij, "Acute and Subacute Psychotomimetic Effects," 41.

CHAPTER TWO

1. Schultes et al., "Cannabis," 23.

2. Clarke, *Botany and Ecology*, 42, 46; Courtwright, *Forces of Habit*, 39; Grinspoon, *Marihuana Reconsidered*, 35; Schultes, "Random Thoughts," 26.

3. Clarke, *Botany and Ecology*, 46. Quotation is left unattributed by Schultes in "Random Thoughts," 19, but is clearly drawn from Anderson, *Introgressive Hybridization*, 67.

4. Schultes, "Random Thoughts," 16.

5. Schultes et al., "Cannabis," 27. On early archaeological evidence, see Li, "Origin and Use of Cannabis," 53–55; see also his "Archaeological and Historical Account," 438–40. Merlin cites one finding of cord-impressed pottery from "early post-glacial fishing sites" at the Yuan-Shun site in Taiwan dating to about 10,000 B.C. in "Archaeological Evidence," 312. However, Li is quite specific in stating that cannabis was the only fiber-

producing plant in *northern* China, suggesting implicitly that such assumptions cannot be made about more southern areas. It seems that Merlin's claims about this southern area of Taiwan have gone beyond what Li would have considered acceptable, for the latter fails to cite these earlier dates despite surely having knowledge of them at the time of his work on cannabis.

6. Hemp was also cost-effective, for even old, worn-out ropes and waste materials from the manufacturing process could be utilized as oakum for caulking on ships. See Hopkins, *History of the Hemp Industry*; and Mills, *Cannabis Britannica*, 17–18.

7. Clearly, more than "three" traditions came together in the sixteenth century, as each geographic area produced any number of local practices and beliefs. However, for the purposes of this history, a general, tripartite schema as outlined by Aguirre Beltrán is sufficiently precise. See Aguirre Beltrán, "Medicina española," "Medicina indígena," and "Medicina negra," chapters 1, 2, and 3 respectively, in *Medicina y magia*.

8. Ibid., 24.

9. Ibid. Aguirre Beltrán cites Ambrosio Paré (1510–90) as an example.

10. Ibid., 25–35.

11. Mexico's first *protomédico*, Francisco Hernández, most famously made this observation which has now become commonplace. Pardo, "Contesting the Power to Heal," 165.

12. Aguirre Beltrán, *Medicina y magia*, 37, 44–45.

13. Ibid., 37–49.

14. Ibid., 58–72.

15. This ease of mixture has made it extremely difficult to determine exactly which practices derived from which tradition. Aguirre Beltrán argues that syncretism took hold with such a force, beginning with Francisco Hernández's work of the sixteenth century, as to make its unraveling almost impossible today. See *Medicina y magia*, 122. An especially contentious aspect of this problem revolves around the origins of "hot-cold" distinctions in the Americas. For background on this debate, see Chevalier and Sánchez Bain, *Hot and the Cold*, especially xiii–xiv.

16. Aguirre Beltrán, *Medicina y magia*, 78.

17. Ibid., 92–93.

18. Antonio Escohotado emphasizes the importance of the root *pharmakon* in his *Historia general de las drogas* (1996), 1:20. See also *Oxford English Dictionary*, 2nd ed. Paracelsus is quoted in Schultes, Hofmann, and Rätsch, *Plants of the Gods*, 10.

19. Aguirre Beltrán, *Medicina y magia*, 127–29.

20. Quoted in Pardo, "Contesting the Power to Heal," 169.

21. Schultes, Hofmann, and Rätsch, *Plants of the Gods*, 9, 26, 30; Díaz, "Ethnopharmacology of Sacred Psychoactive Plants," 654–55.

22. Aguirre Beltrán, *Medicina y magia*, 48–49, 132–37.

23. F. Cervantes, *Devil in the New World*, 40–41, 84–89.

24. Schultes, Hofmann, and Rätsch, *Plants of the Gods*, 26.

25. On *Solano furioso*, see Pardo, "Contesting the Power to Heal," 170–71. See also Aguirre Beltrán, *Medicina y magia*, 304 n. 33. European understandings of witchcraft soon came to play a powerful role in the New World, as traditions dating back cen-

turies gradually took root among ordinary people in Mexico. On this process, see Aguirre Beltrán, *Medicina y magia*, 111–13. Richard Rudgely argues that the legendary flying of European witches was simply the sensation of flight given by the use of hallucinogens like belladonna (*Atropa belladonna*) and henbane (*Hyoscyamus niger*). See his *Essential Substances*, 106. Escohotado makes a similar argument in *Historia general de las drogas* (1996), 1:286–306. Robin Briggs, on the other hand, is skeptical of psychotropic explanations of witchcraft. See his *Witches and Neighbors*, 56–57.

26. Schultes, Hofmann, and Rätsch, *Plants of the Gods*, 27–29; Wasson, "Notes on the Present Status of Ololiuhqui"; Aguirre Beltrán, *Medicina y magia*, 139.

27. Sahagún, *Historia general de las cosas de Nueva España*, 292–93.

28. Ibid.

29. F. Cervantes, *Devil in the New World*, 13–17, 27–30.

30. Ibid., 105.

31. Escohotado, *Historia general de las drogas* (1996), 1:235–52.

32. Garrett, *Spirit Possession*, 1–5; Browne, "(Ng)amuk Revisited"; Spanos and Gottlieb, "Demonic Possession."

33. V. 333, exp. 35, 1620, INQ. My thanks to Alec Dawson for providing me with a transcript of this document.

34. W. Taylor, *Drinking, Homicide and Rebellion*, 32–33.

35. Ibid., 41–42.

36. Quoted in ibid., 42.

37. Ibid., 29n, 35, 59.

38. Ibid., 34, 41.

39. Ibid., 43.

40. Ibid., 64.

41. Quoted in ibid., 64–65.

42. Ibid., 59–61.

43. This is a phenomenon that has been observed worldwide. See Courtwright, *Forces of Habit*, 13–14, 173–74.

44. W. Taylor, *Drinking, Homicide and Rebellion*, 38, 59.

45. Ibid., 36–38.

46. Ibid., 37.

47. There is some evidence to suggest that cannabis smoking in water pipes had perhaps emerged in East Africa by the fourteenth century, though this evidence is not conclusive. For a review of the evidence and the history of the debate, see Philips, "African Smoking and Pipes."

48. Martínez Marín, "Época prehispánica," 56–58.

49. Quoted in ibid., 59.

50. Céspedes del Castillo, *El tabaco en Nueva España*, 28, 30.

51. Ibid., 25–32, 49–50, 68. Medical applications ranged from tobacco's use as an expectorant and emetic to a remedy against rheumatism, with its healing powers being delivered in poultices, infusions, and powders. In Europe, it was soon being prescribed for more than fifty different ailments.

52. Deans-Smith, *Bureaucrats, Planters, and Workers*, 9. The figure quoted here was

actually from 1748, but there is little reason to believe that consumption patterns changed radically over the next fifteen years.

53. González Sierra, *Monopolio del humo*, 47–48.

54. Céspedes del Castillo, *El tabaco en Nueva España*, 45–47, 63–66. As Céspedes points out, Mexico was also distinct in other aspects of tobacco consumption. Spanish observers, for instance, criticized Mexican smokers for disposing of the butt end of cigarettes without smoking their entire contents. Interestingly, Mexican smokers also stood out to the Spanish during the seventeenth and early eighteenth centuries in that they smoked entire cigarettes by themselves, while the Spanish tended to share a single cigarette among many, like later marijuana smokers, apparently because the price was quite high for tobacco in Spain until the late colonial period.

55. Deans-Smith and Céspedes del Castillo differ somewhat in their accounts of the erection of the tobacco monopoly. However, the finer points of these details are of limited importance to this study. This general account is based in part on both works. See "Monopoly, Tobacco, and Colonial Society," chapter 1 in Deans-Smith, *Bureaucrats, Planters, and Workers*; and "La fase de monopolio estatal (1765–1809)," chapter 3 in Céspedes del Castillo, *El tabaco en Nueva España*.

56. *Recopilación de leyes de los reynos de las Indias* (1973), 117. Cultivation of hemp apparently began in Chile in that same year, and nine years later to the day, another order went out specifically mandating that this cultivation be undertaken in Peru. See "Cédula que manda se Siembre en el Perú lino y Cáñamo y se yle y trate en ello," in Encinas, *Cedulario indiano*, 439.

57. Icaza, *Conquistadores y pobladores*, 114.

58. V. 3, exp. 430, 1587, fs. 201vta-202, GdP.

59. Letter dated May 30, 1777, v. 12, exp. 2, fs. 83–124, IyC (see especially the page marked 6, front and back).

60. The pungent smell of hemp in the fields was often reported to produce headaches and "giddiness" in European hemp workers during that era, so much so that the plant's distinct odor was cited by some as a means of distinguishing its fiber and drug strains, the former supposedly being more odiferous. See Johnston, *Chemistry of Common Life*, 89. See also "Notice of the Hachisch."

61. Letter dated May 30, 1777, v. 12, exp. 2, fs. 83–124, IyC (see especially the page marked 6, front and back).

62. Alzate, "Memoria." Originally published as *Asuntos varios sobre ciencias y artes*, no. 3, Nov. 9, 1772.

63. Letter dated May 30, 1777, v. 12, exp. 2, fs. 83–124, IyC.

64. Serrera Contreras, *Cultivo y manufactura*, 1–61.

65. Quoted in ibid., 63.

66. Num. de reg. 15283, Grupo doc. 11, v. 10, exp. 32, fs. 112–13, Bandos.

67. V. 12, exp. 1, fs. 47–55, IyC.

68. Serrera Contreras cites the following towns in this regard: Tlaxcala, Puebla, Teutitlán, Yahualica, Tacuba, Nochistlán, Miaguatlán, Tetela de Xonotla, Tuxtla, Querétaro, Colima, Aquixmón, Tlalpuzahua, and Xamiltepec. *Cultivo y manufactura*, 97.

69. The growers in Tacuba had attempted to turn a profit by selling the seed in Mexico City but found their produce undercut there by an imported product. By 1775,

they had given up the cultivation. Correspondence received Dec. 2, 1777, v. 12, exp. 2, fs. 123–24, IyC; see also Serrera Contreras, *Cultivo y manufactura*, 97.

70. Serrera Contreras, *Cultivo y manufactura*, 273.

71. V. 12, exp. 2, fs. 112–16, IyC. Spanish authorities recognized this problem and attached explicit directions to the original orders, but they also acknowledged the need for more hands-on guidance. Thus, by the end of 1777, a dozen men experienced with this trade were sent to Mexico from Spain. Workers were sent to Louisiana and Caracas for the same purposes, but cultivation there failed quite early on thanks to war around the former and unfit land in the latter. The stay of the workers in New Spain was conflict-ridden from the beginning, with disputes over their discipline, responsibilities, and remuneration. See "Organización de los cultivos y creación de la Real Fábrica (1780–1784)," "La gran polémica (1784–1786)," and "Cláusura de la Real Fábrica y declive del proyecto (1786–1793)," chapters 4, 5, and 6 respectively, in Serrera Contreras, *Cultivo y manufactura*. See especially pages 65–79 and 136.

72. Serrera Contreras, *Cultivo y manufactura*, 97.

73. For Cholula, see the correspondence dated Mar. 28, 1778, v. 12, fs. 54–55, IyC; for Veracruz, correspondence dated Apr. 30, 1778, v. 12, exp. 1, fs. 64–66, IyC; for San Blas, correspondence dated July 19, 1779, v. 12, exp. 9, f. 229, IyC. Complaints regarding the lack of seeds by the head of the hemp and flax project, Luis Parilla, can be found in the correspondence dated Jan. 14, 1783, v. 127, exp. 3, f. 3, and Dec. 4, 1784, v. 15, exp. 1, f. 33, IyC. The persistence of the problem in the next decade is illustrated by the correspondence dated July 27, 1796, v. 21, fs. 209–10, IyC; and correspondence dated Aug. 27, 1796, v. 183, exp. not clear, fs. 328–29, CV. Perhaps the most interesting of these cases was Philipe Díaz de Hortega of Valladolid, Michoacán, whose enthusiasm for the project, and thus frustration with the lack of seeds, was unmatched, as evidenced by a long string of correspondence in the late 1790s. See, for example, the correspondence dated Aug. 9, 1799, v. 24, fs. 258–61, IyC.

74. See, for instance, the correspondence from Veracruz dated Apr. 30, 1778, v. 12, exp. 1, fs. 64–66, IyC; see also correspondence dated Sept. 23, 1796, from Valladolid, v. 24, exp. 1, f. 10, IyC.

75. Num. de reg. 16120, Grupo doc. 11, v. 8, exp. 63, Bandos. Why a lack of seeds so hounded the endeavors in Mexico is not altogether clear. Some seeds had arrived from Europe rotted from the great humidity on the boats, but at the same time the cultivars had apparently been quite successful in Peru and Chile, as evidenced by the repeated requests made to those regions for seeds during the 1790s. See Serrera Contreras, *Cultivo y manufactura*, 191, 263–65. Furthermore, shortly after the turn of the century, the missions of California began having great success with the cultivation of hemp. The governor of California at this time, Diego Borica, began pushing the endeavor in 1795. That year the district produced the quite modest figure of 5½ fanegas or about 14 bushels of hemp. In 1798, California produced about 640 pounds of hemp. By 1810, this number had ballooned to 220,000 pounds. See Mosk, "Subsidized Hemp Production." Serrera Contreras chalks up the general failure of the industry to four major factors: human, technical, political-administrative, and economic. See his *Cultivo y manufactura*, 267–84.

76. On Papantla, see the correspondence dated Feb. 15, 1778, v. 12, exp. 1, f. 42, IyC;

on San Miguel el Grande, the correspondence dated Apr. 7, 1778, v. 12, exp. 1, fs. 49–50, IyC; for San Blas, the correspondence dated July 19, 1779, and July 31, 1788, v. 12, exp. 9, fs. 286–316, IyC, and v. 24. fs. 68–73, IyC.

77. V. 12, exp. 1, fs. 54–71, IyC; correspondence dated June 23, 1778, Num. de reg. 9561, Grupo doc. 8, v. 127, exp. 4, AHH. Some of these reports don't specify where they were made.

78. On the expanse of land cultivated for hemp and flax, see the correspondence dated Apr. 20, 1787, Num. de reg. 3557, Grupo doc. 11, exp. 15, Tierras. On the seeding, see v. 127, exp. 3, AHH. On production in 1787, see the correspondence dated Apr. 29, 1787, Num. de reg. 9561, Grupo doc. 8, v. 127, exp. 1, AHH.

79. Alzate, *Memorias y ensayos*, 1–8.

80. Alzate, *Obras*, xi–xxxvii.

81. Aguirre Beltrán, *Medicina y magia*, 137–39; Vetancurt, *Teatro Mexicano*, 169.

82. Alzate, "Memoria," 55. I use "their" ("lost *their* mind") rather than "his" or "her" here because the gender of this person is not made explicit in the original.

83. "Expedido en nombre del Provisor de Indios el Dr. D. Manuel Joachin Barrientos, para desterrar Idolatrías, Supersticiones, y otros abusos de los Indios," Edict XII in Lorenzana y Buitron, *Cartas Pastorales*.

84. Alzate, "Memoria," 56.

85. Pratt, *Imperial Eyes*, 24–37; Boorstin, *Discoverers*, 429–42; Davis, "Ethnobotany"; Pérez-Mejía, *Geography of Hard Times*, 12. The Americas had been crucial in the ultimate development of Linnaeus's scheme. The discovery of a new world by European explorers had helped to spur major advancements in the natural sciences already in the sixteenth century. Until that time, Europeans had been relying on fanciful recapitulations of Dioscorides's first-century catalog of Mediterranean species. Reliance on Dioscorides achieved such extremes that authors attempted to fit even familiar northern European plant varieties into the descriptions originally provided by the Greek physician. However, as accounts of exotic plant and animal species returned with explorers, Europeans began to reevaluate what was known about the natural world at that time and to abandon the absolute reliance on Dioscorides's original work. The most important contribution of this period was made by artists who furnished highly accurate drawings of local flora from around Europe, a tremendous improvement over the traditional herbals based on bastardized versions of Dioscoridian representations dating back over a thousand years. See Boorstin, *Discoverers*, 426–27.

86. Alzate, "Memoria," 56–57.

87. *Odyssey of Homer*, 55; Lempriere, *Universal Biography*.

88. Alzate, "Memoria," 57–58. Alzate labels the Fortunate Islands the Canary Islands in the footnote. Furthermore, he extracts a portion of Petit's original text, noting that it was "obscene." "Our language, and even more my station, obliges me to pass over in silence all that affronts modesty." Petit, *Homeri Nepenthes*.

89. Quoted in Alzate, "Memoria," 59.

90. Ibid., 60.

91. Aguirre Beltrán notes a number of important similarities in the descriptions of ololiuhqui and the *pipiltzintzintlis* in the files of the Inquisition. For example, the plants were used in similar fashion, with both substances being ground on a *metate* or

flat stone before being mixed with water and drunk for divination. The geographic distribution of the two substances, in the present state of Morelos and surrounding districts, was also the same, and during the period when the *pipiltzintzintlis* do appear in the records, references to ololiuhqui are absent. Finally, the names of the two drugs, both invoking divinities linked to maize, further suggest the relationship. The main obstacle to his theory, as Aguirre Beltrán readily admitted, was that in the Inquisition archives, the *pipiltzintzintlis* were described as the roots, leaves, and stems of a plant but never the seeds, while the word "ololiuhqui" was used exclusively in reference to seeds. Aguirre Beltrán, *Medicina y magia*, 139. It is worth noting that eighteenth-century European medicine also recommended crushing cannabis seeds and infusing them in water, much like Mexican pipiltzintzintli prescriptions. See 255, n. 8. This brings to mind the difficulties, cited above in note 15, in determining whether certain medical or religious practices derived from European or American roots. It would add an ironic twist if the manner of ingesting the pipiltzintzintlis, so identified with Indian Mexico, actually sprang from European medical recipes for cannabis.

92. Interestingly, *Salvia divinorum* has recently gained notoriety in the United States thanks to hundreds of homemade videos posted on YouTube where individuals smoke the plant on camera. Ingestion apparently results in a series of short-lived hallucinations. For viewers, the experience can be somewhat disturbing, as the users lose control of themselves, often toppling over in a stupor, laughing uncontrollably, or becoming verbally incoherent, a description that conforms quite closely to Vetancurt's 1698 description of the effects of the *pipiltzintzintlis*. Long before the advent of YouTube, Wasson reasoned that the *pipiltzintzintlis* should definitely not be confused with ololiuhqui. Within the Inquisition tribunal, the *pipiltzintzintlis* were always referred to as weeds rather than as vines, the latter being the typical and correct identification of the morning glory that produces ololiuhqui. Furthermore, the sources usually noted that the *pipiltzintzintlis* were cultivated and dioecious, two other traits that distinguished the plant from *Rivea corymbosa*. In the early 1960s, Wasson found *Salvia divinorum* being used among Oaxaca's Mazatecs in a manner that fit the colonial-era descriptions of the *pipiltzintzintlis* quite closely. For example, he observed the grinding of these leaves on a *metate* and their straining into an infusion. Given all of the other evidence that distinguished the *pipiltzintzintlis* from ololiuhqui, he concluded that it was this plant that had produced the famed *pipiltzintzintlis* of earlier times. Wasson, "Notes on the Present Status of Ololiuhqui."

93. Díaz, "Ethnopharmacology of Sacred Psychoactive Plants," 650.

94. J. Ramírez, "Informes de los trabajos ejecutados," 172.

95. Díaz cites other reasons to believe Alzate, noting that his account conformed with relatively recent reports of cannabis being used as a divinatory substance in twentieth-century Mexico. Tim Knab reported that among the Otomis in the Sierra de Puebla, the plant was pruned purposefully to maximize its resinous output and employed in a manner reminiscent of both ololiuhqui and the *pipiltzintzintlis*: "The bush is cut, partially dried and ingested in an infusion. The *curandero* sings during the ceremony, his tone changing as the effects are experienced since his voice then belongs to the supernatural being with whom the plant has put him in contact." Díaz, "Ethnopharmacology and Taxonomy," 78. The quote is Díaz's description of Knab's findings.

It should be noted that the reliability of Knab's report remains somewhat in doubt. Knab's paper on this was never published, but a copy exists in Harvard's botany library. Though it is not completely clear, it appears that Knab did not actually witness the ceremony himself and neither did his informant. At the same time, the informant, an Otomí *brujo*, insisted that marijuana was *not* the plant used in this ceremony: "Kaupp (pers. Comm.) first reported use of cannabis among the Otomí though he had never witnessed the ceremony involved. Cannabis is referred to by the Otomí as *yerba de Santa Rosa*, Santa Rosa's weed. The Otomí *brujo* vehemently denies that the *yerba de Santa Rosa* is *marijuana*, which due to national publicity campaigns he feels is only used by hippies who want to make themselves crazy." Knab, "Lesser Known Mexican Psychopharmacogens." Other divinatory use of cannabis has been reported more reliably. See, for example, Lumholtz, *Unknown Mexico*, 2:125; and Williams-Garcia, "Ritual Use of Cannabis." However, Knab's account most resembles descriptions of the *pipiltzintzintlis* or ololiuhqui use in the colonial era.

96. Lumholtz, *Unknown Mexico*, 2:125; Aguirre Beltrán, *Medicina y magia*, 150. It is of course also suggestive that as the Spanish began encouraging hemp production after 1777, they found widespread belief that the production of the plant was prohibited. Alzate himself noted this very problem in a 1778 letter to Viceroy Bucareli. There he expressed puzzlement at this belief, noting that the 1545 order mandating cannabis cultivation was to his knowledge the only law of relevance to the question. This of course raises an important question: why had Lorenzana's prohibitory decree of 1769 not occurred to him? José Antonio Alzate, "Ensayo sobre la siembra y cultivo del lino y del cañamo por lo respectivo a Nueva España (Reflexiones del autor presentadas al Virrey Bucareli)," 28.03.1778 (Co), v. Indias-Cedulario-t. 25, Ms. 457 [1394], fs. 47 a 70, FR. In a 1795 order encouraging the production of these products in Mexico, a history of legislation on this matter is offered which provides no indication that there had ever been any prohibitions on the cultivation of these products. Num. de reg. 16120, Grupo doc. 11, v. 18, exp. 63, May 21, 1795, Bandos.

97. Aguirre Beltrán, *Medicina y magia*, 133; Wasson, "Notes on the Present Status of Ololiuhqui," 175; Leander J. Valdés III, "The Early History of *Salvia Divinorum*," http://www.sagewisdom.org/earlysdhistory.html (Aug. 24, 2011).

98. Aguirre Beltrán, *Medicina y magia*, 148.

99. Alzate, "Memoria," 61–62.

100. The Arizona Industrial Hemp Council, for example, states clearly on its website that "hemp . . . is not only not marijuana; it could be called 'antimarijuana.'" http://www.azhemorg/Archive/Package/Legal/legal.html (June 9, 2011).

101. Fetterman et al., "Mississippi-Grown *Cannabis sativa L.*"

102. Small, *Species Problem in Cannabis*, 1:79; Fetterman et al., "Mississippi-Grown *Cannabis sativa L.*"; Hemphill, Turner, and Mahlberg, "Cannabinoid Content." One notable exception is a study by Hakim, El Kheir, and Mohamed which reports that plants grown in the Sudan from English seed stocks originally devoid of THC gradually produced greater quantities of THC and less CBD. They attribute their findings to the fact that most other studies have experimented only with tropical strains of cannabis in colder climates. See "Effect of the Climate."

103. Small, *Species Problem in Cannabis*, 1:79.

104. Ibid., 104–5.

105. Ibid., 120.

106. Haney and Kutscheid, "Qualitative Variation." Small makes similar observations, though he argues that "preliminary results suggest that environmental effects are relatively slight." *Species Problem in Cannabis*, 1:119.

107. Turner et al., "Constituents of *Cannabis sativa L.*"

108. Hemphill, Turner, and Mahlberg, "Cannabinoid Content."

109. Fetterman et al., "Mississippi-Grown *Cannabis sativa L.*," 1246.

110. Ernest Small, personal communication, Mar. 2002.

CHAPTER THREE

1. The piece is quoted at length in "El hatchis y la mariguana," *El Universal*, Oct. 1, 1854, 3.

2. See chapter 2, n. 85.

3. San Pío Aladrén, *Mutis and the Royal Botanical Expedition*," 27–28; McVaugh, *Botanical Results of the Sessé and Mociño Expedition*, v.

4. Helferich, *Humboldt's Cosmos*, xvii–xxi.

5. Ibid., xviii–xix; Pérez-Mejía, *Geography of Hard Times*, 11–15.

6. Lomnitz, *Deep Mexico*, 233–34.

7. Humboldt, *Ensayo político* (1984), 290.

8. D. Cervantes, *Ensayo a la materia médica vegetal*, 39. His listed medical applications were for gonorrhea, leucorrhea, and jaundice. J. B. Chomel, a noted European authority, described medicinal cannabis in the following terms: "The most common use of this seed is to crush one ounce in a pint of herbal tea that is given by the glassful in the form of an emulsion to people that have jaundice and obstructions of the liver without fever; this seed pushes also the menses and urine if it is infused and crushed in white wine. Some use it in the treatment of gonorrhea and dysuria; it is given as an emulsion." *Abrégé de l'histoire des plantes usuelles*, 494–96. Juan de Esteyneffer in his *Florilegio medicinal* mentions similar applications and admits to having compiled his work using information from other known texts. He recommends cannabis seeds for the overproduction of milk in mothers and for gonorrhea. See pages 1, 210–11, and 234. Similar properties were noted by the Sessé and Mociño catalog with which Cervantes was involved: "Habitat in Nova Hispania et Europa. Proprietas: Semina narcotica et repercusiva, gonorreae, leucorrheae et ictericiae opitulantur." See Sessé and Mociño, *Plantae Novae Hispaniae*, 159. All information provided by this text must be taken with some skepticism due to the tangled history of its production. Many plants that are included in this text were not actually mentioned by Sessé and Mociño. A recent recataloging of the their findings by Rogers McVaugh, for instance, excludes cannabis. See McVaugh's *Botanical Results*. For background on the confusion surrounding the collection, see the prologue, especially page v. For the rules followed for including and excluding certain species, see page 8.

9. Mociño's address is reprinted in D. Cervantes, *Ensayo a la materia médica vegetal*, 51.

10. Riesgo and Valdés, "Memoria estadística del estado de Occidente," 97; *Ensayo para la materia médica mexicana arreglado por una comision nombrada por la Academia*

*Médico-Quiúrgica de la ciudad de Puebla*, which is reprinted in D. Cervantes, *Ensayo a la materia médica vegetal*.

11. "Noticias estadísticas del Departamento de Aguascalientes."

12. Comisión de Estadística Militar, "Memoria chorográfica," 10–11, 33, 42–44; "Ensayo estadístico sobre el territorio de Colima," 275–76.

13. Prieto, *Memorias de mis tiempos*, includes many vice references but no marijuana. See especially 47–50, 76–85. Prieto's *Musa callejera* is similarly devoid of references to the weed. His *Viajes de orden suprema*, 428–32, provides one exception. See also Payno, *El fistol del diablo*.

14. Bingley, *Travels in North America*, especially 243–44; Brackett, *General Lane's Brigade in Central Mexico*, especially 68–71 and 139–45; Tempsky, *Mitla*, especially 35–36, 86, 189, 234, 256, 263, and 374. See also Covarrubias, *Visión extranjera de México*, which summarizes the accounts of four different foreign residents in Mexico during this period.

15. B. Taylor, *Eldorado*, especially 157–58; B. Taylor, "Visions of Hasheesh."

16. Fossey, *Viage a Méjico*, especially 227–29; Fossey, *Le Mexique*, 405.

17. Humboldt, *Ensayo político* (1836), 319 n. 3.

18. Ibid., 598. The second edition (1822) does not yet include this correction. Humboldt, *Ensayo político* (1822), 376–77, and *Ensayo político* (1836), 372–75.

19. Aguirre Beltrán, *Medicina y magia*, 80.

20. Morales Cosme and Martínez Solís, "Un libro," 134–35. Bustamante edited the list with Pablo de la Llave.

21. Ibid., 134–37.

22. *Farmacopea mexicana*, iv–vii. Note that the introduction to the original *Farmacopea* does not contain page numbers. I counted off the page numbers noted here.

23. Ibid., i–iii.

24. Comisión de Estadística Militar, "Introducción," i–ii. For membership rolls, see *Boletín de la Sociedad de Geografía y Estadística de la República Mexicana* (1850 [1839]), 4, 71–72.

25. *Farmacopea mexicana*, 48.

26. Linnaeus also recognized the existence of the plant elsewhere, writing in the margins of the original work "habitat in India." A later edition added Persia as well. Schultes, "Random Thoughts," 23.

27. *Farmacopea mexicana*, 23.

28. Schultes, "Random Thoughts," 23; Stearn, "Typification," 13–14; Schultes et al., "Cannabis," 29–30. The politics infusing most of the literature on cannabis can be detected even in a mostly botanical text like Stearn's when the author notes that "*fortunately*, during the period of its maximum use in Europe, the narcotic properties of its resin were unknown there" (emphasis mine).

29. Oliva, *Lecciones de farmacología*, 1:8–10. The 1846 report describes marijuana as a novelty that had sparked an "epidemic" of laziness in the military. See "Epidemias," *El Republicano* (México City), Apr. 5, 1846, 1–2.

30. Ibid., 12.

31. Ibid., 15.

32. Ibid., 202–3.

33. Ibid., 200–201.

34. Gutiérrez Ramos, "La prohibición," 61 n. 63.

35. There are other suggestive words in Nahuatl as well, such as *huahuana*, which means "to be striped or branded." Bierhorst, *Nahuatl-English Dictionary*, 127, 128, 195, 204. See also Karttunen, *Analytical Dictionary of Nahuatl*.

36. Santamaria, *Diccionario de mejicanismos*, 697–98. I assume the *H* here was simply a typo.

37. See, for example, Bradford, *Comprehensive Atlas*; Colton, *Colton's General Atlas*; and B. Smith, *Century Atlas*.

38. The initial European usage is evidenced in the "Turin" map of 1523. See Craton, *History of the Bahamas*, 45. See also Craton and Gail Saunders, *Islanders in the Stream*, 1:65. Citations to "Mariguana Island" could still be found in the mid-twentieth century. See, for example, "President Inspects Mariguana Base Site," *New York Times*, Dec. 13, 1940, 26.

39. Earlywine, *Understanding Marijuana*, 126.

40. Hutchinson, "Patterns of Marihuana Use," 174–75.

41. *Dicionário contemporâneo da língua portuguesa*; Leitão, *Dicionário da linguagem de marinha antiga e actual*; Coelho, *Diccionario manual etymologico da lingua portugueza*; J. P. Machado, *Dicionário etimológico da língua portuguesa*; Figueiredo, *Novo dicionário da lingua portuguesa*; Morais Silva, *Grande dicionário da língua portuguesa*; J. P. Machado, *Para o dicionário de português antigo*; Faria, *Novo diccionario da lingua portugueza*; Santa Rosa de Viterbo, *Diccionario portatil das palavras*; Lima, *Pequeno dicionário brasileiro da língua portuguêsa*; Freitas, *Novo diccionario da marinha de guerra e mercante*.

42. Hutchinson, "Patterns of Marihuana Use," 179.

43. For a list of common names for cannabis in Mexico, see Aguilar Contreras and Zolla, *Plantas tóxicas*, 45.

44. Earleywine, *Understanding Marijuana*, 126. Interestingly, "marihuana" does appear in a list of synonyms for tobacco in a recent survey of Mexico's "toxic" plants, though this of course does not prove that this word was used for tobacco prior to being linked with cannabis. See Aguilar Contreras and Zolla, *Plantas tóxicas*, 157.

45. Díaz Cántora, "Mariguana, mota, grifa."

46. Orozco y Berra, *Geografía de las lenguas y carta etnográfica de México*, 293. Interestingly, Orozco y Berra also points out that in 1849, a town by the name of "Miquihuana" was founded in Tamaulipas. See ibid., 291 n. 3.

47. Pimentel, "Vocabulario manual de la lengua Ópata." On the status of Opata language and culture, see Johnson, *Opata*.

48. See Said, *Orientalism*.

49. Tenorio-Trillo, *Mexico at the World's Fairs*, 8.

50. Escohotado, *Historia general de las drogas*, 2:37–44.

51. Ochoa, "Las investigaciones de Crescencio García." García's article was reproduced here apparently for the first time.

52. García, "Fragmentos para la materia médica mexicana," 79.

53. Ibid., 82–83.

54. Ibid., 85–87. García closes his exposition by listing ten medicinal preparations using cannabis, eight of which are clearly from European sources and two of which appear to be of local origin.

55. *Mariguana* was included as part of Querétaro's contribution to the 1855 event. "Exposición Universal de 1855 en Paris," *El Siglo Diez y Nueve*, Sept. 3, 1855, 2. Alfonso Herrera included it in a collection of typical Mexican medicinal plants sent to Philadelphia in 1876. Jackson, "Notes on Some of the Pharmaceutical Products Exhibited." See also the *Proceedings of the American Pharmaceutical Association at the Twenty-Fourth Annual Meeting*, 770; note that the marijuana on display is priced at fifty cents per kilo. In the *Philadelphia International Exhibition, 1876, Mexico Section*, under the "Medicine" heading, it is noted that "mention must be made of the Mexican medicinal plants, sent by the Society of Natural History, among which there are specimens of great therapeutical interest," 61.

CHAPTER FOUR

1. An exception: "Epidemias," *El Republicano*, Apr. 5, 1846, 1–2, cites Jalapa, Ver. See also Orozco y Berra, ed., *Apéndice al diccionario universal*, 2:349. Another geography of Jalisco by Leonardo Oliva, "Flórula del Departamento de Jalisco," 130, also mentions its presence. Marijuana was also included as a "narcotic" for Querétaro's contribution to the 1855 World's Fair. "Exposición Universal de 1855 en Paris," *El Siglo Diez y Nueve*, Sept. 3, 1855, 2. See also "El hospital de San Hipólito," *El Siglo Diez y Nueve*, Nov. 11, 1857, 3.

2. James F. W. Johnston, Ernest von Bibra, and Mordecai C. Cooke all published works on the world's intoxicants during this period and conspicuously excluded Mexico from their lists of countries where cannabis was known to be used. Johnston, *Chemistry of Common Life*, 89; Bibra, *Plant Intoxicants*, 150; and Cooke, *Seven Sisters*, 214. These texts were written for popular audiences and contain not only information on where and by whom each drug was used but also maps laying out the areas of use for particular substances. All three texts indicate that the use of cannabis as an intoxicant was known in Brazil but specifically indicate that the weed was not used in Mexico. See also Wilson, "Narcotic Usages," especially 234–41 and 339–340; and Cheever, "Narcotics," 375–76. A foreign scientific expedition through Tamaulipas also failed to mention it. Berlandier, "Espedición científica." James Frederick Elton describes considerable drinking among French soldiers and tobacco smoking among Mexicans but no marijuana. *With the French in Mexico*, 47, 69, 88, 92, 98, 130. Atypically, the Italian countess Paula Gräfin Kolonitz suggests that the Mexicans were a relatively sober people and suffered only from gambling, laziness, and other more mundane vices. *Un viaje a México*, 95–112. The Colombian Federico Cornelio Aguilar has written on the customs and habits of various Mexican populations, emphasizing drunkenness a number of times without ever referring to marijuana. *Último año de residencia en México*, 63, 107.

3. An 1852 report from Yucatán elaborates on the advantages that henequen offered over cannabis fiber in various areas but says nothing about any local production of the latter despite a detailed discussion of drunkenness and prisons as repositories of vice. See "Estadística de Yucatán," 295, 312–13. A report on Chiapas marvels at Indian

knowledge of medicinal plants and also describes how their fights are usually the result of drunkenness but never mentions marijuana. Pineda, "Descripción geográfica del departamento de Chiapas y Soconusco," 354–55. Clearly, review of such reports isn't a foolproof method of determining marijuana's presence (for example, an 1865 report on Jalisco excludes cannabis, though by then its presence had been well established by Oliva [see Banda, "Estadística de Jalisco"]), but they are suggestive nonetheless. Other sources are also suggestive. The Pachuca Scientific Commission of 1864, for example, also fails to mention cannabis. Almaraz, *Memoria de los trabajos ejecutados*, 249–50. Juan N. del Valle's 1864 "El viajero en México" contains a detailed section on problems within prisons where he emphasizes sloth and prostitution but fails to mention marijuana. Along the same lines, see Manuel Rivera Cambas's "México pintoresco, artístico y monumental." Leopoldo Ortega's medical thesis refers to alcoholism and the smuggling of spirits into the barracks but makes no mention of marijuana. "Breves consideraciones," 25, 27, 33–34. Similarly, Agustín García Figueroa's medical thesis on the causes of syphilis in the army emphasizes the vice in the barracks, including prostitution, homosexuality, and alcoholism as well as the smuggling of various forms of contraband by *soldaderas*, without, however, mentioning marijuana: "She supplies them with sugar, tobacco, bread, and alcoholic beverages, totally mocking the security." "Causas de la frecuencia de la sífilis en el ejército," 8–22, 37. Francisco Domingo y Barrera's thesis on hygiene within the barracks mentions alcoholism without mentioning marijuana. "Ligero estudio sobre higiene de cuarteles," 40.

4. Malda, *Recuerdos de la vida bohemia*, makes dozens of references to drinking, tobacco, prostitution, and the generally vice-ridden environments of Mexico City but fails to mention marijuana. See especially, 141, 144, 216, 248–54, and 310–75. Similarly, see Payno, *Los bandidos del Río Frío*, especially the chapters "San Lunes" and "Delirio," 116–32.

5. Emphasis is in the original and was apparently intended to mock Rébollar's sources. The debate is presented over several issues of the *Gaceta médica de México* beginning with a volley from Rébollar, "Clasificación de heridas y lesiones según el código penal," *Gaceta médica de México* 9, no. 12, June 15, 1874. See especially 53. For these details, I also drew on the following installments of the debate all found in volume 9: no. 6, Mar. 15, 1874, 112–14; no. 11, May 31, 1874, 213–15; no. 12, June 15, 1874, 232; no. 19, Oct. 1, 1874, 373.

6. Pérez, "La marihuana," 10.

7. The collection can be found in Readex/CRL: World Newspaper Archive.

8. On the changing nature of the Mexican press, see P. Smith, "Contentious Voices," 29; and Castillo, "Prensa, poder y criminalidad," 26–32. There is no perfect date for marking the emergence of a more yellow press in Mexico. Alberto del Castillo argues that it was during the 1870s and "especially" the 1880s. Phyllis Lynn Smith emphasizes that changes were occurring during the 1870s and 1880s but that the old era was truly dead only in 1896 with the founding of *El Imparcial*. Given the source base here (as detailed in the appendix), 1880 provides the best dividing line because five of the papers were founded between 1880 and 1896 and only two (*El Monitor Republicano* and *Two Republics*) published on both sides of the 1880 dividing line. Furthermore, those papers published between 1880 and 1896 did contain significantly more "yellow" content than

was found in newspapers of the previous era. However, as the analysis will show, a true boom in yellow content with respect to marijuana also clearly occurred after the founding of *El Imparcial*.

9. Obviously, this is mostly an "elite" measure since most Mexicans were illiterate. According to Alan Knight, in 1895, about 14 percent of Mexicans were literate and about 20 percent in 1910. *Mexican Revolution*, 1:41. Carlos Forment provides somewhat more detailed numbers for the 1890s: "According to the most reliable estimates, in the mid-1890s 14 percent of Mexican citizens over the age of six were literate, with the overall percentage for men slightly higher than for women (17 and 11 percent, respectively). Literacy in Mexico City (40 percent), Puebla (40 percent), Veracruz (34 percent), and other urban areas was roughly three times the national average, while in rural areas it was about 7 percent, although this could vary greatly from one community to the next even within the same state." *Democracy in Latin America*, 387.

10. Lumholtz, *Unknown Mexico*, 2:125. Marijuana is also mentioned by Lumholtz as a kind of charm used to ward off witchcraft. See 2:354. For the many locations in the text where Lumholtz might have been expected to mention marijuana if it was present, see 1:208–14, 253–57, 314, 358, 413, and 437–41.

11. Guerrero, *La génesis del crimen*, 17–18.

12. "Sangriento drama en la cárcel de Belem," which reports on a jailhouse murder linked to marijuana, is discussed in Frank, *Posada's Broadsheets*, 48–50. In addition to examining various published works on Posada's oeuvre, I have also searched through the Getty Research Institute's entire collection of Posada's work. The José Guadalupe Posada Prints, 1880–1943, the Getty Research Institute, Los Angeles, CA. See Tyler, *Posada's Mexico*; and Berdecio and Appelbaum, *Posada's Popular Mexican Prints*.

13. Azuela, *Los de abajo*, 27.

14. Newspaper publishing in general took off during this period, as Phyllis Smith demonstrates. "In 1884, 202 newspapers were published throughout the nation, or one newspaper for every 53,858 people. By 1907, the number of newspapers in the country had risen to 1,571, or one newspaper for every 9,337 Mexicans. Of the 202 newspapers in 1884, 22 percent of those were published in Mexico City; of the 1,571 in 1907, 27 percent were published in the capital. During the thirty-five-year Porfiriato, 100 daily newspapers were published in Mexico City." "Contentious Voices amid the Order," 37–38.

15. Pérez, "La marihuana," 10.

16. "Vendedores de marihuana," *El País*, Nov. 24, 1905, 1; "La policía descubrió todo un plantío de la venenosa marihuana," *Excelsior*, Oct. 10, 1918, 1; "La marihuana y sus terribles efectos," *Excelsior*, Nov. 16, 1919, 14. Upper-class users are also cited in an especially sensational article written by Mexican poet José Juan Tablada in 1908, "Las misas negras de la marihuana," *El Imparcial*, July 23, 1908, 1. See also "Gran contrabando de marihuana descubierto," *La Revista de Yucatán*, Oct. 12, 1918, 2, which also notes that even members of high society had been victims of the drug.

17. Both Mattieu de Fossey and Crescencio García linked marijuana to prisons already in the late 1850s. Reference to marijuana use in the army dates to the first extant reference to marijuana smoking in Mexico. See "Epidemias," *El Republicano*, Apr. 5, 1846, 1–2. See also "Desertores," *El Monitor Republicano*, Nov. 14, 1878, 3. In 1882, *El Monitor Republicano* would declare that "for some time" the use of marijuana by the

troops had been causing real problems. "Buena disposición," *El Monitor Republicano*, June 23, 1882, 3. Genaro Pérez claimed that the drug had caused desertions, insubordination, and attacks on superior officers in the army. Pérez, "La marihuana," 55. In an 1894 book on military law and the question of intent in the commission of a crime, Arturo Paz used marijuana as an example of a substance that might lead one soldier to kill another. Paz, *Breves apuntes sobre derecho penal militar*, 5. And for both the fourth (1910) and sixth (1920) national medical congresses, papers were to be presented on the role and consequences of marijuana use in the military. No paper was apparently presented during the fourth congress but one had been requested. See *Memoria general del IV Congreso Médico N. Mexicano*, 17; and Nieto and Ramírez, "Notas."

18. Nieto and Ramírez, "Notas," 569.

19. Ibid.

20. See also García, "Fragmentos para la materia médica mexicana," 85–86; "Mexican Sports," *Mexican Herald*, Mar. 13, 1910, 9; and "¿Hasta cuando nos veremos libres de la plaga de rateros?" *Excelsior*, Sept. 3, 1917, 1.

21. "Where and What the Peon Eats, Drinks and Smokes," *Mexican Herald*, July 30, 1905, 8, 14. For other references to the practice, see F. Gamboa, *La llaga*, 207–8; and "El raciocinio desaparece de una manera absoluta al fumar la marihuana," *El País*, Apr. 7, 1913, 3, 4.

22. "Pulque of the Shops," *Mexican Herald*, Mar. 24, 1896, 7; "Vendedores y fumadores de marihuana presos," *El Diario*, June 12, 1912, 5.

23. "Los habitantes de la capital eran enloquecidos por la marihuana," *El Imparcial*, July 17, 1908, 1, 8.

24. Gómez Maillepert, "La marihuana," 6.

25. "El mercado del volador," *El Monitor Republicano*, Sept. 7, 1880, 2; "La venta de la marihuana," *La Voz de México*," Sept. 16, 1894, 3; "La lucha por la vida," *El Imparcial*, May 29, 1897, 3; "Venta de marihuana," *El Imparcial*, June 3, 1897, 3; Starr, *Catalogue of a Collection of Objects*, 106; "La marihuana en los mercados," *El Imparcial*, July 18, 1900, 4; "Las 'herbolarias' vigiladas," *El Imparcial*, Dec. 7, 1904, 1; "La venta de marihuana," *La Voz de México*, July 28, 1905, 1; "Where and What the Peon Eats, Drinks and Smokes," *Mexican Herald*, July 30, 1905, 8, 14; "Vendedoras de marihuana," *El Imparcial*, Nov. 23, 1905, 4; "La marihuana en los cuarteles," *El Imparcial*, Dec. 8, 1905, 5; "La venta de yerbas venenosas," *El Imparcial*, Feb. 2, 1906, 3; "Los habitantes de la capital eran enloquecidos por la marihuana," *El Imparcial*, July 17, 1908, 1, 8; Gómez Maillepert, "La marihuana," 5–7; Nieto and Ramírez, "Notas," 576.

26. Sanitary law actually referred to *herbolarias* as "collectors of medicines." See "Intereses profesionales" (no. 18) and "Intereses profesionales" (no. 19). Alfonso Luis Velasco's series *Geografía y estadística de la República Mexicana*, all published in Mexico City by Oficina Tipográfica de la Secretaría de Fomento in various years, provides a wonderful resource for data on wild cannabis growth nationwide. For Michoacán, see vol. 6 (1890), 36–42; for Aguascalientes, vol. 17 (1895), 41, 42, 47; for Sonora, vol. 14 (1895), 52, 54, 60, 166; for México State, vol. 1 (1889), 25, 31–34, 48, 188; for Sinaloa, vol. 2 (1889), 33; for Veracruz, vol. 3 (1890), 48; for Zacatecas, vol. 15 (1894), 54, 55, 62, 166; for Guanajuato, vol. 5 (1895), 31, 32, 34; for Campeche, vol. 16 (1895), 52, 54, 60; and for Colima, vol. 18 (1896), 52–53, 59. Other sources provide a similar picture. For the

presence of cannabis in Guanajuato, Michoacán, and Jalisco, see González Cos, "Estadística del partido de Silao de la Victoria," 315, 566; for Michoacán alone, see Velasco, "El estado de Michoacán de Ocampo" (1887), 172, 173, 185, 191; and Velasco, "El estado de Michoacán de Ocampo" (1888), 148–49, 159, 166; for Jalisco alone, see Bárcena, *Ensayo estadístico del estado de Jalisco*, 702–3; for Aguascalientes, see Busto, *Estadística de la República Mexicana*, 1:cxl, chart, n. 7, cxxxv; see also A. González, *Historia del estado de Aguascalientes*, 11.

27. For petty street dealers, see "Pernicious Drug," *Mexican Herald*, July 29, 1898, 8; "Vendedores de marihuana," *El País*, Nov. 24, 1905, 1; "Vendedor de marihuana aprehendido," *El País*, Sept. 3, 1909, 2; and "Dos comerciantes de marihuana," *El Imparcial*, Aug. 18, 1910, 6.

For sales from private homes, see "Vendían marihuana," *El País*, May 26, 1909, 3; and "Una envenenadora aprehendida," *El Imparcial*, June 17, 1901, 3. For sales in theaters, see "La venta de la peligrosa marihuana," *El Imparcial*, Jan. 23, 1909, 1; *El País*, Sept. 7, 1911, 4; "Se descubrieron dos expendios de marihuana," *El Imparcial*, Oct. 3, 1911, 5; "Vendían marihuana," *El Imparcial*, Nov. 6, 1912, 4; and "Gran contrabando de marihuana descubierto," *La Revista de Yucatán*, Oct. 12, 1918, 2.

For sales in small stores or street stalls, see "Vendiendo marihuana," *El Diario del Hogar*, Oct. 12, 1906, 3; "Vendía marihuana," *El País*, Nov. 12, 1908, 4; "Another Marihuana Dealer Captured," *Mexican Herald*, July 19, 1909, 12; "Waging War against Marihuana in Oaxaca," *Mexican Herald*, Nov. 12, 1909, 9; *El Diario*, Jan. 7, 1910, 6; and *El Diario*, Jan. 7, 1910, 6.

All of these methods are summed up by Gómez Maillepert in "La marihuana," 5–7.

28. For smuggling into prisons or sales there, see "Por vender marihuana," *El Imparcial*, June 25, 1901, 2; "Varias noticias de las comisarías," *El País*, July 18, 1909, 2; "Introducía marihuana y alcohol," *El País*, Mar. 18, 1910, 2; "A beneficio de dos diestros," *El Imparcial*, June 13, 1910, 4; "Woman Sells Marihuana in Guadalajara Prison," *Mexican Herald*, June 13, 1910, 4; "El mercado de la marihuana," *El Imparcial*, Oct. 14, 1911, 4; and "Por cultivar marihuana," *Excelsior*, June 11, 1919, 9.

For smuggling into or sales at the barracks, see "Consignación de expendedoras de marihuana," *El País*, Feb. 24, 1900, 1; "Por un paquete de marihuana," *El País*, Nov. 27, 1905, 3; and "Por cultivar marihuana," *Excelsior*, June 11, 1919, 9.

For smuggling into or sales at the military hospital, see "Varias noticias de las comisarías," *El País*, Aug. 4, 1909, 3.

29. "Captura de dos tercios de marihuana," *El País*, Dec. 15, 1899, 3. See also "Diez arrobas de marihuana," *El País*, Feb. 13, 1906, 6; "Los habitantes de la capital eran enloquecidos por la marihuana," *El Imparcial*, July 17, 1908, 1, 8; "Se descubrieron dos expendios de marihuana," *El Imparcial*, Oct. 3, 1911, 5; "Por vender marihuana," *El Imparcial*, Nov. 5, 1911, 5; "Vendían marihuana," *El Imparcial*, Nov. 6, 1912, 4; "Una fábrica de marihuana," *El País*, Apr. 21, 1912, 9; and "Gran contrabando de marihuana descubierto," *La Revista de Yucatán*, Oct. 12, 1918, 2.

30. "Una envenenadora aprehendida," *El Imparcial*, June 17, 1901, 3; "After Marihuana Sellers," *Mexican Herald*, Jan. 24, 1909, 2; "Los habitantes de la capital eran enloquecidos por la marihuana," *El Imparcial*, July 17, 1908, 1, 8; "El envenenador capturado se dice benefactor público," *El Imparcial*, July 20, 1908, 1, 7; and "Vendía marihuana,"

*El País*, Nov. 12, 1908, 4. On Querétaro as a major center of production, see "La policía descubrió todo un plantío de la venenosa marihuana," *Excelsior*, Oct. 10, 1918, 1. For a huge crop of marijuana discovered in Michoacán, see "Plantío de marihuana," *Excelsior*, Nov. 4, 1919, 11.

31. Authorized sales were sometimes advertised. See the classified ad in *El Imparcial*, Feb. 22, 1906, 4. Unauthorized sales were occasionally reported from pharmacies. See "Venden marihuana," *Mexican Herald*, May 12, 1910, 5.

32. "Desertores," *El Monitor Republicano*, Nov. 14, 1878, 3. For other similar cases, see "Abuso militar," *El Monitor Republicano*, Sept. 23, 1884, 3; and "Sergeant Faced a Firing Squad," *Mexican Herald*, Feb. 12, 1915, 3.

33. *La Voz de México*, Jan. 19, 1888, 3. See also "El escándalo a balazos en San Ildefonso," *El País*, Oct. 12, 1900, 1; "News of Mexico," *Mexican Herald*, Sept. 6, 1902, 3; "Víctima de un desequilibrado," *El País*, Sept. 22, 1905, 2; "La marihuana en Belén," *El País*, Nov. 9, 1905, 1; "El hijo que mató á su padre causó la muerte a la madre," *El Imparcial*, June 7, 1907, 1; "El oficial Amador y el cabo Blasco quedan detenidos por abuso de autoridad," *El Dictamen*, Dec. 16, 1909, 1; "Marihuano," *El Diario*, Aug. 19, 1910, 8; "Hazañas de un marihuano," *El Dictamen*, Oct. 20, 1910, 4; "Furioso, hirió a 3 gendarmes," *El Imparcial*, May 13, 1912, 7; "Enloquecido por la marihuana hirió de muerte a su superior," *El Diario*, Dec. 9, 1912, 1, 4; "Bajo la acción de la marihuana causó un escándalo," *El Imparcial*, Jan. 19, 1913, 4; "Un ex-gendarme criminal," *El Diario*, Mar. 21, 1913, 6; "El coro de la tragedia," *El Imparcial*, Mar. 28, 1913, 3; "Condemned Man Is Saved by Amparo," *Mexican Herald*, Sept. 3, 1913, 2; "Se suicidó en un calabozo," *El País*, Mar. 18, 1914, 5; "Son falsos los desórdenes en Querétaro," *El Imparcial*, Dec. 11, 1910, 13; and "Residents Alarmed in Tlalnepantla," *Mexican Herald*, Sept. 2, 1913, 8.

34. "El jurado de un doble homicida," *El País*, Mar. 21, 1899, 2.

35. "Un soldado loco: Efectos de la marihuana," *El Imparcial*, Dec. 15, 1899, 1. For other similar cases, see "Una de cal y otra de arena," *La Voz de México*, Feb. 16, 1898, 2; "El jurado de un doble homicida," *El País*, Mar. 21, 1899, 2; "A última pena," *El País*, Jan. 30, 1903, 1; "Crazed by Marihuana," *Mexican Herald*, June 8, 1905, 3; "Woman Is Seriously Hurt by Her Husband," *Mexican Herald*, Aug. 19, 1906, 1; "Azañas de un marihuano," *El País*, Nov. 23, 1907, 2; and "Does Remember Having Killed a Policeman," *Mexican Herald*, Nov. 6, 1909, 3.

36. "Un oficial herido,'" *La Voz de México*, Jan. 22, 1891, 2; "Pulque of the Shops," *Mexican Herald*, Mar. 24, 1896, 7.

37. "Efectos de la marihuana," *La Voz de México*, Feb. 16, 1901, 2. For similar cases, see "The Marihuana Curse," *Mexican Herald*, Aug. 8, 1898, 8; "Muchacho marihuano," *El Imparcial*, Aug. 8, 1898, 3; "Fusilado siete veces," *La Voz de México*, Dec. 22, 1901, 2; "Gendarme herido . . . un marihuano furioso," *El Imparcial*, July 30, 1903, 1; "Where and What the Peon Eats, Drinks and Smokes," *Mexican Herald*, July 30, 1905, 8, 14; "Un loco peligroso," *El País*, Feb. 8, 1906, 3; "Marihuana Fiend Found," *Mexican Herald*, June 24, 1907, 12; "Un oficial de gendarmes agredido por un marihuano," *El País*, Oct. 3, 1907, 1; "Los habitantes de la capital eran enloquecidos por la marihuana," *El Imparcial*, July 17, 1908, 1, 8; "Los horrores de la guerra," *El Dictamen*, Feb. 9, 1911, 1; "La sangrienta tragedia de anoche," *El Dictamen*, Feb. 16, 1911, 1; "La tragedia de ayer tarde en la tienda 'la villa,'" *El Dictamen*, May 14, 1911, 1; "Un escándalo en la cárcel de Belén," *El País*, June 10,

1911, 5; "Ciudad Juárez es teatro de atroz espectáculo," *El Diario*, Jan. 3, 1913, 1; "Appalling Crime," *Mexican Herald*, Oct. 16, 1900, 2; "El raciocinio desaparece de una manera absoluta al fumar la marihuana," *El País*, Apr. 7, 1913, 3, 4; "Una tragedia en la penitenciaría de Guadalajara," *El Imparcial*, Dec. 8, 1913, 4; and "Alcoholismo y criminalidad," *Excelsior*, Dec. 13, 1917, 1.

38. "Locos por marihuana," *El Imparcial*, June 8, 1904, 4. See also "Colosal escándalo a balazos," *El País*, Nov. 8, 1904, 2; "News of Mexico," *Mexican Herald*, Jan. 13, 1907, 5; "Gran escándalo promovido por un marihuano," *El Dictamen*, Dec. 3, 1908, 3; "Sangriento crímen," *El Diario*, Jan. 5, 1910, 7; "Los reos del hospital militar quisieron fugarse," *El Diario*, July 14, 1913, 1–2; and "Un loco mató a un individuo e hirió a una mujer," *El Imparcial*, Dec. 4, 1913, 8.

39. "Chewed His Wife's Ear," *Mexican Herald*, Aug. 25, 1903, 1. The same story was reported elsewhere. See "Cabo rabioso—efectos de la Marihuana," *El Imparcial*, Aug. 25, 1903, 1; and "Mordedura de caimán," *El País*, Aug. 25, 1903, 1.

40. "Los habitantes de la Capital eran enloquecidos por la marihuana," *El Imparcial*, July 17, 1908, 1, 8.

41. "Una furia en el cuartel del 260 Batallón," *El Imparcial*, May 24, 1898, 1; "La mujer fiera," *El Imparcial*, May 25, 1898, 1.

42. "El crimen y la mujer," *El Imparcial*, May 26, 1898, 1. See also "Gran escándalo," *La Voz de México*, Oct. 4, 1893, 3; "Efectos de la marihuana," *La Voz de México*, Feb. 16, 1901, 2; "Cabo rabioso—efectos de la Marihuana," *El Imparcial*, Aug. 25, 1903, 1; "Crazed by Marihuana," *Mexican Herald*, Nov. 24, 1904, 5; "Furioso por marihuana," *El País*, Mar. 2, 1906, 1; "Feroz marihuano," *El País*, Mar. 27, 1906, 2; and "La marihuana y sus terribles efectos," *Excelsior*, Nov. 16, 1919, 14.

43. "Efectos de la mariguana," *La Voz de México*, Nov. 18, 1893, 3.

44. "News About Town," *Mexican Herald*, Feb. 21, 1901, 5. See also "Notes on the Passing Day," *Mexican Herald*, Mar. 24, 1902, 8; and "Marihuano," *El Dictamen*, Jan. 11, 1906, 1.

45. "Qué graciosos," *La Voz de México*, July 25, 1893, 3.

46. *Mexican Herald*, Nov. 14, 1896, 2; "Miguel Guttman," *El Imparcial*, Jan. 23, 1897, 3; "Passing Day," *Mexican Herald*, Oct. 22, 1898, 3; "Espiritismo y hechicerías," *El Imparcial*, Feb. 22, 1903 (supplement), 1. Other examples: "Las plantas y la locura," *El Imparcial*, June 8, 1903, 1; "News of Mexico," *Mexican Herald*, Aug. 18, 1903, 3; "News of Mexico," *Mexican Herald*, June 10, 1904, 3; "Pulque and Insanity!" *Mexican Herald*, Sept. 29, 1905, 1; "Diez arrobas de marihuana," *El País*, Feb. 13, 1906, 6; "Poisons Good When Rightly Used," *Mexican Herald*, May 27, 1906, 21; "Por introducir marihuana," *El País*, Oct. 27, 1906, 2; "Las industrias criminales," *El Imparcial*, Mar. 2, 1907, 3; "Would Craze 200 Soldiers," *Mexican Herald*, Nov. 16, 1907, 2; "Translación de corrigendos," *El Imparcial*, Dec. 6, 1907, 1; "Envenenadores," *La Voz de México*, Dec. 15, 1907, 3; "La venta de la peligrosa marihuana," *El Imparcial*, Jan. 23, 1909, 1; "De domingo a domingo," *El País*, July 19, 1908, 1; "Las misas negras de la marihuana," *El Imparcial*, July 23, 1908, 1; "La venta de la marihuana y la venta del alcohol," *El País*, July 24, 1908, 1; "La venta de la peligrosa marihuana," *El Imparcial*, Jan. 23, 1909, 1; "Suicidio de un español," *El Dictamen*, Mar. 31, 1911, 4; and "Unas vendedoras de marihuana," *El Diario*, July 12, 1912, 8.

47. "La venta de la marihuana," *El Diario del Hogar*, Sept. 18, 1894, 1. See also "Crí-

menes," *El Monitor Republicano*, Mar. 11, 1880, 3; and "Mariguana," *El Monitor Republicano*, June 7, 1879, 3.

48. For specific claims that marijuana madness was a temporary affliction, see "News About Town," *Mexican Herald*, July 28, 1901, 11; "Would Craze 200 Soldiers," *Mexican Herald*, Nov. 16, 1907, 2; and "Un 20 dictamen en el caso del Ing. E. Zepeda," *El Imparcial*, Apr. 27, 1913, 1, 5. For rare claims of long-term madness, see "Mixcoac Asylum Godsend to Capital," *Mexican Herald*, Apr. 14, 1910, 2; and "Irá al manicomio," *El Diario*, Dec. 22, 1912, 6.

49. "Asesinato," *El Monitor Republicano*, Feb. 2, 1887, 4; "Efectos de la marihuana," *El Monitor Republicano*, Feb. 19, 1887, 3; "Los efectos de la marihuana," *La Voz de México*, Aug. 3, 1894, 1; "Un marihuano anarquista," *El Imparcial*, Jan. 11, 1897, 3; "Otro asesinato ocasionado por la marihuana," *El Imparcial*, July 17, 1897, 4; "Leon Notes," *Mexican Herald*, Aug. 28, 1898, 8; "Las maniobras en Ixtapalapa," *El País*, Nov. 19, 1900, 1; "Un sentenciado a última pena," *El País*, Dec. 17, 1901, 1; "News of Mexico," *Mexican Herald*, June 13, 1904, 3; "Con una hoz," *El País*, June 21, 1905, 2; "Asesinato de un ministro protestante," *El Imparcial*, Feb. 16, 1906, 6; "Hijo desnaturalizado," *El País*, Oct. 26, 1906, 2; "Drama sangriento," *El País*, Feb. 6, 1907, 2; "Le quitó la piel al cadáver de su víctima," *El Imparcial*, Feb. 23, 1910, 5.

CHAPTER FIVE

1. Mayer, *Campaña y guarnición*, 18–24, 31–32, 41, 83, 109, 159; Ruiz, *American in Maximilian's Mexico*, 46, 79. The American, William Marshall Anderson, emphasized the ubiquity of tobacco smoking as well. He also compared the view from the Mexican mountains to intoxication by hashish and whiskey: "We finally reached the top. . . . What a glorious and grand confusion! All the haschisch . . . and whisky in the world, used to a point just below mental madness, could not conjure up such a lovely chaos." But he never mentioned marijuana. Ibid, 18.

2. "La mendicidad en León" and "Los Perros, los mendigos, las mesalinas," *El Diario del Hogar*, May 1, 1884, 3; "Prohibición de corridas de toros y de peleas de gallos en el estado de Michoacán," *El Diario del Hogar*, May 4, 1888, 3; "El mal negro" and "El vicio del juego en zarzuela," *El Diario del Hogar*, Sept. 2, 1888, 2.

3. Mayer, *Campaña y guarnición*, 31; Almaraz, *Memoria de los trabajos ejecutados*, 79.

4. Domínguez y Quintana, "El alcoholismo," 12–13.

5. Malda, *Recuerdos de la vida bohemia*, 6–8.

6. Ibid., 275. Other allusions mixing passion, madness, and intoxication can be found on 19, 134, 198, 254, 267, and 314–15.

7. Mata y Fontanet, *Criterio médico psicológico*, 57–58. Domínguez y Quintana takes on Mata's views directly, citing the importance of doing so "above all for us Mexicans, because his work resides in the libraries of almost all of our lawyers and judges, who probably judge and sentence with reference to the principles put forward by that eloquent doctor-jurist." "El alcoholismo," 35.

8. For example, the introduction to an 1870 medical thesis on alcoholism began in the following manner: "Like all of the peoples of the world, ours since time immemorial has counted among its defects drunkenness. As the Tartars had their *lumis*; as the indigenous people of Siberia their *braga* and their *quas*; as the Germans have their beer;

the Spanish their old wines; and as the English and French their spirits, we Mexicans have had our pulque." Here we see how a list of the agents in each culture that provide *embriaguez* or "intoxication" are all alcoholic drinks. As we have already seen, by the mid-nineteenth century, the exotic intoxicants of different lands had become a topic of popular discourse in the West, but this list on *embriaguez* refers only to alcohol. Domínguez y Quintana, "El alcoholismo," 7.

9. F. Ortega, *Memoria sobre los medios de desterrar la embriaguez*, 5–7. Other works begin by emphasizing precisely the same themes. See, for instance, Domínguez y Quintana, "El alcoholismo," 8.

10. D. Ramírez, "Noticias históricas," 41.

11. F. Ortega, *Memoria sobre los medios*, 16, 43–44; Domínguez y Quintana, "El alcoholismo," 6. Interestingly, Ortega's thoughts remained influential thanks at least in part to brazen plagiarism. Dr. Máximo Silva, who published several articles on drunkenness for *El Diario del Hogar* around the turn of the twentieth century, copied Ortega's fifty-year-old, prize-winning essay and called it his own. See Silva, "La embriaguez," *El Diario del Hogar*, July 15, 1896, 1.

12. Moisés González Navarro argued that drunkenness was the number one social concern of Porfirian elites. *El Porfiriato*, 72. Alan Knight emphasizes the prohibitionist tendencies of Carranza's proconsuls. *Mexican Revolution*, 2:501–3. See also Piccato, "El discurso."

13. Barrera, "Del alcoholismo," 9–10.

14. Antonio Salinas y Carbó, another medical student who worked on the legal culpability of drunks, also delineates these three stages and specifically cites Hoffbauer in his "Breves consideraciones," 20–26; see also Aranda Díaz, "Algunas consideraciones a propósito del alcoholismo," 18–20. For a translation of one of Hoffbauer's most famous works, which includes a biographical introduction, see Innis, *Semiological Investigations*.

15. Barrera, "Del alcoholismo," 11–12.

16. Ibid., 19.

17. Domínguez y Quintana, "El alcoholismo," 16, 20–21.

18. F. Ortega, *Memoria sobre los medios*, 13–14.

19. Martínez, "Algunas consideraciones sobre el alcoholismo," 38.

20. Rivadeneyra, "Estadística de la locura en México," 28.

21. Payno, *Los bandidos del Río Frío*, 116–31.

22. Salinas y Carbó, "Breves consideraciones," 52.

23. "La Locura de los borrachos," *El Diario del Hogar*, July 10, 1892, 10. Other articles provide similar descriptions of drunkenness. See, for instance, "La embriaguez," *El Diario del Hogar*, Dec. 5, 1890.

24. "Horrible," *El Diario del Hogar*, July 8, 1893, 3; "Ebrio agresor," *El Diario del Hogar*, Oct. 17, 1902, 3; "Loco peligroso," *El Diario del Hogar*, Aug. 5, 1893, 3; "Agresión a un gendarme," *El Diario*, Mar. 23, 1912, 6. Other stories emphasized similar themes. In Spain, a drunk was said to have begun eating his own child alive. "Un antropófago," *El Diario del Hogar*, Jan. 8, 1888, 2. A drunken woman in Veracruz began attacking people randomly and had to be subdued by multiple police officers. "Mujer con rabia," *El Diario del Hogar*, May 20, 1892, 3. "Hombre con dos narices," *El Diario del Hogar*, Feb.

13, 1900, 2, reported that two men in the "first stage of drunkenness" got into a fight; "Siempre la ebriedad," *El Diario del Hogar*, Oct. 20, 1906, casually cites "the second stage of drunkenness."

25. Frank, *Posada's Broadsheets*, 29.

26. Roumagnac, *Los criminales*, 301.

27. "Buena disposición," *El Monitor Republicano*, June 23, 1882, 3.

28. "'Un oficial herido,'" *La Voz de México*, Jan. 22, 1891, 2.

29. "Una furia en el cuartel del 26o Batallón," *El Imparcial*, May 24, 1898, 1.

30. "El jurado de un doble homicida," *El País*, Mar. 21, 1899, 2. For other cases where marijuana and other intoxicants were equated, see "La agresión al Ilmo. Señor Arzobispo de Michoacán," *El País*, Feb. 27, 1901, 1; and "Suicidio de un soldado," *El País*, Feb. 28, 1903, 2.

31. "¿Ebrio ó marihuano?" *El Dictamen*, Jan. 13, 1906, 1.

32. "La sangrienta tragedia de anoche," *El Dictamen*, Feb. 16, 1911, 1.

33. Sánchez Santos, "El alcoholismo," 163–64.

34. "La venta de la marihuana y la venta del alcohol," *El País*, July 24, 1908, 1; "La taberna," *El País*, Dec. 4, 1908, 3, repeats the same argument. That article was then picked up by *La Voz de México*, Dec. 5, 1908, 1. "Alcoholismo y criminalidad," *Excelsior*, Dec. 13, 1917, 1. For other examples of alcohol and marijuana intoxication being essentially conflated, see "La agresión al Ilmo. Señor Arzobispo de Michoacán," *El País*, Feb. 27, 1901, 1; "Como rabioso," *El Imparcial*, June 4, 1902, 2; "Suicidio de un soldado," *El País*, Feb. 28, 1903, 2; "Fuerte escándalo que armó una borracha," *El Diario*, Apr. 2, 1911, 2; "La tragedia de ayer tarde en la tienda 'la villa,'" *El Dictamen*, May 14, 1911, 1; "Sonrió ante el cadaver de su víctima," *El Dictamen*, May 17, 1911, 4; "Iba a asesinar a una señorita," *El Diario*, Jan. 9, 1912, 1; "Gendarme que mata a otro," *El País*, June 4, 1912, 4; "El drama de la calle de regina," *El Diario*, Feb. 7, 1913, 1, 4; "El Sargento Díaz fué condenado a muerte," *El Imparcial*, June 7, 1914, 1, 5; and "Alcoholismo y criminalidad," *Excelsior*, Dec. 13, 1917, 1.

35. "La marihuana y la criminalidad," *El Imparcial*, July 23, 1898, 1.

36. "El boletín del Diario del Hogar," *El Diario del Hogar*, Aug. 2, 1898, 1.

37. "Tragedia en la Cárcel de Belén," *El País*, Dec. 16, 1900, 1. *El Popular* argued that prohibiting alcohol would just lead to the use of marijuana, which was apparently worse. Quoted in "Mexican Press," *Mexican Herald*, Mar. 10, 1902, 4.

38. "Contrabando en la Cárcel de Belén," *El País*, Apr. 23, 1906, 2; "El raciocinio desaparece de una manera absoluta al fumar la marihuana," *El País*, Apr. 7, 1913, 3, 4. See also "Contrabandista y militar," *El País*, July 9, 1906, 1, which vaguely distinguishes the two substances.

39. Domínguez y Quintana, "El alcoholismo"; F. Ortega, *Memoria sobre los medios*; and Emilio Cerda Espinosa, "Algunas consideraciones," 4–7, provide similar lists of outcomes. "Cartilla anti-alcohólica para las escuelas," *El Diario del Hogar*, Feb. 14, 1901, 2. On the various aspects of familial destruction wrought by booze, see also "Hecho infame," *El Diario del Hogar*, July 2, 1902, 2; "Post scriptum II," *El Diario del Hogar*, Jan. 8, 1886, 1; and "Explotación del agave," *El Diario del Hogar*, Mar. 5, 1886, 3. On the health effects of drinking, see "Las causas de la mortalidad," *El Diario del Hogar*, Feb. 24, 1894, 3; and "Efectos de la embriaguez," *El Diario del Hogar*, Mar. 12, 1898, 2.

Pablo Piccato's "El discurso," 112–13, also emphasizes the importance of these issues with respect to alcohol, particularly within the labor and Catholic press. On alcohol as a poison, see "Hombres y bestias," *El Diario del Hogar*, June 6, 1900, 1–2, which actually transcribed an article from Cartagena, Colombia, on the physical consequences of drink; see also "Las causas de la mortalidad," *El Diario del Hogar*, Feb. 24, 1894, 3; and "Efectos de la embriaguez," *El Diario del Hogar*, Mar. 12, 1898, 2.

40. F. Ortega, *Memoria sobre los medios*, 25, 34; "La ignorancia y la embriaguez en nuestro pueblo," *El Diario del Hogar*, Feb. 25, 1898, 1. See also "Una medida de higiene pública relacionada con el abuso del pulque," *El Diario del Hogar*, July 21, 1900, 1; and "Boletín," *El Diario del Hogar*, June 16, 1906, 1.

41. "Bebedores . . . grandes," *El Diario del Hogar*, Mar. 6, 1888, 2; "Menú del diario del hogar," *El Diario del Hogar*, Mar. 5, 1886, 3; "No hay pulque en Tacubaya," *El Diario del Hogar*, Feb. (?), 1906, 2; "El pulque conservado por un Metodo Nuevo," *El Diario del Hogar*, Aug. 17, 1888; "El pulque en paris," *El Diario del Hogar*, Sept. 2, 1888, 3. Tolstoy's "Bebidas venenos," *El Diario del Hogar*, May 15, 1900, 1, points out the various reasons given by proponents of alcohol regarding why its use is healthy.

42. There was a run of Grimault advertisements for "Indian Cigarettes" in *El Diario del Hogar* during 1884–85. For an example, see the issue of May 19, 1884, 4. Many geographies listed marijuana as a medicinal plant. For one example, see A. González, *Historia del estado de Aguascalientes*, 11. It was also listed in the National Pharmacopoeia as such. See *Nueva farmacopea mexicana*, 79. Genaro Pérez also mentioned the medical applications. "La marihuana," 47. See also "Poisons Good When Rightly Used," *Mexican Herald*, May 27, 1906, 21.

43. F. Ortega, *Memoria sobre los medios*, 10–15. Suggesting the continuity that characterized major aspects of this discourse, Ortega's work was plagiarized verbatim by Máximo Silva in 1896; see n. 11 above. See also Martínez, "Algunas consideraciones sobre el alcoholismo," 11. During the Porfiriato, the Federal District's official *Boletín* published a summary of the approaches to the problem in different parts of the world, while the press regularly emphasized its international dimensions. "Leyes vigentes contra el alcoholismo" and "Observaciones sociales sobre puntos referentes al alcoholismo" examine French and Argentine approaches respectively. On the recognition of alcohol as a problem of all civilized nations, see, for example, "Gacetilla: Los secretos del alcoholismo," *El Diario del Hogar*, Nov. 22, 1900, 2; "Remedio para amenguar la embriaguez," *El Diario del Hogar*, May 14, 1902, 3; as well as Leo Tolstoy's short piece, "Bebidas venenos," *El Diario del Hogar*, May 15, 1900, 1.

44. R. Ramírez, *Resumen de medicina legal*, 167.

45. Viesca y Lobatón, "El delirio," 341–42. See also R. Ramírez, *Resumen de medicina legal*, 167, 174–75, which pointed out that this condition often led to violent acts and the commission of serious crimes. "Mania" was also the basic type of madness linked to cannabis by research in India around the turn of the twentieth century. See Indian Hemp Drugs Commission, *Report*, 1:249; and Ewens, "Insanity Following the Use of Indian Hemp," 403.

46. "Suicidio de un presidiario," *El País*, July 6, 1904, 2. See also "El Señor Antonio Marrón—Asesinado por un loco," *El Imparcial*, May 15, 1903, 1–2; "'Un oficial herido,'" *La Voz de México*, Jan. 22, 1891, 2; and "La sangrienta tragedia de anoche," *El Dictamen*,

Feb. 16, 1911, 1. For a similar alcohol story, see "Loco peligroso," *El Diario del Hogar*, Aug. 5, 1893, 2; and "Crímen en alta mar," *El Dictamen*, May 31, 1908, 1.

47. As quoted in "La marihuana y sus terribles efectos," *Excelsior*, Nov. 16, 1919, 14. On the publication date of Silva's book, see Agostoni, *Monuments of Progress*, 147.

48. For the "fakirs" comment, see Oliva, *Lecciones de farmacología*, 1:201. Voisin and Liouville quoted in Pérez, "La marihuana," 34. Emphasis in the original.

49. Pérez, "La marihuana," 34.

50. Ibid., 34–39. Nieto and Ramírez also draw significantly from many of the same French sources in their "Notas acerca del uso de la marihuana," 569–72.

51. Pérez, "La marihuana," 28.

52. Typical of Frías y Soto's argument, his position on marijuana's relationship to madness was somewhat confusing. Though he admitted that the abuse of the drug did eventually lead to madness, he argued that, contrary to the claims of European investigators regarding hashish, "impulsive delirium, mania of persecution or suicide, and melancholia in any of its forms never appear in the case of chronic marijuana abuse." He did not then clarify what kind of madness marijuana did cause. His argument is summarized in ibid., 19–20, 29–30.

53. Olvera, "Expendio libre de yerbas medicinales," 268–70. Here I cite the version of this essay that was reprinted in *La Farmacia*.

54. I'm not aware of Pérez being cited by anyone until the 1930s. In 1938, he was shamelessly plagiarized by Dr. Gregorio Oneto Barenque in "La marihuana ante la psiquiatría," 243.

CHAPTER SIX

1. Adam and Eve provide an obvious starting point. Pick, *Faces of Degeneration*, 18–19.

2. Ibid., 11, 20.

3. Borges, "'Puffy, Ugly, Slothful,'" 236.

4. Lombroso's influence in Mexico has been treated in Piccato, *City of Suspects*, and Buffington, *Criminal and Citizen*.

5. Pick argues that in Europe, degeneration became "the veritable common sense of innumerable scientific and cultural investigations." *Faces of Degeneration*, 67. Similarly, writing on Brazil, Dain Borges points out that "in its late-nineteenth-century heyday, degeneration was an inclusive, much-abused, catchall term," but it nevertheless helped shape the "contemporary Brazilian social-welfare state and many contemporary themes of national identity." See his "'Puffy, Ugly, Slothful,'" 235–36.

6. Pick, *Faces of Degeneration*, 54.

7. Ibid., 53.

8. Ibid., 56–57. The phrase is from Charles de Remusat as quoted by Pick.

9. Ibid., 40, 50, 72, 113–20, 128–29. "Peasants into Italians" is of course a rephrasing of the title of Eugene Weber's history of similar processes in nineteenth-century France. See his *Peasants into Frenchmen*.

10. On the conditions of the Porfiriato, see Katz, "Liberal Republic and the Porfiriato." Here I am suggesting a vision of the "modern world" along the lines of that forwarded by C. A. Bayly in *Birth of the Modern World*. The situation also resembles what

Lauren Benton, in "No Longer Odd Region Out," has referred to as "wormholes" in global history.

11. Nye, *Crime, Madness, and Politics*, 144. Borges also emphasizes the importance of the vision of degeneration as a health problem among citizens that threatened the well-being of the entire nation. "'Puffy, Ugly, Slothful,'" 235–36. See also Piccato, *City of Suspects*, 68–69.

12. Said, *Orientalism*, 207. This critical passage is identified by Pick in *Faces of Degeneration*, 39.

13. Pick, *Faces of Degeneration*, 39.

14. Tenorio-Trillo, *Mexico at the World's Fairs*. On the degeneration of the Indians, see page 70. Tenorio-Trillo also points out that among the "exotic peoples" on display at the 1889 World's Fair in Paris were "the European nations' own folk peoples," 82. On comparisons to Egypt, see 85 and 91. Buffington also illustrates the importance of the idea of Indian degeneration to the criminological discourse of the Porfiriato. See *Criminal and Citizen*, 145–49.

15. F. Gamboa, *La llaga*, 61. The Gómez de la Puente version contains no date of publication, but its dedication, by Gamboa, is dated 1910. On the confusion over the publication date, see Pacheco, *Diario de Federico Gamboa*, 27.

16. Pick, *Faces of Degeneration*, 50–51.

17. The term "born criminal" was actually coined by Enrico Ferri in 1880, four years after Lombroso's *Criminal Man* was published for the first time. However, the basic idea is found in Lombroso's seminal work. See Lombroso, *Criminal Man*, 9.

18. Quoted in Pick, *Faces of Degeneration*, 122; see also 109–39 for a more detailed description of Lombroso's views and their origins.

19. Buffington demonstrates the great mixture of influences that characterized Mexican "scientific" criminology during this period. See his "Scientific Criminology: Consolidating the Criminological Paradigm," chapter 2 in *Criminal and Citizen*.

20. "Degeneración de la especie," *El Diario del Hogar*, July 29, 1892, 2, reprints a French article articulating the great anxiety among the French regarding declining birthrates and the safety of France in the face of aggressive outside powers; the concern over birthrates is also articulated in an article on the health effects of coffee, "A los tomadores de café," *El Diario del Hogar*, Oct. 17, 1902, 2. Arthur de Gobineau's *On the Inequality of the Races* already in 1853 defined degeneration as a weakening of superior races through the admixture of inferior ones; on Gobineau, see Borges, "'Puffy, Ugly, Slothful,'" 236. This continued to be an important French concern; see, for instance, "La decadencia de las razas y el socialismo," *El Diario del Hogar*, Feb. 7, 1896, 3. This idea also gained considerable importance as purely genetic theories on human behavior gained credibility around the turn of the century, an intellectual trend that catalyzed the eugenics movement (which eventually had a strong impact in Mexico). See Stepan, *"The Hour of Eugenics,"* especially 22–27, 55.

21. An article reprinted from a Costa Rican paper agreed with one U.S. assessment that concluded that the "Latin American" race was "cowardly" and even its masculine manifestations were "degenerated" in that they took on savage qualities. "Causas y efectos: La cobardía de nuestra raza," *El Diario del Hogar*, June 8, 1908, 1. A Mexican editorial comment concluded that Arabs came from far too poor a racial stock to be

allowed into Mexico. "Inmigrantes," *El Diario del Hogar*, June 10, 1906, 2. "Boletín," *El Diario del Hogar*, June 2, 1908, 1, called the Mexican race inherently lazy. "La vida entre la raza indígena," *El Imparcial*, Oct. 20, 1899, 1, argued that Indian degeneration could be blamed on Indian leadership prior to the conquest.

22. All of these ideas are brought together by the paper *El Grito del Pueblo* of Guayaquil, Ecuador, but reprinted in Mexico as "Regeneración de la raza," *El Diario del Hogar*, Feb. 27, 1906, 1–2.

23. The idea of a beneficial admixture of many stocks is forwarded in "Regeneración de las razas," *El Imparcial*, Nov. 9, 1899, 1; "Colonización Boera," *El Imparcial*, July 4, 1903, 1; and "Regeneración de la raza," *El Diario del Hogar*, Feb. 27, 1906, 1–2.

24. Pick, *Faces of Degeneration*, 24, 27; Borges, "'Puffy, Ugly, Slothful,'" 238. Domínguez y Quintana describes the descent of the lazy rich into alcoholism in his "El alcoholismo," 13.

25. Fernando Araujo argues that old civilizations eventually die out and leave degenerated populations if they do not make enough effort to continue progressing. "Sociología: Como han decaído las naciones latinas," *El Diario del Hogar*, Jan. 18, 1900, 3.

26. "El Obrero debe tener aspiraciones," *El Diario del Hogar*, Mar. 28, 1906.

27. "Un caso estupendo de atavismo," *El Diario del Hogar*, May 26, 1906, 1.

28. "Boletín," *El Diario del Hogar*, Feb 7, 1908, 1; "El atavismo en acción," *El Imparcial*, June 26, 1898, 3.

29. Borges, "'Puffy, Ugly, Slothful,'" 239, emphasizes the continued importance of Lamarckian notions of evolution in Latin America. Stepan, *"The Hour of Eugenics,"* chronicles the gradual fall of Lamarck in Latin America. See especially 24–27. Charles Hale argues that Lamarck's influence faded slowly in France and thus also had a prolonged life in Mexico. *Transformation of Liberalism*, 207–8.

30. Guerrero was arguing directly against the version of this theory that had been posited by Alfonso Herrera and Daniel Vergara Lope. *La génesis del crimen*, 129.

31. Ibid., 129–32. On monsters in the medieval imagination, see Friedman, *Monstrous Races*.

32. Guerrero, *La génesis del crimen*, 129–37.

33. Ibid., 230–31.

34. Ibid., 234–36.

35. Ibid., 236–55. Quotes on 236–37 and 245–46.

36. On the physical weakening that could lead to the conquest of Europe, see "La temperancia en Europa," *El Diario del Hogar*, Jan. 16, 1904, 2. On the time bomb of degeneration left in the ancestors of alcoholics, see "Como se engendra el alcoholismo," *El Diario del Hogar*, Aug. 30, 1910, 2, and "Los niños que fuman," *El Diario del Hogar*, Dec. 2, 1906, 2. On alcohol as a degenerating impediment to progress on which society should wage war, see "Boletín," *El Diario del Hogar*, June 16, 1906, 1. For similar arguments from the official press, see "El problema del alcoholismo," *El Imparcial*, May 12, 1899, 1; "Las víctimas del alcohol," *El Imparcial*, May 20, 1899, 1; and "Efectos del alcoholismo en el sentido moral," *El Imparcial*, May 24, 1899, 1.

37. R. Gamboa, *La histerectomía*, 339.

38. Sánchez Santos, "El alcoholismo," 163–64, 172. Pablo Piccato also discusses the importance of degeneration with respect to alcohol in "El discurso," 80, 118–20.

39. Jefferson Rea Spell, "Prólogo," in Fernández de Lizardi, *El Periquillo Sarniento*, xiii.

40. Fernández de Lizardi, *El Periquillo Sarniento*, 221.

41. Ibid., 221–22, 231–33, 246.

42. Antonio Castro Leal, "Estudio preliminar," in Payno, *El fistol del diablo*, xxi.

43. Ibid., xxxi.

44. Payno, *El fistol del diablo*, 113–23.

45. Payno, *Los bandidos del Río Frío*, 153.

46. Payno, *El fistol del diablo*, 109.

47. Ibid.

48. García Figueroa, "Causas de la frecuencia de la sífilis en el ejército," 8–10.

49. Knight, *Mexican Revolution*, 1:24–31.

50. Guerrero, *La génesis del crimen*, 96–97. The discussion of the levy comes in a longer section on "administrative incompetence" in general. The phrase is used on pages 82 and 89.

51. L. Ortega, "Breves consideraciones," 6.

52. Velasco, *Porfirio Díaz y su gabinete*, 200; F. Gamboa, *Suprema ley*, 128–29; "La consignacion forzosa al ejército," *El Diario del Hogar*, July 1, 1890, 1; "La religión en el ejército," *La Voz de México*, Nov. 8, 1892, 1.

53. L. Ortega, "Breves consideraciones," 7; García Figueroa, "Causas de la frecuencia de la sífilis en el ejército," 41.

54. Domingo y Barrera, "Ligero estudio sobre higiene de cuarteles," 35–40.

55. García Figueroa, "Causas de la frecuencia de la sífilis en el ejército," 35.

56. Ibid., 15, 17, 24–28, 35. L. Ortega also emphasized the contaminating role of the *soldaderas* in "Breves consideraciones," 27, 30.

57. Regulations for Mexico City's prisons published in 1900 banned the introduction of "intoxicating beverages, mariguana, opium, and any other narcotic or poison." *Establecimientos penales del Distrito Federal*, 15. For some examples of coverage in the press, see "Celadores de Belem destituidos," *El Diario del Hogar*, Feb. 8, 1893, 2; "Venta de marihuana," *El Imparcial*, June 3, 1897, 3; "Venta de marihuana," *El Imparcial*, June 26, 1897, 3; "Alcohol y marihuana para Belem," *El Imparcial*, May 15, 1898, 3; "Un abrazo cariñoso," *El Imparcial*, July 3, 1898, 4; *Mexican Herald*, Dec. 23, 1898, 3; "Las visitas de presos en Belén," *El Diario del Hogar*, May 12, 1900; "Marihuana para un preso de Belén," *El País*, Dec. 29, 1901, 2; "Cigarros de marihuana," *El País*, June 17, 1905, 2; "Una mejora de gran importancia," *El País*, Sept. 6, 1905, 1; "El alcohol y la marihuana en Belén," *El País*, Dec. 13, 1905, 1; "Contrabando en la Cárcel de Belén," *El País*, Apr. 23, 1906, 2; "Vendiendo marihuana y alcohol," *El Imparcial*, Apr. 29, 1906, 7; "Vendedores de marihuana," *El País*, June 11, 1906, 2; "Ingenioso medio de introducir alcohol a la penitenciaría," *Excelsior*, Jan. 8, 1920, 11; and "Notas de los juzgados," *Excelsior*, Jan. 22, 1920, 9. See also Sodi, *Nuestra ley penal*, 288.

58. "Fábrica de cigarros," *El Imparcial*, May 18, 1898, 2; "Female Prisoners," *Mexican Herald*, May 19, 1898, 4; "El jefe de la prisión de Belén," *El País*, Mar. 18, 1899, 2.

59. Memo from the Subalcalde to the Secretario de Gobierno del Distrito Federal, Aug. 17, 1907, exp. 59, ECG. Note that at the time of my visit to the Archivo Histórico del Antiguo Ayuntamiento, these files were being reclassified. I was able to acquire the

desired records with the special intervention of an archivist, based on the box and file number listed in Madrid Mulia, Luna Alvarado, and Estévez Zamora, *Archivo Histórico del Distrito Federal*. Subsequent researchers may find a wholly different system of classification. Here I will first cite the basic information listed with the files (as above) and then in brackets the information provided by the guide. In this case the latter was [c. 17, exp. 526].

60. Memo from M. Vázquez to the Secretario de Gobierno del D.F., Apr. 21, 1908, exp. 193 [c. 22, exp. 766], ECG.

61. Memo to the Secretario de Gobernación, Nov. 8, 1908, no exp. [c. 22, exp. 766], ECG.

62. Memo from Márquez to the Secretario de Gobierno del D.F., Feb. 28, 1909, exp. 52 [c. 32, exp. 1095], ECG.

63. Ibid., Oct. 13, 1910, exp. 108 [c. 41, exp. 1316].

64. Ibid., Aug. 24, 1910, no exp. [c. 41, exp. 1331].

65. Again reflecting the still quite limited place of marijuana even in these establishments, the drug was not mentioned in any of these discussions, though the question of whether or not to allow the entry of cigarettes is discussed. "Prisión militar/cantinas y fondas," c. 1590, Seccion: Prisiones, GyM.

66. Páez, *Proyecto de código de justicia militar*, 157–58.

67. "Buena disposición," *El Monitor Republicano*, June 23, 1882, 3.

68. Pérez, "La marihuana," 55.

69. *Diccionario de jurisprudencia militar*, 192–93.

70. Paz, *Breves apuntes sobre derecho penal militar*, 5.

71. Acta de Sesión, July 4, 1894, c. 8, exp. 1, AS.

72. "La venta de la marihuana," *El Diario del Hogar*, Sept. 18, 1894, 1.

73. Correspondence, July 28, 1895, exp. 995, "Arrestos," c. 1251, Seccion: Batallones, GyM. Correspondence, July 29, 1895, exp. 999, "Asuntos Varios," c. 1251, Seccion: Batallones, GyM.

74. "La marihuana en los cuarteles," *El Imparcial*, Dec. 8, 1905, 5; Nieto and Ramírez, "Notas acerca del uso de la marihuana," 577; "Utiles cambios," *El Diario*, Feb. 18, 1913, 4; Antonio Aguilar, May 23, 1906, c. 0533, exp. 093716, TSJDF; Florentino Aguilar, June 29, 1906, c. 0533, exp. 093737, TSJDF; José Torres, Aug. 15, 1906, c. 0476, exp. 083884, TSJDF; Benigno Cano, Aug. 27, 1907, c. 0629, exp. 110546, TSJDF.

75. Iglesias, "Profilaxia de la fiebre amarilla."

76. Nieto and Ramírez, "Notas acerca del uso de la marihuana," 569–70.

77. *El País* claimed that it was in the prisons that the terrible marijuana vice was introduced to prisoners. See "Tragedia en la Cárcel de Belén," *El País*, Dec. 16, 1900, 1. On the discourse on homosexuality within Belén, see Piccato, "El discurso," 99–101.

78. "Obras en la cárcel de ciudad. Rejas y separos," *La Voz de México*, Apr. 23, 1904, 1; "Utiles cambios," *El Diario*, Feb. 18, 1913, 4; J. Ascención Hernández, July 2, 1906, c. 0546, exp. 095640, TSJDF; Antonio Aguilar, May 23, 1906, c. 0533, exp. 093716, TSJDF; Florentino Aguilar, June 29, 1906, c. 0533, exp. 093737, TSJDF; José Torres, Aug. 15, 1906, c. 0476, exp. 083884, TSJDF; Benigno Cano, Aug. 27, 1907, c. 0629, exp. 110546, TSJDF.

79. Following the French Intervention, surely no single institution better embodied

the reigning discourse on prisons than Belén, which was often portrayed as a society unto itself, with a well-developed social structure, rampant vice, and homosexuality. Belén was the new site to which the old Acordada jail moved in 1862. See Madrid Mulia, Luna Alvarado, and Estévez Zamora, *Archivo Histórico del Distrito Federal*, 7. On the discourse surrounding Belén, see Pablo Piccato, "El discurso," 99–101.

80. On censorship in the press, see P. Smith, "Contentious Voices amid the Order," 33. References to the unhygienic conditions of Belén in *El Diario del Hogar*, a leading oppositionist paper, were ubiquitous; see, for instance, "Prisión del fundador," Dec. 8, 1890, 2; "La sarna de Belem," July 26, 1894, 3; "Belén," May 9, 1893, 2; "La situación de los presos políticos," May 11, 1893, 2; "Los presos de Belén," Oct. 10, 1896; and "La cárcel de Belén," Nov. 12, 1904, 2. On the question of corruption within the prison, see the following articles in *El Diario del Hogar*: "Criminales descubiertos," Apr. 24, 1894, 3; "Celadores de Belén destituidos," Feb. 8, 1893, 2; "La destitución de los alcaides de Belén," Nov. 5, 1893, 1; and "Partida de juego descubierta en Belén," Sept. 2, 1896, 2.

81. "Celadores de Belén destituidos," Feb. 8, 1893, 2, mentions the introduction of marijuana and the problems caused within the prison by the drug; "Belén," May 9, 1893, 2, just mentions the horrible conditions within the prison; "La situación de los presos políticos," May 11, 1893, 2, again refers to the plight of the political prisoners and mentions the use of marijuana within the prison; "La destitución de los alcaides de Belén," Nov. 5, 1893, 1, describes the firing of prison authorities after the political prisoners complained of the illicit introduction of alcohol into the prison, all in *El Diario del Hogar*.

82. James W. Brown writes that in Belén, Frías "became acquainted with marijuana and gambling" without providing further detail. See his *Heriberto Frías*, 18.

83. Frias's biographical details were taken from ibid., 17–22.

84. Antonio Saborit, "Nota introductoria," in Frías, *Crónicas desde la cárcel*, 7–15.

85. Saborit comments on the unquestionable historical value of Frías's account as it was one of the only testimonies ever written from the inside of Belén. Ibid., 7–15. On Frías's taste for morphine, see Brown, *Heriberto Frías*, 24.

86. Frías, *Crónicas desde la cárcel*. On the slow pace of legal proceedings, see 23; on brawls, see 22, 36, and 43; on epidemics, 26; on the bad food, 28; on pederasty and homosexuality, 25, 32, and 36; on corruption, 30 and 33; on alcohol, 70; on the school of crime, 25 and 38; and on the presidents, 42. It should also be noted that Frías provided, in the typical style of the era, some positive commentary on the potential for reform. His articles also noted that the new director of the prison, Colonel Pedro M. Campuzano, was doing an excellent job cleaning up the place by painting the walls, scraping away grease and grime, and even having the journalists' cells cleaned. Campuzano's good work remained a consistent theme in the opposition press during this period. See, for instance, "La cárcel de Belén," *El Diario del Hogar*, Mar. 6, 1896, 2; and "Los presos de Belem," *El Diario del Hogar*, Oct. 10, 1896.

87. Gonzalo Aguirre Beltrán challenges Sahagún's negative characterization, arguing instead that the *nahual* was an ambivalent figure, offering both malevolent and benevolent characteristics, though he does note that it was in the animal state that the *nahual* was known for doing the most harm. Aguirre Beltrán, *Medicina y magia*, 98–103.

88. Frías, *Crónicas desde la cárcel*, 62–71.

89. Ibid., 71–82. Guttman's case was familiar to readers of the Mexico City press, both before and after Frías's chronicles. In the summer of 1894, *El Diario del Hogar* reprinted a story from *La Nación* under the headline "More Madness from a Celebrity Prisoner." According to the report, Guttman had recently tried to light his *bartolina* on fire and in the last few days had attempted to cut up his own hand with a bone from the evening's dinner. When asked why he would do something so unusual, he replied that he had done so in order to "punish himself for his errors and as proof of his love for a woman that he adored but who had made him unhappy." July 26, 1894, 3. Two years later, *El Diario del Hogar* reported that the famous prisoner had attacked a guard who had confiscated a package of marijuana cigarettes from him; a number of guards were necessary to drag him back into his cell. "Guttman en Belén," Sept. 2, 1896, 2.

90. Frías, *Crónicas desde la cárcel*, 47–51.

91. One especially noteworthy outburst of such writing, which drew the attention of city authorities, appeared in 1904. See "La cárcel de Belén."

92. "Ecos de Belem," *El Diario del Hogar*, Aug. 30, 1910.

93. "La cárcel de Belem," *El Diario del Hogar*, Aug. 1, 1910; "Ecos de Belem," *El Diario del Hogar*, Aug. 4, 1910; "Ecos de Belem," *El Diario del Hogar*, Aug. 16, 1910, 3; "Ecos de Belem," *El Diario del Hogar*, Aug. 30, 1910; "Ecos de Belem," *El Diario del Hogar*, Oct. 1, 1910, 1, 4. Various other articles around the same time emphasize similar themes.

94. *Diario de los debates del Congreso Constituyente*, 1:788–92.

95. Bancroft, *Native Races*, 633. This account drew from a report by a certain Dr. Villa that Prieto transcribed in *Viajes de orden suprema*, 428–32.

96. Lumholtz, *Unknown Mexico*, 2:125.

97. Ibid., 354.

98. Alzate, "Memoria," 57.

99. Castro Leal, "Prólogo," in Payno, *Los bandidos del Río Frío*, vii.

100. Payno, *Los bandidos del Río Frío*. Key passages and quotes throughout the next several paragraphs are found on 3–5, 13–14, 16, 19, 25, 26, and 27.

101. Ibid.

102. Pineda, "Descripción geográfica del departamento de Chiapas y Soconusco," 354–55. For Dr. Villa's description, see Prieto, *Viajes de orden suprema*, 436–43.

103. Vetancurt, *Teatro Mexicano*, 174–76.

104. Prieto, *Memorias de mis tiempos*, 214.

105. I have concluded that "active properties" is a more accurate translation here than "energetic effects." It seems to me that the latter too forcefully suggests the kind of out-of-control reactions to substances like alcohol and marijuana so commonly cited later in the century, when in fact the report makes no reference whatsoever to recreational drug use and clearly aims simply to curb unregulated medical practice. "Disposiciones del consejo sobre la venta de plantas medicinales y el ejercicio de la herbolaria," Feb. 1, 1843, c. 2, exp. 44, EM. The committee mentioned two other substances along with hemlock and purging nut, but they are unintelligible in the original, though they are clearly not referring to marijuana.

106. Ibid.

107. Ibid.

108. "Intereses profesionales" (no. 18) and "Intereses profesionales" (no. 19). For the original, see "Proyecto de reglamento de boticas y droguerías," 1884–85, c. 3, exp. 5, IF.

109. "La venta de la marihuana," *El Diario del Hogar*, Nov. 18, 1894, 1; *New York Times*, Jan. 6, 1901, 18; "Espiritismo y hechicerías," *El Imparcial*, Feb. 22, 1903 (supplement), 1. See also "La marihuana en los mercados," *El Imparcial*, July 18, 1900, 4; "La libertad de comercio," *El Imparcial*, Feb. 2, 1903, 1; "Delirum or Death," *Los Angeles Times*, Mar. 12, 1905, V20; "Las industrias criminales," *El Imparcial*, Mar. 2, 1907, 3; "Envenenadores," *La Voz de México*, Dec. 15, 1907, 3; and "Investigaciones en la fábrica de cigarros con marihuana," *El Imparcial*, July 18, 1908, 1.

110. "La misas negras de la marihuana," *El Imparcial*, July 23, 1908, 1, 8.

111. Tenorio-Trillo, "Urban Experience," 193–94.

112. Rubén Darío, "El mundo de los sueños," *La Nación* (Buenos Aires), Feb. 9, 1913, 9.

113. Tenorio-Trillo, "Urban Experience," 282.

114. On the small controversy over the publication date of the novel, see n. 15 above.

115. Hooker, *La novela de Federico Gamboa*, 27–28.

116. Pick, *Faces of Degeneration*, 74–96.

117. Pacheco, *Diario de Federico Gamboa*, 17–18.

118. Ibid., 27–28.

119. F. Gamboa, *La llaga*, 38.

120. Ibid., 54–55.

121. Ibid., 207–8. This passage is clearly reminiscent of Máximo Silva's description of marijuana from his *Higiene popular*. Though not published until 1917, Silva apparently penned it in the 1890s; thus, it's not clear who copied whom here. See the excerpts of Silva's work in "La marihuana y sus terribles efectos," *Excelsior*, Nov. 16, 1919, 14.

122. Ibid., 208–11.

123. I thank Ricardo Pérez Montfort, who suggested the latter possibility after reading an earlier version of this work. Gamboa was, after all, a longtime supporter of the Díaz regime despite his numerous works on the underside of life in Mexico. On his politics, see Pacheco, *Diario de Federico Gamboa*, 17–28.

CHAPTER SEVEN

1. I have searched for such records in both the judicial and military archives of Mexico City. The files of the Tribunal Superior de Justicia del Distrito Federal (TSJDF), housed at the Archivo General de la Nación, though organized and digitally cataloged for easy searching, produced only a handful of cases on marijuana. I used several approaches in that search. First, I did various keyword searches in the digital catalog beginning with "marihuana" (in various spellings), through *ebriedad, embriaguez, locura*, and so on. That search produced some marijuana distribution cases and a few other files of value to this study, including one where marijuana was invoked to facilitate the insanity defense (c. 1078, exp. 191289), but not enough files to provide any definitive conclusions about anything at issue here. Second, I used my extensive newspaper research to produce a list of names of individuals implicated in Mexico City for crimes involving marijuana. Though many press reports failed to name the participants, this

method yielded ninety-six total names that might have been found in the TSJDF archive. Of these, thirty-nine were for incidents involving violence or "mad" behavior, and fifty-seven involved the distribution of the drug. Unfortunately, only twelve of the ninety-six names yielded cases archived within the holdings, six among distribution cases, and six among the others. Furthermore, the files for many of these cases were also fragmentary. Thus, among the arrests for marijuana distribution, only four actually contained significant details on the cases. Most of the violence cases were also lacking in useful detail. For example, the case of Tibercio Martínez, who had been cited in the press for murdering a woman while he was using marijuana, contained information only on some of the technical procedure in the trial with nothing on the case itself (c. 0100, exp. 018204). Similarly, the case file of Rosendo Aldana Sánchez, who had supposedly been in a vicious marijuana-fueled fight in Belén, was lacking any detail on the specific incident, though it mentioned him getting in trouble for injuring another prisoner ("Riña en la cárcel de Belén," *La Voz de México*, Sept. 6, 1907 3; c. 0593, exp. 104578; and c. 0576, exp. 100748). Two arrest files that did include significant detail did not mention marijuana despite the press reports that it had been involved. The first involved a brawl in Belén that the press explicitly blamed on marijuana ("Seis heridos hubo en riña ocurrida en la cárcel," *El Diario*, Mar. 23, 1912, 6), but the arrest file noted only that the individuals were drunk on alcohol (c. 1115, exp. 197591). A second story blamed an attack in the street specifically on marijuana ("Un marihuano agredió a un transeúnte," *El País*, Aug. 8, 1912, 6), but the arrest record again noted only that those involved were drinking pulque. Two other cases are of more interest and have been described in the main text of this chapter. Finally, I was informed by the archivists that many of the records that belong to the collection have yet to be cataloged or made available to the public; thus, some of the key cases may eventually emerge.

Archived military collections also produced frustratingly little of value for this research. Those files were also much more difficult to access efficiently. The files housed at the Archivo Histórico de la Secretaría de la Defensa Nacional (SEDENA) are cataloged only by the names of former soldiers. Thus, one cannot do a search for, say, "marihuana" and view all the records available that involve the subject. Furthermore, the records housed at SEDENA deal only with soldiers of the rank of *subteniente* (sublieutenant) and higher, while most soldiers involved with marijuana appear to have been of the rank and file. Even when desired files could be located, they only rarely involved detailed records related to disciplinary problems. As with the TSJDF files, I spent several weeks at SEDENA seeking dozens of names of soldiers reported by the press to have been involved in marijuana incidents. I also searched through the files more or less at random in hopes of getting lucky. I did not find a single detailed record on marijuana use.

Files for soldiers of the line are available at the Archivo General de la Nación. Unfortunately, the entire collection remains to be cataloged, though one can wade through very large boxes organized by battalion and other similarly broad categories. I spent several days combing through these boxes, again in hopes of getting lucky, but found no detailed records. I also called on the expertise of Stephen Neufeld, whose recent doctoral dissertation explored the Porfirian army in depth. In all of his research, he did not find any detailed files on such incidents either, though he did note plenty of comments about marijuana use in the military along with the typical reports of violence and madness.

Finally, I searched the records of Belén prison housed at the Archivo Histórico del Antiguo Ayuntamiento in Mexico City. While these files produced a few references to violent marijuana incidents, none of them examined those incidents in detail.

2. For literacy numbers in Mexico during this period, see chapter 4, n. 9.

3. Gretton, "Posada and the 'Popular,'" 32–33.

4. Frank, *Posada's Broadsheets*, 191.

5. Ibid., 191–201; Tyler, *Posada's Mexico*, 137.

6. Sewell, "Concept(s) of Culture."

7. The phrase is from an exhibition at the Art Institute of Chicago. See Art Institute of Chicago, *Posada, Printmaker to the Mexican People*. On Posada's adoption by Diego Rivera and others, see Rothenstein, *Posada*, 16–17.

8. Frank, *Posada's Broadsheets*, 5–7, 19.

9. Ibid., 20–21. On the attraction of crimes by women that challenged traditional gender roles, see Piccato, "El discurso," 105–10.

10. Frank, *Posada's Broadsheets*, 191.

11. Don Chepito's likely French precursor, Honoré Daumier's Robert Macaire, was always looking to "fleece the public" by any means necessary. Ibid., 194. A *charrasca* was a cheap blade often used in street brawls, while *cascarrabias* means "short-fused" or "irritable."

12. Grinspoon, *Marihuana Reconsidered*, 51–52. Grinspoon argues that law enforcement officials in the United States were especially likely to claim that marijuana dilates the pupils. See also Earleywine, *Understanding Marijuana*, 115; and Hall and Solwij, "Adverse Effects," 1612.

13. Gilman, *Seeing the Insane*, 57.

14. These and other images can be found in Berdecio and Appelbaum, *Posada's Popular Mexican Prints*, plates 155–65.

15. Frank describes this lithograph and provides an image of its front side in *Posada's Broadsheets*, 48–50.

16. "Picoteando," *La Prensa*, July 31, 1913, 3.

17. Bustamante, *Bajo el terror huertista*, 126.

18. While no evidence exists to suggest that Huerta actually smoked marijuana (in contrast, his alcoholism was well documented), Meyer argues that the general might have tried that drug from time to time. Meyer, *Huerta*, 127–31, 228. For other references to Huerta as the *marihuano*, see "El pueblo celebró entusiasmado la gloriosa fecha de ayer," *El Dictamen*, Feb. 6, 1915, 1; "Sombras chinescas," *El Dictamen*, June 24, 1915, 3; and "Simón Bolívar saluda al ciudadano Venustiano Carranza," *El Dictamen*, June 25, 1915, 1.

19. For example, Jonathon Green, in his book *Cannabis*, states that in 1895, "supporters of the Mexican rebel Pancho Villa celebrate[d] marijuana use in their song 'La Cucaracha,' which tells how one of Villa's men goes looking for his '*marihuana por fumar.*'" Ernest Abel writes, "The song was adopted as Villa's battle hymn after his capture of Torreon and subsequent overthrow of the Mexican government because many of his men had smoked marihuana before going into battle, much like other soldiers drinking alcohol before battle." *Marihuana*, 201. Jack Herer writes that the song "tells the

story of one of Villa's men looking for his stash of 'marijuana por fumar' (to smoke!)."
Herer sees the association with Villa in an eminently positive light: "If true (the association between Villa's army and marijuana), this means that marijuana helped to overthrow one of the most repressive, evil regimes Mexico ever suffered." *Hemp and the
Marijuana Conspiracy*, 26, 69. Similarly, Martin Booth writes, "Villa's troops, almost to
a man, came from peasant stock like himself and smoked marijuana both to relax and
to prepare themselves for battle. A well-known Mexican folksong immortalizes them.
Called 'La Cucaracha' ('The Cockroach'), it tells in its original form the story of one
of Villa's foot soldiers, colloquially known as cockroaches." *Cannabis*, 159. All of this is
quite ironic since, as Friedrich Katz has pointed out, Villa was a famous teetotaler who
"neither smoked, drank, nor took drugs." *Life and Times of Pancho Villa*, 76.

20. W. Smith, *Little Tigress*, 102-3.

21. "La cucaracha," Num. de reg. 78037, Grupo doc. 126, Num. de Soporte 284, 1915,
Propiedad Artística y Literaria, AGN.

22. Claes af Geijerstam notes that "La Cucaracha" was one of many songs that during the revolution were "equipped with newly written texts, loaded with symbolism."
*Popular Music*, 67.

23. W. Smith, *Little Tigress*, 102. The 1915 version cited in n. 21 also spoke of a "baker
who went to church, and not knowing what to ask of the Virgin, he asked for marijuana
to smoke."

24. Several different varieties of *Datura* have been and continue to be referred to as
toloache in Mexico. See Schultes, Hofmann, and Rätsch, *Plants of the Gods*, 78, 106-11.

25. Pilgrim, "Does the Loco-Weed Produce Insanity?"

26. Altamirano, "Plantas que producen locura," 210-13.

27. "Referente al robo de la 'Suiza,'" *La Voz de México*, May 22, 1889, 3; "Bien Preso,"
*El Imparcial*, July 3, 1897, 4; "El jurado de un doble homicida," *El País*, Mar. 21, 1899, 2;
"Un proceso ruidoso," *El Imparcial*, Mar. 15, 1907, 3; "El hijo que mató á su padre causó
la muerte a la madre," *El Imparcial*, June 7, 1907, 1; "Pena capital al matador de su
mujer," *El País*, Sept. 15, 1912, 10; "Irá al manicomio," *El Diario*, Dec. 22, 1912, 6; "Es irresponsable de su delito el Ing. E. Zepeda," *El País*, Apr. 4, 1913, 3; "Un soldado asesina a
otros dos soldados," *El Diario*, May 6, 1913, 4.

28. José del Moral, Oct. 27, 1908, c. 0729, exp. 128284, TSJDF.

29. Roumagnac, *Los criminales*, 209-10.

30. Ibid., 191.

31. Ibid., 168.

32. Piccato, *City of Suspects*, 81.

33. Pérez, "La marihuana," 43. Emphasis in the original. Evidence significantly removed in time from Pérez's work also suggests the legitimacy of this testimony. The
"mischievous intentions" of soldiers (i.e., the lacing of other men's tobacco with marijuana), for instance, was also reported as a typical practical joke in the army during the
1930s. In these later cases, soldiers claimed to force their colleagues to smoke the drug
just for entertainment's sake, apparently anticipating some kind of "crazy" behavior
from novice users. Salazar Viniegra, "El mito de la marihuana," 229-30.

34. Roumagnac, *Los criminales*, 209-10.

35. "Un 20 dictamen en el caso del Ing. E. Zepeda," *El Imparcial*, Apr. 27, 1913, 1, 5.

Román Ramírez defines "dementia" as "almost always . . . the last period of the other forms of mental derangement." *Resumen de medicina legal*, 189.

36. Nieto and Ramírez, "Notas acerca del uso de la marihuana," 570–71, 573.

37. Ibid., 574.

38. Ibid., 575.

39. Ibid., 575–76. I noted two such cases in note 1 above. I'm aware of two other such cases. In the first, the *Mexican Herald* initially reported that marijuana had been involved in a murder, though this was refuted by *El País* two weeks later and by the court proceedings. "Appalling Crime," *Mexican Herald*, Oct. 16, 1900, 2, followed by "El suceso sangriento en la Concordia," *El País*, Nov. 3, 1900, 1; Leocadio Gaspar, Oct. 23, 1902, c. 0152, exp. 025461, and Feb. 24, 1903, c. 0233, exp. 040684, TSJDF. In a second case, the newspaper strongly implied that a violent incident had been caused by marijuana, noting that the involved man smoked the drug frequently and became out of control in the process, but it never specifically blamed the episode on the weed. The arrest file confirms that marijuana was not involved. See "Un agente de la policía reservada mató a un ratero de un balazo," *El País*, Nov. 17, 1909, 1; Juan Hernández, Nov. 17, 1909, c. 0910, exp. 159396, TSJDF.

40. Roumagnac, *Los criminales*, 159 n. 1.

41. Genaro Pérez, leg. 54, exp. 40, FEMyA.

42. Pérez, "La marihuana," 40. Emphasis in the original.

43. Ibid. This phrase presents a difficult translation: "Indudablemente influía sobre ellos el temor de que en su Batallón se les tuviera por viciosos." *Vicioso* can mean "drug addict" or one of as many different vice-ridden characters as there were types of vice. "Drug addicts" in some ways conveys the meaning here, but this translation would also be misleading because the "drug addict" or even "drug abuser" was not yet a widely cited social type in Mexico. If the soldiers feared being identified as *viciosos*, they probably feared being seen as the type of person who could become excessively intoxicated on a given occasion rather than as "drug addicts" or "drug abusers," per se.

44. Ibid., 42.

45. Ibid.

46. Ibid., 51.

47. Ibid., 55.

48. Piccato, *City of Suspects*, 85–86.

49. Páez, *Proyecto de código de justicia militar*, xiii.

50. *Diccionario de jurisprudencia militar*, 192–93.

51. *Código penal para el Distrito Federal* (1871).

52. On the thinking behind these articles and precedent in Mexican and other law, see Medina y Ormachea, *Código penal mexicano*.

53. Ibid.

54. "Referente al robo de la 'Suiza,'" *La Voz de México*, May 22, 1889, 3; "Bien preso," *El Imparcial*, July 3, 1897, 4; "El jurado de un doble homicida," *El País*, Mar. 21, 1899, 2; "El hijo que mató á su padre causó la muerte a la madre," *El Imparcial*, June 7, 1907, 1; "Pena capital al matador de su mujer," *El País*, Sept. 15, 1912, 10; "Irá al manicomio," *El Diario*, Dec. 22, 1912, 6. For military examples, see "Un proceso ruidoso," *El Imparcial*, Mar. 15, 1907, 3; and "Un soldado asesina a otros dos soldados," *El Diario*, May 6, 1913, 4.

55. "El jurado de un doble homicida," *El País*, Mar. 21, 1899, 2.

56. "Un soldado asesina a otros dos soldados," *El Diario*, May 6, 1913, 4.

57. "Un crímen sin nombre fue el epilogo de la vida de Gabriel Hernández, tan llena de trágicos capítulos," *El Imparcial*, Mar. 27, 1913, 1–3; "El coro de la tragedia," *El Imparcial*, Mar. 28, 1913, 3; "Fue internado ayer en la penitenciaría el ingeniero Don Enrique Zepeda," *El Imparcial*, Mar. 28, 1913, 1, 8; "El subalcaide Johnson y el teniente villa fueron declarados presos," *El Diario*, Mar. 29, 1913, 1, 8; "Spirit of the Mexican Press," *Mexican Herald*, Mar. 30, 1913, 4; "Es irresponsable de su delito el Ing. E. Zepeda," *El País*, Apr. 4, 1913, 3; "El proceso del ingeniero Enrique Zepeda," *El Imparcial*, Apr. 5, 1913, 7; "Se declaró agotada la instrucción del procesos Zepeda," *El Diario*, Apr. 8, 1913, 7; "Se decretó cerrada la instrucción en el proceso del Ing. Enrique Zepeda," *El Imparcial*, Apr. 8, 1913, 5; "Zepeda no fumó marihuana el día trágico," *El País*, Apr. 8, 1913, 1, 3; "Las últimas diligencias en el proceso del ingeniero Enrique Cepeda," *El País*, Apr. 9, 1913, 1, 3; "Habla el exgobernador," *El Diario*, Apr. 8, 1913, 1; "Lauro Islas o Francisco Castro dieron a Zepeda el cigarro de marihuana," *El Imparcial*, Apr. 10, 1913, 1, 5; "Islas no explotará a Cepeda," *El País*, Apr. 11, 1913, 3; "El proceso de Zepeda y el asunto de la marihuana," *El Imparcial*, Apr. 11, 1913, 7; "Temporary Insanity Is Zepeda's Plea at Trial," *Mexican Herald*, Apr. 12, 1913, 1; "Con la marihuana, Cepeda perdía el conocimiento," *El País*, Apr. 17, 1913, 1–2; "En el proceso del Ing. Cepeda," *El País*, Apr. 18, 1913, 5; "El fallo de los médicos legistas fue adverso al ingeniero Enrique Zepeda," *El Diario*, Apr. 26, 1913, 7; "Acerca de la mariguana, los médicos rinden un dictamen," *El Diario*, Apr. 27, 1913, 5; "Las declaraciones del defensor de Zepeda," *El País*, Apr. 29, 1913, 5; "Cuatro médicos han dictaminado que Zepeda obró en un acto de locura," *El Diario*, May 20, 1913, 7; "La facultad médica preocupada en el caso Zepeda," *El Imparcial*, May 20, 1913, 1, 5; "Se interpone otro amparo en el asunto Zepeda," *El Diario*, May 28, 1913, 7; "Se rindió por fin el dictamen en el asunto Cepeda," *El País*, Aug. 31, 1913, 7; "Zepeda's Crime Condoned," *New York Times*, Nov. 6, 1913, 6; "La absolución de Enrique Zepeda," *El Imparcial*, Aug. 5, 1914, 5.

58. "Puebla," *El País*, Mar. 25, 1903, 2; "Otro paso más en la represión de la embriaguez," *El País*, Mar. 28, 1903, 1. See also "Un triunfo de la moral," *La Voz de México*, Mar. 31, 1903, 1.

59. Pontón, *Disposiciones complementarias del Código Penal del estado de Puebla*, 66–67; *Código penal del estado de Puebla*.

60. Browne, "(Ng)amuk Revisited," 147–48. See also Simons, "Introduction: The Sudden Mass Assault Taxon."

61. Kahn, "Mexican Mining Practice," 43.

62. Nicolás Cháves, Aug. 29, 1911, c. 1078, exp. 191289, TSJDF.

63. "Appalling Crime," *Mexican Herald*, Oct. 16, 1900, 2; "El suceso sangriento en la Concordia," *El País*, Nov. 3, 1900, 1; Leocadio Gaspar, Feb. 24, 1903, c. 0152, exp. 025461, and c. 0233, exp. 040684, TSJDF.

64. "El suceso sangriento en la Concordia," *El País*, Nov. 3, 1900, 1.

65. "Un agente de la policía reservada mató a un ratero de un balazo," *El País*, Nov. 17, 1909, 1; Juan Hernández, Nov. 17, 1909, c. 0910, exp. 159396, TSJDF.

66. Juan Hernández, Nov. 17, 1909, c. 0910, exp. 159396, TSJDF.

67. Piccato, *City of Suspects*, 81.

68. In 1967, Howard Becker hypothesized that perhaps something like this was occurring during the 1920s and 1930s in the United States. He posited that the many cases of reported psychosis among marijuana users during that era had likely been based on real negative outcomes experienced by users. These, he argued, would not have been produced by the drug alone but by the "secondary anxiety" caused by unfamiliarity with it, along with its widespread reputation for causing madness. He argued that something similar was probably happening during the 1960s in relation to the many reported cases of LSD-linked psychosis. By the middle of that decade, major medical centers reported that as many as one-third of their patients had landed there thanks to LSD and other strong psychotomimetics. Becker predicted that as the fear of these drugs began to diminish, so would the negative reactions that had put so many people in the hospital. He proved prophetic. Though the numbers of new users of psychotomimetics would continue to rise sharply until around 1973, in the late sixties, as their use became more mainstream, the numbers of people hospitalized with psychotic reactions to these substances dropped precipitously. See his "History, Culture and Subjective Experience." See also Zinberg, *Drug, Set, and Setting*, 11–12, 173–74.

### CHAPTER EIGHT

1. See, for example, Toro, *Mexico's "War" on Drugs*, 6–7; Astorga, *Drogas sin fronteras*, 353; and G. González, "Drug Connection," 2.

2. See Art. 73, XVI, 4a, in "Constitución Política de los Estados Unidos Mexicanos."

3. Schendel, *Medicine in Mexico*, 85–86.

4. Risse, "Medicine in New Spain," 15; see also Tepaske, "Regulation of Medical Practitioners," 55–56.

5. Schendel, *Medicine in Mexico*, 99.

6. *Recopilación de leyes de los reynos de las Indias* (1774), 160.

7. Tepaske, "Regulation of Medical Practitioners," 56.

8. Schendel, *Medicine in Mexico*, 113. In a much more recent work, Paul Ross disagrees, placing the rise of "modern" medicine firmly within the modern nineteenth century. See his "From Sanitary Police to Sanitary Dictatorship," chapter 1.

9. Febles, *Noticia de las leyes*, 23–27, 32, and the appendix "Petitorio farmacéutico que observa el Proto-Medicato."

10. Ross, "From Sanitary Police to Sanitary Dictatorship," 34.

11. Alonso Gutiérrez del Olmo, *Guía general del Archivo Histórico*, 29. On the *proto-medicato*, see Agostoni, *Monuments of Progress*, 5.

12. Ross, "From Sanitary Police to Sanitary Dictatorship," 70–72, 79–80.

13. "Aviso del gobernador del Distrito Federal y el presidente del Consejo Superior de Salubridad," May 26, 1868, c. 1, exp. 73, IF.

14. Ibid.

15. While I have not been able to find complete versions of either the 1842 or 1846 regulations, the *Farmacopea mexicana* of 1846 was officially sanctioned and did contain lists of substances that should be "on hand in the pharmacies of the Department of Mexico." This suggests conformity with the guidelines laid out by the regulations of 1842 and 1846. From this, I have assumed that marijuana was also included in the list of "typical medicines" that the council inspected on its regular visits to pharmacies.

*Farmacopea mexicana*, 19–57. I drew other details on these laws from the municipal government's explicit reiteration of them in an 1868 declaration. See "Aviso del gobernador del Distrito Federal y el presidente del Consejo Superior de Salubridad," May 26, 1868, c. 1, exp. 73, IF; and "Circular del Consejo Superior de Salubridad," Mar. 1870, c. 2, exp. 8, IF. Castillo Velasco, *Colección de bandos*, 289.

16. *Farmacopea mexicana*, 417–36. For records of dozens of inspections during this period, see c. 1, exp. 8, IF.

17. *El Diario del Imperio*, Oct. 11, 1866. Some doubt remains on this point as the surviving version of this order is remarkably vague. While the list does include specific references to opium, morphine, and digitalis, the majority of its entries refer to broad categories like "Indigenous and Foreign Medicinal Flowers." Martínez Cortés, *De los miasmas*, 79, mentions this regulation and cites a file at the Archivo Histórico de la Secretaría de Salubridad y Asistencia, but the citation refers to a now-obsolete filing system. Within the new catalogs, I was unable to locate this document, and there exists no way to link the old classification system with the new. The 1878 regulation is reprinted in "Intereses profesionales" (no. 17). Unfortunately, *La Farmacia*, in its republication of this regulation, omits the list of medicinal substances that should be on hand in every pharmacy, citing the similarity between this list and the one found in the 1883 regulation, which it had simultaneously republished.

18. "Intereses profesionales" (no. 17). Interestingly, jimsonweed (toloache), which did appear as restricted in 1846, also was excluded in 1878.

19. Ibid., 275. "The persons who dedicate themselves to the gathering and sale of medicinal plants and animals cannot sell those substances which are poisonous or harmful except to pharmacists." The actual list of plants included under this provision explicitly cites *herbolarias* as the collectors. "Intereses profesionales" (no. 18) and "Intereses profesionales" (no. 19).

20. "Intereses profesionales" (no. 18).

21. Ibid.

22. Ibid.

23. Informe del Consejo Superior de Salubridad, Oct. 11, 1877, c. 2, exp. 33, ML.

24. Medina y Ormachea, *Código penal mexicano*, 1:552.

25. Burns, *Las Siete Partidas*, 1346.

26. Medina y Ormachea, *Código penal mexicano*, 1:553.

27. Ross, "From Sanitary Police to Sanitary Dictatorship," 70–74.

28. Martínez Cortés, *De los miasmas*, vi–vii.

29. "Aviso del gobernador del Distrito Federal y el presidente del Consejo Superior de Salubridad," May 26, 1868, c. 1, exp. 73, IF; "Circular del Consejo Superior de Salubridad," Mar. 1870, c. 2, exp. 8, IF.

30. "Bando del gobernador del D.F. que publica el reglamento del consejo," c. 4, exp. 34, SEC.

31. Ibid.

32. Correspondencia del Consejo Superior de Salubridad, Nov. 1880, c. 2, exp. 30, IF.

33. Ibid.

34. For an excellent overview of politics during these eras, see Katz, "Liberal Republic and the Porfiriato."

35. For an in-depth treatment of these processes, see Hale, *Transformation of Liberalism*.

36. *Constitución Federal de los Estados Unidos Mexicanos*. Article 14 protected citizens against retroactive law enforcement; Article 19 protected citizens against detention for more than three days; Article 21 made law enforcement the exclusive provenance of the judicial authorities except in certain cases; and Article 26 protected citizens against the seizure of property by the military or the obligatory housing of soldiers during peacetime. All four articles referred to specific provisions that were to be determined by "the legislature," much like Articles 3 and 4.

37. See chapter 6 of book 2 (on local sanitary administration), Title 1 (on the sanitary administration of the capital of the Republic), in *Código sanitario de los Estados Unidos Mexicanos* (1891).

38. Ibid.; *Código sanitario de los Estados Unidos Mexicanos* (1903).

39. On "canabina," see *Nueva farmacopea mexicana*, 74.

40. "Intereses profesionales" (no. 6).

41. "International Opium Convention."

42. Spillane, "Building a Drug Control Regime," 11. Spillane dates the earliest such pharmacy laws to Britain's Pharmacy Act of 1868.

43. *Código sanitario del estado de Chihuahua*; *Código sanitario del estado de Michoacán de Ocampo*; *Código sanitario del estado de Tabasco*. The 1896 sanitary code from Yucatán is quite similar to the federal version but not a nearly identical copy as are the others cited here; see *Código sanitario del estado de Yucatán*. See also "Ley para la venta de sustancias medicinales" (Nuevo León); "Reglamento de droguerías" (Michoacán); and "Reglamento para las boticas" (Estado de México), 543–44.

On the Federal Penal Code and state adoptions of it, see Medina y Ormachea, *Código penal mexicano*, 1:iii–vi. See also Medina y Ormachea's second volume with an appendix of the states that had adopted the code by that point and the changes made in each. Many other states adopted most of the code after Medina y Ormachea's publication. See, for example, *Código penal y de procedimientos* (Aguascalientes); *Código penal* (Durango); *Código penal* (Guanajuato); *Código penal* (Hidalgo); *Código penal* (Chihuahua); *Código penal* (Jalisco); Baranda, *Código Penal* (Michoacán); *Código penal* (Morelos); *Código penal* (Tlaxcala); *Código penal* (Veracruz); *Código penal* (Yucatán); and *Código penal* (Querétaro).

44. Olguín Alvarado, "El control de las drogas," 46.

45. *Colección de leyes*, 300–301.

46. *Reglamento de policía del Distrito de Cosalá*, 8–9.

47. Marín, "Influencia de las medidas profilácticas," 737.

48. *Actas de cabildo*, 174, 212.

49. Lámbarri, *Directorio general de la ciudad de Querétaro*, 112.

50. *Reglamento de policía del Distrito de Culiacán*, 14.

51. "La venta de la peligrosa marihuana," *El Imparcial*, Jan. 23, 1909, 1; "After Marihuana Sellers," *Mexican Herald*, Jan. 24, 1909, 2.

52. "Correspondencia particular," *El Monitor Republicano*, Nov. 14, 1878, 1.

53. "La libertad de comercio," *El Imparcial*, Feb. 2, 1903, 1.

54. "La venta de la marihuana y la venta del alcohol," *El País*, July 24, 1908, 1. *El País* later reiterated the point. "La taberna," *El País*, Dec. 4, 1908, 3.

55. "Efectos de la marihuana," *El Monitor Republicano*, Feb. 19, 1887, 3; "La venta de la marihuana," *El Diario del Hogar*, Sept. 18, 1894, 1; "Passing Day," *Mexican Herald*, Aug. 30, 1898, 3; "Las 'herbolarias' vigiladas," *El Imparcial*, Dec. 7, 1904, 1.

56. *La Voz de México*, Apr. 20, 1886, 3; "Fabricante de locos," *La Voz de México*, Apr. 21, 1886, 3; "Consignación de expendedoras de marihuana," *El País*, Feb. 24, 1900, 1; "Una envenenadora aprehendida," *El Imparcial*, June 17, 1901, 3; "Por vender marihuana," *El Imparcial*, June 25, 1901, 2; "News About Town," *Mexican Herald*, July 28, 1901, 11; "Cigarros de marihuana," *El País*, June 17, 1905, 2; J. Ascención Hernández, July 2, 1905, c. 0546, exp. 095640, TSJDF; Antonio Aguilar, May 23, 1906, c. 0533, exp. 093716, TSJDF; Florentino Aguilar, June 29, 1906, c. 0533, exp. 093737, TSJDF; José Torres, Aug. 15, 1906, c. 0476, exp. 083884, TSJDF; "Vendiendo marihuana," *El Diario del Hogar*, Oct. 12, 1906, 3; Angela Sánchez, Dec. 20, 1906, c. 0475, exp. 083256, TSJDF; "Fumador de marihuana," *El Dictamen*, May 3, 1907, 2; "Los efectos de la marihuana," *El Dictamen*, May 10, 1907, 2; *El País*, Jan. 21, 1909, 2; Manuel Sánchez, Feb. 19, 1908, c. 0724, exp. 127204, TSJDF; "Por vender marihuana," *El Imparcial*, Nov. 5, 1911, 5; "Un envenenador público que es castigado," *Nueva Era*, Dec. 28, 1911, 4; "Conmutación de penas a unos reos," *El País*, Sept. 14, 1912, 6; "Notas de Policía," *El Dictamen*, Mar. 26, 1915, 2; "Se descubrió un contrabando de marihuana," *Excelsior*, Apr. 11, 1919, 1.

57. "Envenenadoras de marihuana," *La Voz de México*, Feb. 25, 1900, 3.

58. Aug. 27, 1907, c. 0629, exp. 110546, TSJDF.

59. Oct. 9, 1907, c. 0484, exp. 085477, TSJDF.

60. Medina y Ormachea, *Código penal mexicano*, 1:608.

61. This was the case as long as the sanitary council was in charge of regulating drug distribution. Theoretically, under Article 4 of the constitution, the executive had the right to ban certain professions nationwide (i.e., "marijuana dealing"), but since marijuana and the other drugs of interest were accepted medicines at this time, such a course was not really in the cards. The federal legislature also had the right to pass laws related to public health under Article 72, Fraction 21. That fraction was clearly intended so that the legislature could take steps to control epidemics and national emergencies of that nature. The states were otherwise completely in control of their "internal affairs," and therefore a national law enforcement provision like the prohibition of marijuana or any other drug would have been a truly radical departure from the spirit of the constitution. For an excellent comparison of the constitutions of 1857 and 1917, see Branch and Rowe, "Mexican Constitution."

62. Rodríguez's original military commission, in 1895, was at the rank of major and coincided with the granting of his medical degree after studies at both the National School of Medicine and the military hospital. See Martínez Cortés and Martínez Barbosa, *Del Consejo Superior*, 36–41. Further biographical information is available in Niemeyer, *Revolution at Querétaro*, 186–87.

63. *Diario de los debates*, 2:616.

64. Ibid. Rodríguez was quoted as saying "inverse proportion," but clearly his meaning was "in proportion."

65. Ibid., 619–20.

66. Knight, *Mexican Revolution*, 2:495.

67. *Diario de los debates*, 2:653–57; Niemeyer, *Revolution at Querétaro*, 42.

68. "Constitución Política de los Estados Unidos Mexicanos."

69. Acta de la sesión, June 25, 1919, c. 19, exp. 3, AS.

70. For Carranza's order, see Acta de la sesión, Aug. 4, 1919, c. 19, exp. 3, AS. For the longer debate on the alcohol question, revenue, and other related issues, see the Actas de la sesión for Mar. 16, June 16, and June 18, 1919, c. 19, exp. 3, AS. For a summary of the debate on alcohol prohibition at the Constituent Congress, see Niemeyer, *Revolution at Querétaro*, 181–97.

71. Acta de la sesión, Apr. 25 and July 1, 1919, c. 19, exp. 3, AS.

72. "La limitación en la venta de alcohol," *Excelsior*, Oct. 31, 1918, 1.

73. Acta de la sesión, Dec. 31, 1919, c. 19, exp. 3, AS. Emphasis in the original.

74. Ibid., Jan. 10, 1920, c. 19, exp. 4.

75. Departamento de Salubridad Pública, "Disposiciones sobre el cultivo y comercio de productos que degeneran la raza."

76. Correspondence dated May 17, 1912, III-502–5(I), SRE.

77. Summary of Mexico's participation in the Hague Convention, III-502–5(I), SRE.

78. A. Taylor, *American Diplomacy*, 209; Walker, *Drug Control in the Americas*, 50.

CHAPTER NINE

1. Gieringer, "Forgotten Origins."

2. Bonnie and Whitebread, *Marihuana Conviction*, 28, 37, 52, and chapter 7.

3. Musto, *American Disease*, 219; Bonnie and Whitebread, *Marihuana Conviction*, 52.

4. See, for example, Escohotado, *Historia general de las drogas* (1997), 2:322–24; Booth, *Cannabis*, 131–35; Abel, *Marihuana*, 203–8; Gray, *Drug Crazy*, 76; Gordon, *Return of the Dangerous Classes*, 25; and Bertram et al., *Drug War Politics*, 80. Davenport-Hines in his *Pursuit of Oblivion* follows Bonnie and Whitebread in arguing that xenophobia inspired marijuana laws, but he argues that the weed did make users "loud, obstreperous and disorderly," though the "more extreme anecdotes of drug-crazed violence are unsubstantiated, and resemble the more dramatic police reports that the Indian Hemp Drugs Commission of the 1890s had dismissed after investigation." 153–54, 186–87.

5. Bonnie and Whitebread, *Marihuana Conviction*, 33–34; Musto, *American Disease*, 218; Walker, *Drug Control in the Americas*, 6.

6. On the development of the word and its relationship to the Bahamian island now called Mayaguana, see chapter 3. I know of only two U.S. sources to mention the word *marijuana* with reference to the drug prior to the 1890s: Jackson, "Notes on Some of the Pharmaceutical Products Exhibited," 770; and Bancroft, *Native Races*, 633.

7. The paper was also published in Veracruz, though its reporting was clearly centered in Mexico City.

8. "Pulque of the Shops," *Mexican Herald*, Mar. 24, 1896, 7.

9. "The Mexican Manufacture of Pulque, Mescal and Tequila—A Report on

the Same," *Mexican Herald*, Aug. 11, 1896, 2; Crittenden, "Manufacture of Pulque in Mexico," 403.

10. "A Tale of Doctors," *Mexican Herald*, Nov. 28, 1897, 4; "Bakery Riot," *Mexican Herald*, May 26, 1898, 4.

11. "The Marihuana Curse," *Mexican Herald*, Aug. 8, 1898, 8; "A Bad Mexican Habit," *Broad Ax* (Salt Lake City, UT), Oct. 29, 1898, 3.

12. "Along the Border, Curious and Interesting Things on the Mexican Frontier," *Ohio Democrat* (New Philadelphia), Nov. 18, 1897, 1.

13. "A Seductive Weed," *Spirit Lake (IA) Beacon*, Jan. 21, 1898, 4; "Gleanings," *Spirit Lake (IA) Beacon*, Feb. 25, 1898, 4.

14. "A New Opiate," *Marysville (OH) Tribune*, Mar. 23, 1898, 3.

15. Cited in Pilgrim, "Does the Loco-Weed Produce Insanity?" 280–81. For a more recent description of locoweed's effects, see "Loco Intoxication."

16. Schultes, Hofmann, and Rätsch, *Plants of the Gods*, 106–11.

17. Quotes from this story throughout the following paragraphs are from Janvier, "Flower of Death," 126–27, 129–31, 135–36, 142, and 151–52.

18. Pilgrim, "Does the Loco-Weed Produce Insanity?" 275–79.

19. Ibid., 279.

20. Ibid., 281.

21. Chestnut, "Problems in the Chemistry and Toxicology of Plant Substances," 1025–26.

22. Charles Richardson, "Fighting the Loco," *Marshall (MI) Daily News*, Oct. 14, 1903, 2; "Tried New Experience," *Laredo Times*, Aug. 11, 1905, 1; Guy Elliott Mitchell, "Poisonous Plants of the United States," *Denton (MD) Journal*, Jan. 13, 1906, 8.

23. "Loco Weed Hoodoos Horses," *Washington Post*, Dec. 17, 1911, 2. For other references to the locoweed during these years, see "Goverment Trying to Solve Mystery of Loco Weed," *Rio Grande Republican* (Las Cruces, NM), Oct. 29, 1909, 5; "Finds a Sleepy Grass," *Chillicothe (MO) Constitution*, Dec. 6, 1909, 2; and Lewis, *Wolfville Days*, 178–83.

24. R. Smith, *Report of Investigation*, 46.

25. "Dangerous Mexican Plants," *Charlotte (NC) Daily Observer*, Jan. 24, 1905, 8; "Madness in Plants: Mexican Weed Will Drive Men Crazy," *Gettysburg (PA) Compiler*, Apr. 12, 1905, 7; "Madness in Plants: Mexican Weed Will Drive Men Crazy," *Indiana (PA) Weekly Messenger*, Apr. 26, 1905, 7; "Madness in Plants: Mexican Weed Will Drive Men Crazy," *Xenia (OH) Daily Gazette*, Apr. 3, 1905, 2; "Madness in Plants: Mexican Weed Will Drive Men Crazy," *Columbus (GA) Enquirer-Sun*, May 31, 1905, 5; "Smoking That Maddens," *Estherville (IA) Vindicator and Republican*, Nov. 16, 1910, 7; "Loco Weeds of Mexico," *Davenport (IA) Morning Star*, Feb. 9, 1905, 7; "Dangerous Mexican Weeds," *Janesville (WI) Daily Gazette*, Mar. 2, 1905, 4; "Dangerous Mexican Weeds," *Perry (IA) Daily Chief*, Mar. 8, 1905, 4; "Madness in Plants," *Austin (TX) Daily Herald*, Mar. 23, 1905, 2; "Dangerous Mexican Plants," *Waterloo (IA) Daily Courier*, Mar. 25, 1905, 11; "Madness in Plants," *Hamilton (OH) Sun*, Apr. 14, 1905, 11; "Madness in Plants," *Titusville (PA) Herald*, Apr. 14, 1905, 6; "Danger in Mexican Plants," *Stevens Point (WI) Daily Journal*, Apr. 20, 1905; "Madness in Plants," *Indiana (PA) Weekly Messenger*, Apr. 26, 1905, 7; "Crazed from Smoking a Weed," *Waterloo (PA) Daily Courier*, May 16, 1905, 6;

"Madness in Plants," *Sioux County (IA) Herald*, June 28, 1905, 8; "Madness in Plants," *Lima (OH) Daily News*, Aug. 8, 1908, 2; "Danger in Mexican Plants," *Soda Springs (ID) Chieftain*, Aug. 8, 1905, 4; "Smoking That Maddens," *Massillon (OH) Evening Independent*, Oct. 21, 1910, 4; "Smoking That Maddens," *Gettysburg (PA) Times*, Oct. 18, 1910, 3; "Smoking That Maddens," *Naugatuck (CT) Daily News*, Oct. 22, 1910, 5; "Smoking That Maddens," *Williamsport (PA) Gazette and Bulletin*, Dec. 5, 1910, 9; "Smoking That Maddens," *Lumberton (NC) Robesonian*, Dec. 19, 1910, 5; "Smoking That Maddens," *Coshocton (OH) Daily Tribune*, Jan. 7, 1911, 2; "Plants Cause Madness," *Washington Post*, Mar. 9, 1913, 38; "Evil Mexican Plants That Drive You Insane," *Salt Lake City Tribune*, Mar. 16, 1913.

26. For example, "Dangerous Mexican Weed to Smoke," *Petersburg (VA) Daily Progress*, Apr. 10, 1905, 3; "Dangerous Mexican Weed to Smoke," *Glenwood (IA) Opinion*, July 28, 1904, 6; "Mexican Weed Dangerous," *Alyria (OH) Chronicle*, Aug. 1, 1904; "Mexican Weed Dangerous," *Rake (IA) Register*, May, 8, 1904, 4; "Dangerous Mexican Weed to Smoke," *Racine (WI) Daily Journal*, Aug. 16, 1904, 7; "Dangerous Mexican Weed to Smoke," *Petersburg (VA) Daily Progress*, Apr. 10, 1905, 3; and "War on Mexico Weed," *Chillicothe (MO) Constitution*, Aug. 20, 1907, 4. Another story that made the rounds reported on various violent street scenes around Mexico involving marijuana: "Soldier Runs Amuck Killing Wealthy Citizens," *San Antonio Gazette*, Mar. 23, 1907, 3; "War on Mexico Weed," *Chillicothe (MO) Constitution*, Aug. 20, 1907, 4; "War on Marihuana Smoking," *Eau Claire (WI) Leader*, Aug. 6, 1907, 7; "Insanity and Death in Use of Marihuana Weed of Mexico," *Fort Wayne Sentinel*, June 5, 1907, 5.

27. "Marihuana to Be Grown in Texas," *Pacific Drug Review* 21, no. 5 (1909): 68. The story was also reported under various headlines, including "Use for Deadly Weed," "Use for Deadly Plant," and "To Farm Insanity Plant," in the following outlets: *Warren (PA) Evening Mirror*, Oct. 9, 1908, 2; *Centralia (WA) Daily Chronicle*, Oct. 19, 1908, 6; *Marysville (OH) Tribune*, Oct. 22, 1908, 4; *Trenton (NJ) Evening Times*, Oct. 26, 1908, 12; *Atchison (KS) Daily Globe*, Nov. 6, 1908, 6; and *Frederick (MD) News*, Oct 8, 1908, 4.

28. "Terrors of Marihuana," *Washington Post*, Mar. 21, 1905, 21.

29. "Professor Starr Is Sensational," *Elyria (OH) Reporter*, Aug. 18, 1905; Cole, "Frederick Starr."

30. See, for example, "Weeds That Cause Insanity," *Washington Post*, June 15, 1914, 6, which appeared under the same or similar headlines in the following publications: *Colorado Springs Gazette*, June 28, 1914, 4; *Anaconda (MT) Standard*, June 29, 1914, 11; *San Antonio Light*, July 26, 1914, 23; *Frederick (MD) News-Post*, Feb. 25, 1915, 4; *Syracuse Herald*, Apr. 17, 1915, 19; and *Lake Park (IA) News*, May 11, 1916, 8. "De La Huerta Puts Ban on the 'Cigarette Jag,'" *Santa Fe New Mexican*, Nov. 5, 1920, 4.

31. *Abilene Daily Reporter*, Sept. 13, 1911, 5; *San Antonio Light*, July 20, 1913, 27.

32. Terry, *Terry's Mexico*, ccxxix; Alfred Henry Lewis, "Wolfville," *Cosmopolitan Magazine* 55, June–Nov. 1913, 645; Hendryx, *Connie Morgan in Alaska*, 153–54. For other examples, see Fyfe, *Real Mexico*, 149–50; and O'Shaughnessy, *Diplomatic Days*, 36–37, 322. It is perhaps indicative of marijuana's developing prevalence in the public discourse that the three previous book-length installments of Lewis's "Wolfville" series, published a decade earlier than his *Cosmopolitan* piece, did not contain any references to marijuana. See *Wolfville*, *Wolfville Days*, and *Wolfville Nights*.

33. *Reports of Cases Determined*, Crim. No. 2187, In Bank.—Dec. 31, 1918.

34. R. Smith, *Report of Investigation*, 16–17, 29–30, 41, 45.

35. "News of the Week," *Christian Advocate*, Dec. 28, 1905, 2096; *Journal of the Medical Society of New Jersey* 2, no. 8 (1906): 258; "War on Mexico Weed," *Chillicothe (MO) Constitution*, Aug. 20, 1907, 4; "Soldier Runs Amuck Killing Wealthy Citizens," *San Antonio Gazette*, Mar. 23, 1907, 3; "The Casual Casuist," *San Antonio Light*, July 21, 1908, 4; "Use for Deadly Weed," *Frederick (MD) News*, Oct. 10, 1908, 4. See also "Madness in Plants: Mexican Weed Will Drive Men Crazy," *Naugatuck (CT) Daily News*, Apr. 13, 1905, 4.

36. "Official Murder Shocks Mexico," *New York Times*, Mar. 28, 1913, 1; "Ultimatum by Wilson to Huerta," *New Castle (PA) News*, Nov. 14, 1913, 1.

37. "Huerta Refused to Interfere," *Naugatuck (CT) Daily News*, Mar. 28, 1913, 1.

38. "Private Parks Slain by Maass' Men; Second Soldier May Also Be a Victim" *New York Times*, May 9, 1914, 1; "Funston's Report on Parks," *New York Times*, May 10, 1914, 2; "Brutal Murder of Sam Parks," *El Paso Times*, May 18, 1914, 6.

39. "Poison Put in Cigarettes," *New York Times*, May 10, 1914, 4.

40. "Poisoned Cigarettes," *New York Times*, May 13, 1914, 10. The story also hit the wire service and appeared in the *Baltimore Sun*, *El Paso Times*, and surely other publications as well. See "Poison Mexicans Put in Cigarettes," *El Paso Times*, May 22, 1914, 6, which drew on the *Sun*'s coverage.

41. "Mexican Sidelights," *Logansport (IN) Pharos-Reporter*, May 25, 1914, 6.

42. "Is the Mexican Nation Locoed by Peculiar Weed?" *Odgen City (UT) Standard*, Sept. 25, 1915, 13. The *Galveston (TX) Daily News* would make a similar argument on Dec. 14, 1919, in "Fight, Food, Siesta and Fight Again Favorite Method of the Battle-Loving Mexican Rebels," 26.

43. Subcommittee of the Committee on Foreign Relations of the United States Senate, Sixty-Sixth Congress, 457–64; "Mexico, Cradle of Bolshevism and Bandits; Safe Only for Germans," *Sandusky (OH) Register*, Aug. 31, 1919, 11; "Carranza Rule Like Uniformed Thug's [*sic*], Spy Says," *Lima (OH) Times Democrat*, Sept. 5, 1919, 12.

CONCLUSION

1. Salazar Viniegra, "El mito de la marihuana."

2. "Se acusa al Dr. Salazar Viniegra de dar mariguana a los locos de la castañeda," *Excelsior*, Nov. 1, 1938, 1. That report was refuted the next day by public officials. "No se ha hecho fumar mariguana a los enfermos del Hospital de Toxicómanos," *Excelsior*, Nov. 2, 1938.

3. Oneto Barenque, "La marihuana ante la psiquiatría." In fact, Oneto plagiarized key sections of Genaro Pérez's 1886 medical thesis on the subject in order to support his views. Oneto does cite Pérez but then claims to have recently performed the experiments that Pérez actually carried out in the 1880s. See pages 240–43 and compare to Pérez, "La marihuana."

4. "Escándalos y polémicas que dieron calor al mexicano 1938," *Excelsior* (Magazine Dominical), Jan. 1, 1939, 1.

5. Figures of this kind are always dubious, but Peter Reuter and David Ronfeldt argue that between the 1930s and 1960s, Mexico supplied 95 percent of the marijuana on the U.S. market. See their "Quest for Integrity."

6. Walker, *Drug Control in the Americas*, 83.

7. Ibid., 122–27; Astorga, *El siglo de las drogas*, 45–46.

8. Mark Stevenson, "Marijuana Big Earner for Mexico Gangs," *USA Today*, Feb. 21, 2008.

9. "Mexican Official: 34,612 Drug-War Deaths in 4 Years," Associated Press, Jan. 13, 2011.

10. Astorga, "Drugs and Politics."

11. Wasson, "Seeking the Magic Mushroom."

12. Hoberman and Rosenbaum, *Midnight Movies*, 261–62.

13. Rielly, *1960s*, 32; Morgan, *60s Experience*, 197–99.

14. Samuels, *Midnight Movies*, 97.

15. Bertram et al., *Drug War Politics*, 105–6.

16. This history is recounted in Massing, *Fix*.

17. Michelle Alexander, *New Jim Crow*.

18. See Bertram et al., *Drug War Politics*, especially "Part One: Confronting Denial."

19. Tracy Wilkinson, "25 Bodies Found in Acapulco, 15 Decapitated," *Los Angeles Times*, Jan. 9, 2011.

20. "Las drogas en la opinion pública," *Parametría*, http://www.parametria.com.mx/ DetalleEstudio.php?E=4233 (Jan. 14, 2011); "New High of 46% of Americans Support Legalizing Marijuana," Gallup, Oct. 28, 2010, http://www.gallucom/poll/144086/New-High-Americans-Support-Legalizing-Marijuana.aspx (Jan. 14, 2011).

21. DeGrandpre, *Cult of Pharmacology*.

# Bibliography

ARCHIVES AND COLLECTIONS

Acervo Histórico Diplomático de la Secretaría de Relaciones Exteriores, México, D.F.
    Archivo Histórico Genaro Estrada
Archivo General de la Nación, México, D.F.
    Documentación de la Administración Pública, 1821–1910
        Justicia
        Propiedad Artística y Literaria
    Documentación de la Administración Pública, 1910–88
        Dirección General de Gobierno
        Secretaría de la Defensa Nacional
    Documentación de las Instituciones Coloniales
        Archivo Histórico de Hacienda
        Bandos
        Correspondencia de Virreyes
        General de Parte
        Guerra y Marina
        Industria y Comercio
        Inquisición
        Tierras
    Órganos Autónomos y Archivos Judiciales
        Tribunal Superior de Justicia del Distrito Federal
Archivo Histórico de la Facultad de Medicina de la UNAM, México, D.F.
    Fondo Escuela de Medicina y Alumnos
Archivo Histórico del Antiguo Ayuntamiento, México, D.F.
    Cárceles
        Belén
    Gobierno del Distrito
        Fábricas
    Justicia
        Cárceles, Boleros y Menores
Archivo Histórico de la Secretaría de la Defensa Nacional, México, D.F.
    Sección de Cancelados
Archivo Histórico de la Secretaría de Salubridad y Asistencia, México, D.F.
    Salubridad Pública
        Actas de Sesión
        Ejercicio de la Medicina
        Inspección de Farmacias
        Medicina Legal
        Presidencia (Secretaria)

Biblioteca Miguel Lerdo de Tejada, México, D.F.
    Fondo Reservado
Biblioteca Nacional de México, México, D.F.
    Fondo Reservado
Centro de Estudios de Historia de México, México, D.F.
    Archivo Venustiano Carranza
Fideicomiso Archivos Plutarco Elías Calles y Fernando Torreblanca, México, D.F.
    Colección documental de Estados Unidos en Mexico, 1918–28
    Fondo Joaquín Amaro
    Fondo Plutarco Elías Calles
    Fondo Soledad González
    Fondo Alvaro Obregón
    Fondo Presidentes
    Fondo Fernando Torreblanca
Getty Research Institute, Los Angeles, CA
    The José Guadalupe Posada Prints, 1880–1943
National Archives and Records Administration, College Park, MD
    Records of the Department of State Relating to Internal Affairs of Mexico,
        1910–29
    RG 16: Records of the Office of the Secretary of Agriculture
    RG 59: Department of State Central Decimal File, 1910–29
    RG 84: Records of Foreign Service Posts
    RG 88: Records of the Food and Drug Administration
    RG 170: Records of the Drug Enforcement Administration

NEWSPAPER DATABASES
Newspaperarchive.com
Readex/CRL: World Newspaper Archive

SELECTED PERIODICALS

*Anales del Instituto Médico Nacional* (México, D.F.)
*Boletín de la Sociedad Mexicana de Geografía y Estadística* (México, D.F.)
*El Boletín del Consejo Superior de Salubridad* (México, D.F.)
*Chicago Daily Tribune*
*Criminalia* (México, D.F.)
*El Diario* (México, D.F.)
*El Diario del Hogar* (México, D.F.)
*El Diario del Imperio* (México, D.F.)
*El Diario de México* (México, D.F.)
*Diario Oficial de la Federación* (México, D.F.)
*El Dictamen* (Veracruz)
*El Paso Times*
*Excelsior* (México, D.F.)
*La Farmacia* (México, D.F.)
*Gaceta médica de México* (México, D.F.)
*El Imparcial* (México, D.F.)
*El Litigante* (Guadalajara)
*Los Angeles Times*
*Mexican Herald* (México, D.F.)
*El Monitor Republicano* (México, D.F.)
*La Naturaleza* (México, D.F.)
*New York Times*
*Nueva Era* (México, D.F.)
*El País* (México, D.F.)
*La Patria* (México, D.F.)
*La Prensa* (San Antonio, TX)

*La Revista de Yucatán* (Mérida)     *El Universal* (México, D.F.)
*El Siglo Diez y Nueve* (México, D.F.)     *La Voz de México* (México, D.F.)

WORKS CITED

Abel, Ernest L. *Marihuana: The First Twelve Thousand Years*. New York: Plenum Press, 1980.

*Actas de cabildo del Ayuntamiento Constitucional de México: Enero a junio de 1896*. México, D.F.: Imprenta de la Escuela Correccional, 1899.

Agostoni, Claudia. *Monuments of Progress: Modernization and Public Health in Mexico City, 1876–1910*. Calgary: University of Calgary Press, 2003.

Aguilar, Federico C. (Federico Cornelio). *Último año de residencia en México*. México, D.F.(?): Grupo Editorial Siquisirí, Consejo Nacional para la Cultura y las Artes, 1995.

Aguilar Contreras, Abigail, and Carlos Zolla. *Plantas tóxicas de México*. México, D.F.: Instituto Mexicano del Seguro Social, 1982.

Aguilar Plata, Blanca. "La imagen de Porfirio Díaz en la prensa capitalina de su tiempo." In *La prensa en México: Momentos y figuras relevantes*, edited by Laura Navarrete Maya and Blanca Aguilar Plata, 141–60. México, D.F.: Addison Wesley Longman, 1998.

Aguirre Beltrán, Gonzalo. *Medicina y magia: El proceso de aculturación en la estructura colonial*. 1st ed. Colección de Antropología Social. México, D.F.: Instituto Nacional Indigenista, 1963.

Alexander, Michelle. *The New Jim Crow*. New York: New Press, 2010.

Almaraz, Ramón. *Memoria de los trabajos ejecutados por la Comisión Científica de Pachuca en el año 1864*. México, D.F.: J. M. Andrade y F. Escalante, 1865.

Alonso Gutiérrez del Olmo, José Félix. *Guía general del Archivo Histórico de la Secretaría de Salud*. México, D.F.: Secretaría de Salud, 1994.

Altamirano, F. "Plantas que producen locura." *Revista Ibero-Americana de Ciencias Médicas* 6, nos. 11 and 12 (1901): 210–13.

Alzate, José Antonio de. "Memoria sobre el uso que hacen los indios de la pipiltzintzintlis." In *Memorias y Ensayos*, edited by Roberto Moreno, 53–62. México: UNAM, 1985.

———. *Memorias y ensayos*, edited by Roberto Moreno. México, D.F.: UNAM, 1985.

———. *Obras*, edited by Roberto Moreno. México, D.F.: UNAM, 1980.

Anderson, Edgar. *Introgressive Hybridization*. New York: John Wiley Sons, 1949.

Andréasson, Sven, Ann Engström, Peter Allebeck, and Ulf Rydberg. "Cannabis and Schizophrenia: A Longitudinal Study of Swedish Conscripts." *Lancet* 330, no. 8574 (1987): 1483–86.

Anslinger, H. J. "Marihuana: Assassin of Youth." *American Magazine*, July 1937.

Aranda Díaz, Francisco. "Algunas consideraciones a propósito del alcoholismo." Medical thesis, Escuela Nacional de Medicina de México, 1898.

Art Institute of Chicago, ed. *Posada, Printmaker to the Mexican People: An Exhibition Lent by the Dirección General de Educación Estética, México*. Chicago: Lakeside Press, 1944.

Astorga, Luis. *Drogas sin fronteras*. México, D.F.: Grijalbo, 2003.

———. "Drugs and Politics." In *The Political Economy of the Drug Industry: Latin America and the International System*, edited by Menno Vellinga, 85–102. Gainesville: University Press of Florida, 2004.

———. *El siglo de las drogas*. México, D.F.: Espasa-Calpe, 1996.

Azuela, Mariano. *Los de abajo: Novela de la Revolución Mexicana*. 40th ed. México, 2000.

Bancroft, Hubert Howe. *The Native Races of the Pacific States of North America: Wild Tribes*. Vol. 1. New York: D. Appleton and Company, 1874.

Banda, Longinos. "Estadística de Jalisco." *Boletín de la Sociedad Mexicana de Geografía y Estadística* 11 (1865): 245–80.

Baranda, Joaquín, ed. *Código penal del estado de Michoacán*. Vol. 15 of *Codificación de la República Mexicana*, edited by Joaquín Baranda and Melesio Parra. México: Tipografía de las Escalerillas, 1899.

Bárcena, Mariano. *Ensayo estadístico del estado de Jalisco*. Vol. 9 of *Anales del Ministerio de Fomento de la República Mexicana*. México, D.F.: Oficina Tipográfica de la Secretaría de Fomento, 1891.

Barrera, Jesús. "Del alcoholismo y algunas de sus formas." Medical thesis, Escuela Nacional de Medicina de México, 1870.

Baudelaire, Charles. *Artificial Paradise: On Hashish and Wine as a Means of Expanding Individuality*. Translated by Ellen Fox. New York: Herder and Herder, 1971.

Bayly, C. A. *The Birth of the Modern World, 1780–1914: Global Connections and Comparisons*. Malden, MA: Blackwell, 2004.

Becker, Howard S. "History, Culture and Subjective Experience: An Exploration of the Social Bases of Drug-Induced Experiences." *Journal of Health and Social Behavior* 8, no. 3 (1967): 163–76.

———. "Marihuana: A Sociological Overview." In *The Marihuana Papers*, edited by David Solomon, 66–79. New York: New American Library, 1966.

Benavie, Arthur. *Drugs: America's Holy War*. New York: Routledge, 2009.

Benton, Lauren. "No Longer Odd Region Out: Repositioning Latin America in World History." *Hispanic American Historical Review* 84, no. 3 (2004): 423–30.

Berdecio, Roberto, and Stanley Appelbaum, eds. *Posada's Popular Mexican Prints*. New York: Dover, 1972.

Berlandier, Sr. "Espedición científica del General Teran a Tejas." *Boletín de la Sociedad Mexicana de Geografía y Estadística* 5, no. 3 (1857): 125–33.

Bertram, Eva, Morris Blachman, Kenneth Sharpe, and Peter Andreas. *Drug War Politics: The Price of Denial*. Berkeley: University of California Press, 1996.

Bibra, Baron Ernst von. *Plant Intoxicants*. Rochester, VT: Healing Art Press, 1995.

Bierhorst, John. *A Nahuatl-English Dictionary and Concordance to the Cantares Mexicanos with an Analytic Transcription and Grammatical Notes*. Stanford, CA: Stanford University Press, 1985.

Bingley, William. *Travels in North America*. London: Harvey and Darton, 1821.

Bonnie, Richard J., and Charles H. Whitebread II. *The Marihuana Conviction: A History of Marihuana Prohibition in the United States*. Charlottesville: University Press of Virginia, 1974.

*The Book of the Thousand Nights and a Night.* Translated by Captain Sir R. F. Burton. Edited by Leonard C. Smithers. 12 vols. London: H. S. Nichols & Co., 1894.

Boon, Marcus. *The Road of Excess: A History of Writers on Drugs.* Cambridge, MA: Harvard University Press, 2002.

Boorstin, Daniel J. *The Discoverers.* New York: Random House, 1983.

Booth, Martin. *Cannabis: A History.* New York: St. Martin's Press, 2003.

Borges, Dain. "'Puffy, Ugly, Slothful and Inert': Degeneration in Brazilian Social Thought, 1880–1940." *Journal of Latin American Studies* 25, no. 2 (1993): 235–56.

Bournhill, C. J. G. "The Smoking of Dagga (Indian Hemp) among the Native Races of South Africa and the Resultant Evils." Medical thesis, Edinburgh University, 1913.

Brackett, Albert G. *General Lane's Brigade in Central Mexico.* Cincinnati: H. W. Derby & Co., 1854.

Bradford, T. G. *A Comprehensive Atlas Geographical Historical & Commercial.* Boston: William D. Ticknor, 1835.

Branch, H. N., and L. S. Rowe. "The Mexican Constitution of 1917 Compared with the Constitution of 1857." *Annals of the American Academy of Political and Social Science (Supplement)* 71 (1917): i–116.

Briggs, Robin. *Witches and Neighbors: The Social and Cultural Context of European Witchcraft.* New York: Viking, 1996.

Brown, James W. *Heriberto Frías.* Boston: Twayne, 1978.

Browne, Kevin. "(Ng)amuk Revisited: Emotional Expression and Mental Illness in Central Java, Indonesia." *Transcult Psychiatry* 38, no. 2 (2001): 147–65.

Bueno, Christina. "On the Selling of Rey Momo: Early Tourism and the Marketing of Carnival in Veracruz." In *Holiday in Mexico: Critical Reflections on Tourism and Tourist Encounters,* edited by Dina Berger and Andrew Grant Wood, 77–106. Durham: Duke University Press, 2010.

Buffington, Robert M. *Criminal and Citizen in Modern Mexico.* Lincoln: University of Nebraska Press, 2000.

Burns, Robert I., ed. *Las Siete Partidas.* Vol. 5. Philadelphia: University of Pennsylvania Press, 2001.

Bustamante, Luis. *Bajo el terror huertista.* San Luis Potosí(?), 1916.

Busto, Emiliano. *Estadística de la República Mexicana, estado que guardan la agricultura, industria, minería y comercio, resumen y análisis de los informes rendidos á la Secretaría de Hacienda por los agricultores, mineros, industriales y comerciantes de la república y los agentes de México en el exterior en respuesta a los circulares de 10 de agosto de 1877.* Vol. 1. México, D.F.: Imprenta de Inacio Cumplido, 1880.

"La cárcel de Belén." *Boletín Oficial del Consejo Superior de Gobierno del Distrito Federal* 3, no. 40 (1904): 639–41.

Carr, John E. "Ethno-Behaviorism and the Culture-Bound Syndromes: The Case of *Amok.*" In *The Culture-Bound Syndromes: Folk Illnesses of Psychiatric and Anthropological Interest,* edited by Ronald C. Simons and Charles C. Hughes, 199–224. Dordrecht: D. Reidel, 1985.

Castillo, Alberto del. "Prensa, poder y criminalidad a finales del siglo XIX en la

Ciudad de México." In *Hábitos, normas y escándalo: Prensa, criminalidad y drogas durante el porfiriato tardío*, edited by Ricardo Pérez Montfort, 15–74. México, D.F.: Plaza y Valdés, 1997.

Castillo Velasco, José M. de. *Colección de bandos, disposiciones de policía y reglamentos municipales de administración*. México, D.F.: Imprenta de V. G. Torres, 1869.

Castle, David, and Nadia Solowij. "Acute and Subacute Psychotomimetic Effects of Cannabis in Humans." In *Marijuana and Madness: Psychiatry and Neurobiology*, edited by David Castle and Robin Murray, 41–53. Cambridge: Cambridge University Press, 2004.

Cerda Espinosa, Emilio. "Algunas consideraciones sobre el alcoholismo." Medical thesis, Escuela Nacional de Medicina de México, 1899.

Cervantes, D. Vicente. *Ensayo a la materia médica vegetal de México*. México, D.F.: Oficina Tipográfica de la Secretaría de Fomento, 1889.

Cervantes, Fernando. *The Devil in the New World: The Impact of Diabolism in New Spain*. New Haven: Yale University Press, 1994.

Céspedes del Castillo, Guillermo. *El tabaco en Nueva España: Discurso leído el día 10 de Mayo de 1992 en el acto de su recepción pública*. Madrid: Real Academia de la Historia, 1992.

Cheever, D. W. "Narcotics." *North American Review* 95, no. 197 (1862): 374–415.

Chestnut, V. K. "Problems in the Chemistry and Toxicology of Plant Substances." *Science* 15, no. 391 (1902): 1016–28.

Chevalier, Jacques M., and Andrés Sánchez Bain. *The Hot and the Cold: Ills of Humans and Maize in Native Mexico*. Toronto: University of Toronto Press, 2003.

Chomel, J. B. *Abrégé de l'histoire des plantes usuelles: Dans lequel on donne leurs noms différens, tant françois que latins*. 4th ed. Paris, 1731.

Chopra, Gurbakhsh S., and James W. Smith. "Psychotic Reactions Following Cannabis Use in East Indians." *Archives of General Psychiatry* 30 (1974): 24–27.

Chopra, I. C., and R. N. Chopra. "The Use of the Cannabis Drugs in India." *Bulletin on Narcotics* 9 (Jan.–Mar. 1957): 4–29.

Clarke, Robert Connell. *The Botany and Ecology of Cannabis*. Ben Lomond, CA: PODS Press, 1977.

*Código penal del estado de Jalisco*. Guadalajara: Tipografía de la Escuela de Artes y Oficios del Estado, 1907.

*Código penal del estado de Morelos*. Cuernavaca: Imprenta del Gobierno de Morelos, 1899.

*Código penal del estado de Puebla*. Puebla: Tipografía de la Escuela de Artes y Oficios del Estado, 1907.

*Código penal del estado de Veracruz*. Llave Xalapa-Enriquez: Oficina Tipográfica del Gobierno del Estado, 1896.

*Código penal del estado de Yucatán*. Mérida: Imprenta Literaria Dirigida por Gil Canto, 1871.

*Código penal del estado libre y soberano de Chihuahua*. Chihuahua: Imprenta del Gobierno, 1905.

*Código penal del estado libre y soberano de Durango*. México: Tipografía y Litografía "La Europea," 1900.

*Código penal del estado libre y soberano de Guanajuato.* Guanajuato: Imprenta del Estado, 1891.

*Código penal del estado libre y soberano de Hidalgo.* México: J. Gaspar de Alba, 1895.

*Código penal del estado libre y soberano de Querétaro Arteaga.* Querétaro: Imprenta de Luciano Frías y Soto, 1894.

*Código penal del estado libre y soberano de Tlaxcala.* Tlaxcala: Imprenta de Luis G. Salazar y C., 1885.

*Código penal para el Distrito Federal y Territorio de la Baja-California: Sobre delitos del fuero común, y para toda la Republica sobre delitos contra la Federación.* México: Imprenta del Gobierno, en palacio, 1871.

*Código penal y de procedimientos penales [Aguascalientes].* México: Talleres de "La Ciencia Jurídica," 1899.

*Código sanitario del estado de Chihuahua.* Chihuahua: Imprenta del Gobierno á cargo de G.A. de la Garza, 1905.

*Código sanitario del estado de Michoacán de Ocampo.* Morelia: Imprenta del Gobierno en la Escuela Industrial Militar Porfirio Díaz, 1895.

*Código sanitario del estado de Tabasco.* San Juan Bautista, Tabasco: Tipografía del gobierno dirigida por F. Abalos, 1900.

*Código sanitario del estado de Yucatán.* Mérida: Imprenta "Loret de Mola," 1896.

*Código sanitario de los Estados Unidos Mexicanos.* México: Imprenta de Eduardo Dublán, 1903.

*Código sanitario de los Estados Unidos Mexicanos.* México: Imprenta de "La Patria," 1891.

Coelho, Adolfo. *Diccionario manual etymologico da lingua portugueza contendo a significação e prosodia.* Lisboa: P. Plantier, 1890.

Cole, Fay-Cooper. "Frederick Starr." *American Anthropologist* 36, no. 2 (1934): 271.

*Colección de leyes, decretos, circulares y otras disposiciones dictadas por el gobierno del estado.* Vol. 11. Oaxaca: Imprenta del Estado en la Escuela de Artes y Oficios, 1887.

Colton, Woolworth. *Colton's General Atlas.* New York: J. H. Colton and Company, 1857.

Comisión de Estadística Militar. "Introducción." *Boletín de la Sociedad Mexicana de Geografía y Estadística* 1, no. 2 (1857 [1849]): i–iv.

———. "Memoria chorográfica y estadística del estado de Guanajuato." *Boletín de la Sociedad Mexicana de Geografía y Estadística* 1, no. 2 (1857 [1849]): 3–58.

*Constitución Federal de los Estados Unidos Mexicanos adicionada por el 70 congreso constitucional.* México: Imprenta del Gobierno, 1877.

"Constitución Política de los Estados Unidos Mexicanos, que reforma la de 5 de febrero de 1857." *Diario Oficial* 5, no. 3 (Feb. 5, 1917): 149–62.

Cooke, Mordecai C. *The Seven Sisters of Sleep.* Lincoln, MA: Quarterman, 1989.

Costain, William F. "The Effects of Cannabis Abuse on the Symptoms of Schizophrenia: Patient Perspectives." *International Journal of Mental Health Nursing* 17 (2008): 227–35.

Courtwright, David T. *Forces of Habit: Drugs and the Making of the Modern World.* Cambridge, MA: Harvard University Press, 2001.

Covarrubias, José Enrique. *Visión extranjera de México, 1840–1867: El estudio de las costumbres y de la situación social.* Vol. 1. México, D.F.: Instituto Mora, 1998.

Craig, Richard. "U.S. Narcotics Policy toward Mexico: Consequences for the Bilateral Relationship." In *The Drug Connection in U.S.–Mexican Relations*, edited by Guadalupe González and Marta Tienda, 71–92. San Diego: Center for U.S.-Mexican Studies, 1989.

Craton, Michael. *A History of the Bahamas.* 3rd ed. Waterloo, Ont.: San Salvador Press, 1986.

Craton, Michael, and Gail Saunders. *Islanders in the Stream: A History of the Bahamian People.* 2 vols. Athens: University of Georgia Press, 1992.

Crittenden, Thomas. "Manufacture of Pulque in Mexico." *Consular Reports* 51, no. 190 (1896): 396–404.

Daftary, Farhad, ed. *The Assassin Legends: Myths of the Isma'ilis.* London: I. B. Tauris, 1994.

Davenport-Hines, R. P. T. *The Pursuit of Oblivion: A Global History of Narcotics, 1500–2000.* London: Weidenfeld and Nicolson, 2001.

Davis, Wade. "Ethnobotany: An Old Practice, a New Discipline." In *Ethnobotany: Evolution of a Discipline*, edited by Richard Evans Schultes, 40–51. Portland, OR: Dioscorides Press, 1995.

Deans-Smith, Susan. *Bureaucrats, Planters, and Workers.* Austin: University of Texas Press, 1992.

DeGrandpre, Richard. *The Cult of Pharmacology.* Durham: Duke University Press, 2006.

Denq, Furjen, and Hisao-Ming Wang. "The War on Drugs in Taiwan: An American Model." In *Drug War American Style: The Internationalization of Failed Policy and Its Alternatives*, edited by Jurg Gerber and Eric L. Jensen, 149–68. New York: Garland Publishing, 2001.

Departamento de Salubridad Pública. "Disposiciones sobre el cultivo y comercio de productos que degeneran la raza." *Diario Oficial* 14, no. 63 (1920): 1189–90.

*Diario de los debates del Congreso Constituyente.* Edición de la Comisión Nacional para la Celebración del Sesquicentenario de la Proclamación de la Independencia Nacional y del Cincuentenario de la Revolución Mexicana. 2 vols. México, 1960.

Díaz, José Luis. "Ethnopharmacology and Taxonomy of Mexican Psychodysleptic Plants." *Journal of Psychedelic Drugs* 11, nos. 1–2 (1979): 71–101.

———. "Ethnopharmacology of Sacred Psychoactive Plants Used by the Indians of Mexico." *Annual Review of Pharmacology and Toxicology* 17 (1977): 647–75.

Díaz Cántora, Salvador. "Mariguana, mota, grifa: Tres arabismos mexicanos." Paper presented at La Academia Mexicana de la Lengua, Jan. 25, 2001.

*Diccionario de jurisprudencia militar de la República Mexicana, ó sea el Código de Justicia Militar, puesto en forma de diccionario, por el Lic. Juan Manuel Díaz Barreiro, Apoderado del H. Ayuntamiento de la Ciudad de México.* México, D.F.: Imprenta de las Escalerillas Número 20, 1893.

*Dicionário contemporâneo da língua portuguesa.* 3rd ed. Rio de Janeiro: Editora Delta, 1974.

Domingo y Barrera, Francisco. "Ligero estudio sobre higiene de cuarteles e indicación de las condiciones que guardan los de la Capital y medios que se dan para mejorarlas." Medical thesis, Escuela Nacional de Medicina de México, 1880.

Domínguez y Quintana, Manuel. "El alcoholismo: Su historia, causas, efectos patológicos, sociales, su terapeútica y recursos legales para evitar el vicio." Medical thesis, Escuela Nacional de Medicina de México, 1870.

Duke, Steven B., and Albert C. Gross. *America's Longest War: Rethinking Our Tragic Crusade against Drugs*. New York: G. P. Putnam's Sons, 1993.

Dumas, Alexandre. *The Count of Monte Cristo*. New York: The Modern Library, 1996.

Earleywine, Mitch. *Understanding Marijuana: A New Look at the Scientific Evidence*. New York: Oxford University Press, 2002.

Elton, James Frederick. *With the French in Mexico*. London: Chapman and Hall, 1867.

Encinas, Diego de. *Cedulario indiano*. Vol. 1. Madrid: Ediciones Cultura Hispánica, 1945.

"Ensayo estadístico sobre el territorio de Colima." *Boletín de la Sociedad Mexicana de Geografía y Estadística* 1, no. 10 (1850): 244–306.

*Ensayo para la materia médica mexicana, arreglado por una comisión nombrada por la Academia Médico-Quirúrgica de la ciudad de Puebla el año de 1832*. México: Oficina Tipográfica de la Secretaría de Fomento, 1832.

Escohotado, Antonio. *Historia general de las drogas*. 2nd ed. 3 vols. Madrid: Alianza Editorial, 1996.

———. *Historia general de las drogas*. 3rd ed. 3 vols. Madrid: Alianza Editorial, 1997.

*Establecimientos penales del Distrito Federal: Decretos y reglamentos*. México, D.F.: Imprenta del Gobierno, 1900.

"Estadística de Yucatán: Publícase por acuerdo de la R. Sociedad de Geografía y Estadística, de 27 de enero de 1853." *Boletín de la Sociedad Mexicana de Geografía y Estadística* 3 (1852–53): 237–340.

Esteyneffer, Juan de. *Florilegio medicinal de todas las enfermedades*. México: Herederos de J. J. Guillena Carrasco, 1712.

Ewens, G. F. W. "Insanity Following the Use of Indian Hemp." *Indian Medical Gazette* 39 (1904): 401–13.

Falk, John L. "The Discriminative Stimulus and Its Reputation: Role in the Instigation of Drug Abuse." *Experimental and Clinical Psychopharmacology* 2, no. 1 (1994): 43–52.

Faria, Eduardo Augusto de. *Novo diccionario da lingua portugueza: O mais exacto e mais completo de todos os diccionarios até hoje publicados . . . seguido de um Diccionario de synonymos*. Lisboa Imprensa Nacional, 1855–57.

*Farmacopea mexicana formada y publicada por la Academia Farmacéutica de la Capital de la República*. México: Imprenta a cargo de Manuel N. de la Vega, 1846.

Febles, Manuel de Jesús. *Noticia de las leyes y órdenes de policía que rigen a los profesores del arte de curar*. México: Imprenta del Ciudadano Alejandro Valdés, 1830.

Fernández de Lizardi, José Joaquín. *El Periquillo Sarniento*. México, D.F.: Editorial Porrúa, 2002.

Fetterman, Patricia S., Elizabeth S. Keith, Coy W. Waller, Oswaldo Guerrero, Norman J. Doorenbos, and Maynard W. Quimby. "Mississippi-Grown *Cannabis sativa L.*: Preliminary Observation on Chemical Definition of Phenotype and

Variations in Tetrahydrocannabinol Content versus Age, Sex, and Plant Part." *Journal of Pharmaceutical Sciences* 60, no. 8 (1971): 1246–49.

Figueiredo, Cândido de. *Novo dicionário da lingua portuguesa*. 6th ed. Lisboa: Livraria Bertrand, 1937.

Forment, Carlos. *Democracy in Latin America, 1760–1900: Civic Selfhood and Public Life in Mexico and Peru*. Chicago: University of Chicago Press, 2003.

Fossey, Mathieu de. *Le Mexique*. Paris: H. Plon, 1857.

———. *Viage a Méjico*. México: Imprenta de Ignacio Cumplido, 1844.

Francoeur, Nathalie, and Cynthia Baker. "Attraction to Cannabis among Men with Schizophrenia: A Phenomenological Study." *Canadian Journal of Nursing Research* 42, no. 1 (2010): 132–49.

Frank, Patrick. *Posada's Broadsheets: Mexican Popular Imagery, 1890–1910*. Albuquerque: University of New Mexico Press, 1998.

Freitas, Antonio Gregorio de. *Novo diccionario da marinha de guerra e mercante, contendo todos os termos maritimos, astronomicos, construcção, e artilheria naval, com um appendice instructivo de tudo que deve saber a gente do mar*. Lisboa: Imprenta Silviana, 1855.

Frías, Heriberto. *Crónicas desde la cárcel*. México: Breve Fondo Editorial, 1995.

Friedman, John Block. *The Monstrous Races in Medieval Art and Thought*. Syracuse, NY: Syracuse University Press, 2000.

Friman, H. Richard. *Narcodiplomacy: Exporting the U.S. War on Drugs*. Ithaca: Cornell University Press, 1996.

Fyfe, Hamilton. *The Real Mexico: A Study on the Spot*. New York: McBride, Nast and Company, 1914.

Gamboa, Federico. *La llaga*. México: Eusebio Gómez de la Puente, 1910(?).

———. *Santa*. México: Grijalbo, 2001.

———. *Suprema ley*. México, D.F.: Vda. de C. Bouret, 1896.

Gamboa, Ricardo Suárez. *La histerectomía*. Monografías de Clínica Quirúrgica. México, D.F.: Tipografía de la Oficina Impresora del Timbre, 1899.

García, Crescencio. "Fragmentos para la materia médica mexicana, 1859." *Relaciones, Estudios de Historia y Sociedad (El Colegio de Michoacán)* 1, no. 4 (1980): 79–99.

García Figueroa, Agustín. "Causas de la frecuencia de la sífilis en el ejército, y medios de disminuirla." Medical thesis, Escuela de Medicina de México, 1874.

Garrett, Clark. *Spirit Possession and Popular Religion*. Baltimore: Johns Hopkins University Press, 1987.

Geijerstam, Claes af. *Popular Music in Mexico*. Albuquerque: University of New Mexico Press, 1976.

Gerber, Jurg, and Eric L. Jensen. "The Internationalization of U.S. Policy on Illicit Drug Control." In *Drug War American Style: The Internationalization of Failed Policy and Its Alternatives*, edited by Jurg Gerber and Eric L. Jensen, 1–18. New York: Garland Publishing, 2001.

Gieringer, Dale. "The Forgotten Origins of Cannabis Prohibition in California." *Contemporary Drug Problems* 26 (1999): 237–88.

Gilman, Sander L. *Seeing the Insane*. Lincoln: University of Nebraska Press, 1996.

Gómez Maillepert, Eugenio M. "La marihuana." *Ethnos* 1, no. 1 (1920): 5–7.

González, Agustín R. *Historia del estado de Aguascalientes*. México: Librería, Tipografía y Litografía de V. Villada, 1881.

González, Guadalupe. "The Drug Connection in U.S.-Mexican Relations: Introduction." In *The Drug Connection in U.S.-Mexican Relations*, edited by Guadalupe González and Marta Tienda, 1–18. San Diego: Center for U.S.-Mexican Studies, 1989.

González, Guadalupe, and Marta Tienda, eds. *The Drug Connection in U.S.-Mexican Relations*. Vol. 4 of *Dimensions of United States–Mexican Relations*. San Diego: Center for U.S.-Mexican Studies, 1989.

González Cos, Jesús. "Estadística del partido de Silao de la Victoria." *Boletín de la Sociedad de Geografía y Estadística de la República Mexicana* 4 (1872): 301–16, 717–73.

González Navarro, Moisés. *El Porfiriato: La vida social*. Edited by Daniel Cosío Villegas. 2nd ed. Vol. 4, *Historia moderna de México*. México: Editorial Hermes, 1970.

González Sierra, José. *Monopolio del humo: Elementos para la historia del tabaco en México y algunos conflictos de tabaqueros veracruzanos: 1915–1930*. Xalapa, Ver.: Universidad Veracruzana, 1987.

Gordon, Diana R. *The Return of the Dangerous Classes: Drug Prohibition and Policy Politics*. New York: W. W. Norton, 1994.

Gray, Mike. *Drug Crazy: How We Got into This Mess and How We Can Get Out*. New York: Random House, 1998.

Green, Jonathon. *Cannabis*. New York: Thunder's Mouth Press, 2002.

Gretton, Thomas. "Posada and the 'Popular': Commodities and Social Constructs in Mexico before the Revolution." *Oxford Art Journal* 17, no. 2 (1994): 32–47.

Grinspoon, Lester. *Marihuana Reconsidered*. 2nd ed. Cambridge, MA: Harvard University Press, 1977.

Grose, Mr. *A Voyage to the East Indies*. 2 vols. London: S. Hooper, 1772.

Guerrero, Julio. *La génesis del crimen en México: Estudio de psiquiatría social*. México: Librería de la Viuda de Ch. Bouret, 1901.

Gutiérrez Ramos, Axayácatl. "Consumo y tráfico de opio en México, 1920–1949." Bachelor's thesis, UNAM, 1996.

———. "La prohibición de las drogas en México: La construcción del discurso jurídico, 1917–1931." Master's thesis, Instituto de Investigaciones Doctor José María Luis Mora, 1996.

Hakim, H. A., Y. M. El Kheir, and M. I. Mohamed. "Effect of the Climate on the Content of a CBD-Rich Variant of Cannabis." *Fototerapia* 52, no. 4 (1986): 239–41.

Hale, Charles. *The Transformation of Liberalism in Late-Nineteenth-Century Mexico*. Princeton: Princeton University Press, 1989.

Halikas, J. A., D. W. Goodwin, and S. Guze. "Marijuana Effects: A Survey of Regular Users." *Journal of the American Medical Association* 217, no. 5 (1971): 692–94.

Hall, Wayne, and Louisa Degenhardt. "Is There a Specific 'Cannabis Psychosis'?" In *Marijuana and Madness: Psychiatry and Neurobiology*, edited by David Castle and Robin Murray, 89–100. Cambridge: Cambridge University Press, 2004.

———. "What Are the Policy Implications of the Evidence on Cannabis and Psychosis?" *Canadian Journal of Psychiatry* 51, no. 9 (2006): 566–74.

Hall, Wayne, and Nadia Solwij. "Adverse Effects of Cannabis." *Lancet* 352, no. 14 (1998): 1611–16.

Haney, Alan, and B. Kutscheid. "Qualitative Variation in the Chemical Constituents of Marihuana from Stands of Naturalized *Cannabis sativa L.* in East-Central Illinois." *Economic Botany* 27 (Apr.–June 1973): 193–203.

Helferich, Gerard. *Humboldt's Cosmos.* New York: Gotham, 2004.

Hemphill, John K., Jocelyn C. Turner, and Paul G. Mahlberg. "Cannabinoid Content of Individual Plant Organs from Different Geographical Strains of *Cannabis sativa L.*" *Journal of Natural Products* 43, no. 1 (1980): 112–22.

Hendryx, James B. *Connie Morgan in Alaska.* New York: Putnam's Sons, 1916.

Herer, Jack. *Hemp and the Marijuana Conspiracy: The Emperor Wears No Clothes.* 10th ed. Van Nuys, CA: Hemp Publishing, 1995.

Hides, L., S. Dawe, D. Kavanagh, and R. M. Young. "Psychotic Symptoms and Cannabis Relapse in Recent-Onset Psychosis: Prospective Study." *British Journal of Psychiatry* 189 (2006): 137–43.

Himmelstein, Jerome L. *The Strange Career of Marihuana.* Westport, CT: Greenwood Press, 1983.

Hoberman, J., and Jonathan Rosenbaum. *Midnight Movies.* New York: Harper and Row, 1983.

Holmstedt, Bo. "Introduction to Moreau de Tours." In *Hashish and Mental Illness,* edited by Bo Holmstedt, ix–xxii. New York: Raven Press, 1973.

Hooker, Alexander C., Jr. *La novela de Federico Gamboa.* Madrid: Plaza Mayor, 1971.

Hopkins, James Franklin. *A History of the Hemp Industry in Kentucky.* Lexington: University of Kentucky Press, 1951.

Humboldt, Alejandro de. *Ensayo político sobre el reino de la Nueva España.* México, D.F.: Editorial Porrúa, 1984.

———. *Ensayo político sobre el reino de la Nueva-España.* Vol. 2. Paris: J. Smith, 1822.

———. *Ensayo político sobre Nueva España.* Vol. 2. Paris: Librería de Lecointe, 1836.

Hutchinson, Harry William. "Patterns of Marihuana Use in Brazil." In *Cannabis and Culture,* edited by Vera Rubin, 173–84. Chicago: Mouton, 1975.

Icaza, Francisco A. de, ed. *Conquistadores y pobladores de Nueva España: Diccionario autobiográfico sacado de los textos originales.* Vol. 1. Madrid: El Adelantado de Segovia, 1923.

Iglesias, Manuel S. "Profilaxia de la fiebre amarilla." *Gaceta Médica de México* 2, no. 2 (1907): 41–67.

Indian Hemp Drugs Commission. *Report of the Indian Hemp Drugs Commission.* 8 vols. Simla: Government Central Printing Office, 1894.

Innis, Robert E., ed. *Semiological Investigations, or Topics Pertaining to the General Theory of Signs.* Amsterdam: John Benjamins Publishing Company, 1991.

"Intereses profesionales." *La Farmacia* 1, no. 17 (1891): 261–65.

"Intereses profesionales." *La Farmacia* 1, no. 18 (1891): 277–87.

"Intereses profesionales." *La Farmacia* 1, no. 19 (1891): 318–21.

"Intereses profesionales." *La Farmacia* 2, no. 6 (1892): 90–92.

"International Opium Convention." *American Journal of International Law* 6, no. 3 (1912): 177–92.

Isbell, H., et al. "Effects of delta-9-trans-tetrahydrocannabinol in man." *Psychopharmacologia* 11 (1967): 184–88.

Jackson, John B. "Notes on Some of the Pharmaceutical Products Exhibited in the Philadelphia Exhibition of 1876." *Pharmaceutical Journal* 6 (1877): 997–98.

Janvier, Thomas A. "The Flower of Death." In *Stories of Old New Spain*, 126–59. New York: D. Appleton, 1891.

Johnson, Jean B. *The Opata: An Inland Tribe of Sonora*. University of New Mexico Publications in Anthropology, no. 6. Albuquerque: University of New Mexico Press, 1950.

Johnston, James F. W. *The Chemistry of Common Life*. Vol. 2. New York: D. Appleton, 1855.

Kaempfer, Engelbert, and Carrubba, Robert W. *Exotic Pleasures: Fascicle III, Curious Scientific and Medical Observations*. Carbondale: Southern Illinois University Press, 1996.

Kahn, I. S. "Mexican Mining Practice from a Tubercular Point of View." *Boston Medical and Surgical Journal* 158 (1908): 41–47.

Karttunen, Frances. *An Analytical Dictionary of Nahuatl*. Austin: University of Texas Press, 1983.

Katz, Friedrich. "The Liberal Republic and the Porfiriato, 1867–1910." In *Mexico Since Independence*, edited by Leslie Bethel, 49–124. Cambridge: Cambridge University Press, 1991.

———. *The Life and Times of Pancho Villa*. Stanford, CA: Stanford University Press, 1998.

Keeler, Martin H. "Adverse Reaction to Marihuana." *American Journal of Psychiatry* 124, no. 5 (1968): 674–77.

Kirsch, Irving. *The Emperor's New Drugs: Exploding the Antidepressant Myth*. New York: Basic Books, 2010.

Knab, Tim "Lesser Known Mexican Psychopharmacogens." Unpublished manuscript, 1978. Harvard University Botany Libraries.

Knight, Alan. *The Mexican Revolution*. 2 vols. Lincoln: University of Nebraska Press, 1993.

Kolonitz, Paula Gräfin. *Un viaje a México en 1864*. Translated by Neftalí Beltrán. México: Secretaría de Educación Pública, 1976.

Lámbarri, Miguel M. *Directorio general de la ciudad de Querétaro y almanaque para el presente siglo*. Querétaro: Tipografía de Miguel M. Lámbarri, 1903.

Leitão, Humberto. *Dicionário da linguagem de marinha antiga e actual, pelo comandante Humberto Leitão com colaboração do comandante José Vicente Lopes*. Lisboa: Centro de Estudos Históricos Ultramarinos, 1963.

Lempriere, J. *Universal Biography*. Vol. 2. New York: Sargeant, 1810.

Lewis, Alfred Henry. "Wolfville." *Cosmopolitan Magazine*, June-Nov. 1913.

———. *Wolfville*. New York: Grosset and Dunlap, 1897.

———. *Wolfville Days*. New York: Grosset and Dunlap, 1902.

———. *Wolfville Nights*. New York: Grosset and Dunlap, 1902.

"Leyes vigentes contra el alcoholismo." *Boletín Oficial del Consejo Superior de Gobierno del Distrito Federal* 4, no. 48 (1905): 49–52.

"Ley para la venta de sustancias medicinales." In *Leyes, decretos, y circulares expedidas por el Gobierno del Estado desde enero de 1889, hasta diciembre de 1891*, 527–59. Monterrey: Tipografía del Gobierno, 1894.

Li, Hui-Lin. "An Archaeological and Historical Account of Cannabis in China." *Economic Botany* 28 (1974): 437–48.

———. "The Origin and Use of Cannabis in Eastern Asia." In *Cannabis and Culture*, edited by Vera Rubin, 51–62. The Hague: Mouton, 1975.

Lima, Hildebrando de. *Pequeno dicionário brasileiro da língua portuguêsa*. 9th ed. Rio de Janeiro: Editora Civilização Brasileira, 1957.

"Loco Intoxication: Indolizidine Alkaloids of Spotted Locoweed (*Astragalus lentiginosus*)." *Science* 216 (1982): 190–91.

Lombroso, Cesare. *Criminal Man*. Translated by Mary Gibson and Nicole Hahn Rafter. Durham, NC: Duke University Press, 2006.

Lomnitz, Claudio. *Deep Mexico, Silent Mexico*. Minneapolis: University of Minnesota Press, 2001.

Lorenzana y Buitron, D. Francisco Antonio. *Cartas Pastorales y Edictos*. México: Impresas con Licencia, 1770.

Lowes, Peter D. *The Genesis of International Narcotics Control*. Geneva: Librairie Droz, 1966.

Lumholtz, Carl. *Unknown Mexico*. 2 vols. New York: Scribner's Sons, 1902.

Lupien, John Craig. "Unraveling an American Dilemma: The Demonization of Marihuana." MA thesis, Pepperdine University, 1995.

Lyons, Michael J., Rosemary Toomey, Joanne M. Meyer, Alan I. Green, Seth A. Eisen, Jack Goldberg, William R. True, and Ming T. Tsuang. "How Do Genes Influence Marijuana Use? The Role of Subjective Effects." *Addiction* 92, no. 4 (1997): 409–17.

Machado, José Pedro. *Dicionário etimológico da língua portuguesa: Com a mais antiga documentação escrita e conhecida de muitos dos vocábulos estudados*. Lisboa: Livros Horizonte, 1977.

———, ed. *Para o dicionário de português antigo*. Lisboa: Edição da Revista de Portugal, 1964.

Madrid Mulia, Héctor, Rosa María Luna Alvarado, and Leonor Estévez Zamora, eds. *Archivo Histórico del Distrito Federal, Catálogo de Documentos, Cárcel de Belén (1900–1911)*. México, D.F.: Gobierno del Distrito Federal, 2000.

Malda, José Gabriel. *Recuerdos de la vida bohemia. Páginas íntimas*. México: J. M. Aguilar y Ortiz, 1869.

Marín, Ricardo. "Influencia de las medidas profilácticas, en la propagación de los enfermedades infecto-contagiosas." In *Memorias del 20 Congreso Médico Pan-Americano verificado en la ciudad de México, D.F. Nov. 16–19, 1896*, 2:735–52. México, D.F.: Hoeck y Compañía, 1898.

Martínez, Mariano M. "Algunas consideraciones sobre el alcoholismo en México." Medical thesis, Escuela Nacional de Medicina, 1898.

Martínez Cortés, Fernando. *De los miasmas y efluvios al descubrimiento de las bacterias patógenas: Los primeros cincuenta años del Consejo Superior de Salubridad*. México, D.F.: Bristol Myers Squibb, 1993.

Martínez Cortés, Fernando, and Xóchitl Martínez Barbosa. *Del Consejo Superior

*de Salubridad al Consejo de Salubridad General.* Vol. 3. México, D.F.: SmithKline
  Beecham, 2000.

Martínez Marín, Carlos. "Época prehispánica." In *Historia y cultura del tabaco en
  México,* edited by María Concepción Amerlinck, 55–103. México, D.F.: Secretaría
  de Agricultura y Recursos Hidráulicos, 1988.

Marzolph, Ulrich. "Preface." In *The Arabian Nights in Transnational Perspective,* edited
  by Urlich Marzolph, ix–xvi. Detroit: Wayne State University Press, 2007.

Massing, Michael. *The Fix.* Berkeley: University of California Press, 2000.

Mata y Fontanet, D. Pedro. *Criterio médico psicológico para el diagnóstico diferencial de
  la pasión y la locura.* Vol. 1. Madrid: R. Berenguillo, 1868.

Mayer, Edelmiro. *Campaña y guarnición: Memorias de un militar argentino en el ejército
  republicano de Benito Juárez.* México, D.F.: Secretaría de Hacienda y Crédito
  Público, Dirección General de Prensa, Memoria, Bibliotecas y Publicaciones, 1972.

McAllister, William B. *Drug Diplomacy in the Twentieth Century.* London: Routledge,
  2000.

McLaren, Jennifer A., Edmund Silins, Delyse Hutchinson, Richard P. Mattick,
  and Wayne Hall. "Assessing Evidence for a Causal Link between Cannabis and
  Psychosis: A Review of Cohort Studies." *International Journal of Drug Policy* 21,
  no. 1 (2010): 10–19.

McVaugh, Rogers. *Botanical Results of the Sessé and Mociño Expedition.* Vol. 7 of
  *A Guide to Relevant Scientific Names of Plants.* Pittsburgh: Hunt Institute for
  Botanical Documentation, 2000.

Medina y Ormachea, Antonio A. de. *Código penal mexicano: Sus motivos, concordancias
  y leyes complementarias.* 2 vols. México: Imprenta del Gobierno, 1880.

*Memoria general del IV Congreso Médico N. Mexicano.* México, D.F.: Tipografía
  Económica, 1910.

Merlin, M. D. "Archaeological Evidence for the Tradition of Psychoactive Plant Use
  in the Old World." *Economic Botany* 57, no. 3 (2003): 295–323.

Meyer, Michael C. *Huerta: A Political Portrait.* Lincoln: University of Nebraska Press,
  1972.

Mikuriya, Tod H. *Excerpts from the Indian Hemp Drugs Commission Report with
  Centennial Thoughts on Indian Hemp and the Dope Fiends of Old England.* San
  Francisco: Last Gasp of San Francisco, 1994.

Mills, James H. *Cannabis Britannica: Empire, Trade, and Prohibition, 1800–1928.*
  Oxford: Oxford University Press, 2003.

Morais Silva, António de. *Grande dicionário da língua portuguesa.* Lisboa: Editorial
  Confluência, 1949–59.

Morales Cosme, Alba, and Sandra Martínez Solís. "Un libro de texto para la cátedra
  de Historia Natural: Proyecto de Alfonso Herrera, 1873." In *Alfonso Herrera:
  Homenaje a cien años de su muerte,* edited by Patricia Aceves Pastrana, 133–47.
  México, D.F.: Universidad Autónoma Metropolitana, 2002.

Moreau, Jacques-Joseph. *Hashish and Mental Illness.* Translated by Gordon J. Barnett.
  New York: Raven Press, 1973.

———. "Recherches sur les Aliénés en Orient." *Annales Médico-Psychologiques*
  1 (1843): 103–32.

Morgan, Edward P. *The 60s Experience: Hard Lessons about Modern America.* Philadelphia: Temple University Press, 1991.

Mosk, Sanford A. "Subsidized Hemp Production in Spanish California." *Agricultural History* 13 (1939): 171–75.

Musto, David F. *The American Disease.* 3rd ed. New York: Oxford University Press, 1999.

Navarrete Maya, Laura. *Excelsior en la vida nacional (1917–1925).* México, D.F.: UNAM, 2007.

Neufeld, Stephen. "Servants of the Nation: The Military in the Making of Modern Mexico." Ph.D. diss., University of Arizona, 2009.

Niemeyer, E. V., Jr. *Revolution at Querétaro: The Mexican Constitutional Convention of 1916–1917.* Austin: University of Texas Press, 1974.

Nieto, Adolfo M., and Eliseo Ramírez. "Notas acerca del uso de la marihuana en el ejército." In *Memoria del VI Congreso Médico Nacional, verificado en la ciudad de Toluca del 14 al 21 de abril de 1920,* 569–78. México: Imprenta Politécnica, 1921.

"Notice of the Hachisch." *American Journal of Pharmacy* 7, no. 1 (1842): 75–77.

"Noticias estadísticas del Departamento de Aguascalientes correspondientes al año de 1837." *Boletín de la Sociedad Mexicana de Geografía y Estadística* 1, no. 8 (1850 [1837]): 171–95.

*Nueva farmacopea mexicana de la Sociedad Farmacéutica de México.* 2nd ed. México: Francisco Díaz de León, 1884.

Nye, Robert A. *Crime, Madness, and Politics in Modern France: The Medical Concept of National Decline.* Princeton: Princeton University Press, 1984.

"Observaciones sociales sobre puntos referentes al alcoholismo." *Boletín Oficial del Consejo Superior de Gobierno del Distrito Federal* 4, no. 12 (1905): 180.

Ochoa, Alvaro. "Las investigaciones de Crescencio García sobre medicina popular." *Relaciones, Estudios de Historia y Sociedad* 1, no. 4 (1980): 76–78.

*The Odyssey of Homer, Arranged from the Translations of Bryant, Worsley, Cowper, Pope and Chapman; With a Prose Narrative by A. J. Church.* Edited by Frederick B. De Berard. New York: Isaac H. Blanchard, 1899.

Olguín Alvarado, Patricia. "El control de las drogas en la ciudad de México (1890–1931)." In *Cuadernos para la historia de la salud,* 37–69. México, D.F.: Dirección General de Recursos Materiales y Servicios Generales, Centro de Documentación Institucional Departamento de Archivo de Concentración e Histórico, 1997.

Oliva, Leonardo. "Flórula del Departamento de Jalisco, escrito en el año de 1859 por el Sr. Dr. Leonardo Oliva y comunicado a esta sociedad, por el Sr. Dr. Alfredo Dugés." *La Naturaleza* 5 (1880–81): 88–133.

———. *Lecciones de farmacología: por el catedrático del ramo en la universidad de Guadalajara.* 2 vols. Guadalajara: Tipografía de Rodríguez, 1853–54.

Olvera, José. "Expendio libre de yerbas medicinales, de venenos y otras drogas peligrosas." *La Farmacia* 6, no. 2 (1897).

Oneto Barenque, Gregorio. "La marihuana ante la psiquiatría y el código penal." *Criminalia* 5, no. 4 (1938): 239–56.

Orozco y Berra, D. Manuel, ed. *Apéndice al diccionario universal de historia y de*

*geografía: Colección de artículos relativos á la república mexicana.* 2 vols. México,
D.F.: Imprenta de J. M. Andrade y F. Escalante, 1856.

———. *Geografía de las lenguas y carta etnográfica de México; precedidas de un ensayo de clasificación de las mismas lenguas y de apuntes para las inmigraciones de las tribus.* México: Imprenta de J. M. Andrade y F. Escalante, 1864.

Ortega, Francisco. *Memoria sobre los medios de desterrar la embriaguez presentada en 30 de Abril de 1846, y premiada en el concurso abierto por Convocatoria del Ateneo Mejicano de 16 Noviembre de 1845.* México: Imprenta de Ignacio Cumplido, 1846.

Ortega, Leopoldo. "Breves consideraciones sobre algunos puntos de higiene militar." Medical thesis, Escuela Nacional de Medicina de México, 1882.

O'Shaughnessy, Edith. *Diplomatic Days.* New York: Harper and Brothers, 1917.

O'Shaughnessy, W. B. "On the Preparations of the Indian Hemp, or Gunjah (*Cannabis indica*)." *Provincial Medical Journal and Retrospect of the Medical Sciences* 5, nos. 122–23 (1843): 343–47, 363–69.

Pacheco, José Emilio, ed. *Diario de Federico Gamboa, 1892–1939.* México, D.F.: Siglo Veintiuno Editores, 1977.

Páez, R. G. *Proyecto de código de justicia militar de los Estados Unidos Mexicanos, formado por disposición de las Secretarías de Guerra y Marina y la de Justicia é Instrucción Pública.* México: Tipografía de Gonzalo A. Esteva, 1879.

Pardo, Osvaldo F. "Contesting the Power to Heal: Angels, Demons and Plants in Colonial Mexico." In *Spiritual Encounters: Interactions between Christianity and Native Religions in Colonial America,* edited by Nicholas Griffiths and Fernando Cervantes, 163–84. Birmingham, UK: University of Birmingham Press, 1999.

Payan, Tony. *The Three U.S.-Mexico Border Wars: Drugs, Immigration, and Homeland Security.* Westport, CT: Praeger Security International, 2006.

Payno, Manuel. *Los bandidos del Río Frío.* 22nd ed. México: Editorial Porrúa, 2003.

———. *El fistol del diablo.* México: Editorial Porrúa, 1999.

Paz, Arturo. *Breves apuntes sobre derecho penal militar.* México: Tipografía, Litografía y Encuadernación de I. Paz, 1894.

Peebles, A. S. M., and H. W. Mann. "Ganja as a Cause of Insanity and Crime in Bengal." *Indian Medical Gazette* 49 (1914): 395–96.

Peet, Preston. *Under the Influence: The Disinformation Guide to Drugs.* New York: Disinformation Company, 2004.

Pérez, Genaro. "La marihuana: Breve estudio sobre esta planta." Medical thesis, Escuela Nacional de Medicina de México, 1886.

Pérez-Mejía, Ángela. *A Geography of Hard Times: Narratives about Travel to South America, 1780–1849.* Translated by Dick Cluster. Albany: State University of New York Press, 2004.

Pérez Montfort, Ricardo. "Fragmentos de historia de las 'drogas' en México, 1870–1920." In *Hábitos, normas y escándalo: Prensa, criminalidad y drogas durante el porfiriato tardío,* edited by Ricardo Pérez Montfort, 143–210. México, D.F.: Plaza y Valdés, 1997.

Petit, Peter. *Homeri Nepenthes.* Utrecht: Rudolph a Zyll, 1689.

*Philadelphia International Exhibition, 1876, Mexico Section, Special Catalogue and Explanatory Notes.* Philadelphia: Dan F. Gillin, Printer, 1876.

Philips, John Edward. "African Smoking and Pipes." *Journal of African History* 24 (1983): 303–19.

Piccato, Pablo. *City of Suspects: Crime in Mexico City, 1900–1931.* Durham, NC: Duke University Press, 2001.

———. "El discurso sobre la criminalidad y el alcoholismo hacia el fin del porfiriato." In *Hábitos, normas y escándalo: Prensa, criminalidad y drogas durante el porfiriato tardío,* edited by Ricardo Pérez Montfort, 75–144. México, D.F.: Plaza y Valdés, 1997.

Pick, Daniel. *Faces of Degeneration: A European Disorder, c. 1848–c. 1918.* Cambridge: Cambridge University Press, 1996.

Pilgrim, Charles W. "Does the Loco-Weed Produce Insanity?" *American Journal of Insanity* 55, no. 2 (1898): 275–81.

Pimentel, Francisco. "Vocabulario manual de la lengua Ópata." *Boletín de la Sociedad Mexicana de Geografía y Estadística* 10, no. 4 (1864): 287–313.

Pineda, Emilio. "Descripción geográfica del departamento de Chiapas y Soconusco." *Boletín de la Sociedad Mexicana de Geografía y Estadística* 3 (1852–53): 341–435.

Pontón, José Mariano, ed. *Disposiciones complementarias del Código Penal del Estado de Puebla, 1873–1903.* Puebla: Imprenta "El Foro de Puebla," 1904.

Pratt, Mary Louise. *Imperial Eyes: Travel Writing and Transculturation.* London: Routledge, 1992.

Prieto (Fidel), Guillermo. *Memorias de mis tiempos.* 4th ed. México, D.F.: Editorial Patria, S.A., 1964.

———. *Musa callejera.* México: Ediciones de la UNAM, 1940.

———. *Viajes de orden suprema por Fidel: Años de 1853, 54 y 55.* México: D.F.: Imprenta de Vicente García Torres, 1857.

*Proceedings of the American Pharmaceutical Association at the Twenty-Fourth Annual Meeting, Held in Philadelphia, PA, Sept. 1876.* Philadelphia: Sherman and Co., Printers, 1877.

Ramírez, D. José Fernando. "Noticias históricas y estadísticas de Durango, 1849–1850." Boletín de la Sociedad Mexicana de *Geografía y Estadística* 5, no. 1 (1857): 6–96.

Ramírez, José. "Informes de los trabajos ejecutados en el Instituto Médico Nacional durante el mes de Octubre de 1899." *Anales del Instituto Médico Nacional* 4, no. 10 (1899): 171–72.

Ramírez, Román. *Resumen de medicina legal y ciencias conexas.* México, D.F.: Oficina Tipográfica de la Secretaría de Fomento, 1901.

Real Academia Española. *Diccionario de la lengua castellana.* Vol. 2. Madrid: Imprenta de Francisco del Hierro, 1729.

Rébollar (hijo), Rafael, and Marino Zúñiga. "Clasificación de heridas y lesiones según el código penal." *Gaceta Médica de México* 9 (1874): 51–56, 72–75, 91–93, 112–14, 125–28, 174–78, 192–93, 213–15, 232–35, 288–93, 330–35, 349–53, 371–73, 398–400, 442–44.

*Recopilación de leyes de los reynos de las Indias.* Vol. 2. Madrid: Antonio Pérez de Soto, 1774.

*Recopilación de leyes de los reynos de las Indias.* Vol. 2. Madrid: Ediciones Cultura Hispánica, 1973.

"Reglamento de droguerías, boticas y establecimientos análogos." In *Recopilación de leyes, decretos, reglamentos y circulares que se han expedido en el estado de Michoacán,* edited by Amador Coromina, 254–91. Morelia: Talleres de la Escuela Industrial Militar Porfirio Díaz, 1903.

*Reglamento de policía del Distrito de Cosalá.* Culiacán: Imprenta de T. Ramírez, 1888.

*Reglamento de policía del Distrito de Culiacán.* Culiacán: Imprenta de Retes y Díaz, 1896.

"Reglamento para las boticas, droguerías y otros expendios de substancias medicinales o para uso industrial." In *Colección de decretos expedidos por el vigésimo congreso constitucional y por el ejecutivo del estado libre y soberano de México,* 537–54. Toluca: Oficina Tipográfica del Gobierno, 1904.

"Report of Committee Appointed by the [Canal Zone] Governor April 1, 1925, for the Purpose of Investigating the Use of Marihuana and Making Recommendations Regarding Same and Related Papers." 1925.

*Reports of Cases Determined in the Supreme Court of the State of California.* Vol. 179. San Francisco: Bancroft-Whitney Company, 1920.

Reuter, Peter, and David Ronfeldt. "Quest for Integrity: The Mexican-U.S. Drug Issue in the 1980s." *Journal of Interamerican Studies and World Affairs* 34, no. 3 (1992): 89–153.

Rielly, Edward J. *The 1960s: American Popular Culture through History.* Westport, CT: Greenwood Press, 2003.

Riesgo, Juan M., and Antonio J. Valdés. "Memoria estadística del estado de Occidente." In *Sinaloa: Textos de su historia,* vol. 1, edited by Sergio Ortega and Edgardo López Mañón, 80–117. México, D.F.: Instituto de Investigaciones José María Luis Mora, 1987.

Risse, Guenter B. "Medicine in New Spain." In *Medicine in the New World: New Spain, New France, and New England,* edited by Ronald L. Numbers, 12–63. Knoxville: University of Tennessee Press, 1987.

Rivadeneyra, Mariano. "Estadística de la locura en México." Medical thesis, Escuela Nacional de Medicina de México, 1887.

Rivera Cambas, Manuel. "México pintoresco, artístico y monumental." *Criminalia* 25, no. 8 (1959): 397–403.

Robertson-Milne, C. J. "Notes on Insanity with Illustrative Cases." *Indian Medical Gazette* 41 (1906): 129–32.

Rosenthal, Franz. *The Herb: Hashish versus Medieval Muslim Society.* Leiden, Netherlands: E. J. Brill, 1971.

Ross, Paul. "From Sanitary Police to Sanitary Dictatorship: Mexico's Nineteenth-Century Public Health Movement." Ph.D. diss., University of Chicago, 2005.

Rothenstein, Julian, ed. *Posada: Messenger of Morality.* London: Redstone Press, 1989.

Roumagnac, Carlos. *Los criminales en México.* México: Tipografía "El Fénix," 1904.

Rudgley, Richard. *Essential Substances: A Cultural History of Intoxicants in Society.* New York: Kodansha International, 1994.

Ruiz, Ramón Eduardo, ed. *An American in Maximilian's Mexico, 1865–1866: The Diaries of William Marshall Anderson*. San Marino, CA: Huntington Library, 1959.

Ruiz-Cabañas, Miguel, I. "Mexico's Changing Illicit Drug Supply Role." In *The Drug Connection in U.S.-Mexican Relations*, edited by Guadalupe González and Marta Tienda, 43–68. San Diego: Center for U.S.-Mexican Studies, 1989.

Sacy, Silvestre de. "Memoir on the Dynasty of the Assassins, and on the Etymology of Their Name." In *The Assassin Legends: Myths of the Isma'ilis*, edited by Farhad Daftary, 136–88. London: I. B. Tauris, 1994.

Sahagún, Fr. Bernardino de. *Historia general de las cosas de Nueva España*. Vol. 3. México, D.F.: Editorial Porrúa, 1969.

Said, Edward W. *Orientalism*. New York: Vintage Books, 1994.

Salazar Viniegra, Leopoldo. "El mito de la marihuana." *Criminalia* 5, no. 4 (1938): 206–37.

Salinas y Carbó, Antonio. "Breves consideraciones sobre la embriaguez bajo el punto de vista médico-legal." Medical thesis, Escuela Nacional de Medicina de México, 1882.

Samuels, Stuart. *Midnight Movies*. New York: Collier Books, 1983.

Sánchez Santos, Trinidad. "El alcoholismo en la República Mexicana." In *Discursos*, 157–269. México: Tipografía de la Compañía Editorial Católica, 1902.

San Pío Aladrén, Ma. Pilar de, ed. *Mutis and the Royal Botanical Expedition of the Nuevo Reyno de Granada*. Bogotá: Villegas Editores, 1992.

Santamaría, Francisco J., ed. *Diccionario de mejicanismos*. México, D.F.: Editorial Porrúa, S.A., 1959.

Santa Rosa de Viterbo, Joaquim de. *Diccionario portatil das palavras, termos e frases que em Portugal antigamente se usárão, e que hoje regularmente se ignorão*. Coimbra: Real Imprensa da Universidade, 1825.

Schendel, Gordon. *Medicine in Mexico: From Aztec Herbs to Betatrons*. Austin: University of Texas Press, 1968.

Schultes, Richard Evans. "Random Thoughts and Queries on the Botany of Cannabis." In *The Botany and Chemistry of Cannabis*, edited by C. R. B. Joyce and S. H. Curry, 11–38. London: J. and A. Churchill, 1970.

Schultes, Richard Evans, Albert Hofmann, and Christian Rätsch. *Plants of the Gods: Their Sacred, Healing, and Hallucinogenic Powers*. Revised and expanded ed. Rochester, VT: Healing Arts Press, 1998.

Schultes, Richard Evans, William M. Klein, Timothy Plowman, and Tom E. Lockwood. "Cannabis: An Example of Taxonomic Neglect." In *Cannabis and Culture*, edited by Vera Rubin, 21–38. Paris: Mouton, 1975.

Serrera Contreras, Ramón M. *Cultivo y manufactura de lino y cáñamo en Nueva España (1777–1800)*. Sevilla, España: Escuela de Estudios Hispano-Americanos de Sevilla, 1974.

Sessé, Martino, and Josepho Mariano Mociño. *Plantae Novae Hispaniae*. México, D.F.: Oficina Tipográfica de la Secretaría de Fomento, 1893.

Sewell, William H., Jr. "The Concept(s) of Culture." In *Beyond the Cultural Turn: New Directions in the Study of Society and Culture*, edited by Victoria Bonnell and Lynn Hunt, 35–61. Berkeley: University of California Press, 1999.

Simons, Ronald C. "Introduction: The Sudden Mass Assault Taxon." In *The Culture-Bound Syndromes: Folk Illnesses of Psychiatric and Anthropological Interest*, edited by Ronald C. Simons and Charles C. Hughes, 197. Dordrecht: D. Reidel, 1985.

Small, Ernest. *The Species Problem in Cannabis: Science and Semantics*. 2 vols. Toronto: Corpus, 1979.

Smith, Benjamin E. *The Century Atlas of the World*. New York: Century, 1897.

Smith, Phyllis Lynn. "Contentious Voices amid the Order: The Porfirian Press in Mexico City, 1876–1911." Ph.D. diss., University of Arizona, 1996.

Smith, R. F. *Report of Investigation in the State of Texas, Particularly along the Mexican Border, of the Traffic in, and Consumption of the Drug Generally Known as "Indian Hemp," or* Cannabis indica, *Known in Mexico and States Bordering on the Rio Grande River as "Marihuana"; Sometimes Also Referred to as "Rosa Maria," or "Juanita."* Washington, D.C.: Department of Agriculture, Bureau of Chemistry, 1917.

Smith, Wallace. *The Little Tigress: Tales Out of the Dust of Mexico*. New York: G. P. Putnam's Sons, 1923.

Sodi, Demetrio. *Nuestra ley penal: Estudios prácticos y comentarios sobre el código del Distrito Federal de 1 de abril de 1872*. Vol. 1. México, D.F.: A. Carranza y Compañía, 1905.

Spanos, Nicolas P., and Jack Gottlieb. "Demonic Possession, Mesmerism, and Hysteria: A Social Psychological Perspective on Their Historical Interrelations." *Journal of Abnormal Psychology* 88, no. 5 (1979): 527–46.

Spillane, Joseph F. "Building a Drug Control Regime, 1919–1930." In *Federal Drug Control Policy: The Evolution of Policy and Practice*, edited by Jonathon Erlen and Joseph F. Spillane, 25–59. Binghamton, NY: Haworth, 2004.

Starr, Frederick. *Catalogue of a Collection of Objects Illustrating the Folklore of Mexico*. London: Folk-Lore Society, 1899.

Stearn, William T. "Typification of *Cannabis sativa L.*" In *Cannabis and Culture*, edited by Vera Rubin, 13–20. Paris: Mouton Publishers, 1975.

Stepan, Nancy Leys. *"The Hour of Eugenics": Race, Gender, and Nation in Latin America*. Ithaca: Cornell University Press, 1991.

Subcommittee of the Committee on Foreign Relations of the United States Senate, Sixty-Sixth Congress, First Session, Pursuant to S. Res. 106 Directing the Committee on Foreign Relations to Investigate the Matter of Outrages on Citizens of the United States in Mexico. In *Investigation of Mexican Affairs*, vol. 1. Washington, D.C.: Government Printing Office, 1919.

"Substance-Induced Psychotic Disorder." In *Diagnostic and Statistical Manual of Mental Disorders, DSM-IV-TR*, edited by Michael B. First. Washington, D.C.: American Psychiatric Association, 2000. http://online.statref.com.proxy.libraries. uc.edu/document.aspx?fxid=37&docid=189 (accessed Aug. 31, 2011).

Talbott, John A., and James W. Teague. "Marihuana Psychosis: Acute Toxic Psychosis Associated with the Use of *Cannabis* Derivatives." *JAMA* 210, no. 2 (1969): 299–302.

Tart, C. T. *On Being Stoned*. Palo Alto, CA: Science and Behavior Books, 1971.

Taylor, Arnold H. *American Diplomacy and the Narcotics Traffic, 1900–1939: A Study in International Humanitarian Reform*. Durham, NC: Duke University Press, 1969.

Taylor, Bayard. *Eldorado, or, Adventures in the Path of Empire.* New York: George P. Putnam, 1854.

———. "The Visions of Hasheesh." *Putnam's Monthly Magazine of American Literature, Science, and Art,* April 1854, 402–8.

Taylor, William B. *Drinking, Homicide and Rebellion in Colonial Mexican Villages.* Stanford, CA: Stanford University Press, 1979.

Tempsky, G. F. von. *Mitla. A Narrative of Incidents and Personal Adventures on a Journey in Mexico, Guatemala, and Salvador in the Years 1853 to 1855 with Observations on the Modes of Life in those Countries.* London: Longman, Brown, Green, Longmans, and Roberts, 1858.

Tenorio-Trillo, Mauricio. *Mexico at the World's Fairs: Crafting a Modern Nation.* Berkeley: University of California Press, 1996.

———. "The Urban Experience in Turn-of-the-Nineteenth-Century Mexico City." Unpublished manuscript.

Tepaske, John Jay. "Regulation of Medical Practitioners in the Age of Francisco Hernández." In *Searching for the Secrets of Nature: The Life and Works of Dr. Francisco Hernández,* edited by Simon Varey, Rafael Chabrán, and Dora B. Weiner, 55–64. Palo Alto, CA: Stanford University Press, 2001.

Terry, T. Phillip. *Terry's Mexico: Handbook for Travellers.* London: Gay and Hancock, 1911.

Toro, María Celia. *Mexico's "War" on Drugs.* Edited by LaMond Tullis. Studies on the Impact of the Illegal Drug Trade. Boulder, CO: Lynne Rienner Publishers, 1995.

Turner, Carlton E., Patricia S. Fetterman, Kathy W. Hadley, and James E. Urbanek. "Constituents of *Cannabis sativa* L. Cannabinoid Profile of a Mexican Variant and Its Possible Correlation to Pharmacological Activity." *Acta Pharmaceutica Jugoslavica* 25 (1975): 7–15.

Tyler, Ron, ed. *Posada's Mexico.* Washington, DC: Library of Congress, 1979.

Valero Palacios, José de Jesús Emmanuel. "Formación de una región productora de enervantes." Bachelor's thesis, Escuela Nacional de Antropología e Historia, 2001.

Valle, Juan N. del. "El viajero en México" (1864). *Criminalia* 25, no. 8 (1959): 387–96.

Valles Ruiz, Rosa María. *Los aires de la transición: Periodismo de opinión, discurso y procesos electorales.* Hidalgo: Universidad Autónoma del Estado de Hidalgo, 2008.

Velasco, Alfonso Luis. "El estado de Michoacán de Ocampo." *Boletín de la Sociedad Geográfica de Madrid* 25, no. 3 (1888): 137–251.

———. "El estado de Michoacán de Ocampo." *Informes y Documentos Relativos a Comercio Interior y Exterior: Agricultura, Minería é Industrias,* no. 28 (1887): 157–99.

———. *Geografía y estadística de la República Mexicana.* 20 vols. México, D.F.: Oficina Tipográfica de la Secretaría de Fomento, 1889.

———. *Porfirio Díaz y su gabinete.* México, D.F.: Tipografía E. Dublán y Compañía, 1889.

Vetancurt, Fray Agustín de. *Teatro Mexicano: Descripción breve de los sucesos ejemplares de la Nueva-España en el Nuevo Mundo Occidental de las Indias.* Vol. 1. Madrid: José Porrúa Turanzas, 1960.

Viesca y Lobatón, Carlos. "El delirio." *Crónica Médica Mexicana* 2, nos. 11–12 (1899): 305–9, 340–44.

Vital, Alberto. "Victoriano Salado Álvarez." In *La república de las letras: Asomos a la cultura escrita del México decimonónico*, edited by Belem Clark de Lara and Elisa Speckman Guerra, 507–20. México, D.F.: UNAM, 2005.

Walker, William O., III. *Drug Control in the Americas*. Albuquerque: University of New Mexico Press, 1981.

Wasson, R. Gordon. "Notes on the Present Status of Ololiuhqui and the Other Hallucinogens of Mexico." *Psychedelic Review* 1, no. 3 (1964): 275–316.

———. "Seeking the Magic Mushroom." *Life*, May 13, 1957.

Weber, Eugen. *Peasants into Frenchmen: The Modernization of Rural France*. Stanford, CA: Stanford University Press, 1976.

Weil, A. T. "Adverse Reactions to Marihuana: Classification and Suggested Treatment." *New England Journal of Medicine* 282, no. 18 (1970): 997–1000.

Weil, A. T., N. E. Zinberg, and J. M. Nelsen. "Clinical and Psychological Effects of Marihuana in Man." *Science* 162, no. 859 (1968): 1234–42.

Weir, William. *In the Shadow of the Dope Fiend: America's War on Drugs*. North Haven, CT: Archon, 1995.

Williams-Garcia, Roberto. "The Ritual Use of Cannabis in Mexico." In *Cannabis and Culture*, edited by Vera Rubin, 133–45. The Hague: Mouton, 1975.

Wilson, Daniel. "Narcotic Usages and Superstitions of the Old and New World." *Canadian Journal of Industry, Science, and Art* 2, no. 10 (1857): 233–364.

Wisotsky, Steve. *Beyond the War on Drugs*. Buffalo, NY: Prometheus, 1990.

Zinberg, Norman. *Drug, Set, and Setting: The Basis for Controlled Intoxicant Use*. New Haven: Yale University Press, 1984.

Zuardi, A. W., R. A. Cosme, F. G. Graeff, and F. S. Guimarães. "Effects of Ipsapirone and Cannabidiol on Human Experimental Anxiety." *Journal of Psychopharmacology* 7, no. 1 (1993): 82–88.

# Index

*Note*: Page numbers in italics refer to illustrations or tables.

medical counterdiscourse, 169, 171–73; to local Mexican marijuana prohibition, 194–95; in Janvier "flower of death" story, 212–13; Salazar "Myth of Marijuana" paper, 225–26; marginalization of, 226–27; NORML as advocate for, 229, 245 (n. 38); popular opinion on legalization, 230–31. *See also* Anti-drug ideology; Harmlessness; Moderation; War on drugs

*Count of Monte Cristo, The*, 13, 16, 67, 71

Craig, Richard, 242 (n. 8)

Crime. *See* Vice; Violence

Crittenden, Thomas, 206

Cuba, 52

"Cucaracha, La," 162–63, 278–79 (nn. 19, 22)

Cult of pharmacology, 8

Cultural history, 157–58

*Curanderos*, 43

Curiel, Luis, 189

Daftary, Farhad, 11

Darío, Reubén, 151

Darwin, Charles, 125

*Datura stramonium. See* Toloache

Dealers. *See* Distribution

Deans-Smith, Susan, 250 (n. 55)

Degeneration: racial degeneration theory, 3–4, 124–28, 181–82, 197; drugs as moral degeneration, 17, 132; newspaper reports of, 96, 237; as scientific/medical designation, 107, 124, 126; marijuana use and, 124, 136–39; *herbolarias* as symbol of, 124, 143, 145–51, 154; atavisms and, 125, 127–28, 130–32, 209–11, 270 (n. 17); hygiene initiative and, 128, 181–82; children of drug abusers and, 132; soldiers/prisoners associated with, 132–39, 151–54; Mexican Revolution and, 196–97; farm animal locoweed addiction and, 214–15; international comparison of, 269 (n. 5). *See also Herbolarias*; Indigenous people; *Marihuanos*; Nationalism

Degenhardt, Louisa, 34, 37

DeGrandpre, Richard, 8, 24, 28

Delirium: early views of cannabis delirium, 14–15, 70–71, 80, 269 (n. 52); cannabis as cure for, 74; in newspaper references to marijuana, 98–99, 101–2, 116, 173; delirium tremens as alcohol effect, 106–12; mania and, 106, 117; scientific/hygienic writings on, 116–21. *See also* Hallucinations

Delta-8-tetrahydrocannabinol, 30

Delta-9-tetrahydrocannabinol (THC), 29–31, 61–63

Delusions: as reported cannabis effect, 8, 18; as medically observed cannabis effect, 20; psychoactive riddle and, 29; as substance-induced disorder, 32–33, 36; newspaper reports as cannabis effect, 100, 114, 218. *See also* Hallucinations

Depersonalization, 20, 28–29

Díaz, José Luis, 60, 253–54 (n. 95)

Díaz, Porfirio, 190, 193–94. *See also* Porfiriato era

Digitalis, 185–86, 283 (n. 17)

Dioscorides, Pedanius, 252 (n. 85)

Distilled spirits, 49, 86, 105

Distribution: by drug cartel networks, 4, 227–28, 231; by informal sellers, 94; by women, 94–96, 95, 100; pharmacy sale of cannabis, 153, 215; freedom-of-commerce discourse and, 195. See also *Herbolarias*; Pharmacies

Domingo y Barrera, Francisco, 135, 258–59 (n. 3)

Domínguez y Quintana, Manuel, 105–6, 265 (n. 7)

Dopamine system, 31

Dose. *See* Overdose/dose

Drunkenness: in pre-Hispanic ritual, 47–48; criminal behavior as result of, 49; insanity/intoxication defense and, 49, 112, 137, 173–75; newspaper coverage as vice, 84, 86; stages of, 105, 107–8; marijuana intoxication and,

as *soldaderas*, 135–36, 195; women as *herbolarias*, 145, 150; in Posada lithographs, 157, 159; toloache as feminine vengeance, 210–11, 220–21; analysis of Mexican newspapers and, 260 (n. 9)

Germany, 198, 265–66 (n. 8)

Gobineau, Arthur de, 270 (n. 20)

Goldmann, Edmond, 212

Gómez Farías, Vicente, 71

Gonorrhea, 61

Grandsagne, Ajasson de, 120

Green, Jonathon, 278–79 (n. 19)

Gretton, Thomas, 156

*Grifo* ("stoned"), 2–3

Grose, John Henry, 9–10, 244 (n. 7)

Guerrero, Julio, 85, 129–32, 135, 151

Guttman, Miguel, 141, 275 (n. 89)

Guzmán, Ignacio, 75–76

Hague International Opium Convention (1912), 193, 200–201

Hale, William Bayard, 221

Hall, Wayne, 34, 37

Hallucinations: as reported cannabis effect, 8, 31–32; Moreau stages of cannabis effects and, 15–16; Vietnam War cannabis reports and, 20–21; Keeler study on, 28–29; overdose and, 32; as psychotomimetic symptom, 34–35, 43–44; Moreau stages of effects and, 74, 120; newspaper reports of, 96, 98, 173, 237; in alcoholic delirium, 106–7; medical reports of, 168. *See also* Delirium; Delusions

Hallucinogens: "strength" of Vietnamese cannabis and, 21; in Mexican religious practice, 39, 42, 43–44; "psychedelic" movement and, 228

Harmlessness: contemporary research on cannabis harm, 5, 243 (n. 15); psychoactive riddle and, 8, 22–23, 37; IHDC study on, 17; Panama Canal Zone study on, 18–19; Cannabis Subcommittee study on, 19; placebo text and, 24, 37; cannabis as psychosis self-medication, 35–36; cannabis-psychosis incidence correlation, 35–37; silence as marijuana effect, 167; Salazar "Myth of Marijuana" paper, 225–26. *See also* Anti-drug ideology; Counterdiscourse; Moderation

Hashish: Sacy etymology of word, 11–13; use in Crusades, 12–13; Dumas account of, 13, 16, 67, 71; Orientalist writings on, 13–14, 70; additive substances in, 16; delirium associated with, 117, 119; madness associated with, 168–69; as early U.S. cannabis term, 205–6, 217–18

Hemlock (*Conium Maculatum*), 69–70, 149, 150, 185–86, 193, 275 (n. 105)

Hemp (*Cannabis sativa*): European agricultural cannabis, 1, 10, 52; Indian hemp, 10, 73, 119–20; maritime needs for, 40–41, 52, 54, 248 (n. 6); cultivation in Mexico, 52–56, 59, 250–51 (nn. 60, 68, 69, 71, 75); THC in hemp cannabis, 61, 254 (n. 102); classification in Mexican botany, 73; Aztec use of, 213

Henbane (*beleño*), 150, 185–86, 248–49 (n. 25)

Hendryx, James B., 218

Henequen, 258–59 (n. 3)

*Herbolarias*: early marijuana distribution and, 94, 96; substances distributed by, 94, 148, 150; as symbol of degeneration, 124, 143, 145–51, 154; regulation of, 149–50, 185–86, 275 (n. 105); freedom-of-commerce discourse and, 195. *See also* Degeneration; Distribution; Indigenous medical practice; Pharmacology

Herer, Jack, 278–79 (n. 19)

Hernández, Francisco, 44, 248 (n. 15)

Hernández, Gabriel, 175, 220

Hernández family (hemp producers), 52–53

Himmelstein, Jerome L., 204

Hoffbauer, Johann Cristoph, 105

Honor, 180

Hottentots, 74, 78
Huerta, Victoriano, 161–63, 175, 278 (n. 18)
Huichols, 144
Humboldt, Alexander von, 69, 71–72
Hurd, Henry M., 207–8
Hygiene (field of science): science of alcohol abuse, 105–8; alcohol as alternative to impure water, 115–16; hygienic education, 118–19; degeneration theory and, 128, 181–82; investigation of *herbolarias*, 149; Mexican Department of Public Sanitation and, 181–82; birth of public health in Mexico, 184; Federal Penal Code, Crimes against Public Health section, 186–88. *See also* Medicine; Sanitary council
*Hyoscyamus niger* (henbane), 150, 185–86, 248–49 (n. 25)
Hysteria, 177–78

IHDC (Indian Hemp Drugs Commission), 16–17, 107, 286 (n. 4)
India: Orientalist references to cannabis in, 9–11; O'Shaughnessy study in, 14; *charas* (cannabis preparation) in, 18; Ewens study in, 18; native cannabis studies in, 18, 35, 106; "amok" concept and, 27; cannabis-madness connection and, 204
Indian hemp (*Cannabis indica*), 10, 119–20, 153, 205–6, 215–16
Indian Hemp Drugs Commission (IHDC), 16–17, 107, 286 (n. 4)
Indigenous medical practice (Mexico): local cannabis terms in, 1–2; Mexican botanical science, 1–2, 2, 41–42, 68–69, 71–73; indigenous botanical knowledge, 69–70, 73–74; geography of early marihuana use, 82, 90–92, 92, 258–59 (nn. 2, 3); *herbolarias* as degeneration symbol in, 124, 143, 145–51, 154; regulation of products in, 149–51, 185; medical uses for tobacco in, 249 (n. 51). See also *Herbolarias*; Pharmacology
Indigenous people (Mexico): alcohol-

drinking practices of, 47–49; "moderation" concept of, 48–49; travel writing on, 70; atavisms and, 125, 127–28, 130–32, 209–11, 270 (n. 17); marijuana as degeneration symbol and, 126–27, 143–44, 149–51, 154, 220; El Nahual prisoner type, 140–41. *See also* Degeneration; *Herbolarias*; Indigenous religion; *and particular groups*
Indigenous religion (Mexico): divinatory substances in, 39, 42, 43–44, 46, 50, 143–44, 253–54 (n. 95); ecstatic experiences in, 41, 46–47; marijuana associated with witchcraft, 42–45, 117, 124, 144–45, 150, 248–49 (n. 25); *curanderos* role in, 43; parallels with Christianity, 44, 46; role of tobacco in, 50; cannabis in preparation for sacrifice, 80; syncretic *herbolaria* beliefs, 147
Inquisition: folk medicine regulation in, 42, 47, 53, 57, 77; records on *pipiltzintzintlis*, 57, 60, 77, 252–53 (nn. 91, 92, 95). *See also* Anti-drug ideology; Catholicism
Intoxication: insanity/intoxication defense, 2, 49, 83, 112–13, 137, 173–75, 220; Johnston/Bibra monographs on intoxicants, 13; set/setting and, 37–38; *embriaguez* term for, 104–5, 137–38, 173–74, 196, 265–66 (n. 8); military law on, 137–38; as aggravating circumstance in crimes, 175–76. *See also* Drunkenness; Excessive use; Overdose/dose; Poison
Isbell, H., 29–30
Islam, 11, 15, 19
Italy, 125–26

Janvier, Thomas A., 208–14, 221
Jimsonweed. *See* Toloache
Johnston, James F. W., 10, 13, 258 (n. 2)
Juana Inés de la Cruz, Sor, 56

Kaempfer, Engelbert, 27–28, 59
Kahn, I. S., 177–78

Katz, Friedrich, 278–79 (n. 19)
Keeler, Martin H., 28–29, 246 (n. 66)
Knab, Tim, 253–54 (n. 95)
Knight, Alan, 260 (n. 9)
Kolonitz, Paula Gräfin, 258 (n. 2)

Lamarck, Jean-Baptiste, 73, 129
Landa y Escandón, Guillermo de, 194
Latin America: acceptance-of-drugs
    stereotype of, 4; botanical expeditions
    to, 69; marijuana as "othering" device,
    216–17; war-on-drugs economics and,
    230; racial depiction of, 270–71 (n. 21)
Laudanum, 113
Laughter/giggling, 13, 14, 80
Laws (general): insanity/intoxication
    defense, 2, 49, 83, 112–13, 137, 173–75,
    220; military law on intoxication,
    137–38; insanity/intoxication as ag-
    gravating circumstance, 175–76; Span-
    ish regulation of medicine/pharmacy
    and, 182–83; recreational vs. criminal
    drug use and, 186, 188; liberalism as
    counterdiscourse to drug regulation,
    194–95; sale vs. possession and, 195. *See
    also* Anti-drug ideology
Laws (particular)
—pre-1521: precedents in Siete Partidas
    (thirteenth century), 187; Spanish tri-
    bunal on medical regulation (1420),
    182; Spanish *protomedicato* judicial
    oversight of medical practitioners
    (1477), 182
—1521–1821: *protomédicos* established
    in Mexico (1520–1831), 182–84; in-
    spection of pharmacies (1528–29),
    183, 185; New Spain hemp cultivation
    proclamation (1545), 1, 54; alcohol re-
    strictions begin (1579), 49; tobacco
    restrictions (1580–1725), 50; peyote
    prohibition (1620), 47; *pipiltzintzintlis*
    prohibition (1769), 57–58, 254 (n. 96);
    reassertion of 1545 cultivation edict
    (1777), 53–54
—1821–57: Facultad Médica replaces

*protomedicato* in Mexico (1831), 184;
    Consejo Superior de Salubridad
    (1841), 184; regulations of pharmacies
    (1842), 189, 191, 282–83 (n. 15); licens-
    ing of *herbolarias* (1843), 149–50; regu-
    lation of medicinal preparations and
    pharmacies (1846), 185, 282–83 (n. 15)
—1857–1917: Constitution of 1857, 188–
    94, 196–98, 283 (n. 19), 285 (n. 61);
    local marijuana bans (1860s–1920),
    193–96; Federal Penal Code, Crimes
    against Public Health section (1871–
    1929), 174, 186–88; regulation of phar-
    macies and *herbolarias* (1878), 185–86,
    190, 283 (n. 17); Military Code of Jus-
    tice insanity defense (1879), 173–74;
    regulation of products sold by *herbo-
    larias* (1883), 149–50, 185, 283 (n. 19);
    Federal Sanitary Code (1891), 192;
    Puebla's Penal Code, *enajenación
    mental* as aggravating circumstance
    (1903), 175–76
—1917 to present: local marijuana bans
    (1860s–1920), 193–96; Federal Penal
    Code, Crimes against Public Health
    section (1871–1929), 174; Mexican
    Constitution provisions for regulating
    drugs (1917), 181–82; cannabis prohi-
    bition in Mexico (1920), 4, 81, 124–25,
    181, 188, 201, 203; cannabis prohibition
    in U.S. (1937), 4, 226
*Lecciones de farmacología* (Oliva), 67–68,
    73, 79
Lewis, Alfred Henry, 218
Li, Hui-Lin, 247–48 (n. 5)
Lindesmith, Alfred, 24
Linnaeus, Carl, 58, 68–69, 71, 73, 252
    (n. 85)
Liouville, Henry, 119
Locoweed, 163–64, 206–18, 222
Lombroso, Cesare, 125–28, 270 (n. 17)
*Lophophora williamsii. See* Peyote
Lorenzana y Buitron, Francisco Antonio,
    57–58, 254 (n. 96)
Love, James, 216

See also Madness; *Marihuana/mariguana*; Running amok; Violence
Martínez, Mariano M., 107
Martínez, Mucio, 175
Martínez Marín, Carlos, 50
Mata, Filomeno, 142–43
Mata y Fontanet, Pedro, 104, 265 (n. 7)
Maximilian, Ferdinand, 188
Mayaguana, 75–76, 205
Mayans, 41–42, 51
McLaren, Jennifer A., 35–36
McVaugh, Rogers, 255 (n. 8)
Medicine: contemporary research on cannabis harm, 5, 243 (n. 15); O'Shaughnessy cannabis study, 14; Moreau cannabis study, 14–16; Spanish conceptions of illness, 41; cannabis curative properties, 61, 74, 79–80, 255 (n. 8); Mexican nationalist medicine, 79; studies on vice and hygiene, 82–83; Mexican reports on marijuana use, 117–18, 163–69, 171–73, 175–80; Pérez study, 169–73. See also Hygiene; Indigenous medical practice; Pharmacology
Melancholia, 15, 117, 119, 269 (n. 52)
Mellowness, 31
Mental illness (as cannabis effect). *See particular disorders*
Mental illness (as psychological disorder): experimental symptoms using hashish, 14–15; schizophrenia misdiagnosis, 19; *marihuanos* with mental disorders, 168–69; Pérez study of asylum users, 172–73
Merlin, M. D., 247–48 (n. 5)
Mescaline, 35
Mestizos, 127, 131
Mexico: botanical science in, 1–2, 2, 41–42, 68–69, 71–73; medical studies in, 2, 79, 83–84, 120–21; racial degeneration theory in, 3–4, 124–28, 181–82, 197; transformation of cannabis's meaning in, 4–5; post-Hispanic medical cultures in, 41–43; Atlixco

hemp cultivation, 52–54; marijuana as adopted indigenous plant in, 68–70, 72–73, 80; pharmacological studies in, 73–75, 77–80; U.S. war-on-drugs effect in, 227; in surveys of world intoxicants, 258 (n. 2). See also Indigenous medical practice; Indigenous people; Indigenous religion; Laws; Nationalism; New Spain; Sanitary council
Meyer, Michael C., 161, 278 (n. 18)
Military. *See* Soldiers
Mill, John Stuart, 17
Mills, James H., 9–10, 244 (n. 7)
*Míxitl*, 45
Mociño, Josepho Mariano, 69–70, 73–74, 255 (n. 8)
Moderation, 17, 47–49, 172. See also Drunkenness; Excessive use; Harmlessness; Overdose/dose
*Montanoa tormentosa (zoapatle)*, 150, 186, 193
Monterola, Ramón, 189–91
Montes de Oca, Francisco, 188
Montiel, Tiburico, 189
Moral, José del, 164
Moreau, Jacques-Joseph, 14–16, 74, 119–20
Morel, Benedict Augustine, 125, 127–28
Morphine, 117, 193, 199–200, 283 (n. 17)
Muñoz, Manuel, 149
Mushrooms, 35, 164, 228
Music: response to, 15–16
Musto, David F., 203–5

Nahual, El (prisoner type), 140–41, 274 (n. 87)
Nationalism (Mexico): botanical science and, 68–69, 71–72; marijuana as native pharmacological product and, 77–80, 258 (n. 55); marijuana as national stigma and, 116, 124–26; degeneration theory and, 124–31, 196–200, 270 (n. 14); *costumbrismo* as descriptive writing style and, 133–34. See also Degeneration; Mexico

National Organization for the Reform of Marijuana Laws (NORML), 229, 245 (n. 38)

Naturalism, 151

Nelson, Judith, 30

Neufeld, Stephen, 277 (n. 1)

New Spain (Spanish colonial civilization): cannabis cultivation in, 1, 52–56, 59, 250–51 (nn. 60, 68, 69, 71, 75); alcohol-drinking practices in, 39, 47–49; tobacco use in, 39, 50; anxiety over hallucinogenic divination in, 41, 45–47; medical cultures in, 41–43; distilled spirits in, 49; regulation of medicine/pharmacy in, 182–84. *See also* Mexico; Spain

Newspapers (Mexico): cannabis violence as subject in, 3, 81–82; recognition of psychoactive cannabis, 67; scarcity of cannabis references, 81–82; marijuana references in, 82, 85, 87–93, *88–92*, 98, 100, 136–37, 173, 236–38; yellow journalism era, 84, *86*, 87, 92–93, 259–60 (nn. 8, 14); references to vice in, 84–87, *86*, 234; English-language *Mexican Herald*, *85*, 88–90, 99–100, 178, 206–8, 214–18; prison conditions as issue for, 142–43; analysis of Mexican newspapers, 233–34, 260 (n. 9)

Nicotine, 31

Nieto, Adolfo M., 91–93, 119, 167, 173

1960s (U.S. cultural era). *See* Counterculture, U.S.

Nixon, Richard, 4, 229–30, 242–43 (n. 12)

NORML (National Organization for the Reform of Marijuana Laws), 229, 245 (n. 38)

*Nuestro Señor*, 61. *See also* Ololiuhqui

Nye, Robert A., 126

"Old Man of the Mountain" legend, 12, 120

Oliva, Leonardo, 67–68, 73–75, 77–79, 119, 258–59 (n. 3)

Olivera, José, 120

Ololiuhqui (*Rivea corymbosa*), 44–45, 47, 60–61, 164, 252–53 (nn. 91, 92, 95)

Oneto Barenque, Gregorio, 225, 289 (n. 3)

Opatas, 76

Opiates: as "hard" drugs, 5; as hashish additive, 16; as Vietnamese cannabis additive, 21; placebo text and, 24; running amok and, 27–28; effects on dopamine system, 31; as native Mexican narcotic, 69–70; newspaper coverage as vice, 86; delirium associated with, 118; prohibition/regulation in Mexico, 181, 185–86, 283 (n. 17); sanitary council on, 193; as poison, 199–200; alternative addiction approaches, 226

Orientalism: *Thousand and One Nights* depiction of cannabis, 8, 10, 12, 243–44 (n. 4); overview, 9–14; Moreau study and, 16; native views of cannabis and, 18; "amok" accounts and, 27–28; influence on Mexican nationalism, 78–79; in Pérez thesis, 120; degeneration theory and, 126, 131–32, 150–51; othering of Latin America and, 216–17; Mexican stereotypes in U.S., 223; marijuana as countercultural symbol and, 228

Orozco y Berra, Manuel, 76

Ortega, Francisco, 104–5, 107, 116, 135, 268 (n. 43)

Ortega, Leopoldo, 258–59 (n. 3)

O'Shaughnessy, William Brooke, 14, 74, 119

Othering, 216. *See also* Orientalism

Otomis, 253–54 (n. 95)

Ott, Isaac, 212

Overdose/dose, 32, 37–38. *See also* Drunkenness; Excessive use; Intoxication; Moderation

Palafox, Juan de, 51–52

Panama Canal Zone, 18–19

Panic, 20, 22–23, 28–29

Paranoia: Vietnam War cannabis reports and, 20; Talbott and Teague on, 21; Keeler study on, 28–29; overdose and, 32; cocaine/amphetamine use and, 35; disputes of honor and, 180

Payno, Manuel, 70, 107, 134, 145

Paz, Arturo, 260–61 (n. 17)

Peet, Preston, 243 (n. 12)

Pérez, Genaro, 83, 119–21, 166, 169–73, 260–61 (n. 17), 279 (n. 24), 289 (n. 3)

Pérez Montfort, Ricardo, 242 (n. 8)

Persia, 8–9, 244 (n. 7)

Peru, 50, 250 (n. 56), 251 (n. 75)

Petit, Peter, 59

Peyote (*Lophophora williamsii*): European discovery of, 44–45; as preparation for combat, 45; prohibition of 1620, 47; *pipiltzintzintlis* prohibition and, 58; cannabis as substitute for, 60–61, 144; newspaper coverage as vice, 86; ritual use of, 144

Pharmacies: cannabis in Mexican pharmacies, 55, 94, 137, 153, 263 (n. 31), 282–83 (n. 15); regulation of Spanish pharmacies, 182; regulation of Mexican pharmacies, 182–85, 189–92, 282–83 (n. 15); cannabis in U.S. pharmacies, 215. *See also* Distribution; Pharmacology

Pharmacology: international cannabis reports, 8; Johnston/Bibra monographs on intoxicants, 13; double blind experimental protocol, 30; eaten vs. smoked cannabis studies, 30, 32, 93; survey of cannabis effects, 31–32; healing/poison duality in, 43; pharmacological vs. supernatural effects, 58–59, 61–62; Love research press coverage, 216. *See also* Hallucinogens; *Herbolarias*; Indigenous medical practice; Medicine; Pharmacies; Psychoactive riddle; Set/setting; *and particular cannabis effects*

Piccato, Pablo, 166

Pick, Daniel, 125

Pilgrim, Charles W., 163, 211–15

Pineda, Emilio, 148

*Pipiltzintzintlis* (Mexican medico-religious cannabis term): early use in Mexico, 1; European rediscovery of, 44, 53, 58–59; as divinatory substance, 53, 56–58; Inquisition records on, 57, 60, 252–53 (nn. 91, 92, 95); as local medico-religious substance, 59–60; botanical identity of, 60; appearance/disappearance of name of, 61, 64–65, 77

Placebo text, 24, 37, 47

Poison: marijuana poisoning reports, 23, 96–97, 110, *111*, 163; healing/poison duality in pharmacology, 43, 183–84; farm animal cannabis poisoning, 55, 214–15; *herbolarias'* substances as, 94, 148, 150; Empress Carlota poisoning, 163, 215, 218; del Moral counterdiscourse and, 164; sanitary council on, 193, 198–200; as "locoweed" effect, 208–9, 214–18, 222; tobacco-marijuana preparation, 213; toloache poisoning reports, 221–22; newspaper reports of, 238. *See also* Intoxication

Polo, Marco, 12

Porfiriato era: newspapers in, *85*, 87–88; Gamboa depiction of, 85–86; alcoholism as concern of, 105–12, 268 (n. 43); marijuana as issue in, 106, 114–15; degeneration theory and, 107, 126, 133–35, 139, 270 (n. 14); prison conditions as issue in, 142–43; sanitary council and, 190. *See also* Díaz, Porfirio

*Portable Instructions for Purchasing the Drugs and Spices of Asia* (1779), 9–10, 244 (n. 7)

Portugal, 75

Posada, José Guadalupe: references to cannabis in work of, 87; depiction of drunkenness/madness in work of, 109, *110–11*; Don Chepito character in work of, 156–57, *157–58*, 159–60, *160–61*, 203; reflection of popular attitude in work of, 157–59; critique of European influence on Mexico, 203

Positivism, 190

Prieto, Guillermo, 70, 149

Prisoners (as cannabis users): early reports of cannabis use by, 70–71, 80, 85; in newspaper references to marijuana, 91, 98–99, 260–61 (n. 17), 275 (n. 89); "marijuana madness" as popular conception and, 112; associated with "vice" environment, 124; degeneration theory and, 132–42, 151–54; interviews with, 165–66; marijuana-prison discourse in U.S., 205, 207; archival research on, 276–78 (n. 1)

Psychedelic mushrooms, 35, 164, 228

Psychoactive riddle: defined, 8, 26; Weil's cannabis research and, 22–23, 37–38; voluntary vs. compelled usage and, 25; running amok as culture-bound syndrome, 27, 176, 179–80; deficiency of experimental models and, 29; "marijuana madness" as popular conception and, 112. See also Pharmacology; Set/setting

Psychosis: Ames cannabis experiments and, 19–20, 30; Talbott and Teague on, 20–21; panic reactions and, 22–23; Weil deviance thesis and, 22–23; as reported cannabis effect, 31–32; cannabis psychosis, 32–35; psychotomimetic symptoms and, 34–35, 117. See also particular psychoses

Pulque: use by indigenous people, 48; newspaper coverage as vice, 86; marijuana-pulque combined effects, 114; newspaper support for, 115–16. See also Alcohol

Quadrado, Pedro, 1, 52

Quimichpatli, 45

Race: racial degeneration theory, 3–4, 124–28, 181–82, 197, 270–71 (nn. 14, 17, 20, 21); castas (mixed races) in hemp cultivation, 54; hygienic theories of delirium and, 118–19; mestizos, 127, 131; crack cocaine as war-on-drugs target and, 230; genetic theory and, 270 (n. 20)

Ramírez, Eliseo, 91–93, 119, 167–68, 173

Ramírez, José, 60

Ramírez, José Fernando, 105

Ramírez, Román, 116–17

Reagan, Ronald, 4, 230, 242–43 (n. 12)

Rébollar, Rafael, 83–84, 120, 259 (n. 5)

Recreational drugs: global recreational use of tobacco, 51; recreational vs. medicinal use, 186, 188; sanitary council on, 193; "street" drugs as narcotics, 204; Western 1960s boom in, 228

Reefer Madness, 228–29

Religion. See Catholicism; Indigenous religion; Islam

Rivea corymbosa (ololiuhqui), 44–45, 47, 60–61, 164, 252–53 (nn. 91, 92, 95)

Rodas, Manuel de, 52

Rodríguez, José María, 197–200, 285 (n. 62)

Rope (as hemp product), 1, 40, 52, 54, 248 (n. 6)

Rosa María (Mexican local cannabis term), 1–2, 60–61, 74–75, 76–77, 144, 194

Roumagnac, Carlos, 110, 165–66, 169, 173

Rudgley, Richard, 248–49 (n. 25)

Ruiz-Cabañas, Miguel I., 242 (n. 9)

Running amok: Malay use of term, 13, 27, 99; psychoactive riddle and, 26–27; as culture-bound syndrome, 27, 176, 179–80; accounts with no drug involvement, 28; in newspaper references to marijuana, 99–100, 114, 238; medical studies and, 176; "marijuana madness" compared with, 176–77, 179. See also Madness; "Marijuana madness" as popular conception

Sacy, Silvestre de, 11–13

Sahagún, Bernardino de, 44–45, 60, 140, 274 (n. 87)

Said, Edward W., 126, 216
Sails (as hemp product), 1, 40, 52
Salazar Viniegra, Leopoldo, 225–26
Salinas y Carbó, Antonio, 107
*Salvia divinorum*, 60–61, 253 (n. 92)
Samuels, Stuart, 229
Sánchez Santos, Trinidad, 132
Sanitary council (Mexico): cannabis pro-
    hibition in Mexico, 4, 81, 124–25, 181,
    188; regulation of pharmacies, 94; hy-
    gienic education campaign, 118; regu-
    lation of *herbolarias*, 149–50, 185–86,
    275 (n. 105); history of, 184, 188–90;
    degeneration theory and, 196–200;
    scope of legal power of, 285 (n. 61).
    *See also* Hygiene
Santa Anna, Antonio López de, 131, 134
Santamaría, Francisco J., 75–76
*Santa Rosa María*, 61, 77. *See also* Peyote
*Santísima Trinidad*, 61. *See also* Peyote
"Schedule 1" drugs, 4–5, 243 (n. 14)
Schendel, Gordon, 183
Schizophrenia: misdiagnosis of, 19;
    Keeler study and, 29; compared to
    psychotomimetic symptoms, 34–35;
    cannabis as risk factor for, 35; and self-
    reported effects of cannabis use, 36;
    cannabis-schizophrenia incidence
    correlation, 36–37
Schultes, Richard Evans, 40
Science. *See* Botany; Hygiene; Medicine;
    Pharmacology
*Semilla de la Virgen*, 61, 77. *See also*
    Ololiuhqui
*Senecio canicida* (*yerba de la puebla*), 150,
    186
Sessé, Martino, 69–70, 255 (n. 8)
Set/setting: psychoactive riddle and, 8,
    23–24; Vietnam War report and, 21;
    environmental cues and, 25–26, 168;
    social status and, 26, 155; experimen-
    tal prejudice and, 30; overall intoxi-
    cation experience and, 37–38; in hy-
    gienic studies, 118–19; popular opinion

on legalization and, 230–31; Becker
    "secondary anxiety" thesis, 282 (n. 68).
    *See also* Pharmacology; Psychoactive
    riddle
Sewell, William H., Jr., 157–58
Silva, Máximo, 118–19, 268 (n. 43), 276
    (n. 121)
Sixties (U.S. cultural era). *See* Counter-
    culture, U.S.
Small, Ernest, 63–64
Smith, James, 32–34
Smith, Phyllis Lynn, 259–60 (nn. 8, 14)
Smith, Wallace, 162–63
Smoking (of cannabis): eaten vs. smoked
    cannabis studies, 30, 32, 93; devel-
    opment of cigarettes, 51, 93, 136, 250
    (n. 54); first Mexican references to,
    70, 73–74, 79–80; Caribbean origin
    theory, 75; water pipes, 75–76, 249
    (n. 47); yellow-journalism-era canna-
    bis smoking practices, 92–93; com-
    mercial marijuana cigarettes, 153;
    Aztec use of, 213; tobacco-marijuana
    smoking, 213, 215; early U.S. reports of,
    215, 219; cannabis-infused cigarettes as
    practical joke, 279 (n. 33)
*Solanum manicum* (*Solano furioso*/stra-
    monium), 44
*Solanum Nigrum* (*yerba mora*), 69–70,
    150, 186
*Soldaderas*, 94, 100, 195, 258–59 (n. 3)
Soldiers (psychoactive drug use):
    Panama Canal Zone study of, 18–19;
    American Vietnam War soldiers,
    20–21; Sweden schizophrenia study
    of, 37; Mexican-American War mari-
    juana use, 70; marijuana use (Mexico),
    82, 85, 90–91, *91*, 98, 100, 136–39, 166,
    169–71, 219–20, 260–61 (n. 17), 279
    (n. 33); Mexican literary references
    to, 87; *soldaderas* as sellers of cannabis,
    94, 100, 195, 258–59 (n. 3); alcohol use
    (Mexico), 103, 136–39; associated with
    "vice" environment, 124; degenera-

tion theory and, 132, 134–39; as *viciosos*, 170, 280 (n. 43); archival research for, 276–78 (n. 1)

Solowij, Nadia, 37–38

South Africa, 19–20

Spain: as origin of New World cannabis, 1; conceptions of illness in, 41–42; cannabinoid-infiltrated seed strains from, 64; Mexican atavisms and, 131; regulation of medicine/pharmacy in, 182; tobacco-smoking practices in, 250 (n. 54). *See also* New Spain

Spencer, Herbert, 125

Starr, Frederick, 216–17

Stramonium (*Datura stramonium*). *See* Toloache

Stramonium (*Solanum manicum*), 44, 213

Stroup, Keith, 228

Suárez Gamboa, Ricardo, 132

Sudan, 254 (n. 102)

Suicide, 2–3, 12, 27, 96–97, 103, 127, 186, 218, 269 (n. 52)

Suppression of psychoactive drugs. *See* Anti-drug ideology

Sweden, 36–37

Syncretism, 42–43, 147, 248 (n. 15)

Tablada, José Juan, 150, 260 (n. 16)

Taínos, 50

Talbott, John A., 20–21

Taylor, Bayard, 12–13, 70

Taylor, William B., 47–48, 50

Teague, James W., 20–21

Tempsky, G. F. von, 70

Tenorio-Trillo, Mauricio, 78, 127, 150–51, 270 (n. 14)

*Tenxoxoli*, 45

*Teonanácatl*, 44–45

Tepecanos, 144

Terry, Phillip, 218

THC (tetrahydrocannabinol), 29–31, 61–63, 254 (n. 102)

*Thevetia peruviana* (*cabalongas*), 186, 193

*Thevetia yccotli* (*codos de fraile*), 186

*Thousand and One Nights, The*, 8, 10, 12, 243–44 (n. 4)

*Tlápatl*, 45

Tobacco: harm from overindulgence, 4–5; tobacco-schizophrenia incidence correlation, 37; Mexican colonial government and, 39; native and colonial use of, 50–51; global recreational use of, 51; tobacco industry emergence, 51–52, 250 (n. 55); as Mexican "vice," 70, 265 (n. 1); "marihuana" as synonym in Mexico, 75, 257 (n. 44); in marijuana experiments, 170; sanitary council regulation of, 185–86; tobacco-marijuana preparation, 207, 213, 215, 221; medical uses for, 249 (n. 51); smoking practices for, 250 (n. 54)

*Tochtetepo*, 45

Toloache (*Datura stramonium*): as indigenous Mexican narcotic, 69–70, 279 (n. 24); newspaper coverage as vice, *86*; sanitary council regulation of, 150, 185, 193; as cause of madness, 163–64, 221–22; in English-language news, 206–7; in Janvier "flower of death" story, 208–9

Travel writing and ethnography: depictions of Mexican indigenous groups, 70; accounts of Mexican cannabis "vice," 82–83, 85, 258–60 (nn. 2, 3, 4, 10), 265 (n. 1); report of Starr Venezuelan ethnography, 216–17; English-language Mexican travel guides, 218

Tunis, 120

Turkey, 64, 120

*Tzitzintlápatl*, 45

United Kingdom, 16–17, 53, 116, 265–66 (n. 8)

United States: cannabis prohibition in, 4, 226; "Schedule 1" drugs in, 4–5, 243 (n. 14); alcoholism as problem in, 116; cultural archetypes in, 130, 131–32; Mexican study of U.S. prisons, 134;

regulation of opiates in, 193; history of marijuana in, 203–5, 219, 286 (n. 6); Mexican "marijuana madness" discourse in, 204–5, 208–23, 286 (n. 4); pharmacy sale of cannabis in, 215; cannabis associated with Mexican revolutionaries in, 222–23; Mexican stereotypes in, 223; 1960s recreational drug boom in, 228

U.S. Federal Bureau of Narcotics, 13, 19, 204, 226–27

Unreality, 12, 13–14, 15–16, 238

Vallarta, Ignacio Luis, 191

Valle, Juan N. del, 258–59 (n. 3)

Velasco, Alfonso Luis, 135

Venezuela, 216–17

*Veratrum frigidum* (*cintul*), 186

*Veratrum officinale* (*cebolleja*), 186

Vergara Flores, Luis, 108

Vetancurt, Agustín de, 57, 148, 253 (n. 92)

Vice: in foreign accounts of Mexican drug use, 70, 82–83; overview of Mexican media references to, *86*, 103–4, 234; as medical subject, 104; "marijuana madness" and, 112, 117–18; *viciosos*, 236; delinquency as marijuana effect, 246 (n. 66). *See also* Violence

Viesca y Lobatón, Carlos, 117

Vietnam, 20–21

Villa, Dr., 148, 275 (n. 95)

Villa, Pancho, 162–63, 278–79 (n. 19)

Violence: in newspaper references to marijuana, 2–3, *96*, 97–102, 238; *marihuanos* propensity for, 3, 123–24, 154, 159–60; drug cartels and, 4, 227–28, 231; Sacy "assassin" theory and, 11–13, 19; in Crusades, 12–13; Moreau stages of cannabis effects and, 15–16; IHDC study on, 17; in cannabis reports by indigenous people, 18; Vietnam War cannabis reports and, 20–21; peyote as preparation for combat, 45; alcohol use and, 48–50, 105, 108–9,

198–99; Mexico City urban violence, 49–50; *pipiltzintzintlis* associated with, 57; "serious consequences" issue (Rébollar-Zúñiga debate), 83–84; *panela* preparations and, 93; hygienic theories of delirium and, 118–19; prison marijuana users and, 165; in Pérez experiments, 171; honor disputes and, 180; Mexican marijuana-violence discourse influence in U.S., 204–5; Becker "secondary anxiety" theory on, 282 (n. 68). *See also* "Marijuana madness" as popular conception; Running amok; Vice

Virgin of Guadalupe, 147–48

Voisin, Auguste, 119–20

Walker, William O., 242 (n. 8)

War on drugs: as U.S. vs. international phenomenon, 4–5, 226–27, 242–43 (nn. 8, 12); Mexican marijuana ban and, 181; recreational vs. medicinal use and, 186; Federal Sanitary Code and, 200–201; early "war on marijuana" usage, 220; Nixon "public enemy" declaration, 229–30; crack cocaine as target of, 230; profit paradox and, 230; conspiracy theories of, 243 (n. 15). *See also* Anti-drug ideology; Counterdiscourse; Law

Wasson, R. Gordon, 60, 228, 253 (n. 92)

Water pipes, 75–76, 249 (n. 47)

Weil, Andrew, 22, 28, 30, 37–38, 168, 180

Whitebread, Charles, 203–5, 219, 286 (n. 4)

Witchcraft, 42–45, 117, 124, 144–45, 150, 248–49 (n. 25), 260 (n. 10)

Withdrawal, 24–25

*Yerba de la puebla* (*Senecio canicida*), 150, 186

*Yerba de Santa Rosa* (Otomi cannabis term), 253–54 (n. 95)

*Yerba María*, 61, 77. *See also* Peyote

Yerba mora (*Solanum Nigrum*), 69–70, 150, 186

Zapotecs, 41–42
Zinberg, Norman, 30

Zoapatle (*Montanoa tormentosa*), 150, 186, 193
Zola, Emile, 151
Zúñiga, Marino, 83–84

Made in the USA
Columbia, SC
25 August 2024

41108610R00189